20% SAVINGS

SAVE 20% OFF OUR REGULAR PRICE IF YOU ORDER NOW!

Use the order card on reverse side to get your copies of Volumes 2, 3, and 4 of

INVESTING AND MANAGING MONEY IN INTERNATIONAL CAPITAL MARKETS

FUNDAMENTAL ANALYSIS WORLDWIDE

Fundamental Analysis Worldwide

Investing and Managing Money in International Capital Markets

Fundamental Analysis Worldwide

Investing and Managing
Money in International
Capital Markets

VOLUME I:
Financial Statement Analysis

Haksu Kim

Pacific Investment Research, Inc.
Cranbury, New Jersey, U.S.A.

John Wiley & Sons, Inc.
New York • Chichester • Brisbane • Toronto • Singapore

This text is printed on acid-free paper.

Copyright © 1996 by Haksu Kim
Published by John Wiley & Sons, Inc.

REQUIREMENTS:
An IBM, PC/AT 386 or higher computer or compatible computer with
4MB RAM, 2MB hard disk space, 3.5″ high-density floppy drive,
PC DOS or MS DOS Version 3.1 or later, Microsoft Windows and Excel 5.0
for Windows.

Microsoft®, Excel for Windows®, is a trademark of Microsoft Corporation.

Library of Congress Cataloging-in-Publication Data:
Kim, Haksu.
    Fundamental analysis worldwide : investing and managing money in
international capital markets / Haksu Kim.
      p.   cm.
   ISBN 0-471-12229-7 (v. 1 with disks, 3.5″)
   ISBN 0-471-12232-7 (v. 2)
   ISBN 0-471-12233-5 (v. 3)
   ISBN 0-471-12977-1 (v. 4)
   ISBN 0-471-12224-6 (pbk. : alk. paper : set)
   1. Investments, Foreign. 2. Investment analysis. 3. Financial
statements. 4. Corporations, Foreign—Accounting. 5. Corporation,
Foreign—Finance—Information services. I. Title.
HG4538.K463 1996
658.15′99—dc20   95-6439

Printed in the United States of America

10 9 8 7 6 5 4 3 2 1

Subscription Notice

This Wiley product is updated on a periodic basis with supplements to reflect important changes in the subject matter. If you purchased this product directly from John Wiley & Sons, Inc., we have already recorded your subscription for this update service.

If, however, you purchased this product from a bookstore and wish to receive (1) the current update at no additional charge, and (2) future updates and revised or related volumes billed separately with a 30-day examination review, please send your name, company name (if applicable), address, and the title of the product to:

Supplement Department
John Wiley & Sons, Inc.
One Wiley Drive
Somerset, NJ 08875
1-800-225-5945

For customers outside the United States, please contact the Wiley office nearest you:

Professional & Reference
 Division
John Wiley & Sons Canada, Ltd.
22 Worcester Road
Rexdale, Ontario M9W 1L1
Canada
(416) 236-3580
1-800-263-1590
Fax 1-800-675-6599

Jacaranda Wiley Ltd.
PRT Division
P.O. Box 174
North Ryde, NSW 2113
Australia
(02) 805-1100
FAX (02) 805-1597

John Wiley & Sons, Ltd.
Baffins Lane
Chichester
West Sussex, PO19 1UD
United Kingdom
(44) (243) 779777

John Wiley & Sons (SEA) Pte.
 Ltd.
37 Jalan Pemimpin
Block B #05-04
Union Industrial Building
Singapore 2057
(65) 258-1157

About the Author

Haksu Kim was born and educated in Korea. He received his Bachelor of Science degree in Business Administration from Myong Ji University in Seoul. Mr. Kim later came to the United States to pursue his education in accounting, receiving a Master of Science degree from the University of Wisconsin at Madison in 1985. He is licensed as a Certified Public Accountant by the state of Wisconsin and is also a Chartered Financial Analyst.

Mr. Kim began working at the Center for International Financial Analysis and Research, Inc. (CIFAR), of Princeton, New Jersey, in 1987. He contributed substantially to the development of Worldscope, a database of fundamental data on international corporations produced by a joint venture between CIFAR and Wright Investors Services, of Bridgeport, Connecticut. He later helped develop Cfarbase, a similar database project, for CIFAR. While at CIFAR, Mr. Kim contributed to several CIFAR publications, including ''International Accounting and Auditing Trends'' (1989 and 1991) and the Global Company Handbook (1992).

In 1992, Mr. Kim joined Bloomberg LP, of Princeton, New Jersey, where he has continued his work in merging international accounting principles and the construction of global databases of fundamental corporate data for use by the international financial community.

Mr. Kim recently established Pacific Investment Research, Inc., of Cranbury, New Jersey, as an independent vehicle to pursue his international research.

Summary Table of Contents

Contents

Preface

It is difficult to provide advice on how to make sound investment decisions. Until the 1970s most investment activity was generally limited by national boundaries, with the exception of a few generic securities such as commodities. The volume of products exchanged in international markets mounted in the 1960s, the number of exports and imports reaching a peak at the end of the 1970s. As the realization grew that the exchange of resources between countries was beneficial, it became increasingly apparent that the world economy had needs beyond free trade, including a growing demand for capital. As a consequence, direct foreign investment became quite active at the end of the 1970s.

Direct foreign investment raised many issues related to the transfer of capital from one country to another. Foreign exchange controls became the main focus of efforts to improve the process. In the 1980s, demand for capital exchanges increased and wider participation was encouraged. The growing involvement of the general public in this process required an infrastructure to assure the fair dissemination of investment information. As a consequence, regulatory authorities in many countries became increasingly active in the 1980s. Yet the complexity of the process remained far beyond the ability of most individuals to fully grasp. As a result, indirect public involvement in the world's capital markets through the use of mutual funds became popular, a compromise that left the decision-making process to professionals.

Ironically, one of the obstacles to making investment decisions is the flood of financial information regularly released to the public by companies reporting the results of their operations. These corporate reports on financial results are provided annually, semiannually, or quarterly. Other company information is disseminated continuously to the public by the media, including the trading activity of stock markets around the world.

Corporate financial information, however, is prepared according to the unique accounting standards, tax laws, and commercial code prevailing in each country. Therefore, there is significant variation in the way such information is presented. Each country's financial reporting requirements are the product of its own cultural background, economic circumstances, and social needs. Although the "global village" has become a "global marketplace," few have seriously considered the growing need for a global enforcement agency with powers equivalent to those of the Securities and Exchange Commission of the United States.

In the early 1980s a few organizations active in the global integration of the investment community decided to act. Working with limited information, they combined imagination and skill and attracted the attention of academics and financial analysts to the need for some form of global conformity in corporate financial reporting. In the beginning a small number of private organizations tried to implement this concept on a regional basis. Their efforts were eventually rewarded when the European Union (E.U.) adopted its various community-wide Directives on financial reporting.

Obviously, there is no reason to limit such efforts to a single region. These activists, whose numbers include financial analysts, international accountants, researchers, and others, continued to press for nothing less than a global standard in corporate financial reporting. The author has himself been involved in such efforts since the late 1980s and is eager to establish an international dialogue on the subject. Various viewpoints on financial reporting practices have been incorporated in the volume and, it is hoped, others will be added in subsequent editions.

The main goal of this effort is make *more comparable information* available beyond national boundaries. For many reasons, this will be a long, perhaps never-ending, process. In the meantime, while the ideal of internationally comparable corporate financial data stands before us, investments decisions cannot be delayed.

This volume combines the author's own experience, in working with financial data from many countries, with the "local" expertise of numerous professionals who understand how corporate financial reports are prepared in individual countries. The result is an attempt to find a *compromise solution* that makes international corporate data as comparable as possible, given the many existing obstacles.

Detailed comparisons of different national accounting standards have been the subject of substantial academic research. This has contributed to a process of integration as accounting practices in one country have gradually been embraced by others. Sometimes this cross-fertilization has been limited and narrowly focused; one country's acceptance of another's foreign currency translation method is an example. In other cases, change has been sweeping, as exemplified by the adoption of the EU Directives.

In the meantime, international investors who must make daily decisions no doubt have little time for academic discussions. The reference material provided in this book has been developed for global investors seeking the "best solution" currently available when working with today's often confusing corporate financial statements. It has been written by researchers who work daily with such data. They regularly consult public auditors and financial analysts who are familiar with the fine points involved in implementation of accounting standards at a national level. They also maintain contact with academicians who are continuously formulating standard refinements. Some points raised in this book may be impossible to implement, possibly because of financial or other technical constraints. Some readers may be reluctant to follow the recommendations put forward here simply because there is no empirical evidence of the benefits to be derived from the specific research approach. What can be guaranteed is the effort of all contributors to this book to combine all of the information available today, while anticipating future changes, to assist investors in making judicious decisions.

This book, volume one, offers a general overview of corporate financial statement analysis. Its aim is to broaden the reader's horizons and, it is hoped, to point to new areas that investors and other researchers might usefully explore. It provides comparisons of different financial reporting practices in many countries. Rather than offering a series of statistical tables, this volume is presented in a format the author hopes will be of equal interest to investors and would-be investors, financial analysts, professional accountants, and other researchers. It also offers guidance in the design and development of a database structure to be used with the more detailed, country-specific discussion and actual research examples presented in later volumes. Although this first volume bears the name of a single author, it is in fact the product of continuous discussion with all of the researchers who have contributed to succeeding volumes. Each of the volumes that follow is devoted to a specific economic, rather than geographic, region of the world. Experts provide a review of the financial reporting practices in each country in the region, giving actual examples.

Chapter 1 traces the history of financial management in the twentieth century and provides a rationale for the continuing development of standard financial reporting methods. It goes on to explore the fundamental approach used in research to harmonize the various accounting methods around the world.

Chapter 2 addresses general economic information and offers suggestion on how to choose appropriate economic variables for security analysis.

Chapter 3 focuses on company-specific information, the issues it raises, and how those issue relate to financial analysis. Readers without a strong background in the technical aspects of accounting will find Chapter 3's Section 3.2.2, "Financial Reporting and Accounting Principles," of particular interest. It offers an extensive review of practical accounting issues and explanations of the accounting options preferred for purposes of financial analysis. Representative examples from many countries are provided.

Chapters 4 through 6 review, respectively, three central elements to understanding a company's financial condition: the income statement, the balance sheet, and the cash flow statement. These chapters are fashioned to assist in the development of a database, with companies arranged into four categories: industrial, banks, insurance, and other financial services. This segregation is necessary because the reporting formats of financial services differ significantly from those of other businesses. Although a single reporting format would be ideal for making comparisons of companies in all business sectors, many important aspects unique to one industry or another would be lost in such an approach.

Each of the data items surveyed in Chapters 4 through 6 is uniquely defined to make possible international comparisons. Each data item has a four-digit code, included to facilitate database development by the reader. These codes also agree with codes both in the electronic spreadsheet supplement to this book and in the ratio analysis in Chapter 11. Database users may choose the format with which they are most comfortable. For example, regardless of the sequence of account numbers used in this book, readers may use either the increasing liquidity order or the decreasing liquidity order in balance sheets as they see fit.

Chapters 7 to 10 are brief, each addressing a specific subject matter, as reflected in their respective titles: "Diversification of Operating Activities," "Diversification of Capital," "Shareholders Information," and "Management Information."

Chapter 11, "Research Procedures," provides guidance on the use of the data sets constructed in Chapters 4 through 10. Sample ratios are provided but may be modified as needed. The data structure design should accommodate such changes, because each data item is uniquely defined.

For easy reference, the Appendix organizes data structure for an income statement, balance sheet, cash flow statement, and other data into four formats. Each format is used for a separate industry: industrial, banks, insurance, and other financial services. The Appendix also lists a variety of ratios applicable to each industry.

The methods of investment analysis outlined in this book are based solely on publicly available information. This includes annual company reports and other disclosures required by stock exchanges or commercial codes. Although privately obtained information from interviews with management and other "insiders" is often very useful in detailed analysis, it is extremely difficult to obtain. This book offers a method to structure and analyze the vast amount of publicly available information.

Subsequent volumes in this series will cover, country by country, the following geographic areas: Europe, the United States and Canada, Asia, Latin America, and Emerging Markets in Africa and Europe.

For each country, there is a review of general issues, including the country's capital market structures, procedures for setting accounting standards, and financial reporting practices. Research procedures in each country are illustrated, and representative sample companies are selected and segregated by industry sector. A sample company is used for detailed examination, and unique issues are reviewed along with guidance on how they should be treated in the database.

These volumes are designed for financial analysts who themselves analyze corporate financial reports or supervise research staffs who do. Auditors often raise objections to research approaches of a particular country or reject reported corporate financial results as unreliable because they are not verified. The author takes the position that every company has an obligation to report reasonable financial statements and that they should be treated as reasonable by readers whether or not they are audited.

Written suggestions from readers, which are both encouraged and appreciated, will contribute to the continuing improvement of this work. For the use of any material in this book, as a reference or for other purposes, please contact:

HAKSU KIM
Pacific Investment Research, Inc.
5 Tanager Lane, Cranbury, NJ 08512 U.S.A.
Telephone 609-799-5860   Fax 609-799-8464

Acknowledgments

First, I would like to express my deep appreciation to all the researchers who sacrificed a substantial portion of their free time—evenings, weekends, and even vacation time—over many months to share their expertise with others.

I am equally indebted to Bloomberg, LP, my employer, which has applied many of the concepts discussed in this work in its own global database project and was willing to share the experience with a wider audience through this book.

Many local offices of Arthur Andersen, but especially the London office, deserve sincere thanks for providing a prodigious amount of raw material in the form of national and international accounting, tax, and other regulations, along with detailed descriptions of financial reporting practices in many countries.

I cannot overstate the contributions of Sieglinde and Larry Heinzerling, who combined their respective accounting expertise and writing skills to edit each line of this book. Integrating the reports of numerous researchers with diverse backgrounds was a formidable task. Their editing bridged barriers of accountancy, culture, and language to present these findings on today's practices in international financial reporting.

I am most grateful to John Wiley & Sons for its continuous encouragement and support at every level. Without it, this work could not have been put in your hands.

Finally, a very special thanks to my family, Namsoug, Christine, and Benjamin, and the families of each researcher. They provided endless support during our extended efforts to complete this project.

Fundamental Analysis Worldwide

Investing and Managing Money in International Capital Markets

VOLUME I:
Financial Statement Analysis

Introduction and Research Approach

1

1.1 INTRODUCTION

Although we live in a time of instant communication, when the touch of a finger flashes a message around the globe, the world of financial analysis and investment has not kept pace with the electronic age. The speed and reach of an investor's decision-making powers have dramatically increased in recent years, thanks to new technologies and information delivery systems. Yet the supply of meaningful corporate financial information, on which investors everywhere rely, remains relatively backward. Internationally, information is slow in transmittal, lacks uniformity in presentation, and is subject to varying, sometimes conflicting, accounting standards.

Although the necessity for uniform corporate data is obvious, investors must live with the information made available to them. This book is written in the hope it will help investors and financial analysts to make the best possible use of that limited information.

In contrast to the long history of economics, financial management is a twentieth-century phenomenon. The need for a finance theory first arose when U.S. Steel Corporation required a huge infusion of capital in the early 1900s. Although the recession of the 1930s created a need to manage large-scale capital and contain the risks to such resources, it was not until the 1960s that modern concepts of capital market theory or portfolio theory developed and then took off.

The portfolio theory won many followers in the developed economies of the United States and the United Kingdom by the 1970s, but was limited to domestic investments. In the 1980s, great leaps in technology and dramatic reductions in cost made computers widely available. At the same time, the cost of international telecommunications plummeted. Combined, these developments made the quick processing and intercontinental delivery of information a vast, economical enterprise for financial analysts and for everyone else.

The simultaneous and rapid development of capital markets in many countries inevitably led to a change of focus, from "domestic" to "international" investment. In 1970, the United States accounted for 65 percent of the global market value while 35 percent was held by all other countries. Today these figures are exactly the reverse.

The globalization of capital markets and the parallel international expansion in trade has produced a truly worldwide market for goods and services. In contrast, national differences—cultural, political, and economic—persist, although there are significant efforts to harmonize them within large economic blocs.

One of the differences, a major obstacle faced by financial analysts around the world, is the method, or, rather, the bewildering variety of methods, by which corporations report their financial performance. The legal status granted to corporations in any country is accompanied by regulations requiring disclosure of their performance to "interested parties." In times when a company borrowing capital was beholden to a small circle of private lenders or banks, the circulation of its financial status was limited.

Today, especially when it comes to publicly traded corporations, tens of thousands of shareholders are involved and the information the companies are obligated to provide is carefully monitored by regulators at the national level.

Nevertheless, the presentation and quality of corporate information internationally varies in so many ways that it remains problematic. Despite individual national efforts to protect and inform shareholders and other interested parties, it remains an almost impossible task to assure equal treatment of "global" investors located in scores of other countries. There is no legislative body and, therefore, no law to impose uniform financial reporting requirements worldwide. Compounding the problem is the fact that national regulations, formed by culture, tradition, and domestic political considerations, reflect varying and sometimes conflicting perceptions of what is necessary in the way of financial disclosure by corporations. Although there is growing agreement among some countries regarding the accounting standards by which the preparation of corporate financial statements should be governed, consensus is slow in coming.

The law in many countries obliges corporate financial reporting to conform to tax reporting requirements. Yet it is impossible, for example, to expect all countries to have exactly the same tax regulations, which are, of course, linked to national economic priorities. Some countries, the United States and the United Kingdom among them, encourage corporations to prepare their financial statements showing approximate "true earnings" rather than "taxable earnings" and to report the difference as "deferred taxes" (not corporate income taxes).

Regardless of the differences in financial reporting standards, investors will continue to seek profitable opportunities across national frontiers. It is therefore in their interest to be broadly informed about these variations in financial reporting practices and to develop a means to convert "foreign" financial data to measuring units of their own.

This book explores these differences in some detail and seeks to educate investors and financial analysts about them. This is not, of course, the first time this subject has been examined. There has been considerable academic research in the field for a number of years.

Cataloging differences in financial reporting standards, reviewing the political, social, and economic circumstances in which they developed, and studying the resulting codes of regulations are important steps. Yet, as informative as such studies may be, they do not provide practitioners any tools with which to reconcile the differences and make financial statements, no matter their origin, to some acceptable degree comparable. Global investors, as well as the analysts upon whom they depend for advice, lack the patience (and perhaps the life span) to wait for the differences to be eliminated, country by country. The goal of this book is to provide an interim "best solution" for which, as investment horizons continue to expand around the globe, the need grows daily.

Global investment will continue to expand for several reasons:

- Regulations in many countries facilitate the liberalization of domestic economies.
- International investment has become more popular, encouraged by free trade agreements embracing large economic blocs, such as the European Union, the North American Free Trade Agreement (NAFTA) countries, and the unofficial Asian Pacific Economic Cooperation (APEC) group.
- More information than ever before is available today about companies everywhere.

In tandem with expanding global investment activities, there is a growing need for more effective and speedier communication of corporate financial information. Many steps are still necessary to achieve global transparency in corporate financial reporting, a cause to which it is hoped this book will contribute.

1.2 RESEARCH APPROACH

Essentially, investors want to know the intrinsic value of a company so that they can transfer that value to each share of company stock. Then, if the forecasted intrinsic value of the stock rises above the current market price, investors buy shares. If the forecasted value drops, they sell.

There are basically two approaches to predicting the future intrinsic value of a corporation and its securities: the fundamental approach and the technical approach. Both research methods investigate past performance and seek to predict future events.

Fundamental analysts compare a company with others in the marketplace and focus on its historical and projected financial positions, its competitiveness, its production and distribution facilities, and the economic climate in which it must operate. The assumption is that the price of a company's stock will sooner or later reflect the fundamental strengths or weaknesses of the company.

Technical analysts, in contrast, focus entirely on the price of a company's stock and chart its movement over time in search of patterns. They assume that the effects of whatever information is publicly available are already reflected in stock prices and appear as patterns on computer charts tracking price changes.

When it comes to maximizing return on investments, there is no single approach to follow. Using both approaches, separately, can prevent mistakes in valuation and timing and provide a disciplined, superior method of selecting stocks.

This book focuses on the fundamental approach, exploring ways of determining a company's relative financial strength. In particular, it proposes solutions to overcome the complex problems posed by the need to compare corporate financial data prepared in different countries using a variety of often conflicting reporting standards. Step by step instructions in the construction of a model database are discussed in Chapters 4–10. Chapter 11 proposes various uses of the database.

The emphasis will be on the appropriate interpretation of historical data contained in publicly available financial statements disclosed in company reports. These data are the basis for meaningful forecasts of a company's future performance.

The relationship of corporate financial data to other information sources, such as macroeconomic variables and trading information from stock exchanges, is also reviewed. The globalization of capital markets means dealing with a large number of companies in search of a few investment opportunities. Guidance is provided in organizing large amounts of data for various research activities, including what information to compile and how it should be organized in a database.

Despite efforts to harmonize, there continue to be too many differences in financial reporting formats and accounting standards. These differences range from inconsistency in a company's name, a relatively minor problem, to such incurable practices as the use of the Moving Average Method and the First-In-First-Out (FIFO) Method of inventory valuation within the same industry.

International investment requires facing an especially great number of new issues, as compared with domestic investment. These issues, which must also be addressed in compiling data, thus adding further complications to the construction of a database for purposes of analysis, include the following:

- The vast amount of data to be compiled: 20,000 to 30,000 listed companies exist worldwide. There are 40,000 to 100,000 listed securities.
- The lack of expertise in working with capital markets in so many countries.
- The sheer variety of capital markets and of the cultures in which they function.
- Numerous unique issues, including currencies, languages, regulations, accounting standards, economic development and history.

Extensive amounts of data are freely available, but they must be reduced to manageable levels and sorted to serve specific research purposes. Routine procedure should include the following:

1. Setting research objectives
2. Reducing the sample size by using representative variables
3. Further analysis of the reduced number of samples selected

It is necessary to define and maintain a certain number of variables. These should include all basic information sufficient to implement steps 2 and 3.

The data to be gathered may be divided into two categories:

1. General economic data: macroeconomic data by country and by industry (discussed in Chapter 2)
2. Company-specific data: management strategy as well as publicly available financial information (discussed in Chapters 4–10)

General Economic Information

2

2.1 ECONOMIC DATA

Each business is a part of a local, national, and global economy. Each economy is composed of individuals, corporations, and government. The corporations, the focus of this book, are closely intertwined with the other two components of the economy, with which they interact to exchange resources and generate goods for consumption.

Capital for corporations is supplied mainly by individuals, and corporations produce goods for individuals and the government. These activities take place within economic environments regulated by government and through contracts between corporations and government, between corporations and individuals, and between corporations themselves. The net outcome is then distributed to the individuals who have provided the capital to make the entire process possible in the first place.

Local, national, and global economies today are solidly integrated. No company performs its business in isolation. Security analysis therefore involves monitoring changes in the economic policies of local authorities and national governments. The globalization of markets for goods and services, and for capital, requires close attention to international political developments as well.

Establishing the intrinsic value of a company's stock, an investor's primary goal, depends on the company's performance, but performance cannot be assessed without analyzing the economy in which it operates. Thus, fundamental analysis should begin with economic analysis.

The intrinsic value of a security is based on a company's future earnings. Logically, economic analysis should focus not on the current economic situation but on possible future economic developments. This process is called **economic forecasting.**

The following section defines the nature of economic forecasting and categorizes its elements. It also isolates representative economic factors critical to security analysis and provides further details regarding fundamental analysis.

2.2 ECONOMIC FORECASTS FOR SECURITY ANALYSIS

Economic factors underlying the value of stocks and bonds include Gross National Product (GNP), Gross Domestic Product (GDP), inflation rates, interest rates, industry growth, and corporate profits. More precisely, the outlook for corporate earnings is affected by economic factors determining how much the company sells and how much it costs to produce the products for sale. These are called supply factors and expenditure factors, respectively. Forecasts for these factors range from a few quarters to 10 to 20 years. The degree of accuracy fluctuates drastically, depending on the extent of the forecast.

2.2.1 Supply Factors and Expenditure Factors

Supply factors are mainly determined by GNP, which indicates how much an economy can produce. The level of production an economy achieves is determined by the resources available to it and the productivity available to convert resources into final products.

Resources available for production include materials, a labor force, and capital. **Materials** are limited for all organizations, yet materials, as an economic resource, are not limited to natural resources. Materials are continuously being transformed by one organization after another. That is, materials transformed by one company become new materials for the next stage of production, with value added at each stage of the process. The **labor force,** another important factor in production, is determined by demographics: population, age distribution, and education level. **Capital,** that is, money as a financial resource, is another supply factor, essential to bringing the other two factors together. Although capital is an invisible factor, it has value and its use commands a price. Capital allows companies to combine the other input factors and to sustain the risks involved in production.

In addition to these three input factors, **productivity** must also be considered in determining the level of GNP. Productivity is the efficiency of the transformation process using the three input factors to generate products. Productivity of the transformation is also determined by technology and innovation. Emerging countries have plenty of resources, but their GNP is not as high as others' because of a lack of accumulated technology.

These four factors combined determine how much an economy can produce, and disaggregation of the real GNP to industries and companies determines how much it will cost to support the products a company can sell. The **expenditure side of an economy** determines how much companies sell. Contrary to the usual definition of expenditure, the term here refers to how much consuming groups spend on company products and, therefore, how much companies can sell.

Expenditure levels are the result of income distribution among subgroups—individuals, corporations, and government—and, in focusing on a national economy, any foreign sector as well. Each of the subgroups participates in the production process, and earnings from their participation are divided into disposable income, taxes to government, and the inflow and outflow to and from the foreign sector. The total expenditure is divided into durable goods, nondurable goods, and services, and is also segregated by industry and company.

2.2.2 Forecasting Changes in Economic Factors

Having identified major economic factors and their relationships to determine the level of change in each, the next question is how to forecast changes. Simply put, forecasting addresses the level of real GNP and how the GNP is distributed among industry sectors and companies. Forecasting techniques differ considerably, depending on the time frame. Usually, short-term forecasts are for one to two years, mid-term forecasts are for two to five years, and long-term forecasts are for beyond five years.

Because **long-term forecasts** cover more than five years, it may be difficult to determine a specific level of real GNP in a given year. However, long-term forecasts can predict a direction based on likely changes in the development of new materials, demographic shifts, or significant innovations. None of these events is likely to occur every year. For example, the productivity of small companies has increased significantly as a result of the development of personal computers in the early 1980s. No one could foresee such innovation in the 1960s. Who today can possibly predict when superconductivity or nuclear fusion technology will be commonplace in our day-to-day lives? How long will it take to improve a country's general education level?

No matter how sophisticated economic models have become, it is no easy task to make even reasonably accurate long-term forecasts, which can have a direct impact on the analysis of securities. However, long-term forecasts can provide insights to future potential growth and structural changes. Because of the long-term nature of stocks and bonds and, especially, pension funds, long-term forecasts should not be ignored.

Mid-term forecasts cover two to five years, the most reasonable time span to use in determining the level of real GNP. Coincidentally, typical economic cycles since World War II have ranged from four to six years, meaning that mid-term forecasts can eliminate cyclical factors. In addition, the results of corporate investments in plans or government implementation of new economic policies take about five years to be fully evaluated. The level of real GNP and its growth rate can be easily translated to nominal GNP, which takes inflation into account. Obviously, for global investments, potential change in other countries and economic blocs in the mid-term should not be ignored. Long- and mid-term forecasts are the speciality of a few organizations on which most financial analysts rely.

Short-term forecasts range from one to two years, therefore reflecting only a portion of a typical four-to-six-year economic cycle. Short-term forecasts should estimate an accurate real GNP and the distribution of the GNP among sectors and industries. They do not assume any significant structural changes, such as shifts in the quality of a labor force or significant new technology development, for the forecast period. Short-term economic forecasting models are generally manageable by financial analysts themselves.

2.3 LINKAGE BETWEEN ECONOMIC FORECASTS AND ANALYSIS

Once an economic cycle is identified by mid-term forecasts and a real GNP level and inflation rates are determined by short-term forecasting, a nominal GNP can be forecast. The nominal GNP is divided among sectors, and the personal consumption level of each sector is calculated. The nominal GNP level is the total production of each sector (i.e., agriculture, mining, construction, the manufacture of durable and nondurable goods, transportation, utilities, wholesale and retail services, and other services from the private sector and government). It also includes net balances with foreign sectors.

For a given forecasting period, several factors related to longer forecasts are assumed to remain fixed at certain levels. These include, for example, production capacity, the skill of the labor force, national regulations on fiscal policy (e.g., tax rates) and monetary policy (e.g., interest rates and currency rates), price levels of natural resources (e.g., oil), and international political factors.

Personal consumption levels can be disaggregated among durable goods (e.g., motor vehicles, furniture, and other household equipment), nondurable goods (e.g., food, textiles, gasoline, and other fuels), and services (e.g., housing, utilities, transportation, medical care, financial services, and insurance). The apportioned consumption levels can be more narrowly defined and further segregated by industry group. The demand on each industry can be distributed among the companies of each industry group according to their competitiveness. Competitiveness is gauged by each company's production capacity and cost efficiency. Personal consumption can be satisfied by imports if domestic products are not competitive.

Once a company's sales volume is determined, corporate earnings can be estimated. After first setting up all the necessary financial data components surveyed in Chapters 2 to 10, a forecaster can use the analytical procedures summarized in Chapter 11, "Research Procedures."

In a global investment environment, the relative value of a currency is an important factor. Changes in currency values are caused mainly by deficits in a country's balance of trade. However, the issue of trade deficits is sometimes abused by politicians, which can mislead security analysts. As companies become increasingly active internationally, the distinction between exports and imports becomes blurred. The calculation of trade deficits, that is, exports minus imports, is often misleading in terms of who benefits. For example, most of Japan's electronic giants have established manufacturing facilities outside the country. Half-finished or finished products are imported by Japan, and the final products are later exported to the United States or Europe. What portion of these products should be regarded as exports and what portion should be considered imports? For example, when Nike manufactures shoes in South Korea or China and either imports them for domestic consumption or sells them to European countries, the level of GNP and the actual benefits to the public are not always consistent.

There are a few cases, examples of which are cited below, in which conventional forecasting techniques are not applicable. Corporate earnings for these companies are not greatly affected by the level of GNP or cost efficiency. Some examples follow.

Companies offering high-technology products such as cellular phones are less affected by cyclical economic fluctuations but are heavily dependent on obtaining a government license and delivering the product to the market. The license is a formality. Successful competition with international companies is the key to success.

The success of pharmaceutical companies in the United States depends, more than anything else, on the approval of licenses by the Federal Drug Administration. The earnings of utility companies depend on national regulations, which seek to balance the benefits between capital providers and the public. The defense industry is affected by national priorities, whereas financial institutions are faced with regulations limiting the scope of their operating activities.

Some natural resources, such as oil, copper, and diamonds, are located in only a few countries. The political and economic stability of these countries decides the fate of companies dependent on those resources. Elsewhere, the competitiveness of some products is determined by the level of government subsidies they receive.

2.4 LIMITATIONS ON ECONOMIC FORECASTS

Forecasting procedures are not as straightforward as they might appear. A few factors can cause difficulties, and the outcomes they produce are of limited use. Consider, for instance:

1. Most forecasts are based on historical data, which is then projected. History, however, rarely if ever repeats itself in precisely the same way. For example, false assumptions may be made that previously existing national regulations, technology development, and political conditions in other countries remain unchanged.
2. Most data used in forecasts are statistically calculated and are, therefore, not authentic. Many factors are involved, and their interrelationship is not always clear. For example, the impact of tax rate changes on specific investments can sometimes be unexpected.
3. Many alternative decisions are possible at each level of calculation, and personal judgment is only as good as the capability of each analyst. The knowledge of each individual who contributes to the judgment process is limited to certain areas. As a result, some of the many decisions made actually fall into the ''less likely'' category and outcomes should be recomputed.

For investors, the focus of financial analysis is company-specific information, but the performance of an individual company should be analyzed in the context of the larger economy in which it operates. Appropriate macroeconomic variables, especially those useful in forecasting, should be selected for purposes of continuous comparison.

Company-Specific Information

3

3.1 GENERAL INFORMATION

The first task in financial analysis is to identify the companies to be analyzed. This may appear uncomplicated in dealing with a small population of companies, but it is one of the most important and difficult tasks faced by global database developers. The problem lies in the sheer number of companies traded worldwide. It is next to impossible to remember every company in the Standard & Poor's (S&P) 500 index, let alone the 40,000 to 100,000 publicly traded equity securities worldwide, and the number increases dramatically when corporate fixed income securities are also considered.

Another obstacle lies in the lack of an internationally accepted company identification system. Ticker or security identification numbers are assigned by many different organizations, mostly on a country-by-country basis. In addition, these numbers are often changed as a result of company mergers and acquisitions or, sometimes, because a company changes its name. Since it is nearly impossible to track specific entities over time without a structured identification system, the method adopted must be carefully considered by a database developer.

General information about a company is relatively stable. Once the information is collected, it does not have to be updated until a major event, a merger or new listing, for instance, occurs.

3.1.1 Identification of Companies

At least three items are required for the identification of a company. These are the company's name, its industry classification, and its history and background.

Names

The names of companies can often be confusing. The following examples illustrate this problem.

"The" or "Cie." Many companies begin their formal names with "The," and some alphabetically ordered lists honor this convention while others do not. A person searching for a specific company may be unlikely to think of looking under "The." The problem becomes more complex with French companies whose names may begin with "Le," "La," or "Cie." (for "Compagnie"). Companies in Denmark often begin their names with "A/S," standing for "Aktieselskab" (Incorporated), which is unnecessary for purposes of identification.

It is recommended that "The," "Cie.," or "A/S" be attached at the end of a name in parentheses; for instance, Coca Cola Company (The). However, the name of the L'Oréal company should retain the "L'" because it would not otherwise be recognized.

Name of a Person. A person's name is commonly used as a part of a company's name. For a company such as Merck & Company or Philip Morris there is no alternative, but what about E. I. Du Pont & Company, which is generally known as Du Pont? What is the best way to establish a representative name?

If a family name is used, the family name or names should be maintained. But if both the first (given) name and the family name are used, the family name should take precedence and the first (given) name should be attached in parentheses, as in Disney (Walt) & Company, except when the full name, as in Philip Morris, is the company's complete name.

The database developer must also consider the use of a period or periods when an initial is used for the first and/or middle name. For example, which one of the following is best: J. P. Morgan, J P Morgan, JP Morgan, Morgan (J. P.), Morgan (J P) or Morgan (JP)? Many variations are used by newspapers and electronic data distributors. Morgan (JP), or, similarly, Warburg (SG), is recommended.

Translation of Names in Foreign Language. Irrespective of the problems involved in storing foreign-language names in a database, how does one search for the second largest airline company in Japan, All Nippon Airway? Most Japanese investors and others familiar with Japanese know the company as Zenniku rather than All Nippon Airway. Japanese companies, fortunately, have unique English names for the benefit of international investors.

What about such companies as Fuji Spinning and Nitto Boseki? (The word *boseki* means "spinning.") When the local language names and the English names of both companies are known, which should be used? Faced with such complexities, researchers will have to make several attempts at locating the right company in a database. This problem is not limited to Asian companies. French and Italian company names are often translated into English and also confuse investors.

Abbreviations and Shortened Names. There may be no problem matching IBM to International Business Machines, or ATT to American Telephone & Telegraph. What about matching NTT to Nippon Telephone & Telegraph, or DG Bank to Deutsche Genossenschafts Bank? It may not be simple if one is unfamiliar with Japanese or German. The full name of the Suez Group, Cie. Financière de Suez, illustrates such problems, as does STET, a telephone company in Italy whose full name is Societa Finanziaria Telefonica. It is obvious that abbreviations and shortened names will have to be used in a database along with formal company names.

Alphabetization of Foreign Languages. Because it is impossible to know all the world's languages, foreign company names should be expressed in a familiar language. For those familiar with the Roman alphabet, cataloging European companies by their local names would seem reasonable. If one can read Chinese, company names from China, Japan, or Korea in Chinese is possible, assuming the computer being used accepts Chinese characters.

For those planning to keep all names in one script, for instance, English, alphabetization of companies with foreign language names is a difficult task. For example, "Nippon," meaning Japan, may also be spelled "Nipon" and "Nihon." Yet, in fact, the alphabetization of Japanese companies is quite consistent, because an official English version of each Japanese name is required by Japan's Ministry of Finance. Chinese and Korean names can be even more complex. In many cases the same character is written in different ways reflecting, in China, for example, various dialects. Someone versed in the language may be able to recognize which company is meant, but computers are less versatile and would require significant programming.

The alphabetization problem is not limited to languages with other than Latin script. For example, *ö* in German may be alphabetized as *o,* but phonetically it would be *oe.* Some thought should be devoted to establishing a consistent approach.

When a consistent method of expressing foreign names has been established, all applicable companies should be listed in a database with the following details:

> Full name
> Abbreviation
> Publishing name (the name used by a major index in the country may be selected)
> Name in local language, or spelling of the name based on local pronunciation

The publishing name is the name without the usual Co., Inc., Ltd., AG, S.A., Plc, or other abbreviation, attached. A company's publishing name, usually widely recognized, is useful in writing articles about that company. Endings such as that attached to the names of manufacturing companies in Turkey, "Sanayi ve Ticaret A.Ş." (Industrial and Commercial Company, Incorporated), are also best eliminated from the publishing name.

To simplify operation of a database, a company identification number is needed in addition to names and descriptions. Each company identification number should be unique, and the identification of securities issued by the company should be related to that number (see Section 3.1.2, which follows).

Industry Classification

A company's industry classification should be based on the major product or service it provides. Multiple industry classifications for a single company are inevitable when its activities are diversified into separate fields of equal importance.

Holding companies that manage investments in many subsidiaries but have little significant operating activity of their own should be classified according to the activities of the major subsidiaries. Some highly diversified or multiproduct companies, such as BAT Industries or ITT Corporation, may appropriately be classified as "diversified."

Standard Industry Classification (SIC) codes used in the United States (see Chapter 7 for examples) constitute one system of industry classification. Many other classification systems, established by various organizations, are used in other countries. In adopting a classification system for database use it is important to select one flexible enough to allow reclassification of industries for different types of research.

Company History and Background

Identification of a company must also include its history and background. The following items constitute this component:

Site of incorporation
Location of the home office and of major operating activities
Initial public offering (IPO) date for newer companies
Major merger and acquisition activities

3.1.2 Identification of Securities

Companies may issue many different types of securities. Some may be publicly traded and others may be privately placed. The securities discussed in this book are limited to common equity securities, preferred securities, and corporate bonds.

To identify each security and the company to which it is related, it is necessary to collect security identification numbers, security identification codes, security names, the stock exchange(s) where the securities are traded, and each security's basic terms and conditions.

Security Identification Numbers

Once a company is identified, it is necessary to create a list of the securities it has issued. Lists of security identification numbers are provided by major stock exchanges or database providers, but no list is really complete and the numbers are continually being changed. Because electronic databases depend heavily on identification numbers, such changes are often critical and must be connected to one another in the databases. An additional complication is that securities listed on several stock exchanges have different identification numbers at each exchange.

Because of the many companies with multiple securities and the need to avoid confusion, the identification numbers of securities should be related to company identification numbers. The following table provides examples developed by several different organizations. The numbers are used by local stock exchanges to provide information by computer.

A few internationally used security identification numbering systems are illustrated in the following table, but each local stock exchange has its own identification number. The local numbers also are assigned to foreign securities if the stock exchange trades securities issued by foreign companies.

The following are examples of security identification number systems in local markets. Some are used by several stock exchanges in the country and, in some cases, in neighboring countries as well.

SECURITY IDENTIFICATION NUMBERS

Security ID System	Issuer	Coverage by Country	Structure
CUSIP	Abbreviated from Committee on Uniform Securities Identification Procedures		
	Standard & Poor's under license from American Bankers Association in the United States	United States and Canada	First 4 to 6 digits of company ID number, plus security ID, plus 1 check digit[1]
VALOREN	Issued by Telekurs, a Swiss bank consortium and data provider		
	Telekurs AG	All countries	6 digits of company ID, plus 3 digits of security ID
CINS	CUSIP International Number System		
	Standard & Poor's and Telekurs	Non-North American equity and debt instruments	Structure similar to CUSIP assigned to Telekurs database to provide complete coverage internationally
SEDOL	Abbreviated from Stock Exchange Daily Official List		
	International Stock Exchange in London	All countries except United States and Canada	First 4 to 5 digits of company ID, plus security ID
ISIN	Abbreviated from International Security Identification Numbers		
	International Organization for Standardization	All countries	Two characters for country ID, plus a local security ID up to 9 digits, plus 1 check digit

[1] A check digit is used at the end of a series of numbers to confirm by computer that the preceding digits are correct.

WPK Nummer	Used by stock exchanges in Germany and Austria (Wertpapierkenn-Nummer)
SICOVAM	Used in French stock exchanges (SICOVAM = Société Interprofessionel pour la Compensation de Valeurs Mobilières)
SVM	Used by Belgian stock exchange (Secretariat des Valeurs Mobilières)
Euro SVM	Used for international companies by Belgian stock exchange (Euro-clear Operations Center)
CEDEL	Used in Luxembourg (Centrale de Liveraison de valeurs Mobilieres S.A.)

The stock exchanges of Japan, Korea, and Taiwan issue four-digit identification numbers which are only used locally. Some ID systems are international, some are local-regional, and some, such as those in Asia, purely local. There are so many numbering systems it becomes quickly apparent that none of them is adequate to handle the volume required by global researchers. As a result, many researchers develop numbering systems of their own. In considering numbering systems and their appropriate use in fundamental analysis, it is necessary to be aware of the following principles:

1. All systems assign numbers only to publicly traded securities. If a specific security is not traded publicly, it is of no interest to an investor; however, it should be assigned an artificial number. All of a company's sources of capital should be identified for analysis.
2. Derivative securities are not covered. For example, warrants, options, and rights are not systematically covered even though the securities are publicly traded. A number related to the original security should be assigned.
3. If a security is traded in more than one stock exchange, multiple numbers are assigned so as to receive information from each stock exchange. With cross-exchange listings proliferating in response to increasingly active global financing, the systematic organization of such numbers becomes crucial to efficient data operations.
4. As the status of companies changes because of mergers and acquisitions, security identification numbers will also change. The numbers should be well linked to their companies to avoid the loss of information related to the company under research.

Security Identification Codes

In addition to identification numbers, most stock exchanges assign an alpha character code called the *ticker* to identify specific securities. The ticker is usually composed of a few characters and should be easy to remember. A ticker is usually an acronym or initials representing a company's name, such as IBM for International Business Machines, or GM for General Motors. Some stock exchanges have hundreds of securities to handle, and tickers are the only tool with which to deliver information.

However, tickers have problems similar to those of security identification numbers. The combinations of characters sometimes bear no relationship to the names of the companies they represent.

Security Names

When a company's securities consist only of common stock, a preferred stock, and a few bonds, identifying a specific security is easy. Many utility companies in the United States, on the other hand, issue a series of preferred stocks, and assigning a unique and systematic name to each security is necessary.

Stock Exchange Trading

In order to receive market information, it is necessary to know where specific securities are traded. A few stocks are traded in perhaps a score of stock exchanges, and trading units on each stock exchange may be different. Of course, depending on the location of the exchanges, trading currencies may also differ. In this connection, American Depository Receipts or similar instruments also should be noted. Trading in several stock exchanges is an indication of global financing.

Basic Terms of Conditions

Securities have distinctive features and may differ significantly. Distinctions between common stocks, preferred stocks, and fixed income securities are discussed throughout Chapter 5. However, the following information is required for each security:

Common Stocks	Par value
	Dividend rights
	Voting rights
	Liquidation rights
Preferred Stocks	Par value
	Dividend feature
	Possible voting feature
	Issue date
	Reimbursement date
	Conversion feature if applicable
	Liquidation rights
Fixed Income Securities (Bonds)	Par value
	Total amount issued
	Interest feature
	Issue date
	Reimbursement date(s)
	Early retirement conditions if applicable
	Conversion feature if applicable
	Securities as collateral (if any)

3.2 FINANCIAL INFORMATION

Most of the information provided by companies to the public consists of detailed financial data. The following sections discuss this information as it relates to various categories: market data, financial reporting and accounting principles, and the sources of the various pieces of information needed by analysts.

3.2.1 Market Data

Market information is continuously provided by companies, stock exchanges, ticker services, various electronic data delivery systems, and the media. Trading information is provided constantly while stock exchanges are open. Some trading systems allow transactions beyond specific trading hours.

Stock Exchanges

Daily activity on stock exchanges generates information on stock prices, the volume of stocks traded, cash dividends, stock splits, and stock dividends. Although relatively few types of data are available, the amounts are vast. Aggregate information based on various indices is also available. Many data providers, from small, private operators to global distributors such as Reuters, Bloomberg, and Telerate, monitor the information on-line with computers via international communication networks.

The ability to compare current with historical information obviously requires background in such things as stock dividends, stock splits, rights issues, options, and warrants. Information on dividends and stock splits is readily available. Information on rights issues, options, or warrants is not as easily obtainable and, even when available, it is a complicated process to compute the impact on stock prices.

News Releases and the Media. Most publicly traded companies are obligated to reveal any major event affecting the company—from mergers, acquisitions, and new products, to legal actions, major achievements in research and development, and substantial changes in earnings. How this information is distributed varies. Company news releases are often faxed, mailed in advance, or hand delivered to major news distributors such as newspapers and news agencies.

Although announcements on earnings are major events for the financial community, they usually contain only limited information. They are significant, nevertheless, because earnings reports give some indication of a company's performance. Earnings, however, must be seen in the wider context of subsequent financial statements.

3.2.2 Financial Reporting and Accounting Principles

The most comprehensive source of company-specific information is the annual report and any interim reports the company may issue. In many countries this is a well-organized body of information, and it is usually verified by a third party. Annual reports are produced for many different reasons. As custodians of the capital provided by investors and creditors, a company's management is obligated to report on its use. Tax authorities and other government agencies, as guardians of the public interest, also have an interest in the activities of corporations. There are some differences in the methods of financial reporting, depending on the purpose, but the underlying theme is that companies should openly disclose their activities. A certain consistency is required in reporting corporate activities, and the basic rules, discussed later in detail, will be used throughout this book. The focus will be on the financial reporting rules applied to corporations, especially those that are publicly traded.

The frequency of company reports varies by country and by purpose. Some company reports are issued to meet regulatory requirements, whereas others are aimed at specific interest groups. Publicly traded corporations are required to issue their financial statements regularly. The United States and Canada require quarterly reporting, and most other countries require semiannual reporting. A few countries require only annual reporting. But analysts, investors, and others, especially in the United States, challenge the need for quarterly reporting and question whether the increased volume of information is relevant. What is needed, they insist, are regulations that concentrate on the quality and usefulness of the information provided to investors.

The format of financial reports varies by country and company. Financial analysts bear the burden of this accounting diversity. There is no perfect set of accounting standards for analysts. Even if all the world's divergent accounting standards were reduced to one set of "perfect" standards, they would not be universally understood. For one thing, no one is trained to deal with the existing multitude of accounting standards. And even if they were harmonized, how could they be understood and adopted by each individual country?

Accounting may not be a science, but a scientific analysis of each issue will help to construct a coherent set of accounting standards for global financial analysis. The following section explains common rules for preparing and understanding financial statements.

General Accounting Procedures

General accounting procedures apply to the generation of accounting information for financial statements. Their preparation and distribution adhere to the following steps:

Procedures for Setting Accounting Standards. Many interested groups are involved in setting accounting standards. In most countries, the standards are set by an authoritative government body. In a few countries, standards are developed by private groups, such as associations of certified public accountants. There is a significant movement worldwide for countries to cooperate in order to further internationalize capital markets. The European Union (EU) and the International Accounting Standards Committee (IASC) have been especially active in this effort. However, most continental European countries require that company financial reports conform, to some extent, to reports required for tax purposes. Thus, tax laws have a significant influence on financial statements, which complicates international harmonization.

The focus of financial reporting differs slightly, depending on each country's history. In some countries, banks were often the most significant source of capital for companies, which led financial reporting to focus on the liquidity of assets. As a result, the balance sheet was highlighted. In other countries, equity capital, provided by a few families, as in Italy and Sweden, or by a large number of unknown shareholders, grew more significant. Consequently, emphasis was put on various measures of income, leading to an increased focus on the income statement. In recent years, an increase in bankruptcies and in mergers and acquisitions in some countries has led investors to be more interested in a company's cash position. This, in turn, has elevated the importance of the cash flow statement.

In summary, accounting standards vary around the world because of differences in capital and credit market structures, and in how companies obtain financing. There are many historical reasons for accounting diversity. Since World War II, however, the rise of global communications has broken down national boundaries and increasingly opened up a truly international capital market. As more and more capital providers cast their eyes beyond their own national borders to assess investment opportunities, the growing need for internationally accepted accounting standards becomes ever more apparent. The development of such standards, however, has lagged. Easy, meaningful comparisons of corporate financial results around the world remain a distant goal.

Preparing Financial Statements. The financial condition of small, self-financed companies owned by an individual or a family is of little public interest, but whoever has stewardship of someone else's money has to account for how it is managed. When bank loan financing was the major source of a company's capital, equity holders and management were typically the same party and financial statements were prepared by the owner/manager. The focus was on the liquidity of assets controlled by the company, and thus their availability for loan repayments. As equity financing became more popular, management was increasingly separated from ownership and the preparation of financial statements became the responsibility of management. Company managers became professional custodians of the capital they managed.

Verification of Information Prepared by Management. Attestation functions, or verification of information prepared by management, are relatively insignificant to creditors, inasmuch as their focus is on a company's ability to repay loans no matter how well the company is doing. As long as assets and income are conservatively recorded, creditors are comfortable. On the other hand, the relationship of management to equity holders requires public reporting on all aspects of management's activities. The attestation function is performed by independent public auditors. The degree of credibility attached to financial statements prepared by public auditors varies by country and by company size. There is, however, significant consensus on verification procedures around the world because of the influence of major international accounting firms.

For the analyst who uses financial statements, verifying the numbers reported is no longer necessary. Ideally, auditors should not limit themselves to the attestation minimally required by the regulations of each country. Auditors should encourage managers to prepare financial statements aimed at satisfying the needs of all.

Dissemination of Information to the Public. As diverse parties—not just investors—increasingly focus attention on corporate activities, the dissemination of information to the public has grown in importance. These so-called stakeholders, with widely varying agendas, range from environmental groups and communities hoping to expand their corporate tax base, to unions seeking to preserve jobs. The demand for more and more corporate information has become most pressing, perhaps, from those seeking to reduce, if not eliminate, insider trading. Such trading activity has become a major issue in some countries, and regulators now aggressively seek to limit the practice. Nevertheless, the use of inside information is still tolerated in some countries. For the globalization of capital markets to work, everyone in the market must have access to the same information. Progress in electronic data transmission is improving the process, but those who prepare and distribute corporate information, as well as those who consume it, should be committed to full public disclosure.

Accounting Principles

Financial reporting is based on general accounting principles. Sometimes, however, as the later discussion of consistency, comparability, completeness, relevance, and reliability will show, trade-offs are made between various principles or priorities. Different countries tend to emphasize one principle over another. How these principles are applied, therefore, is often a relevant dimension in the comparison of accounting systems.

Matching Principle. There is no reason for a company to use resources without expecting some form of benefit. The best accounting method for measuring the performance of an activity is to compare total cash receipts with total cash disbursements. However, cash is transformed into different types of assets before it returns to the company as cash. If all transactions are completed and returned to the company as cash in the same year, the usual length of an accounting period, measuring the performance of the transaction is not difficult. But what about a transaction that takes several years to complete? Then the resources spent as expenses have to be allocated to the period in which the benefits are returned to the company. This process of matching expenditures to the resulting benefits is based on the Matching Principle.

The Matching Principle is linked to another accounting standard, the Periodicity Principle. This principle says that accounting is divided into several periods (usually one year each). Without periodicity there would be no need for matching. If the operating cycle in an industry is one year or shorter, all activities for the year are accumulated and presented as operating activities. If the operating cycle for an industry is longer than one year, expenditures for the activities are allocated as expenses to the extent that the benefits from the activities are reasonably assured.

In preparing financial statements, the Matching Principle has an additional implication. Providers of capital change continuously in modern capital markets. Those who provide resources during a specific period have the right to receive the benefits from that contribution. The benefit could be in the form of interest, a dividend, or capital appreciation. The Matching Principle ensures the appropriate allocation of profit. For the relationship between matching and conservatism, see ''Conservatism'' in a later section.

Monetary Unit. All transactions by an entity are recorded in monetary units, which are usually expressed as a local currency. The monetary unit, a convenient standard in expressing changes in resources for financial reporting, assumes the currency is reasonably stable. When it is not stable, current cost accounting (or inflation accounting specific to local conditions, e.g., in Brazil) is often used. If transactions by an entity involve multiple currencies, the foreign currency gain or loss is computed.

Historical Cost. A company's cash is exchanged for other types of assets. The assets, in turn, may be transformed several times within or outside the organization and are eventually converted back to cash. This is called an operating cycle. During an operating cycle such assets as products waiting to be sold, or amounts to be collected from sales, have a relatively short life. These are called current assets, and they are not significantly affected by price levels or market value changes. Noncurrent (or fixed) assets, such as manufacturing equipment, remain significantly longer with a company. The process of allocating usage of such assets is often unverifiable. The Historical Cost Principle records the value of assets or liabilities at their purchase price as long as they stay with the organization.

The historical purchase price is verifiable and reliable. Under this convention, all allocation of usage of the assets is also based on the historical cost. In some countries, when the market price of an asset significantly changes after it has been purchased, revaluation of the asset is permitted. However, because the revaluation process is not verifiable, the gain or loss resulting from such revaluations should be treated differently from other, more evident transactions.

Recently, there has been a development toward increased use of market value. An example is market value accounting for equity and fixed income securities on insurance company balance sheets.

Consistency and Comparability. *Consistency* means that similar transactions are treated in a similar fashion in different periods. Consistency over time makes information comparable and, therefore, useful for analysis. However, consistency can sometimes be difficult to achieve. Regardless of a company's efforts, changes in regulations or in the scope of the entity (the size or composition of the company) may not allow consistent reporting. Inconsistency resulting from a change in regulations is expressed either as a prior period adjustment or as a restatement of the previous year's information. Inconsistency resulting from change in an entity is often ignored.

Comparability, the characteristic that allows one to make accurate comparisons, is the most important need of a financial analyst, especially in developing a database. Yet accurate comparisons in such a crucial matter as the relative profitability of companies are extremely complex. For example, the level of an investor's profit should not depend on whether his capital is invested in a bank or a toy factory, or in a developed or an emerging market, but only on the risk he is willing to take. Investors are penalized, nevertheless, because net income is computed quite differently from country to country and even from company to company. There are numerous reasons for this incomparability of net incomes:

- No two businesses are identical.
- Businesses may operate within different environments, in terms of economy, social structures, political, and juridical systems.
- There are significantly different regulations for banks and insurance companies, as compared with industrial firms.
- Different businesses have different accounting standards.

No two entirely comparable earnings per share (EPS) ratios could ever be produced for analysis unless all the transactions in both companies were prepared by the same people using the same accounting standards. Therefore, a major goal of this book is to assist analysts in the preparation of ''more comparable'' company information for analysis.

Conservatism. *Conservatism,* in regard to preparing a business's information for analysis, means that when doubt exists, the solution least likely to overstate assets and income and least likely to understate liabilities should be chosen. When this dictum is followed, companies tend to record less rather than more income. This offers a convenient approach for accountants.

Conservatism requires that an asset be valued at historical cost (see the earlier section "Historical Cost"). Revaluation is appropriate only when the asset's market value is lower than its purchase price.

Conservatism may conflict with the Matching Principle (as described in an earlier section). Whereas the Matching Principle produces the most accurate estimate of a period's revenue and expense, conservatism results in an estimate in which revenues are low and expenses are high. For equity investors, the Matching Principle usually provides the best estimate of the income-generating ability of a company. Conservatism, on the other hand, is preferred by creditors, because it often provides a minimum value that can be extracted from the company in the case of insolvency.

Completeness. Information should be *complete and sufficiently explained* so that it can be used by prudent decision makers. It also should be balanced with relevance (see "Relevance and Reliability" in the following section).

The level of detail used in accounting information is important to those who prepare financial statements. It is also important to financial analysts and database designers. It is impossible to construct a database that includes all accounts disclosed by all industries and that also meets the needs of all database users.

In accounting, as a general rule, a related account on one side of a balance sheet must not be used to cancel or reduce another on the opposite side of the balance sheet. For example, accounts receivable cannot be used to offset accounts payable. Yet there are rare cases when it is better to combine closely related accounts and show net amounts. For example, deferred tax assets and deferred tax liabilities may be netted, because they are so similar in nature. They represent potential future payables and receivables to the same government agency.

Relevance and Reliability. Information in financial reporting should be *relevant*. Such information affects decisions. It should assist in predicting future results and help to confirm or correct earlier expectations. To be relevant, all information needed by a reasonably prudent decision maker should be fully disclosed. Normally, for example, the consolidation of subsidiaries is desirable, because their operations represent a single economic entity. However, when an industrial parent consolidates a financial services subsidiary, the result is irrelevant. Interest expense for bank loans is a financial expense to an industrial company, whereas it is an operating expense to a bank. The aggregate information is therefore less useful.

The information that companies provide should also be *reliable and verifiable*. Information users heavily rely on public attestation functions, such as auditing, for primary information in financial statements. Ratios that companies compute from primary data should be fully explained to users, thereby making the ratios verifiable.

Some balance is needed in the entire costly process of producing corporate financial statements that are subsequently evaluated in depth by analysts. Both companies and analysts must measure the costs and benefits of this process. Companies could devote infinite resources to computing a theoretically accurate depreciation of an asset to little additional benefit. Similarly, database developers must weigh the degree of accuracy desired and the expense involved in processing and analyzing the data. This is true even though computer technology has made it cheaper to build and maintain databases.

DEFINITIONS IN U.S. ACCOUNTING STANDARDS[1]

Qualitative Characteristics of Accounting Information

Relevance	Information is relevant to a decision if it makes a difference to the decision maker in his/her ability to predict events or to confirm or correct expectations.
Reliability	Information is reliable if it is verifiable and neutral, and if users can depend on it to represent that which it is intended to represent.
Consistency	Consistency is an inter-period comparison which requires the use of the same accounting principles from one period to another.
Comparability	Comparability allows the users of accounting information to assess the similarities and differences either among different entities for the same period or for the same entity over different periods.
Conservatism	When in doubt choose the solution that will be least likely to overstate assets and income and least likely to understate liabilities.

---

[1] From: "*Statements of Financial Accounting Concepts #2*" of the Financial Accounting Standards Board (U.S.), May, 1980.

Application of Accounting Principles

From the general principles that form the basis of accounting practice, various accounting standards have been developed to provide practical guidance for those preparing and those verifying financial statements. This section discusses general issues regarding the application of accounting standards, and the following section focuses on more specific issues.

Inclusion of Assets and Liabilities. An important issue in the preparation of financial statements is what criteria to use in recording assets and liabilities. Bookkeeping procedures inevitably generate many intermediate accounts until the final financial statements are produced.

To be classified as an asset, an item must have probable future economic benefit to the organization, and it must be recorded at the value that reflects that benefit. For example, fixed assets are presented on the asset side of the balance sheet at historical cost less accumulated depreciation, their contra account. If fixed assets were shown at their historical value on the asset side and the contra accounts were presented in the liability side, both sides of the balance sheet would be overstated.

A liability is an estimable and reasonably predictable future obligation that consumes a company's assets. For example, a possible negative outcome of a pending lawsuit is not recorded as a liability unless the outcome is reasonably predictable and can be estimated.

What about companies that buy back their own stock or bonds? In some countries, companies present the bonds or stock they have bought back as an investment in the current or long-term asset section of the balance sheet. In such cases the total assets and total stockholders' equity are overstated. (See accounts related to shareholders' equity in Chapter 5.)

The inclusion of assets and liabilities is sometimes confused with the full disclosure requirement. Full disclosure does not mean that all intermediate accounts must be disclosed. If a certain item is classified as an asset and becomes a part of a company's total assets, it should have service potentials and future benefits. The future benefits should belong to the company, and the company should have legally enforceable claims on the benefits.

Liabilities can be seen as the mirror image of assets. They are future obligations, resulting from past or current transactions, and are payable by the reporting entity. The main difference between accounting for assets and accounting for liabilities is related to conservatism (see the earlier section "Conservatism"). A stronger probability of realization is needed to record an asset than a liability. Assets are recorded only if it is highly probable that they will be realized in the future and can be estimated. Liabilities, on the other hand, are generally recorded as soon as they can be estimated, but they also must be probable. If a potential liability is less than probable, it is recorded as a contingent liability off the balance sheet.

Classification of Items. Numerous transactions occur in a large organization. However, financial statements should not list each individual account. Materiality, that which is material or meaningful, typically determines which items should be classified separately.

If the aim is to describe the activities of an entity to interested outside parties, financial statements should not ignore their audience. Of course, many diverse groups have an interest in large organizations and one set of financial statements cannot satisfy all of them. Financial statements for special-interest groups can be produced by analysts with the assistance of a database when such statements are not provided by the company itself. Databases are well suited to selecting and organizing general information for specific users. In just this way, data in financial statements can be reorganized for the specific needs of users.

Substance over Form. In interpreting the transactions of an entity, there is a choice between focusing on economic substance or on legal form. For the purposes of financial analysis, the former is generally preferable. It should be noted, however, that emphasis on either substance or form varies by country.

Typical instances of when an emphasis of substance over form is appropriate are the consolidation of subsidiaries and the capitalization of long-term leases. If the resources of a subsidiary are substantially directed by another organization, past or future economic performance of the organization cannot be evaluated without disclosure of the relationship. This is sometimes problematic when, for example, tax regulations in most countries require companies to report their taxable income on a single-company basis. The reason is that governments often contribute to a company's earnings in a specific way, for example, by providing infrastructure. Thus, tax authorities focus on legal structure rather than economic substance. Equity holders also have claims on residual earnings from all sources in which the company has invested.

When a company uses an asset—machinery, for example—that it substantially owns on a long-term lease basis, and the potential future services will be substantially used by the company, the machinery qualifies and should be recorded as an asset by the company regardless of how the purchase was financed.

Estimation of Ongoing Earnings. One of the most important tasks of financial analysts is to estimate a company's future ongoing earnings. Thus, the reliability, accuracy, and relevance of the information provided are all important in compiling data. Revenue and expenses should be organized in a way that gives analysts enough information to estimate ongoing earnings in future years.

Earnings, whether referring to net income or profits, is an accounting term widely used in financial statements. However, an examination of how such earnings are calculated reveals many different methods. Each method has its own justification. The term is quite often defined by the requirements of tax regulations. No matter what the method of calculation, however, data compiled for analysts should be relevant to an estimate of ongoing earnings.

Ongoing earnings are often defined as "earnings before extraordinary items." This term implies earnings from the use of all earning capacities in a company. If the facility is maintained in reasonable condition, the amount of future earnings can be easily estimated. This assumes that earnings take into consideration the results of nonoperating activities, not only income from excess cash temporarily invested, for example, but also such costs as interest payments for borrowing. Extraordinary activities, such as losses from natural disasters or the restructuring of a significant portion of a company's manufacturing facilities, should not be included.

Sometimes there are incentives for company management to manipulate earnings. This can be accomplished by pushing revenues and expenses into different periods, thereby overstating or understanding the income of the current period. Therefore, caution is needed in using historical earnings to estimate future earnings.

Impacts on Cash Positions. In recent years, many analysts have been increasingly concerned about the cash positions of companies. Growing merger and acquisition activities are the reason. As a result, the cash flow statement has become one of the most important components of a financial statement. The use of accrual accounting, which is sometimes far removed from cash accounting, reduces the clarity of a company's cash position. All elements of a company's financial statements must be organized in a way that provides sufficient information to predict its future liquidity.

Issues Related to Specific Accounting Policies

This section addresses problems that arise when specific accounting standards are applied in practice. The issues are not directly linked to any single item appearing in financial statements. This discussion starts with an explanation of why standards differ between countries, then examines individual issues. Issues related to disclosure of information are covered in the following section, and those related to specific financial statement items are discussed subsequently in Section 3.2.3.

General Accounting Standards Followed by Individual Countries. The development of accounting standards in any specific country is based on the needs of that country. In some countries the development of standards is historically related to tax regulations, rather than economic justification or conceptual accounting theory. For example, the Debit-Credit Format for income statements, still used in some countries, was the prevailing method in many countries in earlier years. The Debit-Credit Format does not express any justification of income or expenses, nor is it based on the accrual method of accounting. Reversal of provisions are recorded as income rather than adjustments of expenses, for example.

Among the major accounting standards of the world are those of the United States, the United Kingdom and the Commonwealth, and those of continental Europe. U.S. standards aim to present true earnings, which implies some reliance on economic theory. Accounting in the United Kingdom and the former British Commonwealth, which included all of Britain's former colonies in Africa and Asia, and is now known simply as the Commonwealth, is based on the concept of "true and fair" financial statements. This concept is defined relative to the society in which it is applied, which makes it a somewhat political concept. Continental European accounting is often influenced by tax law. In recent years, the distinctions between British and continental European standards have faded somewhat as a result of European Union Directives that apply to both (see the following box). The specific accounting standards of the European Commission and the International Accounting Standard Committee are provided at the beginning of Volume II.

EUROPEAN UNION DIRECTIVES

A goal of the European Union (EU) is to create a unified business environment among member states, including harmonization of corporate accounting laws. To achieve this goal, several directives regarding financial reporting have been issued. These are the Fourth Directive, which regulates formats and rules of accounting, and the Seventh Directive, which regulates consolidation accounting. The legal status of these directives is such that whereas they have been adopted by the European Commission (an EU body), all member states must incorporate them into their own law within a specified time. Thus, there was to be a strong legal basis for enforcing directives. In practice, however, the intent of the Commission has not always beeen carried out, because the same legal text has been interpreted quite differently by courts in various countries. In addition, the original directives themselves provide room for flexibility.

The Fourth and Seventh Directives were adopted by the European Commission in 1978 and 1983, respectively. By the early 1990s, all member countries had incorporated them into their own laws, so both directives are currently in force throughout the EU.

INTERNATIONAL ACCOUNTING STANDARDS COMMITTEE

The International Accounting Standard Committee (IASC), a global, private-sector organization, was founded in 1973 and is based in London. IASC membership is made up of national associations of public accountants and bases its authority on private-sector regulation.

The IASC develops accounting standards and promotes their implementation around the world. In developing standards, there is a due process, similar to that of national standard setters such as the Financial Accounting Standards Board (FASB) in the United States. IASC statements now cover many different areas in its efforts to promote international accounting standards. However, because international agreement is needed to adopt a particular standard, the IASC sometimes allows many different alternative accounting treatments. This makes the standards easier to implement, but reduces their harmonizing effect. The inability to enforce standards is a central problem for the IASC. It has no authority of its own and must rely on that of its member professional bodies. The IASC can only urge companies to observe IASC standards.

A criticism often leveled at the IASC is that it is influenced mostly by the accounting environments of the United States and the United Kingdom. Individuals from both countries are among the most active in the organization. By and large, it is unlikely that many accountants are familiar with the content or status of IASC standards.

Scope of Entities. Even companies whose main operations do not involve investing money may decide to invest a significant portion of their assets. If an investment is simply to use temporarily available cash, the assets can be used for operations whenever the company needs them. However, if the investment is long-term and controls another organization, such as a supplier, or simply duplicates the same type of business in other countries, investment income from the assets is insufficient to analyze the company's future performance. Many companies are connected, horizontally or vertically, with other companies.

For a meaningful analysis of the financial status of such entities, operating activities of all related entities must be consolidated. The method of accounting for such investments varies, depending on the degree of dominance a company exercises over another company's decision-making process. The consolidation of subsidiaries that are significantly controlled by a company is generally accepted worldwide. The application of consolidation accounting varies, and different methods have been adopted at different times. This creates problems in analyzing historical data on a global basis.

Valuation of Investment Assets. Investment assets in a company are classified as short-term or long-term securities, depending on the length of the holding period (intention to hold rather than actual holding period), whereas equity securities, fixed income securities, and other investments, including real estate investments, are classified by asset type.

The method of placing a value on the equity securities of one company held by another depends on the purpose of the holding. Although there are variations, typical valuation methods may be illustrated as follows:

Valuation of Equity Securities

Dominant holding	Greater than 50%	A. Full consolidation
Joint ventures	Combined control	B. Proportional consolidation
Substantial holding	20% to 50% holding	C. Equity Method
Minority holding	Less than 20%	D. Cost Method
Short-term holding	Insignificant	E. Mark to market or Lower of Cost or Market (LCM)

Valuation of Fixed Income Securities

Long-term holding	Amortized cost method
Short-term holding	Mark to market with LCM

Valuation of Other Investments

Real estate for leasing	Rental income

A. FULL CONSOLIDATION

When 50 percent or more of a company's voting power is held by another company, the decision-making process is dominated by the investing company and the two companies should be treated as one. In accounting, the process is called *consolidation*.

The Full Consolidation Method dictates that the parent company must include all of the subsidiary's operating results in its own. All line items in the subsidiary's balance sheet must be included in the parent company's balance sheet. The parent's investment in the subsidiary will be replaced by the shareholders' equity in the subsidiary. Further procedures eliminate all intercompany transactions such as the purchase or sale of merchandise, as well as receivables and payables between the companies.

If the parent company's ownership is less than 100 percent, the remaining ownership is treated as a minority interest. The income statement will set aside the earnings of the minority shareholders from the current earnings, and the balance sheet will accumulate the undistributed earnings as minority interests.

However, the nominal ownership of capital is not the sole criterion for consolidation. The substance of the relationship between the two companies, which of the two actually exercises control, should be the standard in deciding whether to consolidate. Suppose, for example, a

(continued)

(continued)

company owns 80 percent or 100 percent of a company in a politically unstable country. In such a case, exercising control may be impossible or impractical and full consolidation would distort the quality of assets included in the parent company's consolidated financial statement. Another example is a corporation that owns 49 percent of a company in an emerging country whose government owns the other 51 percent. If the government merely owns the stock and is passive in the company's operations, the Full Consolidation Method is more appropriate because dominant control is exercised with 49 percent ownership.

B. PROPORTIONAL CONSOLIDATION

When a company has a significant influence on the decision-making process but does not dominate, the situation is a little tricky. Typically, the relationship has the form of a joint venture, whereby all parties have equal voting powers, that is, 50 percent for each of two parties, one-third each for three parties, and so forth.

The parent company may include all sales and assets of the joint venture and set aside the portion not owned by the parent company as a minority interest, using the Full Consolidation Method. However, the Full Consolidation Method may be misleading as to the ownership of assets in the consolidated financial statements, because the parent company can not exercise full ownership.

An alternative is to include the portion of sales and assets to the extent of the ownership. This is called the Proportional Consolidation Method. This process will not create any minority interest in the consolidated financial statements.

C. EQUITY METHOD IN CONSOLIDATION

If a company has a significant influence on another company's decision-making process but is not dominating, the Equity Method may be used. This process is also called *consolidation* in many countries.

In using the Equity Method, sales and expenses of the owned company are not included in the parent company's income statement, nor assets and liabilities in a parent company's balance sheet. The parent company's investment account is adjusted by the proportion of the owned company's earnings or losses. Actual distribution of the earnings by the invested company will reduce the investments.

Determination of whether significant influence is present is based on the degree of control rather than legal ownership percentage. Typically, 20 percent to 50 percent of voting rights is a criterion for the determination of significance, but this should be based on ownership of other shareholders of the subject company. Another consideration is whether the investment is limited to the equity investment, or whether it also includes loan investment.

The quality of the investments adjusted by equity earnings is not the same as that of other assets, and they must be treated differently from other investments.

(continued)

(continued)

D. COST METHOD IN OTHER LONG-TERM INVESTMENTS

Investments can be long-term or short-term in nature. Whether an investment is long-term or short-term is determined by the intention of the investor rather than the actual holding period.

Long-term investments without any significant influence on the invested company should be valued by the Cost Method. The investments should be recorded at purchase price unless there is any significant impairment of their value in the market. Any distribution from the invested company will be accounted for as dividend income.

E. MARK TO MARKET OR LCM

Short-term investments, such as marketable equity securities or marketable fixed income securities, are investments owned temporarily in a company, which the investor intends to sell as soon as it is profitable to do so. Ideally, the value of short-term investments should be established by the market, but this is prevented by the conservatism dictated by general accounting principles and by the difficulty of setting a fair market value when certain securities are not actively traded. Usually, the lower of either the cost or the market value determines their value. Temporary declines in value must be recorded at the end of the accounting period. Recovery of the write-down in value is allowed in most countries.

Foreign Currencies. Foreign currency gains and losses are generated by companies that operate internationally or own foreign subsidiaries. Foreign currencies have an impact on two separate accounting areas, transactions and translations. Transactions, such as imports and exports, involve buying and selling in foreign currencies. Translation, on the other hand, involves consolidating the financial statements of foreign subsidiaries into the parent company's statements when the functional currency of a subsidiary is different from the parent's.

Gains or losses from operations involving foreign currencies are included in the income statement regardless of the accounting method used. Losses can be minimized by hedging.

The translation of financial statements of foreign subsidiaries is required if they use local currencies as their functional currencies. Translation methods vary by country. However, the method recommended in Statements of Financial Accounting Standards (SFAS) 52 of the FASB of the United States is followed by many countries. Modifications of the Current Rate Method, as it is known in the United States, or the Closing Rate Method, as it is known in the United Kingdom, are used in some countries, especially those experiencing high inflation. In other countries, these two standard methods are used but are known by other names.

Gains or losses from the Current Rate Method directly adjust shareholders' equity. There are exceptional cases when a subsidiary is located in a country with hyperinflation. Then, gains or losses are accounted for in the income statement. However, there are fewer exceptions now. Most countries that suffered hyperinflation in the mid-1980s have much lower inflation rates today.

Foreign Currency Transaction Gain/Loss. The conversion of foreign currency transactions is fully explained by SFAS 52. (See the following box.) This statement is applicable to exports, imports, and foreign loans that are denominated in a currency other than the reporting currency. Gains or losses from such transactions are reported in the income statement.

Foreign currency transactions can be hedged by purchasing futures or forward contracts. Completely hedged foreign currency transactions do not result in foreign currency gains or losses. The difference between the forward exchange rate and a spot rate at the time of a transaction is treated as an amortized discount or premium and accounted for as a separate revenue or expense in the income statement.

FUNCTIONAL CURRENCY AND REPORTING CURRENCY (SFAS 52), DECEMBER 1981

The most important issue addressed by SFAS 52 is how to determine a functional currency. Transactions in foreign currencies must be translated into the parent company's reporting currency. However, all of the financial transactions or financial statements of the foreign entity should be measured in terms of that entity's functional currency before they are translated into the reporting currency.

The functional currency of an entity is the currency used in the economic environment in which the entity operates. The functional currency is used to record the major activities of the entity; it is determined by considering cash flow, sales, sales market, expenses, financing, or any other significant events in the entity.

If the functional currency is not the same as the reporting currency in certain transactions, the historical rate of exchange is used for the translation and the gain/loss is reported in the income statement. Exporting or importing activities belong in this category. If most of the foreign entity's transactions are recorded in a foreign currency, the foreign currency will be the functional currency.

If the functional currency of the foreign entity is different from the reporting currency of the parent company, the Current Rate Method is used and any foreign exchange gains or losses from the translation of the foreign entity's results should be treated as retained earnings.

The currency of companies in hyperinflation countries is unstable and does not qualify as a functional currency. The company should therefore use the reporting currency as its functional currency. The Temporal Method (SFAS 8) should be used to convert the company's financial statements.

Current Rate (Closing Rate) Method. The Current Rate (Closing Rate) Method is well explained in SFAS 52 of the U.S. Generally Accepted Accounting Principles (GAAP). The balance sheet is translated at the fiscal year-end rate of exchange, and the income statement is translated at the average exchange rate for the period. Although this is not called the Current Rate Method in some countries, the substance of the methods used is similar. Gains or losses resulting from foreign currency translations are directly accounted for in shareholders' equity and have no impact on the income statement.

As noted earlier, SFAS 52 contains a clause covering the special cases of subsidiaries located in hyperinflation countries. In such cases, SFAS 52 says the Temporal Method (SFAS 8) should be applied and gains or losses from translation should be included in the income statement.

Temporal Method. The Temporal Method is also known as the Monetary/Nonmonetary Method. Monetary assets and liabilities are translated at the current rate of exchange, and nonmonetary assets and liabilities are translated at historical rates. Gains or losses are accounted for in the income statement. Before the Monetary/Nonmonetary Method was adopted, current/noncurrent segregation was used.

However, the two methods classified some items differently, among them inventories and long-term debts. Either current/noncurrent or monetary/nonmonetary segregation was widely accepted, but eventually was replaced by the Current (Closing) Rate Method, which most countries now use.

EXCHANGE RATES USED IN THE TRANSLATION OF FOREIGN FINANCIAL STATEMENTS

	Current/ Non-current	Monetary/ Non-monetary	Temporal	Current (Closing)
Fixed Assets	Historical	Historical	Historical	Current
LT Receivables	Historical	Current	Current	Current
ST Receivables	Current	Current	Current	Current
Liquid Assets	Current	Current	Current	Current
LT Liabilities	Historical	Current	Current	Current
ST Liabilities	Current	Current	Current	Current

Deferred Income Taxes. In many countries there are significant timing differences, some permanent and others temporary, between financial accounting and tax accounting. In order to measure the true performance of a company in a specific period, the impact of tax obligations on earnings for the period must be considered. Use of the Matching Principle, which requires accrual accounting, promotes interperiod income tax allocation.

Permanent differences (see box below) between accounting rules and tax regulations, however, are not subject to deferred income taxes. Amortization of goodwill and excess entertainment expenses are examples. Special tax treatment under current cost accounting is a separate issue and, in view of its complexity, is not covered here.

In some countries there is little difference between financial accounting and tax accounting, and thus no significant timing differences. Tax authorities in these countries require that corporate financial statements conform in key respects to reporting procedures prescribed by tax regulations. Therefore, the results disclosed are of little relevance to investors trying to determine the true performance of a company.

Accounting for timing differences is defined in Accounting Principles Board (APB) Opinion 11. FASB's Statement of Financial Accounting Standards (SFAS) 96, promulgated in 1987, did not clarify some areas, and its actual adoption was postponed several times. SFAS 96 was not widely implemented and was eventually replaced by SFAS 109 in 1992. Most countries follow U.S. practice regarding deferred income taxes.

Several methods of accounting for deferred income taxes are available. The Deferred Method, based on the tax rates in effect when the timing differences originate, has been widely used since APB Opinion 11 was issued in December

---

Permanent Timing Differences

Revenues or expenses that are recognized for financial accounting purposes but are not recognized for tax purposes are classified as *permanent differences*. This classification varies, depending on the regulations in each country.

For example, income from government-issued securities is recognized as income for financial accounting purposes, but is not recognized as income for tax purposes. With respect to expenses, special benefits to key employees, amortization of goodwill (although this is recognized as an expense for tax purposes in a few countries), and excess entertainment expenses are recognized as expenses for financial accounting purposes but not for tax purposes.

If current cost accounting is used, any gain from the revaluation of assets is usually recorded as follows, which in the Netherlands, for example, is called a "semipermanent" timing difference:

Debit: Assets	100	
Credit: Revaluation Reserves (60%)		60
Deferred Tax (40%)		40

Temporary Timing Differences

Revenue or expense in some transactions is allowed for financial reporting purposes during the year, but is postponed for tax purposes. The timing differences between financial reporting and tax accounting are temporary. A common example of temporary differences involves depreciation, for which methods used for tax and financial reporting often differ.

The transactions that can cause such timing differences depend on the regulations of each country. There are significant differences between countries in the level of conformity required in financial reporting and tax accounting. Because Germany and Austria, for example, require a high level of conformity, timing differences in those countries are rare, whereas deferred tax liabilities and the resulting timing differences are common in the United States, the United Kingdom, and the Netherlands.

1967. This is a comprehensive but impractical method for companies with many transactions, and therefore a change of method was seen as necessary. The complications were compounded by transactions encouraged by special tax incentives.

The Liability Method is linked to the balance sheet. Actual tax liabilities are estimated on the balance sheet date. This method uses probable tax rates at the time of reversal.

The Net-of-Tax Method does not record any amount of deferred tax, assets, or liabilities on the balance sheet. Deferred taxes are taken directly as an adjustment to related assets, liabilities, revenues, or expenses. This method has been accepted academically but has never been adopted in practice. It does not present potential true benefits of assets or burdens of liabilities.

Deferred tax assets are avoided as a result of conservatism. However, deferred tax assets are generally allowed to be recorded as an offset against deferred tax liabilities. Generally speaking, they can also be recognized if it is likely that they will be realized in the future. In Australia, deferred tax assets are recorded as future income tax benefits, rather than being netted against deferred tax liabilities.

Deferred Method

The Deferred Method focuses on the income statement. The originating tax rate for each account is applied to all temporary timing differences, and a resulting deferred tax liability (or asset) is recorded on the balance sheet. If, in later years, tax rates change, no adjustment is made in the balance sheet. Thus, after a few years of changing tax rates, the deferred tax amounts in the balance sheet tend to become meaningless. Often a deferred tax liability will be recorded, even though it may never actually be paid. However, the method is valid in the income statement.

Liability Method

The Liability Method centers on the balance sheet. The deferred tax liability (asset) is continuously updated for possible changes in tax rates at the time of reversal. Thus the liability (asset) is always current, and there is an expectation that the recorded amount will actually be paid (received). The income statement, however, will be distorted by gains and losses resulting from changes in tax rates, that may not have anything to do with the operations of the company.

Net-of-Tax Method

The Net-of-Tax Method focuses on the tax effect of individual assets and liabilities, rather than using a company-wide approach, as do the Deferred and Liability Methods. For example, if an asset is bought for $1,000 and the tax rate is 40 percent, the asset would be recorded on the balance sheet at $600. The reason is that the total value of the depreciation expense over the life of the asset will be $400.

EPS Computation. Earnings per share (EPS) is one of the most widely used figures in the financial community, but there are many definitions of EPS and many people use them differently. Earnings per share is simply computed by dividing net income by the number of shares for the period. However, different earnings per share can be computed by choosing different earnings or different numbers of shares. The appropriate EPS depends on the purpose of analysis.

Selection of Earnings. If the purpose is to analyze the competitiveness of companies with different lines of business activity but similar capital structures, *operating income* should be selected. This is a good measurement of operating performance, but the capital structures must be analyzed separately.

Earnings before extraordinary items should be used if the aim of analysis is to consider the capital structure as well as to assess ongoing operating performance. The earnings, including nonoperating gains/losses, are a good measurement of a company's long-term growth and cash position.

Net income after extraordinary items is one of the most common earnings numbers used around the world. It embraces all activities, including extraordinary activities. If operations in a company do not change significantly in a specific year, these all-inclusive earnings will not differ much from continuing earnings (earnings before extraordinary items). These earnings also provide a dependable indication of a company's ability to pay dividends in a specific year. A company's short-term overall performance and cash position will be directly related to this earnings number.

Number of Shares. The most popular method of computing EPS is to use a *weighted average number of shares*. Ideally, the shares' weighted average should be calculated on a daily basis during the subject period. That is important for companies with active capital transactions such as options, rights issues, or convertible securities. In some countries such derivative securities are not popular and the weighing process is ignored. The impact on EPS will not be significant in such cases.

Often, the computation of EPS is based on the *number of shares outstanding* at the end of the fiscal year, rather than on the weighted average number of shares. This is justified when changes in the level of capital are infrequent. There is another argument for using the number of shares outstanding instead of the weighted average number of shares for comparing the current EPS to the future estimated EPS, in that most current shares are valid in future years. This approach is acceptable as long as most companies in a country follow the same practice and investors understand the limitations of the EPS figure based on the number of shares outstanding. However, the number of shares should be weighted to meet international acceptance. That is the best way to improve communication between those who prepare financial statements and those who analyze them. In countries with hyperinflation, however, weighted average numbers will not work because of the necessary restatement of capital, and only the year-end number of shares is relevant.

Treasury Stocks. Shares owned by the company that issues them should not be considered shares outstanding, and the company therefore should not claim extra capital for its operations for the period. This treatment of treasury stocks is nevertheless found in the presentation of EPS computations in many countries.

There is a counter point of view that argues that temporarily owned treasury stocks are insignificant and that a market for the stocks is always available. It maintains that treasury shares qualify as assets that can bring in cash, like any other short-term investment, whenever the company needs it. If the treasury shares qualify as assets, capital should not be reduced on the balance sheet and the stocks qualify for the EPS computation.

Both arguments can be made, but the second is weak because it suggests that any dividend would be paid to the company itself. To compare companies in different countries, a reduction of share capital by the amount of treasury shares is preferable.

Substantive, permanently owned treasury stocks are different and, with the exception of subsidiaries, it is accepted in most countries that companies should reduce shareholders' equity accordingly. In substance, however, there is no difference between stocks owned by a company itself and stocks owned by a subsidiary if they are consolidated. The stocks owned by consolidated subsidiaries should not inflate assets in the consolidated financial statements.

Stocks owned by an Employee Stock Option Plan (ESOP) or a company's own pension plan raise another issue. How these shares are accounted for may depend on how one judges the relationship between the the company and the pension trust. Obviously, the two organizations are legally independent, and the trust is supposed to have full authority to invest the funds in the most profitable securities. However, in reality, the trust's board of directors is under the strong influence of the company's management. In practice, it is common to use this influence in mergers or management buy-outs, and the amounts are often significant. Such an approach may encounter resistance from companies, but shares owned by an ESOP or a company's own pension fund trust should be treated as treasury stocks, and shareholders' equity should be reduced accordingly. The number of shares used to compute EPS should also be reduced by the number of treasury shares.

EARNINGS PER SHARE (EPS)

For financial analysts, EPS is one of the most convenient indicators to use in comparing the performance of companies. EPS is also used for other ratio computations. However, there is no single definition of EPS, and this complicates matters. Which definition of EPS is used depends on the purpose of analysis.

The methodology is to compute earnings applicable to the securities analyzed, divided by the number of shares that have contributed to those earnings. The varieties of EPS include primary EPS, fully diluted EPS, or EPS from ordinary activities. Possible adjustments for stock splits, stock dividends, or right issues need to be considered for historical comparisons.

Primary EPS
The computation of primary EPS is based on earnings for common shares divided by the weighted average number of common shares outstanding

(continued)

(continued)

for the period. Earnings for common shares is the net income after all operating expenses, interest expenses, income tax expenses, minority interests, and dividends to preferred stocks. Dividends to preferred stocks should reduce earnings because they are, from the point of view of common shareholders, a type of fixed expense.

The difference in most countries between interest expense for bonds and preferred dividends for preferred stocks is that interest expense is computed before tax and preferred dividends are after-tax amounts. In some countries, particular preferred dividends are before-tax amounts.

The number of shares used in EPS computations is usually the daily weighted average number of common shares outstanding for the period. The computation of this number varies slightly in different countries. Only a few countries use the number of shares outstanding at the end of the period.

Fully Diluted EPS

As capital markets become more sophisticated, there tend to be more hybrid securities, which raise important accounting issues. Obviously, these securities are issued by mutual agreement between capital providers and capital users, for whom the accounting of the securities is a secondary issue.

If hybrid securities can be converted to common stock, however, the possible conversion should be considered in EPS computations. These securities include convertible bonds, convertible preferred stocks, warrants, options, and other rights.

The concept of fully diluted (FD) EPS is not applied in many countries because:

- Most investors are not familiar with FD EPS.
- Dilutive securities are not issued in the particular country.
- No regulations require the disclosure of FD EPS.

Earnings should be adjusted as the type of shares used for EPS computations are changed. If convertible securities are included in an EPS computation, expenses related to the convertible securities should be added back to the earnings for EPS computation. For example, dividends for convertible preferred stocks should be added back to earnings for common shares if the convertible preferred stocks are included in the FD EPS computation. Another example is interest expenses for convertible bonds, which should be added back to earnings for common shares. Tax increases resulting from higher income should also be considered in the latter case.

The number of shares for an EPS computation should be increased to the full extent of the possible dilution. The possible exercise of outstanding options or warrants will increase the number of shares unless they are antidilutive. The dilution is computed using the Treasury Stock Method. The Treasury Stock Method assumes that the options or warrants are exercised at the beginning of a year or, if later, at the date of issuance.

ADJUSTMENTS FOR STOCK DIVIDENDS AND STOCK SPLITS

If there is an increase in the number of shares but the recipients of those shares do not contribute additional money to the company, the transaction should be treated as a stock dividend or a stock split. The existing shareholders have absolute preemptive rights to receive the additional shares. The stock dividend or stock split effects must be reflected in historical per share information.

A stock split is an example of the distribution of additional shares to existing shareholders uniformly, without any additional capital contribution to the company. Although not required, the par value is usually adjusted according to the distribution rate.

Stock dividends are distributed to current shareholders in proportion to the number of shares they hold. Typically, companies transfer accumulated reserves, such as asset revaluation reserves, to share capital. Stock dividends in lieu of a cash dividend should be treated as two separate transactions, that is, as a cash distribution and as a new issue. If the stock is priced lower than the current market price, the difference should be treated as a discounted issue.

A discounted stock issue (issue price is less than market price) resulting from certain rights or options should be treated as a partial stock dividend. For example, Japanese companies often issue bonus shares at 5 or 10 percent less than the current market price. The discounted portion should be treated as a stock dividend. Computation of the stock dividend ratio is complicated.

The following is an example of bonus shares issued to all shareholders at the same time; the computation process of the dilution is relatively easy.

Nippon ABC Co.

Number of shares outstanding	15 million
Current market price	2,500
Bonus shares issued	2 million
Issue price for bonus shares	2,200

$$((2,500 - 2,200) \times 2,000,000) / (2,500 \times 15,000,000)$$

$$= 0.05 \text{ (about 5 percent)}$$

When a company issues rights or options to buy shares at a fixed price, the rights or option holders may exercise them irregularly and it is therefore not easy to compute the dilutive portion, a process this book does not address.

Multiple Shares. Companies usually have one type of common share, and the remaining securities have a fixed income component, such as preferred shares, bonds, or bank borrowing. However, there are a significant number of companies with more than one type of common share.

What are multiple common shares? A common share is defined as a security that has claims to a company's residual earnings during an ongoing operating period and has the least privilege in regard to assets at liquidation. Dividends to common shares are paid after all fixed obligations. The amount of a dividend varies, depending on the company's performance during the year. If a company has several shares with these characteristics, they are called multiple shares.

Multiple shares are differentiated by various features, such as dividends per share, voting rights, and aspects in conversion to another stock. Sometimes, all of a company's multiple shares are traded at the stock exchange(s) and each is traded at a different price because of its different status. In some companies, one type of multiple share is owned only by a particular group of shareholders and is not traded, while another stock is publicly owned and traded on the stock exchange. In some cases, shares are restricted to certain investors. In Mexico and China, for example, there are restrictions on foreign ownership, whereas Brazil has restrictions on private ownership.

The bottom line for multiple shares is dividend rights, and dividends for a specific share depend on each year's operating performance. Most companies in Brazil and Korea, for example, have participative preferred shares. They have no voting rights but participate almost every year in the residual earnings after a designated amount is distributed as dividend payments to common shareholders. The substance of these preferred shares is no different from the Swiss or Austrian participation certificates or French investment certificates, and they all should be classified as a type of multiple share.

Companies in the United States create multiple shares to give existing shareholders the privilege of double voting rights when the company makes an initial public offering. In Belgium, dividends from AFV (Avantage Fiscal/Fiscaal Voordeel) shares are given favorable tax treatment. Dividends for registered shares, bearer's shares, and participation certificates in Switzerland are calculated in proportion to their par values.

Typical Multiple Shares in Various Countries

Austria	Common share, participative preferred share, participation certificate
Belgium	Ordinary share, AFV
Brazil	Ordinary share, participative preferred share
China	A Share, B Share, H Share
France	Ordinary share, investment certificate
Greece	Common share, participative preferred share
Italy	Ordinary share, savings share
Korea	Ordinary share, participative preferred share
United States	A and B common shares
Sweden	A and B shares (no segregation between restricted and free shares since January 1993)
Switzerland	Registered share, bearer's share, participation certificate

---

What do multiple shares mean to analysts? Multiple shares vary in the rights they grant to claims on a company's earnings or liquidation value, and they have a different intrinsic value. There are a number of key factors that determine their value. For financial analysts, the economic value of the shares must be the most important factor. For ongoing companies, dividend rights must be considered the most important. For example, double voting rights do not mean shareholders receive twice the dividend.

For financial analysis, a company's earnings should be distributed among the multiple shares, and earnings for a class of shares should be divided by the number of that class of shares outstanding to calculate earnings per share. To spread total earnings for a company among the multiple shares, relative claims on earnings for each type of share must be determined. This creates significant problems, because the relative claim on earnings among shares often is not clear. Relative ownership can be measured by many possible criteria, including dividend right parity and voting right parity. A relative value can be assigned based on an analyst's estimate of the stock's value, which in turn is based on the stock's economic benefit to shareholders. Whereas voting rights can play a significant role in the decision-making process of corporations, dividend rights parity can have an immediate and direct impact on the wealth of shareholders.

What are the problems for analysts? Are there practical solutions?

1. Dividend rights parity should be determined in terms of gross dividend rather than net of taxes. For example, AFV shares in Belgian companies are differentiated by varying withholding tax rates.
2. For U.S. companies with A common shares and B common shares, there is sometimes a slight difference in dividend rights parity between the two classes of shares. The stock price will be slightly higher for the higher-dividend shares, but the distribution of earnings for EPS calculation should generally not differentiate between the two classes. This will make price/earning (P/E) ratios differ slightly, and analysts should consider the implications.
3. Registered shares and bearer's shares in Swiss companies, and restricted and unrestricted shares in Finnish companies, also differ slightly in their market value because of restrictions on trading. Recently, Swiss companies began removing restrictions on registered shares and now allow them to be converted to other types of shares. In such cases the relative values are so minor that it is impractical to assign different values.
4. Deferred shares in the United Kingdom are usually established temporarily following mergers or acquisitions, and dividend rights are suspended until they are converted to ordinary shares. Usually, the number of shares is not significant. Therefore, the deferred share is better described as a preferred share with zero dividend. For analysis, except for the aspect of possible conversion, such shares should be ignored.
5. When all common shares are traded in the market, determining their relative value is much easier because significant evidence from the market is available. Sometimes, however, one type of share is traded in the market and another is not. In such cases, total market capitalization cannot be determined. If shares representing the majority of capital are traded, and other shares are not traded, the dominant share should be treated as a primary share.

   However, the common shares of some companies (BNP in France, for example) are not traded in the market. Only investment certificates are traded. If we accept the market value of the investment certificates as representing the total market capitalization of the company, we lack a complete picture of the company for purposes of analysis. A solution in this case is to assign the assumed relative value to the untraded shares based on the dividend right parity.

Similar cases exist elsewhere. For example, Japan's NTT is often identified as the world's largest company in terms of market capitalization. But only a fraction of NTT's shares are traded on the market. The great majority of shares are owned by the Ministry of Finance. It is impossible to know what the price of a share would be if all of the shares were traded in the market, but it must be assumed that the price of the majority of shares owned by the Ministry of Finance will be the same as the price of the traded shares. Similarly, most French subsidiaries of foreign companies are owned by their parent companies and only a fraction of the subsidiaries' shares are traded on the French market. The subsidiaries, of course, are consolidated by their parent companies, so it would be rare to encounter them individually for analysis. Therefore, "floating" stock is extremely important in determining a company's liquidity and real market value.

6. Another special case is the organization comprising Royal Dutch Petroleum in the Netherlands and Shell Transport and Trading in the United Kingdom. Essentially, the company has no nationality. Its shares are independently issued in the United Kingdom, the Netherlands, and the United States. There is only one set of combined financial statements, yet earnings for the company are distributed in the three different markets. If we convert the prices of the shares into a single currency, they are basically the same price (five shares of Shell Transport are the equivalent of one Royal Dutch Petroleum share). To compute the EPS, the same parity (5 to 1) should be used. Unilever, EuroTunnel, and Reed Elsevier constitute similar cases.

7. GM in the United States has three different types of shares: common, E, and H shares. Similarly, Fletcher Challenge in New Zealand has ordinary division and forest division shares. However, each of these shares accumulates earnings from different companies. We can not identify such shares as multiple shares. The practical solution is to break down the companies and re-create three companies by share type. Each type of share should be analyzed separately.

A ratio analysis of companies with multiple shares should be done differently. All of the ratios using per share information will have some reservation because of the arbitrary criteria according to which the assignment of earnings is made. Certain ratios can allow the analyst to avoid using per share information. The use of multiple shares creates additional barriers in capital market efficiency, and many of the countries where they are customary are in the process of eliminating them.

EPS COMPUTATION WITH MULTIPLE SHARES

In order to compute EPS, earnings for the shares and the number of shares have to be computed. However, the distribution of earnings to each share is arbitrary, and although there is no perfect solution, there is a practical approach to this problem.

The method involves identifying a primary share among multiple shares and converting the other shares to primary equivalents. The aggregated primary equivalents can be used for a per share computation, and

(continued)

(continued)

the primary EPS is distributed to each share based on the conversion ratio.

The primary share selected should be the most important of the multiple shares and will be the focus of analysis of multiple share companies. Selecting the most active share is convenient. If one of the shares is traded, that share should be selected. If two are traded, a share from the class containing the most shares should be selected. However, as in the case of BNP, whose secondary share only is traded, the nontraded share should be the primary share.

The selected primary share will have a dividend parity of one, and the remaining share(s) will be converted to the primary equivalents by their parity. The aggregated primary equivalents will be used for EPS computation.

There are several ways to compute EPS, depending on the earnings selected, as discussed in an earlier section. Suppose, for example, that the Swiss ABC Company discloses the following information:

Bearer's share (BR)	Sfr 500 par	2,000,000 shares	Sfr 50 DPS
Registered Share (RG)	Sfr 100 par	4,000,000 shares	Sfr 10 DPS
Participation Certificate (PC)	Sfr 50 par	4,000,000 shares	Sfr 5 DPS
Net Income	Sfr 200,000,000		

STANDARD COMPUTATION

The bearer's share should be selected as the primary share, because it is under no restriction insofar as global investment is concerned. Then the dividend right parity and the primary share equivalents can be computed as follows:

	Dividend Right[1] Voting Right[2]	Shares Outstanding	Primary Equivalents[3]	EPS
BR	1.0/1.0	2,000,000	2.0 mil	= Sfr 62.5[4]
RG	0.2/0.2	4,000,000	0.8 mil	= Sfr 12.5[5]
PC	0.1/0.0	4,000,000	0.4 mil	= Sfr 6.25[6]
Total		10,000,000	3.2 mil	

---

[1] Dividend right is assigned by the relative dividend per share to be received by setting 1.0 for the bearer's share.
[2] Voting right is assigned by the relative voting right by setting 1.0 for the bearer's share.
[3] Primary equivalent (bearer's share as the primary share).
[4] Sfr 200 mil ÷ 3.2 mil shares = Sfr 62.5.
[5] Sfr 62.5 × 0.2 = Sfr 12.5.
[6] Sfr 62.5 × 0.1 = Sfr 6.25.

ALTERNATIVE METHODS FOR EPS COMPUTATION WITH MULTIPLE SHARES

Alternative 1

Earnings after dividends paid are equally distributed among multiple shares.

	DPS	Dividend Paid	Residual EPS[1]	Total EPS
BR	Sfr 50	100,000,000	+ 2.0	= Sfr 52.0
RG	Sfr 10	40,000,000	+ 2.0	= Sfr 12.0
PC	Sfr 5	40,000,000	+ 2.0	= Sfr 7.0
Total		180,000,000		

---

[1] Residual EPS (200,000,000 − 180,000,000) ÷ 10,000,000 shares = Sfr 2.0 per share.

If most earnings are distributed and all of the shares are equally active in the market, Alternative 1 may be acceptable. But how can book value per share or sales per share be computed on the same basis with this alternative?

Alternative 2

In general, the voting right parity should be ignored in per share computation because of the difficulty in quantifying the value. But when voting rights are believed to control the residual earnings, the following computation is possible:

	DPS	Dividend Paid	Voting Rights[1]	Residual EPS	Total EPS[5]
BR	Sfr 50	100,000,000	2,000,000	+ 7.14[2]	= 57.14
RG	Sfr 10	40,000,000	800,000	+ 1.43[3]	= 11.43
PC	Sfr 5	40,000,000	0	+ 0.0[4]	= 5.00
Total		180,000,000	2,800,000		

---

[1] Voting rights = (number of shares outstanding) × (voting right parity).
[2] Residual EPS for bearer's share (200 mil − 180 mil) ÷ 2.8 mil shares = Sfr 7.14
[3] Residual EPS for registered share Sfr 7.14 × 0.2 (voting right) = Sfr 1.43
[4] Residual EPS for participation certificates is zero, because of no voting right.
[5] Total EPS = DPS + Residual EPS.

This process reflects the possible value of voting rights in EPS computation, but it is difficult to incorporate the voting rights in book value per share or sales per share as in Alternative 1.

Pension Accounting. Many corporations provide benefits to their employees at retirement or after termination of their employment. The benefits are earned during the employees' working years and involve varying sums of cash payment. The amount is either paid out entirely at the time of retirement or spread out until the retiree dies.

When benefits are fully paid at retirement—the amount is based on the number of years of employment and the employee's last salary—then the total amount is easily estimated. However, when benefits are spread out over the remaining years of an employee's life, estimating the amount to be paid out is not an easy task. If the employer's contribution to the retirement plan is fixed and the employee simply receives whatever income has accumulated upon retirement, the program is called a *Defined Contribution Plan*. Because the company is not responsible for maintaining a specific level of payment to retired employees, accounting for a Defined Contribution Plan is routine. Companies simply treat the annual contributions as expenses.

When the monthly payment to retired employees is fixed, the program is called a *Defined Benefit Plan*. The company's contribution to the plan fluctuates, based on the assumed income from an accumulated fund. The company makes up any difference between the income earned by the fund and the amount the company is obligated to pay its retired employees. How to account for a defined benefit plan depends on the assumptions made about the income to be earned from the accumulated fund, as well as the number of years payments have to be made to retirees.

The number of years for which benefits are to be paid out depends on the life expectancy of retirees. Estimates regarding benefits are computed by actuarial experts; few accounting issues are involved. Estimates are more complicated when it comes to health care benefits. Another benefit, severance payment, which is paid to employees who leave a company before retirement, is dependent on the employee's salary and number of years of employment. Companies regularly make provisions for such payments. In reality, there benefits are not very different from defined contribution plans.

Accounting for defined contribution plans is relatively simple. How to estimate future payments for defined contribution plans, whether the payment is one fixed amount or a fixed monthly sum, becomes an important accounting issue. Whichever payment method is used, the accrual basis of accounting, which is based on the Matching Principle, requires companies to treat the obligation as an expense each year an employee remains with the company rather than as a single one-time expense at retirement.

Retirement plans may also include contributions from employees. When employees contribute, the arrangement is called a *Contributory Pension Plan*. When they do not, it is known as a *Noncontributory Pension Plan*. Neither creates significant accounting complications.

Retirement plans are also differentiated according to who manages the fund. The level of benefits to be paid out depends on the contract between the employer and the employees and follows the conventions of the country concerned. If an employer pays a relatively low amount, the lower expense may provide a competitive advantage to the company. This has no accounting impact. Whether the company manages its own pension funds or not, however, has significantly different implications.

Externally managed funds provide sure benefits to employees, regardless of the company's future performance, but the company may not treat the fund as an asset. On the other hand, internally managed funds represent a significant liability but also remain an asset within the company. Such assets may be used as security against future borrowing and may also be used to pay debts. There may be restrictions on their use, and employees may have a higher priority claim on them if the company is liquidated. Treating internally managed funds as assets without also acknowledging the liability they represent can have a significant impact on the balance sheet. Financial analysts must take this into consideration.

For example, the assets of Japanese companies are generally overstated because the major portion of their pension obligations is managed by the companies themselves. However, the value of the assets reported is appropriate when it comes to liquidation.

Many countries, including those of Europe and the United States, have government-run pension programs as part of a national social security system. Contributions to the social security fund are shared by employees and employers. This is a form of Contributory Defined Contribution Pension Plan, although contributors are not always beneficiaries.

Some countries with a heavy reliance on pensions managed by a government social security system have gradually introduced private pension plans as a supplement. These funds are usually managed internally, but, gradually, some are being funded outside the company.

Two issues and their implications for financial analysis must be considered: pension liability and underfunded plans. Both will have a significant impact on an analyst's valuation of a company.

Inventory Costing. Inventory is generally valued at the lower of cost or market value. Cost is established in the same way in most countries. It comprises material and the direct and indirect expenses in preparing it for sale. A few cost items, such as interest expenses or remotely related overhead expenses, may be included in some countries but not in others.

In contrast, determining cost flow can differ significantly by industry and by country. Ideally, cost flow accounting should match the actual movement of items when a perpetual inventory costing system is not possible. Cost flow accounting, however, is complex, and most industries, with the exception of a few such as construction, engineering, and expensive jewelry, find that it is expensive to keep track of all inventory items throughout the year.

INVENTORY COSTING SYSTEMS

A *perpetual costing system* is an accounting method used to identify unit costs of each inventory item purchased and sold. It requires each purchase and issue to be recorded in the inventory account. At year end, the balance of the inventory account is transferred to the balance sheet, and the accumulation of issued inventory for the period is the cost of goods sold in the income statement.

A *periodic inventory costing system* leaves the beginning inventory balance unchanged during the year, instead of recording each purchase. At year's end, all purchases are added to the beginning balance, and the ending inventory balance is deducted to arrive at the cost of goods sold.

There are essentially three ways to trace the flow of costs of inventories in the periodic inventory costing system: Last-In-First-Out (LIFO), First-In-First-Out (FIFO), and Average Cost. What distinguishes each of these methods is the assumption made about the order in which inventory items are used. This is especially important when prices change and the same inventory items have a very different cost.

LIFO is used in the United States, but it is not allowed in many other countries. Some European countries use the similar base stock valuation method. Adjusting LIFO reserves at year end offers significant tax advantages but, in this respect, U.S. corporate financial statements must conform to tax regulations.

FIFO and average costing are allowed in most countries. There are some variations in certain industries. For example, the wholesale/retail industry may cost inventory by eliminating sticker price markups because of the many items involved. Hyperinflation countries cost inventory with replacement costs rather than purchase costs. The most important issue for financial analysts seeking comparability is the possible lack of consistency in method among companies under research.

Last-In-First-Out (LIFO)

LIFO assumes that the inventory items bought last are the first to be sold. In times of rising prices, this assumption leads to a low balance sheet value for inventory, but to a high Cost of Goods Sold in the income statement. Thus, this system leads to low net income and low retained earnings. It does reflect a realistic value of inventory consumed during the year for a computation of net income, but inventory on the balance sheet reflects older, lower prices. Earnings can be significantly manipulated by using LIFO reserves as last-minute window dressing.

First-In-First-Out (FIFO)

FIFO assumes that items bought first are the first to be sold. During times of inflation, the effects are just the reverse of those produced by LIFO. FIFO tends to overstate inventory through its use of older (lower) prices.

Average Cost

The Average Cost approach used in inventory costing is based on the average cost of inventory items available for sale to determine an ending balance on the balance sheet. The average cost can be determined in two ways, through the use of either the weighted average or the moving average. The weighted average uses the total cost of purchases, including the beginning balance, divided by the total number of units purchased, including the beginning balance, to compute a unit price. The cost of goods sold and the inventory balance are then computed using the unit price. The moving average is used with the perpetual inventory costing system to produce the same result as given by the FIFO method. Consequently, it is justified when tracing the physical flow of inventory is not feasible.

Depreciation. There are two central issues in comparing the depreciation expenses of different companies: the method of calculation and the number of years used for depreciation.

The two main methods of depreciation are straight-line depreciation and accelerated depreciation. Straight-line depreciation means that the cost of an asset is depreciated in equal amounts annually over its estimated useful life. Accelerated depreciation means that higher amounts of the cost are depreciated in earlier years, and lower amounts in the later years of the life of the asset. If a company continuously replaces its fixed assets, the two methods produce similar results. However, for companies that grow or decline, these methods can have different impacts. For example, the accelerated method gives low asset values, and low net income for growing companies with new capital inflows every year.

Fixed assets represent a manufacturing company's main capital investment. Economic policymakers, using tax regulations, prescribe the period in which they may be depreciated. Often, depreciation schedules and the actual consumption of fixed assets do not correspond.

Depreciation periods vary by country and by company. In the United States and the United Kingdom, for instance, the period is generally based on the useful economic life of the asset, which in turn is estimated by management and auditors. Thus, in those countries, the periods vary by company. In countries such as Germany and Japan, depreciation periods are fixed by tax law and these rates are used for financial reporting, so every company uses the same period (a very short period in Germany) for similar assets.

Capital Leases. A lease transaction involves a lessee and a lessor. The lessee is allowed to use some portion of the lessor's property and pays rents for the usage. This practice was developed for those who cannot afford to purchase an entire property at one time or do not need to use the property for its entire life. Current leasing practices, however, were developed as a strategic financing tool. In accounting, a lessee does not have to record the property on its balance sheet and may simply treat the rental payments as expense.

The periodic payment for usage is recorded as rent. The rental payment is called an *operating lease* if the rental period is shorter than the life of the property. If the rental period is relatively long in terms of the economic life of the property, however, and most of the possible benefits of the property are expected to be used by the lessee company, the usage is considered to be no different from a purchase. In such cases, the lease is simply seen as a form of financing. Accounting rules in most countries require the lessee to record the property on its balance sheet, and the minimum required payment is recorded as a liability. This undertaking is known as a capitalized lease, or finance lease, and is often used as an example of substance over form.

Capitalized leases can provide tax advantages. Some companies exploit this situation by selling a property and promptly leasing it back to claim a tax break. The requirements for capitalizing leases and the degree of tax advantage differs among countries.

A capitalized lease should be recorded as an asset and be depreciated over its economically useful life. The resulting lease payments should be recorded as a liability and their interest portion as interest expense. Because a lease payment is sensitive to the market interest rate, the lease obligation should be treated as long-term borrowing.

DEPRECIATION METHODS

Depreciation is an allocation of the purchase price of long-term assets over their useful years. The accrual accounting convention requires this allocation. Ideally, such allocation should match the actual consumption of assets. The allocation method requires purchase prices, estimated salvage value, useful years, and the rate of consumption. The assumed consumption rate depends on the method chosen, the Straight-Line Method or the Accelerated Method. In practice, tangible assets are often revalued as a result of pervasive inflation, and depreciation in the following years is based on the revalued amounts. The accumulated depreciation is usually disclosed as a reduction in total purchase prices.

The costs of intangible fixed assets are also allocated using similar conventions. However, their disclosure is net of depreciation amounts because their replacement value is difficult to justify.

Straight-Line Method

The Straight-Line Method of depreciation requires that the purchase price of fixed assets, after salvage value, be evenly distributed over the expected time of the assets' use. The actual consumption of assets may vary (estimated lifetime), but the consumption of long-term fixed assets, such as buildings, should be close to this assumption (realistic).

Accelerated Method (Declining Balance Method)

The Accelerated Method of depreciation assumes higher consumption of an asset in earlier years as compared with later years. How extensive the acceleration should be depends on the individual asset. This assumption is generally applicable to machinery, equipment, and vehicles with five to ten years of life. The Accelerated Method depreciates assets by a fixed percentage of the remaining balance, and depreciation expenses gradually decline as the balance declines. This method is known by various names, depending on the fixed percentage used. For example, machinery with five years of life may be depreciated at a rate of 20 percent; this is called the Flat Declining Balance Method. It is interesting to note that depreciation tables provided by the Ministry of Finance of Japan uses a 150 percent rate.

The Sum-of-Digit Method is another variation. Some countries, including Germany, use the double declining rate until the amount using the Straight-Line Method is higher than that using the Accelerated Method, which results in further acceleration.

In practice, accelerated depreciation is used more as a tax incentive for companies than to match the actual consumption of assets.

Goodwill and Intangible Assets. There are several types of intangible assets. Of these, goodwill relating to acquisitions is probably the most common. Other intangible assets include capitalized research and development and trademarks. The first question about intangibles is whether they should be recognized as assets. The second question concerns the amount that should be recorded. A third is that if they are recognized as assets, how and over what time period they should be amortized. If amortized, where should amortization be allocated? To direct cost, indirect cost, or both? The final issue is how to disclose the asset.

Goodwill is a special case. Because it results from acquisition, it must be dealt with. Nonrecognition is not an option. Goodwill is sometimes immediately written off against equity, with no income statement effect. The more common treatment, however, is to amortize goodwill on a straight-line basis. The amortization period can range from a few years up to 40 years.

In considering research and development, as well as trademarks and other intangibles, the main question, as mentioned earlier, is whether to recognize such intangibles as assets or to treat them as expenses. In most cases, they are not capitalized; however, there are exceptions in some industries and countries. Amortization methods vary. Intangible assets are amortized by the Straight-Line Method in most countries, with some exceptions, such as in Australia, where they are periodically revalued by management. Sometimes amortization is based on the assumed life of the underlying asset, such as the expected life of the product being researched and developed. Often, however, a shorter period is used.

GOODWILL

When a company is purchased, the Purchase Accounting Method records the market price of the assets and liabilities acquired. If the total price paid is greater than the aggregated value of assets and liabilities, the difference is treated as goodwill.

Goodwill is either written off against the owners' equity, with no income statement effect, or it is capitalized and amortized. In the latter case, amortization will lower the acquiring company's earnings as long as the amortization continues. In some cases, this could go on for as long as 40 years. Because of the large goodwill amounts created by the many acquisitions of the 1980s, the impact of amortization of goodwill on earnings has been the subject of much debate, especially in the United Kingdom.

Reserves. Reserves, also called provisions, are established to prepare for estimated future payments or use of assets. This book recognizes three types of reserves: operating reserves, capital reserves, and a type somewhat between these two known as nonequity reserves.

Operating reserves (which, ideally, should be called *provisions*) are accounts established to cover particular estimated future operating costs such as doubtful accounts or accumulated depreciation. These accounts are established as contra-accounts for assets. They are estimated internally and provide full disclosure of the use of the assets.

There are various routine types of provisions to meet estimated expenses, but if the expenses are confirmed by a third party they are not considered provisions. Very complicated processes are involved in calculating the necessary provisions for pension obligations and the reserves needed to pay for future benefits in life insurance and other insurance businesses. As part of a company's operating activities, these provisions are legitimate contra-accounts.

If a provision is directly related to a specific asset, the related assets are reduced and the net balance is disclosed in the balance sheet. This avoids an overstatement of total assets. If the provision has no direct relationship to a specific asset, it is disclosed as a liability on the balance sheet.

Capital reserves are related to capital transactions rather than operating activities. Their main purpose is to preserve capital provided by shareholders.

The legal entity created by incorporation is empowered by law to act as an individual in private contracts. The law also seeks to protect parties entering into contracts with the legal entity. Therefore, the law regulates the preservation of the corporation's capital.

As mentioned earlier, a primary purpose of establishing capital reserves is to preserve the capital provided by shareholders. There are two types of capital belonging to shareholders, capital provided during the process of incorporation, and capital made available during later expansion. Under the Ongoing Concern Principle, capital provided by shareholders may not be returned to shareholders. This nondistributable shareholders' equity consists of either nominal capital or a portion in excess of nominal capital. The amount in excess of nominal capital is called a capital reserve or additional paid-in capital. Capital reserves also arise in consolidation as the extra value paid by an acquirer on top of the nominal value of the stocks exchanged.

Shareholders' equity also consists of earnings from capital provided by the shareholders, which are not distributed as dividends. Shareholders who provide capital are supposed to receive any excess earnings from the capital provided by them, but often a part of the earnings is retained within the organization for reinvestment or future distribution.

Many countries require or encourage corporations to reserve some earnings for reinvestment. Quite often there are restrictions on when earnings may be distributed as dividends. The restricted earnings are set aside as an earnings reserve. If the amount is relatively permanent, it can be converted into permanent capital by issuing additional stocks as a stock dividend. Of course, it also can be used for future distributions without liquidating the organization. Corporations are also required or encouraged to set aside capital for other purposes such as future expansion and restructuring.

Nonequity Reserves. In contrast to the two types of reserves discussed, there is another—nonequity reserves—which may be viewed as either a liability or as shareholders' equity. These reserves are neither required for operations nor reallocated from earnings. Operating reserves are before taxes, and capital reserves are either after taxes or not subject to taxes. Nonequity reserves, however, may or may not be taxed. Most countries do not allow such reserves. In some countries they are allowed as a regulatory tool by government, in which case they are often closely related to tax policy.

We can isolate three main types of nonequity reserves. These are revaluation reserves, regulatory reserves, and discretionary provisions.

Asset revaluation reserves, if allowed in a country, are established based on the changes in the general price level. The assets are typically limited to tangible fixed assets and subject to depreciation in the future. The book value of tangible fixed assets is often significantly different from their estimated current market value. This variation, which may result from misallocation of purchase costs or steady inflation, may lead to revaluation, although this contradicts the Historical Cost Principle. Revaluation is allowed in many countries. Notable exceptions are the United States and Japan.

Tangible fixed assets are purchased with the capital provided by either debt holders or shareholders for use in operations. Debt holders expect the tangible assets to generate enough earnings to pay interest and principle. The assets are typically used as security in case of liquidation. On the other hand, equity holders expect the assets to generate enough earnings to provide an excess after debt obligations, which they will receive as dividends or additional shares. When general price levels go up, the unrealized gains from tangible assets are usually excluded from the profit and loss account and are not available for distribution to shareholders.

In contrast, debt holders do have an implied right to take part in any gain in the value of assets in return for the loan provided. Debt holders may have already considered the possible increases in the nominal value of the tangible fixed assets when the loans were provided.

Equity holders also will benefit from the increased nominal value when any excess is left after first providing security for debts. Benefits may flow to equity holders in two different ways. One is through dividend payments after the assets are sold and the gains are accounted for. Benefits through dividend payments should consider tax effects on the gain. The other way is to issue additional shares to equity holders by transferring the asset revaluation reserves to share capital. (Capitalization of this unrealized gain as a reserve is usually allowed if the increases are expected to be permanent.) The tax effects are postponed until the stocks are sold.

There are a number of unique aspects regarding asset revaluation reserves:

1. The amount of asset revaluation is set by management or is based on official tables.
2. Tax charges on the gain are postponed, in some cases for a very long time.
3. Both debt holders and equity holders are beneficiaries of the additional nominal value.

The asset revaluation reserves should be kept within a company to preserve the capital provided by outsiders, but they belong to three parties: the government, through taxes; debt holders, through increased security; and equity holders, through residual gains after considering benefits to the other two parties. For analysis, the reserves should be split among the three parties.

The second type of nonequity reserves are the *regulatory reserves*. Some countries require reserves for regulated industries, such as insurance or utilities, and some allow regulatory reserves in general or for specific industries.

German and Austrian companies show these reserves on the balance sheet between shareholders' equity and liabilities. These nonrequired special reserves are essentially tax havens for profit, established to encourage investment. If the reserves are used as intended by the government, taxes are waived.

The amount of nonequity reserves is determined by the specific regulations applicable, rather than legitimate business reasons. The reserves should be split among beneficiaries, as in the case of asset revaluation reserves. Special reserves in the regulated industries are established to protect policyholders or customers rather than debt holders or equity holders. The amount is determined either by net earnings or by volume of sales, depending on the purpose of the related regulations. The reserves should be assigned to the interested parties for analysis.

Discretionary provisions may be established by management. Examples are the provisions for restructuring or reorganization. In addition to the amounts being discretionary, this is problematic for analysis because the allocations are spread over several periods.

When a company foresees problems facing a sector of its business, management may set aside significant amounts a few years in advance to prepare for the one-time cost of restructuring. From management's point of view, if the restructuring process is expected to result in significant losses or cash needs, early preparation is necessary to smooth the company's earnings or to avoid a cash crisis. From a shareholder's point of view, however, the cost in reduced dividends or stock prices should be borne in the period the restructuring occurs. Although inefficiencies may have accumulated over many years, it is the shareholders during the restructuring period who suffer.

If the creation of restructuring reserves is a legitimate means to ensure a company's survival, how does one determine how much is needed and how should the cost burden be distributed in following years? Is it reasonable to transfer any of the burden to shareholders after the restructuring? Analysis of such reserves should allocate the one-time burden to the appropriate parties.

There is consistency in disclosing reserves within each country. If a specific reserve is to be disclosed as a liability, it is called a provision; if disclosed as a part of shareholders' equity, it is called a reserve. However, each of these reserves and the applicable national regulations under which they were created should be carefully studied, regardless of what they are called, and should be classified appropriately to be useful in analysis.

Issues Related to Disclosure and Presentation of Information

In this section, the emphasis shifts from specific accounting standards to focus on how information is presented in the financial statements and how much information is disclosed. In this regard, we consider current cost accounting, restatement of the previous year's information, discontinued operations, and interim financial statements.

Current Cost Accounting. The Historical Cost Principle forbids revaluation of assets on the books, because repeated revaluation is neither objective nor practical. Many companies were hard hit by the high global inflation of the 1970s fueled by the oil crisis. In a significant diversion from the Historical Cost Principle, they tried to reflect the consequences in their financial statements in the early 1980s. New accounting methods attempted to separate earnings produced by changes in the price level from earnings produced by operations.

Constant dollar accounting seeks to maintain historical cost accounting but adds information about changes in general price levels. As a result of inflation, monetary assets lose purchasing power and monetary liabilities gain purchasing power. The net results are treated as retained earnings. This promotes capital maintenance in terms of constant purchasing power.

Current value accounting abandons historical cost accounting and measures assets at present value or net realizable value based on specific price levels. Realized and unrealized holding gains or losses are measured and accounted for in the income statement. This promotes capital maintenance in terms of operating capacity.

The development of new accounting methods to reflect changes in general price levels subsided in the 1980s as inflation levels dropped around the world. Nevertheless, some countries still allow partial adjustments, such as revaluation of fixed assets, whereas others, including the Netherlands, often supplement such information based on the Current Cost Accounting Method.

Latin American countries continued to experience serious inflation levels into the 1990s, however, and their accounting standards have been completely adapted to reflect changes in general price levels. Financial statements in Latin American countries, therefore, are not comparable to one another or to financial statements elsewhere in the world.

Restatement of Previous Year's Information. Financial statements comprise an income statement, balance sheet, cash flow statement, and related footnotes. They disclose the company's operating results for the period, its financial position at the fiscal year end, and any change in its cash position during a given period. The previous year's information is also provided to give users a comparison. U.S. companies provide figures for two prior years in their annual income statements and for one prior year on their balance sheets, while most other countries require one prior year for both.

It is obvious, however, that if there have been any changes in the size of the company or if the reporting standards have been changed, the figures for prior years are no longer comparable. Sometimes, in such cases, two sets of incomparable figures are provided and all changes are fully disclosed. Users can then determine the usefulness of the figures. An alternative is for the company to restate the previous year's figures as if the changes had already occurred in the previous year.

Restatement is common in the United States and also occurs in the United Kingdom. However, other countries do not readjust the beginning balances of the previous year's financial statements. The main reasons for the frequent restatements in the United States and the United Kingdom are the relatively large number of mergers and acquisitions, discontinued operations and company reorganizations, changes in the scope of consolidation, changes in accounting standards, and different presentation formats.

In countries where no restatements are made, changes in company size are not reflected on the balance sheet. Changes in accounting standards, on the other hand, are disclosed as prior period adjustments below earnings for the EPS computation in the income statement, and the net accumulated effects are directly reflected in retained earnings on the balance sheet.

Each alternative has advantages and disadvantages. Restated figures simplify comparisons of a company's operating performance over the years. Such comparison is more meaningful when we know that the size of the enterprise is the same and that the same accounting standards have been used. Even restated figures, however, present complications for the analyst. Restated figures are based on various assumptions, and some information can not be restated using these assumptions. For example, the stock prices of previous years are not reflected when divulging changes of the entity's size or when different accounting standards are used. So P/E ratio computations, using the price of a company's stock before a merger and its earnings after the merger, will be wrong. Similarly, the dividends paid in the previous year will not be based on the restated earnings figures, and therefore dividend payout ratios based on restated earnings will be incorrect.

For purposes of building a database, both original and restated figures should be available to satisfy different types of analysis. For example, sales or asset growth should be computed using restated figures, and P/E ratios or dividend yields should be computed based on the original figures. (Logically, for analysis, if the stock price already reflects, say, a merger, the P/E should be based on restated figures.)

Industry analysis based on aggregate figures especially should use original figures to avoid duplication of figures or survivor's bias in a specific industry. Because restated figures are simply unavailable in some countries, any global comparative analysis should be based strictly on the original figures.

Discontinued Operations. The communications revolution has dramatically advanced the global exchange of information. Simultaneously, economic cycles have become shorter and shorter. Products once considered capital goods now are regarded as consumer products. Shake-ups of corporate structures have resulted in mergers and acquisitions, or reorganization, and the many attendant discontinuations of operations. These developments have had a significant impact on corporate earnings.

Shareholders want companies to be profitable before they provide new capital. If a certain sector of a company is no longer profitable, or excessive investment has been made in other sectors, the excess capacity should be eliminated to boost future profitability. Elimination of unprofitable sectors and investments in new, profitable sectors should be a natural evolution for corporations. Financial results from discontinued operations are isolated from the ongoing business. These discontinued operations are usually defined as extraordinary activities. Their extraordinary nature arises from the fact that discontinued operations are not related to future performance.

There are some restrictions, however. Whether a discontinued operation qualifies as an extraordinary activity depends on the materiality of its size in relation to the company's total operations. In addition to materiality, discontinued operations should also be defined to mean the closing of a separate sector. If a company closes one of many manufacturing facilities but remains in the same business, the restructuring does not qualify as a discontinued operation unless that restructuring is the result of unpredictable outside factors.

Two factors should be considered regarding the impact of discontinued operations: the operating results from the discontinued operation before complete shutdown and the gain or loss from disposal of the discontinued operations.

The formal presentation of discontinued operations differs significantly from country to country. Most countries separate the operating results of discontinued operations from the gain or loss from the disposal of discontinued operations. The operating results are often included in operating activities until the operation is completely closed, and the gain or loss from the disposal is disclosed as earnings below the EPS computation.

As suggested earlier, the definitions of extraordinary activities and earnings for EPS computation are not the same in every country. The results of discontinued operations are disclosed below earnings for EPS computation by companies in the United States, and they generally qualify as extraordinary activities. Companies in the United Kingdom disclose the results of discontinued operations and the gain or loss from their disposal in a separate column, in accordance with Financial Reporting Standard No. 3. There are two possible reasons for the frequent restructuring by U.S. and U.K. companies. The most obvious is that there is simply more restructuring activity in those particular markets. The other reason may lie in the corporate culture. Managers in the United States and the United Kingdom are under continuous shareholder pressure to produce positive short-term results, and to keep their positions they need to be flexible and sensitive to changes in the corporate structure.

Interim Financial Statements. How often corporations should be required to provide information on how they manage the capital that investors provide them is a subject of endless debate. Regulatory agencies in all countries demand annual financial statements. There is controversy in the financial community, however, because U.S. regulatory agencies require quarterly reporting. Quarterly financial statements are strongly supported by the Association for Investment Management and Research (AIMR) in the United States.

There is also discussion about what should be included in the interim financial statements. U.S. companies include basic financial statements (i.e., income statement, balance sheet, cash flow statement, and related notes), whereas companies in other countries provide very little information. There is no audit requirement in any country for interim financial statements. Nevertheless, many multinational corporations provide voluntary information that exceeds by far the requirements of their home countries in order to satisfy international investors.

There are advantages and disadvantages to quarterly financial reporting. The first advantage is that quarterly reporting provides more timely information to users, especially investors, enabling them to make more timely decisions. The second advantage is that it gives managers preparing the financial statements more frequent information to guide their decisions in allocating resources.

The main disadvantage, of course, is that preparing quarterly financial statements is costly. As a result, more expenses are eventually transferred to investors, and dividends to shareholders, for example, are reduced. It may also reinforce a short-sighted view of resource allocation. U.S. managers, under pressure to produce short-term results, often have difficulty establishing long-term goals that might eventually benefit investors. That is one of the many reasons that German companies (e.g., Deutsche Bank) resist being listed on U.S. stock exchanges. They regard quarterly reporting as emphasizing a short-sighted approach.

How much information is adequate is also debatable. It is clear that a few figures on revenue and earnings or total assets and dividend information would be inadequate. Yet fully audited financial statements would be excessive because of the extensive preparation required. It should also be noted that for the many businesses that have an operating cycle longer than three months, quarterly financial statements would be misleading.

A decision on the necessary content of interim statements should be based on the relationship between investors and management and on what specific information can actually be produced between reporting periods. Modern computer-to-computer communications now make it possible to relay vast amounts of information from management to investors without preparing and mailing out formal financial statements. At the same time, use of such technology would reduce the cost of preparing financial statements, thus making quarterly financial reporting possible at little cost. With timely electronic access to such data, sophisticated investors and analysts would be far better informed.

The author recommends that companies provide formal semiannual financial statements, supported by informal but meaningful quarterly information; that is, less frequent formal reporting (to save costs) combined with information on a more frequent basis, for more effective analysis. The semiannual information should contain full financial statements—income statement, balance sheet, cash flow statement, and related notes. Fewer reporting requirements would reduce preparation costs, and more frequent, detailed information, preferably accessed by computer, would provide sufficient and timely information for analysis.

3.2.3 Financial Statement Items

Bookkeepers compress all corporate transactions into a few numbers that eventually appear in company annual reports. The many activities behind those numbers arc useful to financial analysts. Yet it is impossible to compare these activities, because no two companies are identical. Such information, therefore, can only serve as useful background.

Corporate financial information is routinely made public through annual and interim reports. Most of it is summarized in an income statement, balance sheet, cash flow statement, and related footnotes. The most important consumers of this information are those people and institutions who provide corporations their capital. Governments and regulatory bodies determine what information the statements must include, how they are organized, and how the information can be verified. There are variations in each country. Although national standards are applied to financial reporting, the corporations and the investors that provide them capital are increasingly international in character. This is a complication for companies that need to meet differing reporting standards around the world, and for investors who increasingly need to find a standard measurement of a company's performance.

Operating activities differ significantly from industry to industry, and their uniqueness is reflected in financial statements. It is therefore necessary to segregate companies by industry before attempting to compare their performances. A database format for financial statements can be customized for each industry. However, it is clear that a balance must be maintained between the desire to establish a flexible database to optimize analysis and the cost involved.

All industries can be categorized by five types: industrial, banking, other financial services, insurance, and regulated utilities. Industrial enterprises include all manufacturing, service, and retail/wholesale companies. Utilities are similar to industrial enterprises in cost structure, but their revenue is significantly regulated by government or local authorities and few have diversified or expanded into other countries. Therefore, utilities are placed in a separate category.

When accounting standards were first developed, the focus was on the balance sheet, which discloses a company's financial position at fiscal year end. The reason was that bank loans were then the major source of capital and loan providers were primarily concerned about the security of a company's assets and the company's ability to repay loans. Today, with the rise in importance of equity capital, the focus has switched to the income statement and the cash flow statement. The significance of each type of statement depends on an individual company's main source of capital.

In the following discussion, information is classified by its location in financial statements. Note that each of the seven parts of this section relates to a later chapter in this book.

Income Statement

The income statement is a table that reports all revenue and expense for a given accounting period. It measures a corporation's operating performance. A more important aspect of the income statement for financial analysts is its usefulness in estimating the earnings capability of a corporation in the future.

The basic rules for presenting an income statement are set by the Matching Principle and the Periodicity Principle. These principles determine what revenue may be recognized, that is, how much income is to be recognized and how much expense is associated with that income in a given accounting period.

The income statement records the transformation process of assets, which is the transformation of cash to cash in transactions with third parties resulting in revenue earnings. The outcome of these transactions is recorded on the balance sheet.

Net earnings for an accounting period are available for distribution to capital providers. Any undistributed earnings are transferred to the balance sheet and are used for future distribution or reinvestment.

Revenue Recognition. In accounting on a cash basis, revenue (sometimes called receipts) is recognized when cash disbursed is returned to the organization. Since the adoption of accrual accounting, the revenue recognition process has become more complicated. Revenue is now recognized when the earnings process is "reasonably completed," for example, when products are sold or services have been delivered. In this way, income from the rental of assets is recognized as time passes, not necessarily when payment is received.

In accrual accounting, the point when revenue is recognized is very important because it determines when the use of a company's resources may be expended. The amount expended must relate to the amount of revenue recognized. The resulting recognition of earnings determines how much is to be distributed to the capital providers for the period.

Long-Term Contracts. When it takes longer than a year to fulfill a purchase contract, the buyer and seller may agree to payments before completion of the product, as in long-term construction or shipbuilding. This is an example of revenue recognition before delivery. Accounting treats such long-term contracts in two ways.

The Completed Contract Method is based on full delivery. Revenue is recognized only when the contract is completed. During construction, accumulated costs for the completed portions of a contract are recorded as inventory, and cash received before completion is recorded as an advance payment. This method is acceptable when reliable estimates as to the degree of completion cannot be made over the contract period.

The *Percentage-of-Completion Method* allows revenue to be recognized at interim points during the contractual period, based on costs incurred or other reliable estimates. Billing is allowed to the extent the product is completed, and the amount billed is recorded as an account receivable. Completed or partially completed products for which no bills have been issued are recorded as inventory.

The most important point in the process is a reasonable measurement of the percentage of completion. Precise units of measure can be established in different types of contracts as agreed to by the parties. Sometimes a contract allows billing in excess of completion. This excess should be recorded under "other short-term liabilities." In a long-term contract, any gain is deferred and recognized only at completion. Any loss, under the principles of conservatism, however, must be recognized as soon as it can be estimated. The Percentage-of-Completion Method is accepted for accounting purposes but is generally not accepted for tax purposes.

Installment Sales. In the case of installment sales, a product is delivered but payment is collected over some future period. The resulting uncertainty over payment means that the earnings process is not considered complete until full payment is collected. When installment sales payments include implicit interest, the interest and gross profit portions should be separated and accounted for as distinctly different elements of income.

An installment sale is secured by the product sold, which can be repossessed if the buyer does not pay on time. Repossessed products should be returned to inventory at their recoverable value, and installment accounts receivable must be reduced accordingly. The gain or loss from the canceled sale and the allowance for doubtful accounts should be recognized at the same time and treated as a sales expense.

The *Cost Recovery Method* treats all payments as recovery of costs. Only cash collected after cost has been recovered is recognized as earnings and begins to contribute to net income. This method is the most conservative and is recommended when there is a high degree of uncertainty regarding payment.

The *Installment Method* recognizes revenue and expenses proportionally. There are different accounting treatments for the unrealized portion of deferred profits. On the balance sheet, deferred gains can be presented as liabilities (as current liabilities if the installment sales period is within the company's operating cycle) or as a reduction in accounts receivable on the asset side.

In the income statement, full disclosure entails showing the realized deferred gross profit portion and the unrealized deferred gross profit portion separately and, in addition, separating each by the origin of sales. However, in a database designed for global analysis that includes all types of industries, analysts are forced to treat such deferred gains/losses in a way that allows comparison. One alternative is to reduce sales by the unrealized deferred gains if the earnings process is evidently not completed. Another is to increase cost of sales or selling expenses by the unrealized deferred gains. This approach may not appear to make sense conceptually, but it assures that sales and operating income/loss is not misstated.

Government Subsidies. Federal or local governments support private or quasi-private enterprises in some countries to promote certain industries or to serve the public interest. When subsidies are made available to all industries, they take the form of a reduction in taxes. Temporary tax reductions to lift the national economy from recession or to encourage long-term economic development are not generally regarded as subsidies. They are simply treated as lower tax expenses.

However, subsidies may be made available only to specific industries or specific products. Specific subsidies are sometimes designed to expand public services provided by the private sector, such as railways and airlines. The rationale for subsidies differs by country. Specific subsidies may be made available only to some companies in an industry, or they may be made available to all companies in differing amounts. The differences in subsidies can be a major hurdle in international comparative analysis.

General subsidies are treated by companies as a reduction in tax expense or as a postponement of future tax obligations. No further explanation is necessary. But the treatment of specific subsidies, such as subsidies for railroads or utilities, varies among companies. Some companies treat these subsidies as part of their operating activities, and others account for them as part of their nonoperating activities. Some treat them as an increase in revenue, and others as a reduction in expense.

The treatment of subsidies is determined by the extent to which they are related to a company's operating activities. If a subsidy is not directly related to a specific product or service, it should not be included in the operating performance evaluation. It should be classified as either a reduction in general expense or as a nonoperating gain. On the other hand, if subsidies are granted to support a specific product or service, they should be treated either as an increase in revenue or as a reduction in the cost of sales.

In treating a subsidy as an increase in revenue, sales of goods or services are recorded at full value no matter whether payment comes from the government or from the private sector. However, when treating a subsidy as a reduction in the cost of sales, only the amount the company receives in arm's-length transactions will be recorded as sales, not the full value of goods or services provided. This is a valid treatment when the amount paid by the government has been negotiated in terms of costs involved and not in terms of market price. Both methods will provide appropriate gross margins earned by the company.

Consider, for example, a railroad company whose ticket prices are subsidized by government. The subsidy can be seen as helping the consumer pay the full price, in which case the subsidy is accounted for as sales. On the other hand, the subsidy could be seen as reducing production costs, in which case it is treated as a reduction in costs. The suggested method is to increase revenue, because it is unlikely the company can add any margin to the costs recovered from the government. If a company is not allowed to add any profit in the long run, it will avoid involvement in such transactions.

Unique Revenue Recognition Rules in Various Industries. Conceptually, the revenue recognition rule is similar for all companies, regardless of the industry to which they belong. In the manufacturing and service industries, income is recognized as products or services are reasonably completed and delivered to customers. However, the banking and insurance industries deal with significantly different products.

Banking is essentially buying or gathering money from customers and then reselling the money to different clients. Banks are paid for this process. Income and expenses are generated mainly by the passage of time, which involves risk.

The insurance industry provides two distinctive types of services, property and casualty insurance, and life insurance. Despite some exceptions in North America and Europe, each type is usually offered by separate legal entities and is governed by different sets of regulations.

Property and casualty insurance services are similar to other financial services dealing with risk rather than money. The insurance companies distribute the possible risks of designated events faced by a specific subscriber to the rest of a subscriber pool. Premiums for the services are set, based on the odds of the risk for each client. Premiums are recognized as income by the passage of time, and expenses consist of the actual payments made when the designated events occur.

Life insurance services deal with risks to human life, which are different from risks to property. Different time horizons for income and expense are governed by significantly different rules of recognition. Income is recognized by the passage of time, as in property and casualty insurance, but expenses are recognized based on the actuarial method. Thus income is limited to the policy payment period, but expenses are spread over the projected lifetime of the subscriber.

When organizations provide both types of insurance, the income and expense from the two must not be added. Unfortunately, not all insurance companies follow this rule, and their income statements do not clearly separate the income and expenses of the different types of service. Analysis of information that mixes the types of service is very difficult.

Consolidation of Related Parties. For meaningful analysis of a company's performance, all related entities should be consolidated if the company exercises significant control over them. Whether an entity should be consolidated is determined by economic substance rather than its legal relationship to the company. The consolidation process eliminates intercompany transactions and combines all earnings of the consolidated entity into the parent company's financial statements.

Consolidation ought to eliminate possible manipulation of earnings through intercompany transactions. However, consolidated financial statements are relatively novel, and regulatory bodies in many countries have only recently begun requesting their use. Reasons for the slow implementation of consolidation include the following:

1. Most companies are launched as single entities. If no major subsidiaries are involved, their influence on a consolidated financial statement will be insignificant. This is still true for many small companies.
2. Tax authorities in most countries require companies to file tax returns on a single-company basis.
3. Consolidation is a costly process, and companies try to avoid it unless they need to raise capital internationally.
4. Little academic guidance is available, and consolidation is not well understood by the public in certain countries.
5. Regulations requiring consolidation do not exist in many countries, but it can be implemented on a voluntary basis.

Influences of Other than Equity-Holders. All majority equity holdings should be consolidated in financial statements. But what if outside influence on the decision-making process of a company is achieved through means other than equity ownership? For example, German companies are heavily capitalized by banks and their supervisory boards often include bank representatives. Although the relationship between a company and its bank creditors is substantively similar to its relationship to equity holders, banks are ignored in the consolidation process.

Other examples of outside influence that escape the consolidation process are the *zaibatsu* or *keiretsu* groups in Japan and Korea. Even though the equity ownership is significantly less than a majority holding, member companies of a group are strongly related to each other by intercompany loans or vertical business relationships. The integration of the group members is sometimes stronger than equity-ownership in Western society. They are so closely linked that the entire group may be threatened financially by a mistake by one group member. Regulations in Japan and Korea help to obscure recognition of these outside influences by requiring the consolidation only of subsidiaries that contribute more than 10 percent to the group's operations. This 10 percent hurdle is much higher than the accepted standard.

Significantly Different Industries. A manufacturing company with revenues from banking and insurance subsidiaries will pose significant problems in a consolidated financial statement. For analysis purposes, revenues from financial subsidiaries and sales from manufacturing companies should not be lumped together. If different revenue streams are combined, they should be segregated and further analyzed. Companies in most countries provide segmented information in related footnotes. Methods of analysis in such situations are explained in a later section, "Diversification of Operating Activities."

Another type of income, usually included as "other operating income" in the consolidated income statement, is often provided by a separate company division or subsidiary which runs operations unrelated to the parent company's main operating activities. This income may be included in the parent company's total sales as long as it is derived from third-party customers and the subsidiary has autonomy in its decision-making process.

Revenues from wholesale or retail subsidiaries should also not be added to a parent manufacturer's income consolidation. Wholesale and retail industries depend on a high volume of products, and most of their business efforts add value through sales and general organizational activities only. Their gross margins are very thin, and their sales revenues cannot be compared with those of manufacturing companies.

Changes in Entity (Acquisition or Discontinued Operations). Sales from discontinued or newly acquired operations cause problems in analysis across accounting periods. Obviously, sales from discontinued operations are valid for comparisons to previous years, but not to future years. On the other hand, sales from newly acquired operations are valid for comparisons to future years, but not to previous years. It is necessary in such situations to create multiple records for the same period. These issues are more common in countries where mergers and acquisitions occur frequently, such as the United States and the United Kingdom. Quite often this information is not clearly presented in other countries.

Operating Activities and Nonoperating Activities. A critical issue for analysts is how profitable a company is and how that profitability will develop. Profitability is measured by the performance of operating activities, which must be distinguished from nonoperating activities.

Operating activities are transactions directly related to the main business of a company. To qualify, these activities should be practiced repetitively and must be expected to generate revenue in the future. This means that the profitability of operating activities is crucial to a company's future success. It does not mean that a company is restricted only to operating activities. Sometimes in the course of business companies perform transactions only remotely related to operating activities. These are called nonoperating activities.

A company's operating activities determine the industry to which it belongs. The composition of a company's expenses varies considerably by industry. For example, expenses in the wholesale business are composed mainly of materials purchased to be sold. On the other hand, expenses in textile manufacturing consist of significant labor costs, as well as materials. In an economic sense, operating activities consist of purchasing materials and using labor to process them to sell to users. Naturally, the process requires capital until invested cash is returned as cash. Capital is not provided freely. If capital is provided by external sources, interest or dividends are paid; whereas when it is generated internally, the opportunity cost should be taken into consideration. However, opportunity cost is not treated as expense. In general, resources are economically segregated into materials, personnel, and capital costs.

Most materials are purchased and used within an operating cycle. The total expense for the materials consists of purchases plus/minus changes in inventory during the period. Some materials are consumed over multiple operating cycles. These are called fixed assets, and they are depreciated or amortized over their life based on their usage.

Some personnel expenses are directly related to the number of units produced or sold, and others are only indirectly related. Directly related personnel expenses are called labor expenses. Those that are indirectly related are called personnel expenses.

Expenses for capital are different from material or personnel expenses. As mentioned earlier, capital can be provided internally or externally, and the choice is a financing decision. Therefore, interest expenses are treated as nonoperating expenses except in the financial services industries.

These expenses are composed differently in each industry, and the first step in analysis is setting up a standard cost structure for each industry. Analysts can then compare the relative strength of a company with those standards.

Operating activities are determined by the intention of a company, that is, what it aims to do. If certain activities are frequently performed but are not part of the company's main business, they are not regarded as operating activities. This is not always a simple matter to establish. Conglomerates with many different subsidiaries, which in turn have different operating activities, are involved in multiple operating activities. (See the earlier section "Significantly Different Industries.")

Nonoperating activities are infrequent occurrences only remotely related to operating activities. For example, at some point, a company's fixed assets, used over many years, are either used up or become obsolete. When the assets are sold, their residual value is recovered. Even though the gain from the disposal of the assets adds to the company's net income, the company did not purchase the fixed assets originally to make a gain on their disposal.

The nonoperating section in the income statement combines all income and expense, or gain and loss, from all activities which are irregular, rarely expected to continue, and are not material. If the amount is significant, it is treated as an extraordinary item.

The distinction between operating activities and nonoperating activities also determines the nature of current assets and noncurrent assets in the balance sheet. If assets are used in operating activities and are expected to be consumed within one operating cycle, they are classified as current assets.

An *operating cycle* is defined as the time it takes to complete the cash-to-cash cycle in the revenue earning process. The actual time varies by industry. For example, ice cream sales by peddlers will take a few hours, whereas highway construction will take several years. Current assets and current liabilities in the balance sheet are defined by this time frame, or operating cycle, as is cash from operations.

There are two methods of disclosing expenses related to operating activities: according to the function of the expenses in relation to revenue, and according to the types of resources. The first is called the Functional Method, or Cost of Sales Method; the latter is the Cost Summary Method.

Functional Method Versus Cost Summary Method. An income statement includes operating sections, nonoperating sections, and other items to be included in net income. In the Functional Method, the placement of an expense is determined by its function in relation to the revenue-earning process. In the Cost Summary Method, the placement of an expense is determined by the nature of the resource consumed. A third format, the Debit-Credit Format, is less common but is used occasionally.

The operating section consists of a company's operating revenue and operating expense and the net result, which is called operating income. The items disclosed in the operating section can differ significantly, depending on the type of business and the country in which it is located.

Operating revenue, which is known as sales revenue in industrial companies, represents the principal operating activities of the company. Companies in unique service industries provide more specific revenue descriptions. For example, the franchise industry refers to its ''subscription revenue.'' If the operating activities for a company vary, the different components are listed. The banking industry in particular lists different sources of income, such as interest income, investment income, and commissions and fees. Financial analysts should classify such revenue by type and by industry for analysis purposes.

INCOME STATEMENT WITH FUNCTIONAL METHOD

Net Sales
-        Cost of Sales
-        Selling, General, and Administrative Expenses

Operating Income
- \+   Nonoperating Income
-        Nonoperating Expenses
-        Income Tax Expenses

Income Before Extraordinary Items
- \+/−   Extraordinary Items

Net Income
-        Preferred Dividend

Income for Common Shareholders
Weighted Average Number of Shares for EPS
Earnings per Share

The *Functional Method* is made up of net sales minus the cost of sales minus selling, general, and administrative (SG&A) expenses. This is also called the *Cost of Sales Method;* it is result oriented, segregating all operating activity expense related to sales. Certain characteristics distinguish this method.

1. Costs are summarized by focusing on a company's marketing functions, which are paramount in most companies. The cost of sales is separated from selling, general, and administrative expenses to the degree each relates to revenue.

   The cost of sales is the cost of products sold, regardless of how many units are manufactured or how many units are accumulated in the warehouse. If they are not sold, the costs related to the unsold units will be accumulated as inventories (changes in inventories is considered in the income statement). A few countries, including Turkey and Korea, provide a separate, detailed statement on the cost of sales.

   Selling, general, and administrative expenses are expenses incurred in the completion of sales transactions, but there is no guarantee that they will benefit future sales. Obviously, they cannot be stored as inventory. Usually, general and administrative expenses are only remotely related to the number of units sold.

2. Another aspect of the Functional Method is how costs relate to the number of units sold. The cost of sales varies with the number of units sold, but SG&A expense does not. Indirect manufacturing costs—for example, depreciation expenses of machinery—may be precisely computed by comparing the number of units manufactured with the total capacity of the machinery. Because the machinery is isolated at a manufacturing facility, expenses related to it can conveniently be allocated to each individual unit produced. A similar allocation procedure is not possible for SG&A expenses.

The *Cost Summary Method,* in contrast, focuses on manufacturing. Operating expenses are summarized by type of manufacturing resources. These include materials purchased, personnel expenses, depreciation and amortization, and changes in inventory. This method provides solid information about a company's manufacturing activities for a period. It looks at the process rather than the result. The volume of materials purchased and personnel expenses gauge the volume of production for a given period. The number of units produced plus/minus changes in inventory gives the number of units sold.

However, the Cost Summary Method reveals neither how costs relate to the number of units sold nor the degree of relationship between the two. It implies that all personnel costs are related to the manufacturing process and does not differentiate the roles of employees.

This method is popular in continental Europe, where companies are often manufacturers with mid- or long-term production goals. In these countries, stock trading is less volatile and shareholders take a long-term perspective, which provides companies more stability.

Although the Functional Method is dominant in Anglo-Saxon countries, service-related industries and some other industries use a format similar to the Cost Summary Method. The companies in service industries do not have significant inventory and personnel expenses, and depreciation expenses are emphasized as major operating expenses.

INCOME STATEMENT WITH COST SUMMARY METHOD

Net Sales
   +/−   Changes in Inventory
   +   Other Operating Income
Total Operating Income
   −   Purchase of Materials
   −   Personnel Expenses
   −   Depreciation and Amortization
   −   Other Operating Expenses
Operating Income
   +   Other Income
   −   Other Expenses
Income Before Taxes
   −   Income Tax Expenses
Income Before Extraordinary Items
   +/−   Extraordinary Items
Net Income
   −   Preferred Dividend
Income for Common Shareholders
Weighted Average Number of Shares for EPS
Earnings per Share

INCOME STATEMENT WITH DEBIT-CREDIT FORMAT

Debit	Credit
Purchase of Materials	Net Sales
Personnel Expenses	Other Operating Income
Depreciations and Amortization	Changes in inventory
Other Operating Expenses	
Charges and Provisions	Reversal of Provisions
Financial Charges	Financial Income
Other Charges	
	Exceptional Income
Other Exceptional Charges	
TOTAL CHARGES	TOTAL INCOME
Net Income	
Debit Total	Credit Total

Although uncommon in current accounting practice in almost all countries, the *Debit-Credit Format* depicts the income statement as the portion of the trial balance related to the earnings computation. This format is used occasionally, for example, by some companies in Italy. All incoming revenue or gains are recorded on the credit side and expenses or losses are recorded on the debit side. The format does not link expenses with specific revenue, but because debits and credits balance out, the validity of the bookkeeping process is confirmed. If the information is to be used for financial analysis, restructuring the format is essential.

Extraordinary Items. Earnings from nonoperating activities are disclosed in various ways in different countries. Terms such as *nonoperating gain or loss, gain or loss from unusual activities, exceptional items,* and *extraordinary items* are used confusingly, but there is a trend in favor of stricter definition.

A change in accounting principles, such as SFAS 106, *Accounting and Disclosure of Post-Retirement Benefits Other than Pension,* is regarded as an extraordinary item. However, a change in estimates, such as the gain on disposal of fixed assets, should not be defined as an extraordinary item. Discontinued operations are usually extraordinary activities. However, if one of many facilities are discontinued but the company is still in the same business, the discontinuation should not be considered an extraordinary item.

Extraordinary items are strictly defined as activities that are unusual, infrequent, and material in nature. Any activities not meeting this definition should be classified as "other nonoperating items." However, this definition has not been accepted in all countries, and therefore extraordinary items may include all kinds of unusual activities. The broader concept of extraordinary items can be called "exceptional gain/loss." Most European countries are now redefining extraordinary items following the adoption of the Fourth Directive of the European Union.

For comparative analysis, it is necessary to reclassify the exceptional items as either nonoperating items and truly extraordinary items. In practice, this is often not possible because most companies do not provide enough information for reclassification.

In high-inflation countries, monetary gain/loss can be seen as an extraordinary item. This is a material gain or loss resulting from the adjustment of the value of assets and liabilities because of changes in the price level. It should not be included as an operating item.

UNUSUAL, INFREQUENT, AND MATERIAL EVENTS

An *unusual* event is one that no reasonable businessperson could have predicted. Natural disasters and sudden changes in regulations are good examples. If an activity is anticipated, such as a scheduled closing of a manufacturing facility, it cannot be considered unusual.

An *infrequent* event is one that does not occur in an organization in the normal course of business. Flooding along the Mississippi River is a

(continued)

(continued)

recurring event; therefore flood damage to businesses in the region cannot be considered an extraordinary item. Automobile factory closings (in the United States) was common in the 1980s. Under such circumstances, when a company closes a factory but remains in the same business, the closure should be classified as an operating or nonoperating activity rather than an extraordinary item.

A *material* event is one in which the amount involved is significant in terms of the company's size. Even though an activity is unusual and infrequent, if the result is insignificant in relation to other activities, there is no point in further analysis. The materiality of a specific event depends on the activity involved, but a 10 percent rule is generally applicable. If an activity is related to changes in operations—typhoon damage to crops or changes in pension expenses, for instance—the materiality should be compared to net sales. On the other hand, if an activity is related to the net gain or loss—for example, the gain or loss from disposal of discontinued properties—it should be compared with the operating income.

Balance Sheet

Whereas the income statement measures performance for a period, the balance sheet reports a company's financial position. The balance sheet includes assets, liabilities, and shareholders' equity.

The assets of a company differ by industry, but their nature is similar. Individual assets have their own value and can be used in operating activities through the transformation process or as security to protect capital providers, or they may be exchanged to pay debts. Sometimes the combination of various assets in different industries has a positive synergistic effect, or a negative synergistic effect, depending on how well the mix suits a specific industry.

The balance sheet's presentation of liabilities and shareholders' equity shows how a company's assets are financed. Some assets are financed by day-to-day transactions, and others by long-term capital providers who seek returns on the money they provide. Returns are provided on fixed terms for lenders and through the residual income of common stocks for shareholders. The balance sheet reflects the various combinations of financing chosen by management as best for the company. The combinations expose the influence of the capital providers, what cash flow the company can sustain, and the total cost of capital. They can differ because of developments in the capital markets or simply by the choice of management. Management (which has custody of the assets) and capital providers (who at one time tended to be a company's management as well) have become increasingly separated in developed capital markets in recent decades.

In compiling data, itemizing and grouping assets and liabilities proves helpful in analysis. The valuation method a company chooses for each category is also important. Yet no matter how much effort is expended, an attempt to reconstruct financial statements to suit an analyst is simply not practical. Because of limited public information, for example, the value of inventory under the FIFO Method cannot be converted to the value the inventory would have under the Moving Average Method. The best thing an analyst can do is accept the amount produced under the FIFO method while noting the valuation method. Analysts should also consider the nature of the company's business in reaching a conclusion.

Valuation of Assets and Liabilities. Note that here the term operating assets and liabilities is used interchangeably with current assets and liabilities. This may be confusing to some readers, inasmuch as operating assets and liabilities can have alternative definitions in other situations.

The valuation of assets and liabilities is dominated by the principles of historical cost and conservatism. The value of assets and liabilities changes continuously over the holding period. Their book value, for accounting purposes, is recorded based on the price the company paid when acquiring the assets or incurring the liabilities. However, when there is doubt, the lowest possible value for an asset (i.e., the lower of cost or market value) and the highest possible obligation for a liability are recorded in the books as suggested by conservatism.

Valuation rules on assets and liabilities are quite different for those used in an operating cycle and those used in multiple operating cycles. Assets and liabilities within an operating cycle are adjusted periodically by their turnover, but the those kept for multiple operating cycles require an allocation process for their usage because of periodic reporting requirements.

Assets Used Within an Operating Cycle. Such assets, which are called short-term assets or current assets, are supposed to be turned over and replaced through new transactions. The value of those assets should be set at the new prices at the time of the new transactions. Major components include cash and its equivalents, short-term investments, accounts receivable, inventory, and other current assets. Detailed illustrations of possible valuation methods are provided in Chapter 5. In principle, the purchase cost of the assets and their current realizable value should not differ significantly. If there is any possibility that the net realizable value may be less than the purchase value, however, the net realizable value should be recorded. For example, short-term investment assets should be close to market value, and accounts receivable should be reduced by any doubtful accounts. Inventory should be recorded at the purchase price or construction cost after discounting any obsolescence. However, a possible gain should not be included in calculating the net realizable value unless the industry as a whole takes that approach.

Loan investments in banking and investment assets in the insurance business are both operating assets, but the industries have different operating cycles. The valuation methods applied to such operating assets are defined by industry practice and cannot be compared with the valuation methods applied to operating assets by the manufacturing industry.

Assets Used for Multiple Operating Cycles. Significantly different methods, in different industries and in different countries, are applied in valuing assets used for multiple operating cycles. Noncurrent or long-term assets require more arbitrary judgments for valuation because of periodic reporting requirements, and the valuations will vary. In addition, the valuation method is sometimes driven by economic policy rather than income justification. Regulatory interference is also substantial in many countries.

By definition, noncurrent assets remain with a company longer than an operating cycle. They are composed of tangible fixed assets, financial fixed assets, intangible fixed assets, and "other assets." The purchase prices of tangible fixed assets are allocated to each reporting period based on the rate of their consumption. Ideally, the determination of the rate of consumption should be set close to the rate at which they are used up. In some countries, rates are set by tax regulations or national economic policy.

On the other hand, these tangible fixed assets stay with a company for long periods and are not exposed to outside transactions. Their economic value can change over time, and there are different ways to adjust their book values. For example, companies in the United States, Germany, and Japan delay adjusting book values until the assets are disposed of, a time when there may be a significant difference between their book value and economic value. The differences in value are typically called *hidden reserves*. Companies in such countries as the United Kingdom may make adjustments partially or fully before disposal of the assets, and their new values can be used for future cost allocation. Of course, adjustments without outside transactions can lead to arbitrary valuation amounts.

Financial fixed assets are one-time investments, and their value may be adjusted depending on their nature. Long-term investments by a company with majority control of the decision-making process are integrated with the investor's business in consolidated financial statements. Long-term investments with significant, but not majority, control are adjusted by the proportion of ownership in the investee's earnings each period. However, the relationship between investor and investee may not be simply a pure investment. Instead of the investor's pursuing financial returns on invested money, the relationship may involve cooperation in operating activities between the two companies. The investee's earnings may then be influenced by the investor, and the computation process may not be objective. The investments with significant control should be distinguished from the pure long-term investments seeking a financial return.

Intangible assets definitely qualify as assets, in the sense that they provide contributions to earnings. However, it is not clear how to verify their contribution to the future earnings of a company. The ambiguity of the contribution forces companies to record intangibles at their purchase price, and the number of years for amortization is set arbitrarily. This practice is not consistent from country to country.

Any other assets, especially those not used for operating activities or those not held for normal profits, should be classified as "other assets." These should be recorded at cost until their disposal.

Liabilities Within an Operating Cycle. A major portion of short-term liabilities are financed by trading partners, that is, through accounts payable or prepaid revenue. A simple delay of certain payments can provide some amount of capital without explicit interest expenses. Banks also provide needed cash, but with significant interest expenses attached. Long-term obligations will come due at some point and will then become short-term obligations. If companies fail to meet such obligations in a timely fashion, they quickly draw the attention of financial analysts who focus on possible mergers and acquisitions.

Liabilities in Multiple Operating Cycles. A significant proportion of a company's obligations, usually to be paid out many years later, consists of contracts with capital providers. Many of these liabilities have explicit interest obligations. Long-term borrowing with explicit interest obligations can be financed through private banks or through the issue of bonds to the public. There are also liabilities that have implicit interest obligations.

All types of long-term borrowing are recorded at current value. This means that borrowings with explicit interest are recorded at present value, and obligations without explicit interest are recorded at their discounted value. The total of all liabilities must represent the company's total obligations as if they were payable on the balance sheet date.

There are obligations that are not based on an explicit contract, such as provisions for pensions, which are liabilities based on expected future payments. Provisions for depreciation of fixed assets, in contrast, do not qualify as liabilities, because they do not represent obligations. This kind of provision is simply a contra item reducing the book value of a related fixed asset.

There are also obligations that cannot be considered legitimate, such as arbitrary provisions for a possible plant closing that are set up to prevent a huge, one-time future loss. It is obvious that such obligations become clear only when management realizes a plant is failing. They therefore cannot be reasonably provided for. These types of ambiguous reserves are discretionary.

As capital markets become more inventive, some obligations lie in between liabilities and shareholders' equity. Convertible bonds and convertible preferred equity are two examples. These have the characteristics of both borrowing and equity, and their valuation for security holders is complex.

Shareholders' Equity. All assets, after fixed obligations are deducted, belong to shareholders. A part of these assets is contributed by shareholders, and other parts are acquired through use of the earnings from the capital provided by shareholders. Typically, capital contributed by shareholders is separately earmarked and may not be returned to shareholders before liquidation, because that would violate the purpose of incorporation.

In some countries, companies are required to set aside a portion of their earnings to strengthen the position of the corporations. The status of a corporation is granted by law, and if that status is threatened by financial instability it could disturb the social fabric, leading to bankruptcy and unemployment, for example.

There is no specific valuation method for shareholders' equity, because all residual value belongs to the shareholders. However, segregation between undistributable capital and distributable capital should be clear for financial analysis.

The residual value per share (book value per share) is quite often used for analysis. However, if a company has more than one type of share issued (multiple shares), this ratio loses its validity. A valid ratio can be computed, but the process is complicated. This complication creates inefficiency in the market, and recently many countries have sought to discourage such structures.

Disclosure Formats. The disclosure format in a balance sheet is consistent with the income statement format. If the Functional Method (cost of sales) is used in the income statement, then current and noncurrent (functional) format is used for the balance sheet. If the Cost Summary Method is used in the income statement, the balance sheet is usually organized by types of assets and liabilities.

The balance sheet format is also influenced by the industry to which a company belongs. Most manufacturing industries use the Functional Method to format their balance sheets, but banks and insurance companies classify their assets and liabilities by type.

Assets and liabilities may also be arranged in order of liquidity. Utilities, for example, report in order of increasing liquidity, whereas light manufacturing and service industries report in order of decreasing liquidity. Reporting practices also vary by country; for instance, most European companies report in order of increasing liquidity.

Classification by Functional Method. The Functional Method segregates assets and liabilities in terms of their relationship to operating activities. If assets and liabilities are directly related to operating activities, they are classified as current assets and current liabilities. *Current* is defined as functioning over a one-year period or over an operating cycle, whichever is longer. This understanding is slightly different from *short-term*. *Short-term* and *long-term* are distinguished according to the one-year criterion, which is not very useful for financial analysis if a company's operating cycle is longer than one year. A typical example is accounts receivable for long-term contracts. However, the application of current/noncurrent classifications is limited to operating assets; others, such as financial assets, are classified as short-term/long-term under the Functional Method.

BALANCE SHEET BY FUNCTIONAL METHOD

(Liquidity order may be reversed in many European countries.)

Debit	Credit
Cash	Accounts Payable
Short-Term Investments	Short-Term Borrowing
Accounts Receivable	Short-Term Portion of Long-Term Borrowing
Inventory	Other Current Liabilities
Other Current Assets	**Current Liabilities**
Current Assets	Long-Term Borrowing
Gross Fixed Assets	Deferred Tax Liabilities
Accumulated Depreciations	Other Long-Term Liabilities
Net Fixed Assets	Noncurrent Liabilities
Long-term Investments and Receivables	**Total Liabilities**
Intangibles and Others	Share Capital
	Capital Surplus
	Retained Earnings
	Minority Interests
	Total Shareholders' Equity
Total Assets	**Total Liabilities and Shareholders' Equity**

The Functional Format for the balance sheet is accepted in most countries even if the income statement uses the Cost Summary Method or the Debit-

Credit Format. However, segregation of current/noncurrent and short-term/long-term items is often unclear, if applied at all, when the Cost Summary Method or the Debit-Credit Format is used in the income statement.

The greatest advantage of the Functional Method is its linkage of assets and liabilities to operating cycles. Typically, companies using the Functional Method in their balance sheets split assets and liabilities into those associated with operating activities and those linked to nonoperating activities. However, some of the assets—security investments, for example—are segregated according to the company's intended use of the assets rather than by the actual holding period. Moreover, noncurrent security investments can be as liquid as short-term security investments.

Classification by Types of Assets and Liabilities. A balance sheet may be broken down by types of assets and liabilities, rather than by their relationship to operating activities. This format is difficult for analysis. It is used mostly in the banking and insurance industries. For example, banks segregate assets into security investments and loan investments, and scatter liabilities among deposits, borrowing, and other liabilities. Sometimes short- and long-term segregation is added at some point. Nevertheless, most assets and liabilities can be redefined as current or noncurrent according to their relationship to operating activities, and their reclassification is not difficult.

Classification by Decreasing or Increasing Liquidity. Assets and liabilities can be itemized according to their current or noncurrent nature, but the arrangement within this grouping varies by industry and by country. Most manufacturing companies list their assets starting with cash and near-cash items in order of decreasing liquidity. On the other hand, utilities with heavy equipment start with fixed assets. It makes sense to list the most important assets or liabilities first in order to focus the balance sheet.

Formats vary by country. Most European countries tend to use the increasing liquidity format. The choice of format may depend on tradition or the expectations of users. This is not significant for analysts, because reconstruction of the disclosure format requires little effort and has no impact on ratios. The Vertical Format, in which current liabilities are subtracted from current assets to isolate the working capital, is used in the United Kingdom.

Balance Sheet "After Appropriation." Occasionally, in a few countries, companies present their balance sheets before and after assigning retained earnings to specific reserves. The latter shows the rearrangement of the shareholders' equity section. Within the concept of adequate disclosure, regarded as an underlying principle of financial reporting, disclosing significant events after a balance sheet date might be justified. But can an event that occurs annually be considered "significant"? An additional problem is that the appropriation of retained earnings in fact does not occur on the balance sheet date.

For analysis, information must be taken from a consistent format if the appropriation makes any difference in the results of analysis. In any case, any appropriation is generally disclosed in the statement of shareholders' equity. Especially dividends declared, which are classified as liabilities, should be returned to retained earnings for effective comparison purposes.

Statement of Changes in Shareholders' Equity. Appropriations of retained earnings are disclosed in the statement of changes in shareholders' equity. This statement is issued at the annual shareholders' meeting, well after the balance sheet date. It shows the changes in the beginning balance of capital reserves and retained earnings. Many countries encourage or require companies to save some portion of their earnings for future rainy days before distributing the earnings to shareholders. Such regulations seek to reinforce the corporation's status in society as a contractual party.

In some countries, the statement includes details of remuneration to company directors and key officers. There may be some justification for this, depending on the role of the directors or officers. Generally, however, compensation should not be recorded as an appropriation of retained earnings. If the directors or officers supervise operating activities, compensation should be classified as a general expense. An extreme example is a practice in Greece, whereby income tax expense is classified as an appropriation of retained earnings.

Overall, the statement of changes in shareholders' equity does not provide significant information, and many companies disclose the equivalent information as a continuation of the income statement or in a separate paragraph in the annual report.

Cash Flow Statement

The cash flow statement has a short history as compared with the balance sheet and the income statement, and some countries still ignore the importance of a company's liquidity.

Until the 1930s, bank borrowing or bonds issued were the major sources of capital for a company, and the providers of such capital held the greatest influence in the corporate decision-making process. When a company faced significant losses and had insufficient capital for new investment, the loan providers replenished capital by extending further credit. In those days, such providers received their interest on capital, just as investors now receive dividends on equity.

Today, capital providers include both debt capital providers and equity capital providers. Equity capital providers treat interest expenses as a business expense, and delinquency on interest payment jeopardizes the company. Increased market sophistication has made management's role more important in the corporate decision-making process. Irregular payment of dividends by management drives stock prices downward. The capacity to make dividend payments as well as interest payments has become more significant, and investors watch changes in a company's cash position closely.

The format of the cash flow statement is relatively uniform. However, some countries include a sources and uses statement in a Debit-Credit Format.

Cash Versus Working Capital. The United States led in the development of the cash flow statement as a result of the dramatic changes in capital markets brought about by the Great Depression of the 1930s. In the days when a company in default had a small number of creditors, it could extend its corporate life through the cooperation of its creditors. Current assets and current liabilities could provide enough liquidity for such a company, and the net figure, working capital, determined the level of of a company's liquidity.

The cash flow statement focusing on working capital, called the *fund state-*

ment, disclosed the origin and disposition of working capital from operating and nonoperating activities. All nonoperating activities were separated into two sections under the titles "Sources" and "Uses," which reflected the changes in noncurrent assets, noncurrent liabilities and shareholders' equity.

As capital markets diversified, equity capital became more common. The focus shifted from working capital to more liquid assets and liabilities. Some companies still used working capital, others used cash, near-cash items, or cash minus short-term borrowing. The statement was called the "Statement of Changes in Financial Position" but the "financial position" was variously defined in the transition period of the 1980s. The variety of definition of the financial position drew much attention and comment regarding its usefulness.

The conflict was resolved in 1986, when SFAS 95, *Statement of Cash Flows,* was issued. It defines cash as the only measure of liquidity and requires the nonoperating section to be divided into capital investment and capital financing. U.S. companies have been required to implement these standards since 1988, and many companies worldwide have gradually followed the trend. The cash flow statement is still not a requirement in many countries, and there also remain significant differences in reporting formats. For example, the cash flow statement prescribed by Financial Reporting Standard #1 of the Accounting Standards Board of the United Kingdom has five different sections: operating activities, cash from investment and financing activities, taxes, investing activities, and financing activities. To avoid confusion, *cash flow statement* in this book will refer to the SFAS 95 statement, the focus of which is cash.

Operating Versus Nonoperating Activities. All forms of cash flow statements divide sources of cash into two categories: operating activities and nonoperating activities. The increases and decreases in cash from operating activities can be presented in either of two formats, namely, the direct approach and the indirect approach, as discussed in the following section. Nonoperating activities are segregated either by "source" and "use" of cash or by investing and financing activities. Each format is explained in detail later; however, a view of the segregation of operating activities and nonoperating activities and some unique examples may be helpful at this point.

The cash flow statements of U.K. companies, for example, disclose taxation as a part of their financing activities instead of operating activities. This is due to a different conceptual view of who the owner of the company is. When cash is the focus of the cash flow statement, shareholders become the focal point for the analysis. Interest expenses paid to debt capital are treated as expenses in the operating section, whereas dividends paid to shareholders are treated as the distribution of capital in the financing section. For U.K. companies, dividends paid to shareholders are located in the cash flow statement before net cash from operations, and are treated as expense. This practice implies that equity capital is treated similarly to debt capital. On the other hand, taxation in the United Kingdom is a part of financing activities. This implies that government, by providing infrastructure for business activities, is a partner of the company and taxation is treated as a distribution of income.

Analysts must study all companies on the same conceptual basis. Therefore, reclassification of the format is necessary and must be fully understood.

Direct Approach and Indirect Approach. In addition to the need to determine what are and what are not operating activities, there is the further complication that operating activities may be disclosed through two different approaches. The first format, called the Indirect Approach starts with net income; the second, the Direct Approach, starts with cash generated from sales of goods.

The *Indirect Approach* is used by most companies everywhere. The Indirect Approach for cash from operations assumes that net income is the major source of cash from operations and that it is adjusted by noncash activities, such as depreciation and amortization. The capital invested in fixed assets is expended by usage over its lifetime, but these expenses do not require any cash disbursement. Other noncash activities include provisions for doubtful accounts and severance payments, deferred income tax expenses, and equity earnings from related companies under the equity method. There are a few other cash adjustment items established to avoid double accounting, for instance, gain or loss from sales of assets. In addition to noncash adjustments, changes in noncash working capital, such as changes in accounts receivable, inventory, or accounts payable, also affect cash from operations.

INDIRECT APPROACH

Net Income
 (+)Depreciation and amortization
Other noncash adjustments
 (+)Provisions for doubtful accounts
 (+)Provisions for retirement accounts
 (±)Deferred income tax expenses (credits)
 (±)Minority interest charges (credits)
Other items to avoid double accounting
 (−)Gain from sales of fixed assets (tangible, financial, and intangible)
 (+)Loss from sales of fixed assets (tangible, financial, and intangible)
Changes in noncash working capital
 (−)Increase in accounts receivable
 (−)Increase in inventory
 (−)Increase in other current assets
 (−)Decrease in accounts payable
 (−)Decrease in other current liabilities
 (+)Decrease in accounts receivable
 (+)Decrease in inventory
 (+)Decrease in other current assets
 (+)Increase in accounts payable
 (+)Increase in other current liabilities

Cash from Operations

The *Direct Approach* is seldom used, except in Australia, because the additional disclosure of reconciliation of cash from operations using the Indirect Approach is usually required. The Direct Approach starts with cash receipts from sales of goods or services and deducts cash disbursed for operating activities (e.g., purchase of materials, personnel expenses, and taxes). In practice, sales are adjusted by changes in accounts receivable, and purchases of materials are adjusted by changes in inventory and in accounts payable.

DIRECT APPROACH

    Cash receipts from sales of goods or services
       (−)Cash disbursed for purchase of materials
       (−)Cash disbursements for personnel
       (−)Cash for taxes
       (±)Cash from/to other activities

Cash from Operations

It is not clear whether some items belong to operating or nonoperating activities. For example, most results from extraordinary activities are obviously nonoperating results, but their impact on cash is still included in cash from operations. Losses from discontinued operations are also nonoperating activities, but their impact on cash is disclosed between operating activities and nonoperating activities in U.K. financial reports issued prior to implementation of FRS 1.

Under the Indirect Approach some companies start with income from operations instead of net income. In this case, depreciation and amortization are adjusted back as noncash items and other nonoperating cash activities adjust the cash positions.

Sources and Uses (Applications) Method. With the Sources and Uses Method, cash from nonoperating activities is usually categorized under either Sources or Uses. *Sources* is an itemization of cash inflows. *Total Sources,* the sum of all cash inflows, represents decreases in noncurrent assets and increases in noncurrent liabilities and shareholders' capital, in addition to cash from operations. A decrease in noncurrent assets is reflected in sales of fixed assets and long-term investments. An increase in long-term liabilities reflects the issuance of long-term bonds and share capital.

Uses (Applications) is an itemization of cash outflows. *Total Uses* comprise dividend payment, capital expenditure (increase in fixed assets), reimbursement of long-term debt, and reduction of capital. All of these items should be examined with respect to actual changes in cash.

Investing and Financing Method. In the United States, changes in cash from non-operating activities have been rearranged into Investing and Financing sections ever since the issuance of SFAS 95, when cash was defined as the focus of the cash flow statement. Changes in noncurrent assets are classified as investing activities, and changes in noncurrent liabilities and shareholders' equity are classified as financing activities.

Dividends paid are also included as a financing activity, except in the United Kingdom, as explained earlier. Also included in "cash from financing activities" is any change in short-term borrowing.

Another characteristic of the investing/financing format is its impact on cash from foreign currency translation. Effects on cash from foreign currency translations are disclosed as a separate item below the financing activities to reconcile the ending cash balance.

Diversification of Operating Activities

There are many ways to reduce exposure to risks resulting from economic change. If a company is large enough, small economic fluctuations are generally absorbed. Companies that have diversified into many different sectors, or operate in several different countries, are obviously less exposed to economic risk than those that have not. As any company grows, it tends to try to diversify its products or markets in many different ways. Diversification into different products is called product diversification, and a move into many different markets is called geographic diversification.

It is not clear whether greater product diversification is beneficial. Whereas diversification tends to reduce risk for corporate management, it may not be ideal from an investor's point of view. Investors may be able to diversify more efficiently on their own by establishing a varied and appropriate stock portfolio. The argument could also be made that a high degree of company diversification stretches managerial resources too thin. This point of view has been reinforced by the recent trend of major companies to focus on their core activities.

Product Diversification. Measuring product diversification is not easy, because the relationship between different products in regard to effective diversification is not easily quantifiable. Even though a company's products are classified by sector, there is no proven technique for analyzing the relationship between the sectors in terms of spreading risk.

For data compilation, Standard Industry Classification (SIC) codes are available from the U.S. Government. Companies in many countries are required to disclose the distribution of their products in terms of sales, operating income, and/or identifiable assets by sector. The definition of different product lines is not consistent, however, and the assignment of an SIC code to each sector is difficult. Nevertheless, the differences in classification are often used by financial analysts as a measure of diversification.

The extent of diversification can be expressed as an index, using the relationship between sectors. The validity and usefulness of the index depends on the clarity with which companies report on the sectors in which they operate. Interpretation of the index requires care.

An index computation assumes the independence of each segment, but, in practice, no product is completely independent of another. This problem can be resolved in two steps. First, SIC codes that group segments by sector, (e.g., consumer, industrial, energy, financial services) are consulted. The relationship between sectors can be called *unrelated diversification*.

The next step is to examine the relationship between products in the same sector. For example, there are no obvious benefits of diversification when a healthcare company producing vitamin A begins to produce vitamin C, because the market for the two products hardly differs. But when a textile company producing men's clothes diversifies into the production of women's clothing, some positive effects of diversification can be seen, because the two products have significantly different markets. This type of diversification synergy within a single sector is called *related diversification*.

Total diversification can be computed by combining the two diversification indices, the Unrelated Diversification Index and the Related Diversification Index. This means that the index total will gain value if the products are spread out over different sectors, rather than only within sectors.

If an index expressed in decimal values is not wanted, discrete values can be assigned as follows (with the decimal equivalent in brackets): 0, not diversified at all (0–0.5); 1, somewhat diversified (0.5–1.0); 2, reasonably diversified (1.0–1.5); 3, diversified (1.5–2.0); 4, well diversified (2.0+).

There are other methods to find the diversification index besides using sales. For example, operating income or identifiable assets can be used, or a combined index can be computed using all three measures.

UNRELATED DIVERSIFICATION INDEX COMPUTATION

$$I = \sum_{(j=1 \text{ to } m)} \text{of } P_j \times \text{Ln}(1/P_j)$$

Where P_j = size of jth sector/sum of all sectors,
m = total number of sectors.

The index value assumes that the distance between two sectors is equal for all sectors and that each of the sectors is independent.

For example, ABC company has the following information in terms of sales:

1	Chemical products	235 mil (52%)
2	Electronic products	125 mil (27%)
3	Transportation service	60 mil (13%)
4	Miscellaneous revenue	35 mil (8%)
	Total Revenue	455 mil (100%)

Computation results will be:

Sectors	P_j	$\text{Ln}(1/P_j)$	$P_j \times \text{Ln}(1/P_j)$
1	.52	.6539	.3400
2	.27	1.3093	.3535
3	.13	2.0402	.2652
4	.08	2.5257	.2021
Total	1.00		1.1608

A few things should be noted in the computation process:
1. The contribution from a significant segment is not much different from that of a small segment, which is also true in practice.
2. Equal distribution of sales in many segments maximizes the index value. For example, 10 percent of sales in each of 10 segments will produce the index value 2.303, whereas 25 percent of sales in each of four segments will produce 1.386.
3. The minimum value is zero for a single segment, but the mathematical maximum value is set. If the number of segments becomes significant, the index value will converge to a certain limit because of the nature of the logarithmic function. The maximum limit can be set at approximately 2.5, assuming about 12 equal segments.

RELATED DIVERSIFICATION INDEX COMPUTATION

$$I = \sum_{(j=1 \text{ to } m)} \text{of } P_j \times \sum_{(i=1 \text{ to } n)} \text{of } P_{ij} \times \text{Ln}(1/P_{ij})$$

Where P_j = size of jth sector/sum of all sectors,
$\quad P_{ij}$ = size of ith segment/sum of all segments within jth sector,
$\quad m$ = total number of sectors,
$\quad n$ = total number of segments in each sector.

The computation process for the Related Diversification Index is similar to that for the Unrelated Diversification Index, except for the small segments within a large sector.

Geographic Diversification. Some companies attempt to reduce the risk of economic fluctuations by establishing markets in different countries or continents. Obviously, because of their varying resources and economic policies, not all countries have similar economic cycles.

The geographic distribution of operating activities must be disclosed in some countries and is volunteered information in others. However, there are no specific guidelines as to what to disclose or how to disclose it. Most often, sales, operating income, and/or identifiable assets are disclosed as in product segmentation, but segregation by country or continent is not consistently shown.

Once geographic information is available, a diversification index value can be computed as in product segmentation. Of course, segregation by area should be based on economic blocs, rather than expressed in pure geographic terms.

In geographic segmentation, a few special factors must be considered. If sales or revenue is used in the manufacturing industry as the measure, the origin of products and their markets should be distinguished. Both obviously have diversification effects, but they have different effects. The diversification of production facilities may reduce risks related to production, whereas market diversification may reduce risks related to sales.

Geographic diversification by origin of production can be traced through locations of subsidiaries in different countries. The size or operating results of each subsidiary and its industry will give a reasonably good picture of the diversification of production facilities. Geographic diversification of markets can be seen in export distribution patterns. Many relatively small or medium-sized companies that have only domestic production facilities may export their products to many countries.

For service industries, such as transportation, banking, and insurance, other data items—in addition to sales, operating income, and identifiable assets—may be required. Because of the nature of their operating activities, it is not clear, for example, where the revenue of airlines originates. We may use the origins of freight or the location of ticket sales. Similarly, banking services have two major components: the destination of loans to customers and the origin of deposits. Overall service activities can be traced by the location of branch offices and their size in terms of loans tendered, deposits, or the number of employees at each location.

These factors are valuable in understanding each component and its contribution to diversification, but in practice this method of analysis is complicated. Many steps are involved in gathering information from different sets of tables in a database. A composite index, reflecting all related information that addresses the issue of risk distribution by location, would be preferable. Such a composite is the *Multinational Corporate Index* (MNC Index).

The MNC Index is computed by tracing the most important factor in the industry and determining the degree of diversification. If information in the primary category is not available for a specific company, the next category can be used. The multiple categories of information can be used either step-by-step or as a composite value based on the importance and relevance of each category.

Capital Structure

The composition of the credit side of a balance sheet reveals a company's capital providers. Financial analysts scrutinize this information to compute the cost of capital. A company's management is responsible for managing assets on behalf of capital providers and works with the capital providers. Changes in the composition of the capital providers also change the role of management.

When debt capital providers dominated corporate capital, management worked closely with a limited number of parties (banks and/or private lenders). However, as capital providers have changed from debt to equity and from private to public, the role of management has became more important. Management can now choose how to organize the credit side and the debit side of the balance sheet.

To understand how a company's capital structure will affect both its future performance and a specific category of investors, knowing the level of long-term borrowing or shareholders' equity is not enough. The structure of capital also provides information that makes it possible to estimate future capital needs and the explicit cost of the capital. In addition, it reveals the influential parties in a company.

Short-term capital needs can be met by delays in payment of liabilities, or by loans from banks. Capital providers change continuously, and it is not worthwhile monitoring every transaction. Most corporations have limited credit lines, and a company can overdraw its account when immediate cash is required. However, the short-term portion of long-term loans should be separated. The amount is predictable if the long-term borrowing is well documented.

Long-term capital needs are met by two major types of financing. One type, long-term capital with a fixed return and a fixed date of repayment, is called long-term borrowing. Some long-term loans are privately financed, typically by banks, and others are financed by the public, that is, through publicly traded corporate bonds. Publicly financed capital usually has a lifetime of 10 to 20 years. Most privately financed loans are provided by commercial banks, and the loans may or may not be backed by explicit security. Another type of financing is the leasing of assets. For such commitments, companies are required to disclose the leased assets as the company's assets, and the commitments to lessors are recorded as liabilities. Of course, certain portions are financed by employees (provisions for retirement accounts) or by government (deferred tax liabilities) without explicit interest commitments. Privately placed loans may require substantial long-term commitments, particularly in Europe and in Japan. Companies in emerging markets are often supported by the government to promote economic development.

Each of these loans and the demands they place on income in the form of interest can be traced for every reporting period. The repayment schedule will provide financial analysts with information on a company's future cash needs and its cost of capital for the financing.

Long-term capital with a fixed return but without a fixed repayment schedule is called preferred equity. It lies somewhere between liabilities and shareholders' equity and is sometimes treated as a part of shareholders' equity, depending on how long the capital remains with the company. It is similar to a long-term loan in terms of cost to a company but typically has a lower priority at liquidation. Payment of dividends can also be postponed in a year when earnings are low. If a company is unable to pay the promised dividends, either the preferred equity holders may participate in the corporate decision-making process or the preferred shares are permanently converted to common shares. Each of the preferred stocks should be documented in terms of dividend payment, participation in corporate decision making, or convertability to common shares.

Common equity is the primary source of capital in a corporation's life, and protecting the interests of common shareholders through financial analysis is a primary purpose of this book. Common shareholders take the residual value of a company after paying for all fixed obligations and operating expenses. The common shareholders' equity is divided between the capital provided by shareholders and the retained earnings generated by the capital provided but not distributed.

From the point of view of corporate management, which today holds more power than ever before, dividends to common shareholders are just another cost of capital. Management is rewarded for managing returns to shareholders and indirectly assuring the growth of the company's stock.

In general, the structure of equity capital is relatively simple. If there is only one class of common shares, shareholders' influence on corporate management is directly related to the number of shares owned by each shareholder. Often this one class of shares is publicly traded. However, if a company experiences a major reorganization or goes public, multiple common shares may be issued, some temporarily, others permanently. There may also be different categories of common shares, because of specific regulations governing foreign investors, special tax benefits on dividends, and other factors.

All multiple shares have rights on the residual value in case of liquidation. They do differ in two respects: in the distribution of earnings and in the participation in corporate decision making.

Shareholder Information

As a company's capital structure changes from heavy debt financing to equity financing, the influence of shareholders grows. However, there are numerous shareholders in a publicly traded company, and not all behave in the same way. Notable in this respect are the large investments in the developed capital market made by public and private funds that invest professionally on behalf of clients. These institutional shareholders influence corporations in a significantly different manner than individual shareholders or governments.

Shareholder influence also differs by the size of each holding. Small shareholders pursue economic gains from dividends or the appreciation of stock prices, but major shareholders have interests beyond dividend payments. Companies in some countries, such as Korea, distribute greater dividends to minor shareholders than to majority shareholders.

Information about shareholders can be segregated into three categories. The first is information about *major single shareholders*. When a company is owned in majority by another organization, the majority's shares often are not traded. But the influence of the majority shareholder should not be ignored in any financial analysis. Another instance might be that of a young company, whose majority shareholder is a company director or key officer. Despite regulations on security trading by shareholders with access to inside information, their influence on corporate decisions is significant and must be taken into account. In yet other cases, a government may hold the majority of shares, especially in companies that require significant amounts of capital to be efficient or that compete with foreign companies in the domestic market. Governments sometimes support public services to promote economic development and may assist them by providing capital. When governments have a significant shareholding in a company, corporate decisions will definitely be influenced by government economic policy.

The second category of information about shareholders is the *distribution of shareholders by characteristics*. A company with individuals as majority shareholders and another with institutional majority shareholders differ in their decision-making processes. Information on shares owned by management/insiders can be very important in determining management's incentive to make profits. A third category, *shareholders by size of holding,* can also cause differences. A company with many small shareholders and another with a few large shareholders will have significant differences as to who influences company policy.

When a company's major shareholders rotate often, it is an indication of problems and the Concentration Index (explained in Chapter 9), which reflects the concentration of single shareholders in a company, will help detect such movement. Many Scandinavian companies are dominated by a few shareholders, which may explain their stability and why those countries experience close cooperation between government, business, and labor unions.

Information about shareholders can also be useful for other purposes. The Europe, Asia, and Far East Index (EAFE Index) developed by Morgan Stanley and Capital International is criticized because it is weighted too heavily toward Japan, and because the index does not represent market movement as it was designed to do. One reason is that intercompany shareholdings within *keiretsu* companies can not be eliminated in computing the index. This problem can be solved only with a comprehensive database containing information on shareholders and subsidiaries.

Management Information

Another party to corporate policy-making, probably the most strongly influential, is management. As capital markets become more diversified, a large body of small minority shareholders coupled with huge institutional shareholders is emerging in many countries. As a result, many shareholders are unconcerned about the corporate decision-making process except as it affects the economic gains they may enjoy. In such developed capital markets, management has great influence on corporate decisions.

However, the structure of management and the compensation for managers varies significantly among different countries. Obviously, directors are elected by shareholders and other influential parties, such as debt providers, and management is selected by the directors. A financial analysis of a company's future performance cannot be completed without scrutinizing its decision-making process.

Maintaining the biographical details of all directors and key company officers is not practical. However, the stability of management, the specialties of particular managers, and their success within a company will indicate the direction of future policy. Generally speaking, U.S. and U.K. companies import new managerial skills from outside, whereas continental European and Japanese companies use internal resources.

German companies often include directors from major banks, some of whom hold directorships in several companies. Often ranking government officials also serve as directors.

3.3 RESEARCH OPINION

Research on corporations is performed for many different reasons. The pursuit of investment opportunities is one of the main objectives. Research also assists governments in setting economic policy. Competing companies constantly analyze one another to win an advantage in the marketplace.

The search for investment opportunities is undertaken by "sell-side," "buy-side," or independent research organizations. The sell-sides, typically security brokerage firms, try to attract more clients by providing better information. The buy-sides, such as institutional investors, try to gain economically by selecting better securities. It is the business of independent organizations to provide authoritative opinions to both sides.

In order to estimate a company's future earnings, research starts with an analysis of historical data and the company's investment policy. However, no two estimates will agree, even though they are based on the same information. Each researcher's interpretation of the data will differ from the others. Moreover, these differing estimates of a company's future earnings are constantly updated as new information becomes available. Some organizations combine the independent estimates and statistically establish the "best" number, a median or a mean, from the spread. This information is publicly available at nominal cost.

Estimates on international securities are complicated by the national differences in accounting standards. Of course, the private organizations that collect individual estimates from researchers make significant efforts to mitigate accounting standard differences. For example, estimates of foreign securities listed as American Depository Receipts in the U.S. market may be based on U.S. GAAP, as well as on local accounting standards. Comparing estimates based on different accounting standards requires great caution. An independent analyst deciding on an investment should do his or her own analysis before coming to any conclusion, but the opinions of others can serve as a reference.

Each of the parts of Section 3.2 in this chapter, "Financial Information," relates to a subsequent chapter. Whereas this chapter includes a more conceptual discussion, the following chapters contain detailed descriptions of how individual data items can be extracted from an annual report and be included in a database.

3.4 INSIDE INFORMATION

Trading securities based on "insider information" is explicitly prohibited in many countries, but the ban is not well enforced internationally and "insiders" remain a major obstacle to operating efficient capital markets globally. Different information is often distributed to different groups of interested parties. For example, German companies provide full financial statements to banks but not to the public. In particular, participants in emerging capital markets frequently trade securities based on information withheld from the public.

It may be acceptable that different classes of capital providers are given different types of information in order to protect corporate interests. However, capital providers belonging to the same class must be on an equal information footing in regard to content and the timing of its release. If any information is provided to a selected group ahead of others, that information becomes "inside information."

Insider information is defined by regulators in each country and violators are prosecuted. But there are differences in the definition of inside information around the world, and penalties for its use vary as well. A more significant difference, however, is in the level of enforcement of such regulations.

As companies require capital from a broad range of interested groups, they voluntarily make information public. In global capital markets a constant awareness of the information flow in local markets will remain essential, however, until corporate managers become clearly commited to "fair trade" for all capital providers. For now, most analysts located far from their subjects are limited in their ability to compete with others closely related to a company.

Despite the rapid development in telecommunications and the almost instantaneous movement of information around the world, financial analysts must consider the serious risks presented by insider trading. Increasing cooperation among authorities in different countries may help mitigate such risks. Their success could lead to the eventual development of more efficient capital markets.

3.5 ISSUES RELATED TO DATA COMPILATION

Fundamental analysis of equity and fixed income securities on a global basis requires a huge set of integrated databases to deal with more than 40,000 equity securities and 100,000 fixed income securities. Fundamental information should be compiled for about 20,000 companies, a representative sample of firms around the world. No single researcher could possibly cover all these companies. It would require significant organization of data and computer support to compile sufficient information for efficient use in research.

First, a structure to accommodate efficient research activity must be developed. The necessary functions and related issues, presented in the following list, are reviewed here and examined in further detail in Chapter 11.

> Issues Related to Library Functions
>> Identification of companies
>> Collection of public documents
>> Availability of information to the public
> Issues Related to Research Preparations
>> Industry classification

Industry grouping
Industry formats for data compilation
Issues Related to Research
 Languages of the financial statements
 Currency of the financial statements
 Different fiscal year ends and their changes
 Differences in reporting formats
Issues Related to Analysis
 How many years to compile
 Restated information
 Computed numbers and adjustments

3.5.1 Issues Related to Library Functions

Identification of Companies

Stock exchanges and many research organizations publish numerous lists of companies, but no one organization publishes a comprehensive list of all companies. Even if such a list existed, it would have to be continuously updated to accommodate new listings and delistings. Most existing publications are organized by security rather than by company, and the isolation of individual companies is difficult because some companies issue many different securities. The connection between a company and its securities is usually not readily obvious.

The primary focus of fundamental analysis is those companies with publicly traded securities. Most companies trade one type of common share. Others, in controlled economies or emerging capital markets, are owned by government. Companies with at least one type of publicly traded security should be selected for research.

The listings of companies on the world's many stock exchanges are at times confusing; local subsidiaries owned by a foreign parent company are sometimes listed along with the parent company. For example, IBM–France, listed on the Paris stock exchange, is not the same as IBM–United States, listed on the Tokyo stock exchange. IBM–France is a subsidiary owned by IBM–United States, but the security represents earnings from IBM–France. On the other hand, IBM listed in the Tokyo stock exchange is a security for IBM–United States, which represents IBM's consolidated earnings, including IBM–France's earnings. IBM–France should be treated as an independent company as long as it is listed as a separate entity. Industry analysis should take into account such duplication of two entities.

It is not clear as to where some companies are domiciled or on what stock exchange they are capitalized. Some Israeli companies, for example, are capitalized in the United States and are not listed in their own country, and some U.S. and Hong Kong companies are domiciled in Bermuda but operate elsewhere.

Collection of Public Documents

When a list of companies has been prepared, all public documents about those companies should be collected for further research. The frequency with which companies provide information differs from country to country. U.S. companies report quarterly with reasonably detailed information, but companies in other countries typically report annually. Semiannual reports are few in number and, when issued, limited in content. There are significantly different auditing practices as well. Variations in fiscal year-end reports cause problems in collecting information and in analysis.

Availability of Information to the Public

Whether company documents for the public are produced is one issue; whether the documents are available is another. Large companies in countries with developed capital markets are very publicity conscious and respond well to public requests for information. Small companies are less responsive, especially those marginally interested in attracting global capital. These companies often favor local requests for information while ignoring those from abroad.

Often documents are translated into English for international users. Although these documents are useful, some may be only partly translated, and the abbreviated versions do not contain all the information appearing in the original. Sometimes the annual reports contain little more than pictures and corporate propaganda.

In some countries the documents are superficially prepared for public consumption and differ significantly from documents prepared for the government. Companies in Japan and Korea, for example, prepare reports of less than five pages for shareholders. In certain emerging countries, simply mailing the documents is regarded as too expensive. On the other hand, the annual reports produced by Italian companies after auditing are extremely bulky, and it takes considerable time for them to be printed and to reach the public.

3.5.2 Issues Related to Research Preparations

Industry Classification

Revenue and cost structures differ among industries. A comparison of the outcomes is feasible when companies belong to the same or similar industries. Most companies in the same industry have similar structures; however, no two companies are ever in the exact same business.

Among the larger companies in any country are the conglomerates, which operate a variety of business lines either in a single-entity format or through many subsidiaries. Information about such complex business activities should be separated by the different lines of business. Companies do not always provide this information, and when they do it is often restricted to sales, operating income, and/or identifiable assets.

When a major business activity can be identified, it should be selected for segregation by industry, and business activities can be further segregated by product. However, mixing incomparable industries, such as financial services and manufacturing companies, is pointless for effective financial analysis.

Industry Grouping

How detailed must industry segregation be for efficient financial analysis? Some organizations recognize 40 different industries, others as many as 80. No one set suits all purposes of analysis. Obviously, the larger the initial number of industries, the greater the flexibility that is possible. The segregation should be as detailed as possible, but the capability of regrouping the industries into smaller groups should be maintained. For example, the cost structure of the computer software industry is similar to those of other service industries. A significant portion of operating expenses is devoted to personnel, but marketing is tied to computer manufacturing and technology companies as well. Another example is the relationship between textile manufacturing and the textile retail/wholesale industry. Industries should be regrouped for specific purposes of analysis, and certain conglomerates should be included in the analysis of many related industries.

Industry Formats for Data Compilation

In analyzing a large number of companies, data on a significant number of companies should be collected, and the data compiled obviously should suit the purposes of the research. There is a tradeoff, however, between diversity and simplicity. In opting for simplicity, information on all companies selected can be compiled in a standard format. Such data, however, will not reflect the unique characteristics of the different industries. On the other hand, if the unique characteristics of each company are included, the data will not be useful in synthesizing general industry trends.

Commercially available databases compile data in a company report format. This is advantageous in analyzing a specific company but does not provide the capability of comparing companies. With this approach, especially in global research, the unique characteristics of each company will be mixed up along with differences in accounting standards. Even simple ratios, such as operating income/margin return on equity, will not be comparable between two companies in different countries.

Many industries can be distinguished by two major types of revenue: manufacturing/services and financial services. Revenue from manufacturing/service industries is typically reported as sales or turnover, but revenue from financial services is unique to the type of service the company provides. A characteristic of revenue in financial services is that most revenue is explicitly or implicitly related to interest factors. For more efficient and effective data compilation, industries can be further segregated into four formats, that is, industrial, banking, other financial services and insurance.

The *industrial* format comprises a wide range of businesses, including all manufacturing and commercial services. Most companies within this broad category report their gross revenue as sales or turnover. Manufacturing industries are similar in operations; that is, they purchase materials, manufacture products with the use of personnel expenses and capital equipment, and sell their products. How these factors are combined differs significantly across industries. The differences should be the main focus in analysis.

Revenue in the wholesale business is unique. Wholesale companies deal with huge volumes and a minimal gross margin.

The revenue and expenses in utility industries differ only slightly from those in other commercial services. However, the rate-setting process is heavily regulated by authorities because these industries are public services and monopolistic in character. Data on regulatory factors affecting utilities should be maintained.

Rail transportation and telecommunication services were once regulated everywhere because of their monopolistic positions. Diverse alternatives to these services are now increasingly available, however, because of technological development. In some countries such services remain monopolistic and are dominated by government.

Banking is narrowly defined as commercial banking, which takes deposits from customers and provides loans to customers. Banks deal with financial risks, and both income and expenses are related to interest factors. Their operating activities, however, are quite different from country to country. The services banks may provide in the United States or Japan are carefully regulated by authorities, whereas European banks have greater latitude, and may provide services ranging from commercial loans to travel agencies.

The *insurance business* covers risks to property or life. The industry is regulated by local authorities in terms of how reserves are calculated and, thereby, the rates charged for premiums. Insurance companies in Japan and Korea can provide either property and casualty insurance or life insurance, but European companies can provide both and may go into many other businesses as well.

Other financial services are services other than banking and insurance. The revenue of financial services is generally related to interest or investment income. The personal loan business also depends on interest income but, unlike banks, does not take deposits from customers. Real estate investment or investment trust companies invest their money in real estate or securities in other companies, and most of their income is composed of dividends or gains from investments.

"Holdings" are companies whose major assets are investments in other companies, and their major earnings are the dividends from these investments. If the investee companies are consolidated by the holding company, it would be helpful to analysts if the holding company would use the industrial format in compiling data.

Data Formats	Industries
Industrial Format	All manufacturing industries, retail/wholesale, extraction businesses and other nonfinancial services, utilities
Banking Format	Commercial banking, money centers, savings and loans
Other Financial Service Format	Personal loans, real estate investments, investment trusts, security brokerages, holding companies
Insurance Format	Property and casualty insurance, life insurance
(See the detailed classification of industries in Chapter 7.)	

3.5.3 Issues Related to Research

Languages of the Financial Statements

Obviously, companies prepare financial statements in the language of the country in which their major operations are located. Many companies in non-English-speaking countries publish their financial statements in English for the convenience of international users. Some publish them in the local language and English side by side. No matter what languages are used, translation of the information into an analyst's own language should not be a barrier to research.

In fact, the hurdle is not the translation of financial statements word by word from one language to another, but rather the transfer of the meaning. First, it is necessary to understand the fundamental issues related to the different accounting standards in each country. Individual researchers should be equipped with such skills.

Currency of the Financial Statements

Business transactions are performed in local currency, and gains and losses from operating activities in foreign currencies are converted under the rules of foreign currency transactions. These gains and losses are included in the income statement.

The financial statements prepared in a local currency must be converted to a standard currency for global analysis. No standard method of conversion, however, is specified in any regulations or books on international finance. The English versions of annual company reports sometimes convert financial statements into U.S. dollars or British pounds, but the rates of exchange companies use are at their own discretion.

Usually, the income statement is translated by the year's average rate of exchange, and a fiscal year-end rate is used for the balance sheet. However, the average rate used for the income statement may be, for example, a monthly average rate or, at other times, a daily weighted average rate. Even companies within the same country with the same fiscal year-end dates may use different rates. This may be the case, for example, for the financial statements of foreign companies that issue American Depository Receipts (ADRs) in the United States. Primary data compiled by financial statement users should be in the company's local currency. Analysts should make their own conversion of local currency in financial statements to a currency of their choice, rather than depending on the conversion method used by each company. Certain ratios (e.g., dividend yield), should be computed both in local currency and in the analyst's currency of choice.

Different Fiscal Year Ends and Their Changes

Companies periodically report their operating results and financial positions. Annual financial reporting is required in all countries, but interim reporting is not. In data compilation, the accounting periods should be appropriately assigned, and the data will then be useful for analysis.

A majority of companies issue their annual reports on December 31 of each year, and interim reports are produced accordingly. However, the cut-off dates vary according to differing operating cycles and national traditions. For example, the fiscal year for German companies ends on December 31, but for Australian companies it ends on June 30, and for Japanese companies it ends on March 31. For consistency in databank organization, the year in which the fiscal year end falls should be the year designated in the databank. For example, the year ending March 31, 1993, may be called 1992/1993 by a company, but the data should be treated as 1993 information in the databank.

Cut-off dates can also vary according to company practice. For example, retail businesses typically finish on a convenient Sunday at the end of the calendar year, which results in the inclusion of 52 weeks in one year and 53 weeks in another year. An arbitrary cut-off date is needed, such as January 15. Thus, information for January 3, 1994, would be treated as 1993 information, whereas that for January 16, 1994, would be treated as 1994 information. Opinions may vary according to cultural background, but in the end some date must be set so that data can be realigned and the analysis process can begin.

Sometimes when a company goes through reorganization, the reporting period may be more or less than 12 months. The result is either having to skip a year or having two fiscal years for a specific calendar year. As long as the data compilation process keeps track of such cases, the analysis process can accommodate the irregularity by annualizing the data.

Differences in Reporting Formats

Not all financial reports look alike. The variations are a result of differences in accounting standards or different points of focus. Minor differences are common even between companies in the same industry in the same country. Compiling data by following the formats of company reports will not be useful unless individual data items are characterized by a consistent definition.

Ideally, all data should be compiled with the use of a few standard data sets, and information for all companies should be compiled based on their operating activities. Characterization requires considerable thought, involving a significant number of trained researchers specializing both in specific industries and in specific countries.

3.5.4 Issues Related to Analysis

How Many Years to Compile

The number of years for which data should be compiled depends on the purpose of the analysis. Some information may be comparable for 10 or 20 years, but no country maintains the same accounting standards for so long a time. Changes in emerging countries occur almost every year. Alterations in accounting standards or corporate structures trigger restatements of financial statements, which thus no longer provide comparability between years.

Considering the possible changes in accounting standards and in corporate structures, about six years' information is appropriate for financial analysis and will accommodate five-year compounded growth ratios. When a company is publicly traded for less than six years, the information given for the respective time period is sufficient for analysis. In the case of an initial public offering (IPO), however, one prior year's information is needed for comparison. This is usually provided in the company's prospectus.

Restated Information

The restatement of the previous year's figures may be necessary, not only because of reorganizations but also because of changes in reporting standards or for other similar reasons. Some countries do not allow changes in the beginning balances carried forward from the previous year. Retroactive results from changes in accounting standards or regulations are disclosed as prior period adjustments at the end of the income statement, or a direct adjustment is made to retained earnings. If previously reported numbers are restated, they should be collected in the same way as in the case of reorganization. However, analysis of the data should differentiate the two cases. Usage of restated information for research is explained in Chapter 11, "Research Procedures."

Computed Numbers and Adjustments

Some companies compute ratios for users. To analyze companies on a consistent basis, such ratios should be treated cautiously. A company's computation process may not use the same definitions as others. Only if information is used in a company's ratios that an analyst could otherwise not obtain, should the company's ratios be accepted.

The analyst should also be aware of the nature of company adjustments to per share information following a stock split or stock dividend. The adjustment can easily be computed as long as all required data items are collected. The adjusted numbers disclosed by a company are comparable only for the period covered by the financial statements (usually two years) but are not comparable beyond that.

Income Statement 4

This chapter reviews the income statements of four major industry groups. The income statement, also referred to as *profit and loss account,* summarizes net earnings for a reporting period. It accumulates all revenue/expenses, gains/losses, charges to provisions, and reversals of provisions. This activity is summarized by the Functional Method, by the Cost Summary Method, or in the Debit-Credit Format. Detailed descriptions and discussion of these methods can be found in Chapter 3.

The following discussion of income statements, balance sheets, and cash flow statements focuses on database development. The database design is aimed at making global financial analysis more efficient, while retaining some of the unique qualities of different reporting practices in various countries.

To analyze a single company, the reporting format it uses, no matter which, will suffice. All information a company reports can be organized on a spread sheet, including qualitative and quantitative information, for the analyst's convenience. However, the efficient analysis of a number of companies within particular groups requires that the data for all companies in a group be organized consistently so that results from various companies can be compared to establish the relative strength of each.

Comparability is not limited to a specific industry sector or to a specific country, even though most financial analysts specialize in a single sector. An investor expecting a reasonable return from investments does not care whether the money is invested in the U.S. cyclical sector, European banking, or pharmaceutical companies worldwide. Thus, for comparability, some common key factors across industries and across countries are needed.

The income statement has four components: operating activities, nonoperating activities, extraordinary items, and other periodic reference items. In some countries, such as the United Kingdom, companies present the appropriation of net earnings at the bottom of the income statement, connecting it to the shareholders' equity section on the balance sheet.

The income statement structure in this database is designed using the Functional Method or Cost of Sales Method, rather than the Cost Summary Method or Debit-Credit Format. The information from each company is converted to the Functional Format for effective comparison globally. The conversion process typically is not perfect, because of insufficient disclosure or the incompatibility of company formats, in addition to the fundamental differences in valuation methods. To reflect unique items in different formats or differences in accounting standards in various countries, a few reference items are added.

STRUCTURE OF THE INCOME STATEMENT	
Sections	**Activities**
Operating section	All revenue and expenses related to operating activities in the company.
Nonoperating section	All income/expenses, gain/loss from other than operating activities.
Extraordinary activities	Gain/loss from extraordinary activities.
Reference items	Per-share computation and related information. Other periodic information and reference information related to the main body of the income statement. Items related to the appropriation of net earnings (statement of changes in shareholders' equity) are included here.

The nature of business differs by industry, and different reporting formats are used by various industries even though they issue reports for much the same reason. For example, the reporting formats used in banking and insurance differ significantly from those of industrial companies, mainly in the operating sections because of the differences in operating activities. In other respects their reports are similar. In this book, the formats across industries are segregated into four types: Industrial, Banking, Insurance, and Other Financial Services. The Functional Method is mainly used in designing the Industrial Format, which embraces manufacturing, commercial services, transportation, and utilities. The Cost Summary Method is used in designing the reporting formats for banking, insurance, and other financial services.

The banking and insurance industries have their own reporting formats. Other financial services comprise very diverse sectors, such as securities brokerages (using a format close to that used by banking in the United States and the United Kingdom, but close to a commercial services format in Japan and Korea), personal and commercial loans (using a format close to a banking format), real estate leasing (often mixed with real estate development, which should use the industrial format, as in construction), and investment management firms. A single reporting format should be chosen for the main body of the income statement, and reference items should be used to fill the gaps reflecting characteristics of other formats.

The operating sections and related data are explained in detail in this chapter for all four industry formats. Reference items may be added to reflect unique items in each format. The nonoperating section and the extraordinary section are explained in the Industrial Format only.

Data items in the income statement are the numbers accumulated during the reporting period, rather than those at the fiscal year-end date. The reference section includes a few per-share data computations and supporting information. The per-share data should be computed by analysts if the necessary information is available. The basis for computing earnings per share (EPS) reported by individual companies, however, is often unclear.

Sometimes analysts are confused by the terminology companies use. For example, EPS in U.S. and U.K. companies exclude extraordinary items, but companies in other countries may include extraordinary activities in the numerator. There is no consistency in the definition of EPS, and in some countries it is not disclosed at all. These national differences will be noted in later volumes with specific examples.

4.1 INDUSTRIAL FORMAT

The Industrial Format embraces all industries except financial services (banking, insurance, and other financial services). Thus, the Industrial Format includes agriculture and extractive industries, manufacturing industries, commercial services, wholesale/retailing, transportation, and utilities. Each subcategory has its own characteristics (unique cost structures, for example), which become obvious when the Cost Summary Method is applied.

Costs in the manufacturing industry are spread among materials, personnel expenses, and depreciation expenses, whereas the costs of commercial services are dominated by personnel expenses. Wholesale/retail industries are dominated by the cost of products purchased and transportation companies and utilities are heavily capitalized with fixed assets. The user of the data should evaluate these different cost structures in the analysis process, rather than create a completely different format for compiling data.

The Industrial Format is designed for manufacturing and commercial service companies, but a few conglomerates have significant revenue from financial services as well. Most manufacturing companies do not fully consolidate subsidiaries in such significantly different industries in their financial statements. Instead, the operating results of these other enterprises are added to those of the consolidating entity by the Equity Method. However, consolidation in U.S. companies is all-inclusive, these companies providing separate additional sets of financial statements for the financial service activities. Items in an all-inclusive consolidated income statement are not useful for analysis. For example, although interest expenses are nonoperating expenses for manufacturing companies, they are operating expenses for financial service companies.

Each data item in the following table is assigned a specific account number designed for database development as well as for easy reference when using this book and future volumes. The main body of the income statement up to and including "IS1299 Net Income" adopts the Functional Method structure, and all accounts from individual companies are converted to this format. The remaining reference items explain additional information or absorb unique information from other reporting formats.

This section explains each of the following items, why they were selected, and how they will be used in analysis. Convertibility of information from each company to this standard format will be explained in the forthcoming country-specific volumes.

INCOME STATEMENT IN AN INDUSTRIAL FORMAT

Sections	Data Items	
Operating Section	IS1001	Net Sales
	IS1019	Other Operating Revenue
	IS1020	**Total Revenue**
	IS1021	Cost of Goods Sold or Cost of Sales
	IS1039	Direct Expenses for Other Operating Activities
	IS1040	**Total Direct Expenses**
	IS1050	Selling, General, and Administrative Expenses
	IS1099	**Operating Income**
Nonoperating Section	IS1110	Interest Expenses
	IS1120	Foreign Exchange Loss (Gain)
	IS1130	Loss (Gain) from Associated Companies
	IS1140	Other Nonoperating Loss (Gain)
	IS1150	Income Tax Expenses (Credits)
	IS1160	Reserve Charges (Credits)
	IS1199	**Income Before Extraordinary Items**
Extraordinary Items	IS1210	Loss (Gain) from Extraordinary Activities Before Tax Effects
	IS1220	Tax Effects on Extraordinary Items
	IS1230	Minority Interests
	IS1299	**Net Income**
Reference Items for EPS	IS1310	Cash Dividends to Preferred Stocks
	IS1320	Cash Dividends to Common Stocks
	IS1323	Appropriation to Capital Reserves
	IS1324	Appropriation to Revenue Reserves
	IS1325	Distributions to Directors and Officers
	IS1330	Dividend per Share (DPS)
	IS1340	EPS Before Extraordinary Items
	IS1350	Primary Earnings per Share
	IS1360	Weighted Average Number of Shares for the Primary EPS
	IS1370	Fully Diluted EPS
	IS1380	Number of Shares for Fully Diluted EPS
	IS1390	Special EPS
Other Reference Items	IS1510	Export Sales
	IS1520	Cost of Materials
	IS1530	Personnel Expenses

(continued)

(continued)	IS1540 Depreciation Expenses
	IS1550 Research and Development Expenditure
	IS1610 Capitalized Interest Expenses
	IS1620 Sales from Discontinued Operations
	IS1630 Loss (Gain) from Discontinued Operations
	IS1700 Number of Days for the Period

4.1.1 Operating Section

The first line of the operating section in an income statement for industrial companies is headed by Revenue from Sales. Operating expenses are deducted to derive an operating income. The sales figure is the sum of the sales of the company's various entities. A further breakdown specifies segment information. However, the organization of operating expenses depends on the reporting format chosen by a company.

IS1020 Total Revenue

The term *Total Revenue* does not appear in the financial statements of manufacturing companies. However, it is used throughout this book to provide better comparability among industries. Total revenue is the sum of IS1001 Net Sales and IS1019 Other Operating Revenue. IS1019 is added to absorb revenue from financial services of manufacturing companies.

The Scope of Entities, or the number of subsidiaries included in a parent company's consolidated financial statements, determines the amount of total revenue. Any changes in subsidiaries arising from mergers, acquisitions, divestitures, or changes in the consolidation method, should be noted before analysis is attempted.

The aim is to include all related companies whose activities are significantly influenced by the investing parent company. A discussion of various consolidation methods, found in Chapter 3, are summarized here:

Degree of Ownership	Influence over Investee	Consolidation Method
More than 50% ownership	Dominating	Full Consolidation Method
Joint venture	Equally dominating	Proportional Consolidation Method
20%–50% ownership	Significant influence	Equity Method
Less than 20% ownership	No significant influence	Cost Method

The percentages in the preceding list should not be overemphasized in choosing a consolidation method. Each country uses slightly different percentage criteria to determine the degree of influence of an investor on investees. Joint venture entities with equal influence are consolidated by the Proportional Consolidation Method or the Equity Method, depending on the parent company's view. The more important issue is the need for a consistent application of a consolidation method to provide comparability over the years.

Radical *changes in the Scope of Entities,* such as mergers and acquisitions, discontinued operations, other reorganizations, and changes in the consolidation method, inevitably compromise comparability and should be separately noted. If the restated previous year's information is available, it should be included as an additional set of financial statements with appropriate notes on the source information.

Note should also be taken of the *length of the reporting period* and should be assigned to IS1700 Number of Days for the Period. Any irregular reporting period should be normalized (projected to its regular reporting period) in the analysis process.

Revenue from discontinued operations should not be included here, because it is of no use in evaluating the performance of ongoing activities. As discussed in Chapter 3, there are two sources of income from discontinued operations in the year of disposition. One is the operating results up to the point of disposition, and the other is the gain or loss from the disposition. Revenue and expense from disposed operations could be considered sales and cost of sales, but such information is irrelevant in estimating future operating prospects. Therefore, both the net operating results from the discontinued operations up to the time of disposition, and the gain or loss from the disposition, should be included in extraordinary activities. *Revenue from newly acquired businesses* should be assigned to ongoing revenue, because it is relevant to future operations.

IS1001 Net Sales. IS1001 Net Sales includes all revenues from main operating activities for the reporting period. The operating activities should be the activities that the company pursues day to day and that are expected to generate revenue consistently in the future.

In the consolidated income statement, sales include sales from all subsidiaries after eliminating intercompany transactions. Revenue from significantly different industries, such as financial services, should be excluded and assigned to IS1019 Other Operating Revenue, when the main activities are classified as industrial. In some cases it is not clear as to which of several operating activities is the main one. For example, revenue from financial services at BAT Industries (U.K.) and ITT (U.S.) is as important as the companies' other operating revenues. Some companies with mixed industries ignore gross receipts in presenting their income statement and begin with operating income from each segment. An extreme example is the practice of holding companies that show only investment income received from their subsidiaries. The financial statements of these holding companies follow the financial services format and lose all value for analysis.

Some Commonwealth countries do not disclose sales figures at all, but start with trading profits. Trading profits and sales are not the same thing.

Adjustments. Not all gross receipts from customers are sales for a company. Some portion of gross receipts simply passes through the company and is only temporarily recorded as revenue. Such pass-through revenues or temporary accounts are called *sales adjustments* and must be eliminated to derive net sales.

Sales discounts, returns, and allowances are commonly recorded in accounts separate from sales. This practice is valid for bookkeeping purposes. In the adjustment process, these accounts should be subtracted from gross receipts to generate a net sales figure showing the true results of operating activities. Similarly, *shipping and insurance charges* directly passed on to customers are not revenue and should be subtracted from gross receipts to generate a net sales result.

Excise taxes, sales taxes, value-added tax (VAT), and any other pass-through charges by government should not be included in the operating revenue. These charges take different forms in different countries. The amounts are usually significant in the oil/gas, tobacco, and alcohol businesses.

Subsidies from national and local governments to support public services should be included here, because they are, in effect, sales to government. (See the detailed discussion of government subsidies in Chapter 3.)

There is less emphasis on gross revenue from sales in wholesale businesses. The industry is not common except in Japan and Korea, where companies collect products from *keiretsu* companies and sell them to outside parties. In fact, the industry's gross margin is very low and value added by the wholesale process is marginal. However, that being the nature of the business, the gross sales figures must be used. Analysis must always consider the nature of the business under study.

Sales from industrial companies may include such diverse activities as manufacturing and services, and it is questionable whether they should be combined. For example, sales from computer manufacturing and sales from software production at IBM should, ideally, be kept separate. If necessary, data for each activity can be separated in the product segmentation section of the database.

IS1019 Other Operating Revenue. A particular account is designed for conglomerates whose main activities are in the industrial sector but also derive revenue from financial services through one or more subsidiaries. To be included in IS1019 Other Operating Revenue, the revenue must result from a subsidiary's main operating activity. Otherwise, the net results from such activities should be included in IS1140 Other Nonoperating Loss (Gain).

IS1040 Total Direct Expenses

Total Direct Expenses include all operating expenses directly related to total revenue. "Directly related" means that the expenses increase or decrease according to the change in the volume of sales or other operating revenue. Disclosure of directly related operating expenses varies significantly in different reporting formats. The Functional Method treats them as the Cost of Goods Sold in the manufacturing industry and as the Cost of Sales in the retail/wholesale industry.

Neither the Cost Summary Method nor the Debit-Credit Format distinguishes direct operating expenses from indirect operating expenses. Operating expenses in the Cost Summary Method should be a lump-sum amount in IS1050 Selling, General, and Administrative Expenses. The most significant items of operating expense are shown in the reference items IS1520 Cost of Materials, IS1530 Personnel Expenses, and IS1540 Depreciation Expenses. If a company has revenue from other operating activities, related direct expenses should be segregated and placed in IS1039 Direct Expenses for Other Operating Activities.

IS1021 Cost of Goods Sold or Cost of Sales. Under the *Functional Method,* the uses of resources are segregated by their relationship to sales. For example, materials used in a factory are classified as the cost of products, whereas materials used in administrative offices are treated as general expenses. Financial statements prepared using the Functional Method can easily identify these items. The proportion of resources used directly and the proportion used indirectly for sales are determined by the company. Those preparing financial statements using the Functional Method may have specific criteria and can gauge the functions of each department to establish where resources are employed.

In some countries, including Turkey and Korea, companies produce a Statement of Cost of Sales to clarify the components of the Cost of Sales. A statement can be prepared for each product to identify a unit production cost. This information is useful when a company has relatively simple product lines. Most companies, however, prepare consolidated financial statements, and sales reported on the income statement comprise many different product lines. Such statements are not useful for analysis.

Under the *Cost Summary Method,* operating expenses are not segregated into direct and indirect expenses but are, rather, sorted by types of cost. The types of cost include material purchased from outside and changes in the inventory level of those materials (i.e., increase in cost of material used through decrease in inventory level), personnel expenses, depreciation and amortization expenses, and other operating expenses. If the Cost Summary Method is applied by a company, the Cost of Goods Sold account may not be used. IS1050 Selling, General, and Administrative Expenses should instead account for total operating expenses, and its main components are shown in IS1520 Cost of Materials, IS1530 Personnel Expenses, and IS1540 Depreciation Expenses. Amortization of intangible assets is often difficult to separate from depreciation expenses and may require a footnote.

Whichever method is used, costs should be matched with the scope of entities used in the revenue section. The Cost of Goods Sold should include the expenses corresponding to IS1001 Net Sales.

Although the Functional Method is most widely used for income statements in the United States and Japan, service-oriented industries often use the Cost Summary Method. For example, airlines may disclose the cost of fuel, depreciation of airplanes, and the cost of personnel—the major components of their operating expenses. Sometimes the Cost Summary Method is used for a parent company's financial statements to satisfy local authorities, as in Germany, whereas the consolidated financial statements are prepared by the Functional Method.

IS1039 Direct Expenses for Other Operating Activities. This account should be paired with IS1019 Other Operating Revenue, and assumes the revenue is not generated by a major operating activity of the company. As discussed in the revenue section, other operating revenue in industrial companies comes mainly from financial services.

IS1050 Selling, General, and Administrative Expenses

Selling, general, and administrative expenses, disclosed in account IS1050, are only indirectly related to the level of operating activities and are generated by such departments as sales, accounting, personnel, and research and development (R & D), which support a company's major operating activities. These are operating expenses, but they are not linked to the number of units sold or manufactured during a period.

Expenses for R & D are only remotely related to contributions to sales and should be included in this line item. R & D expenses must not be confused with IS1550 Research and Development Expenditure, which is the total expenditure for the year. Even though most companies expense total R & D expenditure in the year the resources are used, there are exceptional cases that warrant capitalization and amortization over time. IS1550 Research and Development Expenditure focuses on the ratios that explore future growth potential.

In addition, exploration expenses for dry holes in the oil and gas extraction business should be included in IS1050 Selling, General, and Administrative Expenses, as should taxes based on sales or operating volume.

THREE TYPES OF TAX EXPENSE

Pass-Through Taxes

Some taxes "pass through" a company and are unrelated to the company's performance. These include sales taxes, excise taxes, and value-added taxes and should be treated as adjustments to gross sales to derive IS1001 Net Sales.

Taxes Related to Operations

Certain taxes, such as licensing fees or fees related to permits issued by local authorities, are imposed because a company performs certain operating activities. They may be one-time payments or may be remotely related to the level of operating activities. Such expenses should be part of IS1050 Selling, General, and Administrative Expenses.

Income Tax Expenses

Income taxes are based on the level of net earnings, which is taxable income. The tax owed can be a negative number if a company has significant losses in a year, and may include credits for excessive payments in prior years or for future payments. Income tax expenses should be classified as IS1150 Income Tax Expenses (Credits).

As discussed earlier, if the Cost Summary Method is used, the cost of goods sold and cost of sales are not segregated from selling, general, and administrative expenses, and IS1050 will include all operating expenses. The major components are referenced in items, IS1520 Cost of Materials, IS1530 Personnel Expenses, and IS1540 Depreciation Expenses.

If government subsidies are not related to a company's specific products, they should be treated as a reduction in general expenses rather than as increases in sales. Such subsidies are likely to occur in the telecommunication and transportation industries in developing countries.

IS1099 Operating Income

Operating Income is IS1020 Total Revenue minus IS1040 Total Direct Expenses minus IS1050 Selling, General, and Administrative Expenses.

4.1.2   Nonoperating Section

All activities in a company are in some way related to operations. However, activities not related to the company's main objective are called *nonoperating activities*. Consider, for example, a piece of equipment acquired and used for production. When the equipment is worn out or becomes obsolete, it will be discarded or sold. A gain or loss from the disposition of the equipment occurs if the net book value and the actual value are not the same. Turnover of equipment is not a company's objective but a necessary reality in an ongoing business. Therefore, the gain or loss is classified as *nonoperating*. Another example is the expense of borrowing. When a company needs extra capital, many alternatives are available. If the capital is provided through preferred equity or common equity, the related expenses—that is, preferred dividends or common dividends, respectively—will be treated as distributions after net income. However, when long-term bond issuance or bank borrowing is the method chosen, the distribution is accounted for as interest expense. These are financing activities, not operating activities.

Results from nonoperating activities such as IS1110 Interest Expenses, IS1120 Foreign Exchange Loss (Gain), and IS1130 Loss (Gain) from Associated Companies are itemized because of their importance in financial analysis; all others are combined.

The items in the Nonoperating Section are applicable to all industry formats even though the nature of specific items is decided by their relationship to a company's main operating activities. For example, a foreign exchange gain/loss is an operating activity in the Banking Format and a nonoperating activity in the Industrial Format.

IS1110 Interest Expenses

Interest expenses, disclosed in account IS1110, include the cost of short-term and long-term borrowing, issuance expenses, and factoring expenses. They also include amortized premiums or discounts on bonds, because these are the result of differences between the market interest rate and the face rate of the bonds. Interest expenses related to lease financing should also be included.

Interest expenses should be reduced by the capitalized portion, that amount used for internal construction of specific inventory items or fixed assets. In addition, the capitalized portion should be referred to IS1610 Capitalized Interest Expenses to analyze a company's total cash needs for interest payments.

IS1120 Foreign Exchange Loss (Gain)

Account IS1120 includes foreign exchange losses or gains either from foreign currency investment or from transactions in foreign currencies. Gains or losses from foreign currency investment activities may be classified as investment income. For most companies, however, they are related to accounts receivable or accounts payable, denominated in foreign currencies that have not been hedged against a possible fluctuation in rates. A decision not to hedge is a financing decision rather than an operating decision.

This account also includes gains or losses from foreign currency translation using the Temporal Method or the exceptional application of the Temporal Method under the Current Rate Method. However, foreign currency translation adjustments under the Current Rate Method are accounted for in the shareholders' equity on the balance sheet rather than in the income statement.

IS1130 Loss (Gain) from Associated Companies

Also called Equity Earnings from Related Companies, IS1130 Loss (Gain) from Associated Companies reflects the undistributed loss or earnings from investments with 20 percent to 50 percent ownership under the Equity Method. There is increasing use of consolidated financial statements, and use of the Equity Method for investments with 20 percent to 50 percent ownership is now widely accepted. When a company has significant influence over an investee, but no control of voting rights, the Equity Method is used in the consolidation process.

Even when a company owns the majority of shares in another company, the subsidiary may be consolidated using the Equity Method rather than the Full Consolidation Method if the parent company lacks control because of political uncertainties or government interference.

In addition, when a subsidiary's activities are significantly different from the parent company's operations, the Equity Method is preferred to the Full Consolidation Method. In such cases, proportional undistributed earnings from the subsidiaries should be included here.

Of course, whether a gain or loss is operating or nonoperating may be debated. When the main activities of associated companies are directly related to the operating activities of the parent company, earnings from the associated companies should be treated as operating income. However, it must be noted that:

- Net sales and the cost of goods sold from the investee's operations are not included in the parent company's financial statements, and

- The investor has only a significant influence on, but does not dominate, the investee. This means that the investor lacks control over the resource allocations of the investee.

Itemization of IS1130 can help in analyzing the profitability of BS2180 Investments in Associated Companies. (See Chapter 5, "Balance Sheet.")

IS1140 Other Nonoperating Loss (Gain)

Other nonoperating losses or gains include results from nonoperating activities other than those listed for IS1110 through IS1130. In many countries there is no clear distinction between extraordinary items and nonoperating activities, and the account might be called "Exceptional Items," or something similar. These exceptional items should be reclassified and be placed in appropriate accounts under general expenses (IS1050), nonoperating loss (gain) (IS1140) and true extraordinary items (IS1210). A few illustrations of nonoperating losses and gains are given in the following paragraphs.

Interest income: Interest expenses on short- or long-term loans from banks or from the public are common in industrial companies because of their need for cash. Therefore, interest expenses are important enough to be itemized. However, the possibility of a lender providing excess money to increase interest income is slight among industrial companies. If money is loaned to other parties and interest is earned, the interest income should be included in IS1140 Other Non-Operating Loss (Gain), after related expenses are deducted.

Investment income (loss): Even though industrial companies are not in the business of investing money in securities, their excess cash should be invested until the money is needed. Any income from such investments should be included here after the related investment expenses are deducted. This account also includes unrealized losses on security investments.

Gain or loss from sale of investments: When securities are sold, the resulting gain or loss should be included here after related expenses are deducted.

Gain or loss from disposal of fixed assets: When property or equipment used in operating activities becomes outdated or unusable, it is disposed of and replaced. However, the asset's net book value after accumulated depreciation is unlikely to be the same as the market value at the time of disposal. The difference between net book value and market value results in a gain or loss, which should be included here.

IS1150 Income Tax Expenses (Credits)

There are expenses arising from federal, local, and/or foreign taxes, based on a company's earnings. Such taxes are imposed when a company has any taxable income. Taxable income may not be the same as the income figures used for financial reporting purposes. If the income for financial reporting purposes is greater than the taxable income, the deferred income tax expenses belong here as well. Account IS1150 also includes the income tax expenses passed on to subsidiaries if they are consolidated with the parent company.

IS1150 includes only income taxes. It does not include pass-through taxes such as excise taxes, sales taxes, or VAT taxes, as described in "IS1001 Net Sales." Income taxes directly related to extraordinary items should be separated from taxes on ongoing earnings. These tax expenses belong in IS1220 Tax Effects on Extraordinary Items.

IS1160 Reserve Charges (Credits)

Account IS1160 is limited to charges to and reversals of BS2680 Nonequity Reserves (see Chapter 5). Charges to operating reserves should be a part of operating expenses, whereas transactions involving capital reserves do not affect the income statement. For purposes of analysis, BS2680 Nonequity Reserves is introduced in this book. (See Chapter 3). However, companies often establish reserves that are unrelated to operating activities and cannot be classified as operating expenses. These reserve charges vary by country and are often established because of tax incentives or other special regulations.

Charges to these reserves accumulate and can be reversed under certain conditions. This account, IS1160, should include the net of the charges to and reversals of the reserves for a year, and the accumulated reserves should be classified as Nonequity Reserves in the balance sheet. These sometimes ambiguous charges arise as a result of nonoperating activities and are not permitted in most countries.

For example, Austrian tax laws may allow substantial depreciation of an asset with no obvious business justification. This special depreciation must be shown as a revaluation reserve and reverses either when the asset is sold or through annual depreciation charges in the income statement. Some reserves are established with untaxed earnings, and others with taxed earnings. Each of these cases is differently regulated in individual countries. The untaxed allocations are accumulated as untaxed reserves, which will be taxed when they are utilized. Often such tax obligations are forgiven forever if certain conditions are met. They may cause deferred tax liabilities if financial reporting ignores such special treatment. However, regulations in some countries, such as Germany, Italy, and Spain, also require that the accounting standards of company financial reports conform to tax returns and that no deferred tax liabilities are recorded.

Revaluation of fixed assets is not permitted by the Historical Cost Principle. Yet companies in countries experiencing high inflation want to report realistic earnings. In such cases, revaluation of fixed assets and inventory is allowed on a limited basis. If the revaluation results are directly charged to shareholders' equity, as in the United Kingdom and Korea, the income statement is not affected. Otherwise, the gain or loss from the revaluation should be separated and included in account IS1160 in order to distinguish operating results from nonoperating results.

Often, excess depreciation expenses are allowed for the first few years after an initial investment. Excess depreciation reserves are established and reversed in later years when certain conditions are met.

Depending on circumstances, provisions can be assigned to various accounts. In the early 1990s provisions against anticipated restructuring prompted by fears of recession were common in some industries, most notably the auto industry. Such restructuring charges are common in the United States because many manufacturing companies, for example, have moved their factories to southern states to take advantage of lower manufacturing costs. Restructuring expenses should be classified as general expenses if they are not significant and the restructuring occurred within the year. If restructuring is due to unexpected events and the amount is significant, the expenses should be classified as extraordinary items. On the other hand, if such charges are expected and provisions are made in advance, the charges should be classified in this account as reserve charges and should be differentiated from the expenses of current operating activities.

IS1199 Income Before Extraordinary Items

Income before extraordinary items is disclosed in account IS1199. This is a subtotal derived by deducting IS1110 through IS1160 from IS1099 Operating Income.

4.1.3 Extraordinary Items

IS1210 Loss (Gain) from Extraordinary Activities Before Tax Effects

The definition of an *extraordinary item* is inconsistent from country to country. In the United States it is defined as something that is unusual, infrequent, and material (See Chapter 3, Section 3.2.3, for a more detailed discussion). This definition is spreading to other countries, including those of Europe since the adoption of the European Union's (E.U.) Fourth Directive, although it is applied somewhat differently.

IS1210 includes gains (losses) from natural disasters, discontinued operations, and accumulated adjustments resulting from changes in accounting standards. It is useful for analysis to separate the tax impact of extraordinary items from taxes on regular operating results. This account should show the extraordinary item before the impact of income taxes. The taxes should be assigned to account IS1220.

A discontinued operation is often classified as an extraordinary item, but it qualifies as such only if the company closes a specific business sector. Simply closing one or two factories and opening another elsewhere is common practice within conglomerates and should not be classified as an extraordinary item. The results of discontinued operations have two components, operating results from the discontinued operation during the year, and the gain or loss from the disposal of the business. In the United Kingdom, discontinued operations are disclosed in a separate column since the Financial Reporting Standards (FRS) 3 revision in 1992. This account, IS1210, adds the two components of discontinued operations, but each is separately noted in accounts IS1630 and IS1620, respectively.

Accumulated adjustments resulting from changes in accounting standards, such as Financial Accounting Standards Board (FASB) 106, *Postretirement Benefits,* are disclosed in a separate line item as prior period adjustments. Earnings per share (EPS) is computed with and without the adjustments in the United States.

Many countries do not clearly define extraordinary items and have accounts such as *Exceptional Items,* which include all nonoperating items. If these exceptional items are lumped together, the components should be carefully reviewed and separated into nonoperating and extraordinary items for further analysis. In such cases the tax effects of a specific extraordinary item are unlikely to be identified, and this should be noted.

IS1220 Tax Effects on Extraordinary Items

Tax charges and credits relating to extraordinary items included in IS1210 should be disclosed in IS1220 Tax Effects on Extraordinary Items. Many companies do not disclose tax effects separately. The tax impact is sometimes mixed with regular income taxes, or the extraordinary items are net of tax effects and no further information is made available. In such instances, an independent computation of the tax effects is virtually impossible.

IS1230 Minority Interests

Earnings from subsidiaries are fully combined with earnings from the parent company in the Full Consolidation Method. When the parent company does not own 100 percent of a subsidiary, the undistributed earnings and losses that belong to minority shareholders should be segregated from the earnings of the parent company. If a subsidiary incurs a loss, the minority shareholders' portion of the loss should also be allocated and should be a credit to the parent company.

Account IS1230 is sometimes disclosed as an item below Net Income in company reports. No matter where the item is disclosed by a company, it should be assigned to this account to be made comparable internationally.

IS1299 Net Income or Net Profit (Loss)

Net income or net profit (loss) is disclosed in account IS1299. This is a subtotal obtained by deducting IS1210 through IS1230 from IS1199 Income Before Extraordinary Items. It represents earnings that belong to shareholders (preferred shareholders as well as common shareholders).

4.1.4 Reference Items for EPS

IS1310 Cash Dividends to Preferred Stocks

All cash dividends declared for preferred stocks should be included in account IS1310. The international capital market is complex, and various hybrid securities are often issued. The definition of preferred stocks is not always consistent, and it is often difficult to identify them in company reports translated into English. Identification should be based on the characteristics of each security.

Preferred and common stock and the criteria by which they can be identified are discussed in Chapter 3.

One of the characteristics of preferred stocks is a fixed dividend commitment, which will be the defining characteristic for the purposes of this book. This means that participative preferred stocks cannot be classified as preferred stocks as they are, for example, in Germany, Austria, Brazil, Greece, and Korea. Preferred stocks are sometimes granted voting rights, usually when a company fails to make its dividend payments, but the voting right factor will be ignored in this book. Convertible preferred stocks are preferred stocks until they are converted.

In analysis, the dividend should be the amount declared for the year. Actual payment follows the annual shareholders' meeting, which is held three to six months after the end of the fiscal year. Cumulative preferred stocks are entitled to dividends in later years if they cannot be paid because of a loss in any given year. Although it depends on the specific purpose of analysis, generally the loss to current common shareholders should not be increased because of dividends in arrears owed to preferred stockholders. Earnings available to common stock shareholders will be reduced when the dividends are actually declared. The amount paid in dividends for the year is captured in the cash flow statement.

The cash dividends to preferred stocks should be reported as the gross amount, if possible, although some countries may provide an "after withholding" tax dividend.

IS1320 Cash Dividends to Common Stocks

Account IS1320 includes all cash dividends declared to common stocks as a part of the appropriation of earnings. The segregation of dividends into preferred stocks and common stocks should be consistent with the segregation appearing on the balance sheet. The amounts should be those declared to be paid, rather than the actual amounts paid. The actual cash payment will be recorded much later, following the shareholders' meeting, and the amount will be captured in the cash flow statement.

Stock Dividends and Stocks in Lieu of Cash. Dividends consisting of additional stocks or stocks issued following a stock split should not be treated as cash dividends. Stock dividends or stock splits are given special treatment and require an adjustment of historical per share information. However, stock distribution in lieu of cash should be treated as cash dividends. Stocks in lieu of cash combine two transactions, cash distribution and the issuing of new stocks. These stock distributions have no dilutive effect, because the stocks are rendered at fair market value. If the exchange price is lower than the fair market value, the discounted portion may be treated as a stock dividend. However, the computation of dilution is complicated and is usually insignificant.

Gross or Net. Tax regulations regarding dividends vary by country. Companies in all countries must pay income taxes on their earnings. When earnings after corporate income taxes are distributed as dividends to shareholders, the shareholders may or may not pay additional taxes on the dividends received.

If shareholders must pay additional taxes, as in the United States, for example, there is double taxation on the same earnings. Taxation also depends on the status of shareholders. Triple taxation, which is possible when corporate shareholders must pay taxes on dividends received, is usually avoided in practice.

Dividends received may or may not be subject to taxation for individuals, depending on whether the dividends are attached to imputed tax credits. Moreover, the tax credits may or may not be utilized, depending on the individuals' overall income levels in conjunction with marital status, or depending on the status of shareholders as residents or nonresidents. Sometimes the withholding tax rate or the tax credit differs according to the extent of ownership.

In most countries, a percentage of the declared amount of dividends is withheld for tax purposes. The amount differs, depending on whether a domestic or foreign shareholder is involved. Generally, foreign shareholders are deprived of tax credits.

Despite the taxes withheld, IS1320 Cash Dividends to Common Stocks should record the gross dividend. However, the figures can be adapted to the accepted practice of the particular capital market. If the net figure is used, the ratio computation process should consider the withholding tax rate. With few exceptions, the withholding tax rate is the same for all companies within a country. AFV (Avantage Fiscal/Fiscaal Voordeel) shares, which enjoy a lower withholding tax rate in Belgium, are among the exceptions.

MULTIPLE SHARE INFORMATION SET

In order to compile all relevant information about each stock for companies issuing multiple shares, the following data set may be prepared:

STOCK ID	Identification of Security
IS1320	Cash Dividends to Common Stock
IS1330	Dividend per Share
IS1340	EPS before Extraordinary Items
IS1350	Primary EPS
IS1360	Weighted Average Number of Shares
BS2710	Number of Shares Outstanding
BS2720	Par Value
BS2730	Dividend Right Parity
BS2740	Voting Right Parity
BS2770	Number of Treasury Stocks

The account numbers duplicate those in the income statement and balance sheet, because the data sets for specific multiple shares are expected to be stored in a different data set with a specific share identification and company identification.

Whether gross or net cash dividends are used, the amount should be consistent with IS1330 Dividend per Share. In addition, the withholding tax rates should be noted for further analysis.

Multiple Shares. A company usually has one type of common share that has claim to a portion of the company's residual value based on the percentage of holding it represents. This is not always the case, however. There are some companies that may issue two or more types of common shares, called Common A and Common B, or they may have names that make it difficult to identify them as common shares. These should be classified as common shares if they represent a claim on a company's residual value. The multiple shares may have different dividend rights or different voting rights. The most important criterion in determining whether a share should be classified as preferred or common is whether its dividend payment varies according to the performance of the company. "True" preferred stock pays dividends fixed to its par value.

If a company has multiple common shares, dividends for each share must be separately noted in the multiple share information set, and aggregated dividends to each share should be disclosed in account IS1320. Many other issues related to multiple shares are discussed in Chapter 3.

Earnings from current operations are accumulated in unappropriated retained earnings in the balance sheet, and the accumulated earnings are distributed. The most significant distributions are the dividends to common shareholders. Such transactions are commonly summarized in the Statement of Changes in Shareholders' Equity. A few of those important transactions, except dividends to common stocks, described earlier, are collected in the following three accounts.

IS1323 Appropriation to Capital Reserves

Theoretically, companies should distribute all earnings from operations to shareholders because shareholders have a claim on all of a company's residual value in return for their investments. However, most countries impose some restrictions on distributions to preserve capital, and companies may resist distributions in order to weather temporary fluctuations in operating performance. The companies then save some portion of their earnings in a capital reserve until the reserve reaches a legally set level. The appropriation of earnings for capital or legally required reserves should be collected in account IS1323. Specific guidelines will be provided in later volumes.

Capital reserves may be converted to share capital as stock dividends. Alternatively, they may be used to reduce accumulated losses in the future.

IS1324 Appropriation to Revenue Reserves

In addition to capital reserves, companies may set aside additional amounts for general or specific purposes. Reserves for general purposes are called revenue reserves, or earnings reserves, and may be used to reduce accumulated losses.

Reserves for specific purposes are designated by purpose and will be used accordingly. Both types of reserves should be assigned to account IS1324. The Appropriation to Revenue Reserves (after income tax) must be distinguished from IS1160 Reserve Charges (Credits), which are "before income tax" and are included in the computation of IS1299 Net Income.

IS1325 Distribution to Directors and Officers

A company's directors or officers may be paid a cash or stock bonus. Such compensation is not recorded as a personnel expense, because the directors or officers are not considered employees. Often these bonuses are based on corporate performance in the year and treated as a distribution of earnings. These amounts should be placed in account IS1325 Distribution to Directors and Officers.

IS1330 Dividend per Share (DPS)

The dividend declared per share (DPS) should be entered in account IS1330. The DPS should match the definition of gross or net as determined for IS1320 Cash Dividends to Common Stocks.

For multiple shares, dividend per share for each type of share should be disclosed in the multiple share information sheet, not in the income statement. Only the DPS for the primary share equivalent is shown in the income statement, as a useful and easy reference for analysts.

Once per share information is computed, it should be adjusted for stock splits and/or stock dividends for purposes of historical comparison. For example, a 2:1 stock split means that DPS for prior years should be split in half so

---

STOCK PRICE INFORMATION SET

For illustration purposes, daily stock prices should be collected along with the following data items:

STOCK ID	Identification of security
DATE	Date of transaction
OPENING	Opening price
HIGH	High of the day
LOW	Low of the day
CLOSING	Closing price
VOLUME	Volume traded
EX-CHANGE	Exchange where stock or security is traded
CUR-RENCY	Currency of the transaction
RATIO	Stock dividend or stock split ratio
TYPE	Type of dilutive activities

they can be compared with the current DPS. The date the stock price is affected is called the ''Ex-dividend date.'' A split or dividend can occur at any time, which means that data frequency will differ from financial information appearing in periodic (quarterly or semiannual) reports and will therefore require another information set.

In recording stock dividends and stock splits, stock prices should be combined in one data set. The following data table may be used to incorporate the stock dividends and splits with stock price information. Of course, the stock prices can be revised according to an analyst's needs, ranging from continuous updates to annual closing prices with highs and lows.

It is advisable to revise stock prices more frequently than fundamental information, for example, quarterly revisions of stock prices for annual fundamental information, or monthly revisions for quarterly fundamental information. An additional record for each stock dividend or stock split should be created if stock prices are collected less than daily.

To be comparable, the ratio and ex-dividend date at each dilution should be incorporated to adjust all historical per-share information.

Stock splits and stock dividends are straightforward in most cases, and this information can be used in the adjustment process. However, there are more complicated situations in which it is not immediately clear what adjustments should be made.

An example is the *discounted issuance,* which is widely used in Japan. The price of the new issue is usually set lower than the market price at the ex-date as a privilege for existing shareholders. For the historical price adjustment, only the discounted portion should be treated as dilution. Rights issues, warrants, and options should be treated similarly.

IS1340 EPS Before Extraordinary Items

Earnings per share is a widely used indicator of performance in the financial community, but it is not always defined in the same way. It also has varying levels of acceptance in different countries. The purpose of research should determine which definition of EPS is used. Companies in the United States use EPS before extraordinary items (IS1340), but in other countries EPS is based on the net income after extraordinary items. The matter is further complicated by varying definitions of what constitutes an extraordinary item.

The calculation process is quite simple:

Numerator for EPS = IS1199 Income Before Extraordinary Items

  − IS1230 Minority Interests − IS1310 Cash Dividends to Preferred Stocks.

Denominator for EPS = IS1360 Weighted Average Number of Shares

                 for the Primary EPS.

The numerator isolates the earnings before extraordinary items available to common shareholders.

EPS with Multiple Shares. If there are multiple shares in a company, the EPS computation process becomes difficult. First, earnings for the company should be distributed among the multiple shares according to their relative ownership. Shares for GM constitute a very special case, because earnings come from completely different entities. Most companies with multiple shares are a single entity, and earnings by such companies should be distributed among the shares.

If the dividend right parity is used as the measurement of relative privilege, each of the multiple shares can be converted to primary share equivalents. The primary share equivalents are accumulated in IS1360 Weighted Average Number of Shares for the Primary EPS, and the aggregated primary equivalents are used to compute the EPS for a primary share. The primary EPS can be redistributed to each type of multiple share by its dividend right parity. For a more detailed discussion, see Chapter 3.

IS1350 Primary Earnings per Share

Another definition of EPS, primary earnings per share, also known as "net income per share," is widely used in many countries. The denominator can be defined in the same way as in IS1340 EPS Before Extraordinary Items, and the numerator should be defined as follows:

Numerator = IS1299 Net Income − IS1230 Minority Interests − IS1310 Cash

Dividends to Preferred Stocks.

The EPS reported by companies is not always consistent. If the EPS reported is used for IS1350 Primary Earnings per Share, the computation process should be carefully reviewed. If the EPS defined by the company does not match the analyst's definition, it must be recomputed to maintain a consistent data set. EPS for multiple shares can be computed using the procedure described in Chapter 3.

IS1360 Weighted Average Number of Shares for the Primary EPS

The weighted average number of shares (included in account IS1360) is usually provided when a company computes EPS. This figure is difficult for analysts to compute independently in an active capital market. The weighting process must consider the capital increases and decreases on a daily basis. U.S. and U.K. companies are required to disclose EPS and the weighted average number of shares on the face of the income statement. Companies in continental Europe rarely disclose EPS, and when they do, it may not be calculated in a consistent way.

European firms often use the number of shares outstanding at the end of a fiscal year instead of their weighted average. This practice is justified by the argument that their capital structures change less frequently than those of companies in other countries. At the same time, it is argued, the number of shares outstanding at year end are valid for the following year. If the weighted average number of shares is not calculated but the ex-dates of the capital increases are available, the figure can be computed. However, if the exercise of warrants or options is frequent for a company, only approximate weighting can be achieved.

If the ex-dates for capital changes are not available, a simple average between periods can be computed and used instead. For a discussion of multiple shares, see Chapter 3.

IS1370 Fully Diluted EPS

If a company has dilutive securities, that is, convertible bonds, convertible preferred stocks, warrants, options, or rights issues, earnings may be distributed to those securities. An EPS computation based on possible dilution is called "Fully Diluted EPS" (account IS1370). U.S. companies usually disclose the fully diluted EPS in their income statements. The computation process requires adjustments of both the earnings and the number of shares. For example, when convertible bonds are assumed to be converted, their interest expenses should be added back to earnings after tax effects.

The fully diluted EPS cannot be computed by analysts, because financial statements are unlikely to provide all the information required for the computation. If a company does not report the fully diluted EPS—and there are no possible dilutive securities in the capital structure—the fully diluted EPS can be assumed to be the same as the primary EPS. The fully diluted EPS is disclosed in the United States only because dilutive securities are widely used in its capital markets.

IS1380 Number of Shares for Fully Diluted EPS

If the fully diluted EPS is provided, the number of shares used in the computation is provided as well. This information is included in account IS1380.

IS1390 Special EPS

Efforts are under way to define a standard EPS. For example, the Institute of Investment Management and Research (IIMR) in the United Kingdom defines an EPS for "investment community" uses with a few adjustments that emphasize comparability. Companies are encouraged to disclose this EPS as of the 1993 fiscal year.

Another example is the EPS established by the Deutsche Vereinigung für Finanzanalyse und Anlagenberatung/Schmalenbach Gesellschaft (DVFA/SG) in Germany, which eliminates hidden reserves in addition to other adjustments. However, various organizations differ over the definition (and implementation) of the DVFA method. A similar definition of EPS by the Österreichische Vereinigung für Finanzanalyse und Anlagenberatung (ÖVFA) is accepted and used by all companies in Austria.

Individual definitions of EPS are being developed in many countries but remain outside the generally accepted local accounting principles. If documented, these definitions are useful in analysis.

Even though EPS may not be strictly defined in a particular country, some companies compute EPS based on their earnings. Some also provide an EPS based on U.S. GAAP. This adjusted EPS may be used with an appropriate footnote.

American Depository Receipts (ADR), which are foreign stocks traded in the U.S. market through transfer agents, are required to provide an earnings figure calculated using U.S. GAAP, which may then be used to compute EPS. Often one unit of ADR is a multiple of the original share, and earnings per ADR can also be calculated.

4.1.5 Other Reference Items

A cohesive set of data items may be used to derive other types of earnings per share calculations from an income statement. The following reference items should be collected to generate additional information for analysis.

IS1510 Export Sales

The geographic distribution of sales activities can be analyzed in two ways, by origins of sales and by destinations of sales. Each method reveals different aspects of the diversification of risk. Every country has its own economic cycle, and diversification of sales activities among countries is believed to offer considerable risk reduction.

Diversification by origins of sales is based on the sales generated by individual production facilities, each of which faces risks in its local economy. Diversification by origination will be captured later in the geographic segment information set. Diversification of sales by destination, based on a product's many markets, also provides diversification of risks.

Exports are defined as sales produced in the corporate home country and sold in another (included in IS1510 Export Sales). Export information can be a good substitute when a company does not disclose international sales statistics. Exports also include any intercompany sales between the home country and its international offices. However, exports do not include sales from one international office of a company to another. Such activity, defined as international sales, belongs in the geographic segmentation set with intercompany adjustments.

IS1520 Cost of Materials

Account IS1520 consists of all costs of material reported by a company as operating expenses, or, more precisely, the cost of all materials purchased from outside adjusted by changes in inventory. In service industries it also includes services provided by outside organizations. Materials used to construct fixed assets for internal uses should be excluded.

When the Cost Summary Method is used, the cost of materials will be clearly disclosed as a major expense by manufacturing industries. Even when the Functional Method is used by a company, a Statement of Cost of Sales or an additional footnote may disclose this item.

IS1530 Personnel Expenses

All personnel expenses reported as operating expenses, including the wages and salaries of manufacturing, marketing, general, and administrative personnel, are shown in IS1530 Personnel Expenses. This account includes all employment-related expenses, such as social security taxes and contributions to severance and pension plans. The proportions of wages to related benefits in employment contracts vary among countries because of their particular customs.

Personnel expenses that have been capitalized in the inventory and fixed assets under construction should theoretically be excluded from account IS1530. Because this is not possible in practice (the needed numbers are not provided anywhere), IS1520 Cost of Materials must be reduced instead, which will slightly distort the cost of materials figures. Personnel expenses are clearly reported in the income statement under the Cost Summary Method and may sometimes be found in a Statement of Cost of Sales or in a footnote.

IS1540 Depreciation Expenses

Account IS1540 contains the depreciation expenses for tangible fixed assets employed in operating activities. In manufacturing, depreciation expenses are a major operating expense. IS1540 also includes the depletion of assets in the extraction industry. It does not include amortization of intangibles or goodwill, even though depreciation and amortization expenses are combined in the income statement in many countries. If the depreciation expenses are not separately reported by the income statement, a depreciation schedule for all tangible and intangible fixed assets should be available in related notes. The combined total of depreciation and amortization expenses will be reported in the cash flow statement.

Tangible fixed assets employed in operating activities are used over numerous accounting periods, and investments in fixed assets should be allocated each year based on the usage of such assets during their useful lifetime. Depreciation expenses are computed by the Straight-Line Method or the Accelerated Method to reflect the diminution of an asset's value each year. However, which depreciation method is applied is strongly influenced by national economic and fiscal policy. Many countries require a consistently applied accounting method for financial reporting and tax purposes. The Accelerated Method, in particular, is computed at different rates of acceleration in different countries. The specific method employed by each company should be noted for future analysis.

The level of depreciation expenses as compared with the size of operating facilities varies by industry and from country to country as a result of local tax regulations and/or reporting practices. However, accelerated depreciation, allowed by special regulations, does not mean that the diminution of a fixed asset's value is accelerated. For analysis, the expense may be reduced to a common denominator based on industry statistics. Depreciation of financial fixed assets or nonoperating fixed assets should not be included here.

IS1550 Research and Development Expenditure

Research and development (R & D) expenditures are considered operating expenses. They are included in the Cost of Goods Sold if they are directly related to manufacturing activities; otherwise such expenditures are treated as general expenses. Most companies treat as expense all costs of research and development in the year they occur. In a few cases, some of these costs are capitalized and amortized. Even if a portion is capitalized, the total R & D expenditure should be reported in account IS1550, because it will be used to analyze potential for future growth.

Research and development expenditure has different names in different industries. For example, R & D expenditure in the extraction business is called *exploration expense* or *dry hole expense*. Its substance, however, is not different from R & D expenditure in other manufacturing industries. R & D expenditures play a significant role in the analysis of technology industries, such as electronics and pharmaceuticals. The fate of such industries is often decided by developments in technology.

IS1550 should exclude expenditures for R & D activities on behalf of third parties that are performed for fees. Income from such projects should be accounted for as sales, and related expenses should be treated as the cost of sales.

IS1610 Capitalized Interest Expenses

IS1110 Interest Expenses reflects interest payments expended in a given year. If certain operations can absorb a part of the interest expense as an inventory cost or as fixed assets, the capitalized portion belongs to account IS1610. Interest expenses are important in the analysis of a company's cash needs, and Capitalized Interest Expenses should be included in such a study.

IS1620 Sales from Discontinued Operations

The results from discontinued operations are classified as extraordinary items in account IS1210 and have two components: operating results from discontinued sectors, and gains (losses) from the disposal of discontinued facilities. Account IS1620 will capture the sales during the year that operations were discontinued and can be used in comparing the operating performance, adjusted for the length of time, with the previous year's results.

IS1630 Loss (Gain) from Discontinued Operations

IS1210 Loss (Gain) from Extraordinary Activities Before Tax Effects includes the financial impact of discontinued operations. IS1630 is used to isolate the results from discontinued operations from other extraordinary items. The amount should include a gross amount before tax effects as a supplementary account of IS1210; otherwise it must be footnoted.

IS1700 Number of Days for the Period

The number of days in an accounting period should be noted in account IS1700. Some companies change their accounting periods, making it impossible to compare operations in one period with operations in another. The information given here will be used to establish a regular period equivalent.

4.2 BANKING FORMAT

The main function of banks is to lend to and borrow from individuals and other organizations. However, the banking industry has diversified into additional activities, so there is no clear definition of banking anymore. Some banks appear on street corners as cash machines. Some are regional or national in scope, and others are purely local. Money may be borrowed from insurance companies or other financing companies, but these are not banks. The banks referred to in this book are commercial banks, defined as *institutions that take deposits from the public.* All others must be classified as industries other than banking. For example, investment banks, mortgage banks (which issue bonds as a financing source), and merchant banks should be classified as "other financial services."

There are also organizations called "banks" that in reality are not banks, such as export-import banks. These are financed through government-backed bonds and provide loans to medium-sized or small companies to encourage certain sectors in a given country. They are not financed by capital from deposits made by the public. Nor should building societies in the United Kingdom be considered banks. Central banks, which control a nation's money supply and issue currency notes, cannot be classified as commercial banks unless they take deposits from the public. A few commercial banks also exercise central banking functions, such as the Hong Kong Shanghai Bank in Hong Kong (currently based in the United Kingdom after merging with Marine Midland), whose stocks are publicly traded.

In many countries, such as the United States, Japan, and Korea, banks are strictly regulated in terms of the services they may provide and whether they may operate nationally or only regionally. Their functions are limited to commercial banking. Banks in Europe, however, have few limitations. They may provide a wide range of services including those of travel agent, security brokerage, or long-term lending to corporations.

Banks are financed mainly by capital from deposits made by the public, and they provide loans for individual and commercial use. Deposits are usually short-term, and the loans they provide tend to be short-term as well. Many commercial banks also provide mortgages, for individual homes and commercial buildings, which mature in 15 or 30 years. In practice, the duration of such mortgage loans averages between 5 and 7 years, either because home owners change their houses or because the loans are sold to mortgage servicing companies, which belong to the "other financial services" category. These long-term loans are backed by government funds. The banks originate the loans but rely on related commissions and fees for their revenue rather than interest income from the loans. The average duration of commercial bank loans varies, depending on the bank's role in a country.

Banks vary in type from money centers, savings and loans, and credit unions, to institutions with regional, national, and international operations. Post offices also participate in banking in many countries.

INCOME STATEMENT IN A BANKING FORMAT

Sections	Data Items	
Operating Section	IS1011	Interest Income
	IS1012	Trading Account Profit (Loss) and Foreign Exchange Revenue
	IS1014	Investment Income
	IS1015	Commissions and Fees Earned
	IS1019	Other Operating Revenue
	IS1020	**Total Revenue**
	IS1022	Interest Expenses
	IS1023	Provision for Loan Losses
	IS1024	Commissions and Fees Paid
	IS1039	Direct Expenses for Other Operating Activities
	IS1040	**Total Direct Expenses**
	IS1050	General and Administrative Expenses
	IS1099	**Operating Income**
Nonoperating Section	IS1130	Loss (Gain) from Associated Companies
	IS1140	Other Nonoperating Loss (Gain)
	IS1150	Income Tax Expenses (Credits)
	IS1160	Reserve Charges (Credits)
	IS1199	**Income Before Extraordinary Items**
Extraordinary Items	IS1210	Loss (Gain) from Extraordinary Activities Before Tax Effects
	IS1220	Tax Effects on Extraordinary Items
	IS1230	Minority Interests
	IS1299	**Net Income**
Reference Items for EPS	IS1310	Cash Dividends to Preferred Stocks
	IS1320	Cash Dividends to Common Stocks
	IS1323	Appropriation to Capital Reserves
	IS1324	Appropriation to Revenue Reserves
	IS1325	Distributions to Directors and Officers
	IS1330	Dividend per Share (DPS)
	IS1340	EPS before Extraordinary Items
	IS1350	Primary Earnings per Share
	IS1360	Weighted Average Number of Shares for Primary EPS
	IS1370	Fully Diluted EPS
	IS1380	Number of Shares for Fully Diluted EPS
	IS1390	Special EPS
Other Reference Items	IS1530	Personnel Expenses
	IS1620	Revenue from Discontinued Operations
	IS1630	Loss (Gain) from Discontinued Operations

(continued)

(continued)	IS1640 Actual Loan Loss IS1650 Interest Income from Loans IS1660 Interest Expenses to Deposits IS1670 Unrealized Gain (Loss) on Investments IS1700 Number of Days for the Period

4.2.1 Operating Section

IS1020 Total Revenue

Total Revenue is the sum of all revenue from operating activities, including IS1011 Interest Income, IS1012 Trading Account Profit (Loss) and Foreign Exchange Revenue, IS1014 Investment Income, IS1015 Commissions and Fees Earned, and IS1019 Other Operating Revenue. Accounts IS1012 and IS1014 are reduced by related expenses and losses. The net revenue/loss from activities other than financial services belongs in IS1019 Other Operating Revenue, even though some subsidiaries in countries with "universal" banking show this as results from operations.

Attempting to compare this account and the total revenue reported by companies may be useless, because of inconsistency in netting expenses or losses, but IS1020 Total Revenue is created as an equivalent to sales in the Industrial Format. Although no one would try to equate such unrelated businesses as banks and industrial companies, investors should be able to compare the overall profitability of any two companies.

IS1011 Interest Income. As long as lending is the main operating activity in a commercial bank, interest on loans will be its major source of income. Interest income in banking is fundamentally different from interest income in industrial companies. In banking, interest is operating income; in industrial organizations, it is nonoperating income.

When the funds banks have available to lend exceed the demand for loans, the excess should be used in alternate ways. One alternative is for banks to act as wholesalers by lending to other banks. Interbank loans are different from loans to customers in that they are short-term loans. Because the risk involved in interbank loans is minimal and both parties are fully aware of the costs, interest income from interbank loans is lower than interest received from the loans to the public. Interest income from loans to all customers should be placed in IS1650 Interest Income from Loans.

Excess funds may also be used to purchase securities, although many governments, to protect bank depositors, restrict banks from investing in risky equity securities. In principle, income from securities should be recorded in IS1014 Investment Income, but in practice income from fixed income securities (i.e., bonds) is recorded as interest income.

In summary, IS1011 Interest Income in banking may include interest from loans to customers and to other banks, as well as from investments in fixed income securities. If possible, interest income from loans should be included in a separate reference item, IS1650 Interest Income from Loans, to give a better picture of the profitability of each asset category.

If a bank is a capital lessor, the loans should be classified as loans and the interest income they generate should be placed in account IS1011. However, if a bank is an operating lessor, the rental income belongs in IS1019 Other Operating Revenue. Assets used for operating leases should be classified as fixed assets, and their depreciation expenses should be treated as general expenses.

IS1012 Trading Account Profit (Loss) and Foreign Exchange Revenue. Any gain or loss from the sale of marketable equity/debt securities should be included in account IS1012. When marketable securities are valued at Mark-to-Market, the unrealized gain/loss from trading assets should be included here. IS1012 also includes gain/loss from sale of long-term investments. Figuratively speaking, IS1014 Investment Income is the collection of fruit from a tree, and IS1012 Trading Account Profit (Loss) is gain (loss) from the sale of the tree. Investment assets are readily marketable and likely to be valued at market price, and the unrealized gain/loss should be recognized. An unrealized loss is generally recognized in any industry, but an unrealized gain is not recognized as a gain, as a function of conservatism. However, banks, for which dealing in securities is regarded as an operating activity, are permitted in many countries to recognize an unrealized gain.

Consistency in the organization of the balance sheet is important in creating a valuable database for use in analysis. The classification of short-term investments and long-term investments on the balance sheet should be consistent with the income from those assets in the income statement. The classification of an investment as either short- or long-term should be based on the intent of the company. The ongoing income generated by a short-term investment is not likely to be significant. This interest or dividend income may be included with investment income from long-term investments.

Investment in foreign exchange should be classified as a short-term investment, and income from trading in foreign exchange should be included in IS1012. Fees charged for foreign exchange dealing on behalf of customers should be classified as IS1015 Commissions and Fees Earned. Any gain or loss from selling loan investments also should be entered in account IS1012.

The current trend is to value investment assets (especially marketable securities) at the Mark-to-Market instead of at the Lower of Cost or Market amount. Unrealized gains or losses from changes in the market value of investments should be included in IS1012, along with a note reporting that the company follows such practices. Unrealized investment income should be referred to IS1670 Unrealized Gain (Loss) on Investments.

IS1014 Investment Income. Account IS1014 should collect income from all investment assets except income from loan investments, which is treated as IS1011 Interest Income. IS1014 Investment Income should include dividend income from equity securities, interest income from debt securities, and investment income from trading securities.

Equity earnings from investments in associated or related but unconsolidated companies should be excluded from this account and included in IS1130 Loss (Gain) from Associate Companies. These earnings are influenced by the controlling company and should not be mixed with other investment income.

IS1015 Commissions and Fees Earned. Income from customer services, such as commissions and fees, belong to account IS1015. Bank services vary by country because of the various regulations. So-called universal banking in Europe allows a broad range of services, but banks elsewhere are strictly limited. The most common banking services include checking accounts, loan transactions, money transfers, and guarantee services. These services require that banks hold assets on behalf of third parties, which are called customers' acceptance and liabilities (contra items). Commissions and fees paid should not be offset by commissions and fees earned unless the fees paid are directly related to fees earned. The fees paid should be classified in account IS1024. Many banks operate trusts, either their own or through controlled subsidiaries. Trust income should also be included in IS1015 Commissions and Fees Earned.

IS1019 Other Operating Revenue. Account IS1019 includes all other operating income (loss). Income (loss) qualifies as other operating revenue if it is generated by activities, sometimes performed by subsidiaries, that are consistently pursued by the bank. Loans dedicated to capital leases should be recorded as loans, but income from operating leases is classified as rental income and should be included in this account.

IS1040 Total Direct Expenses

Account IS1040 is the sum of IS1022 Interest Expenses, IS1023 Provision for Loan Losses, IS1024 Commissions and Fees Paid, and IS1039 Direct Expenses for Other Operating Activities. The term *Total Direct Expenses* is not used in any published financial statement, but is an account equivalent to the Cost of Sales or Cost of Goods Sold used by industrial companies. A consistent treatment will be useful in global analysis and in comparison of many industries.

IS1022 Interest Expenses. Interest paid to depositors and lenders is included in account IS1022. A bank finances its main activities by borrowing money from depositors and lending money to borrowers. Interest expenses paid to depositors, which constitute a bank's main expenses, should, in addition to being recorded here, be referred to IS1660 Interest Expenses to Deposits. Loans received from other banks are likely to be short-term. Banks operate under the principles of asset management, which match the duration of financing resources to loans. However, banks sometimes issue long-term bonds to the public, especially those offering long-term loans such as mortgages.

It is helpful to collect separate figures for interest expenses incurred for deposits and those incurred for long-term bonds. In practice, however, these figures are not separated consistently.

IS1023 Provision for Loan Losses. Loan losses should be treated in the same way as in setting up a provision for doubtful accounts, as follows:

At fiscal period end,
    (debit) Provision for loan losses   xxxx
        (credit) Loan loss reserves   xxxx

When certain loans are not collectible,
    (debit) Loan loss reserves   xxxx
        (credit) Loans   xxxx

Reserves for outstanding loans should be maintained at a certain level, based on experience, to cover all uncertainties. Banks play a fundamental economic role in society, and the level of reserves they must maintain is often established by law. Banks in the United States, for example, were required in 1989 to make material provisions for loan losses in Latin America. Such provisions should be classified as IS1210 Loss (Gain) from Extraordinary Activities, rather than as normal provisions for loan losses (IS1023) because they are significant but irregular, one-time occurrences arising from accumulated stress in the banking business.

In many countries, provisions for loan losses are set at levels significantly below actual experience. This is because the minimum provisions required under tax regulations, although wholly unrealistic, take precedence over actual experience. Banks either establish the minimum loan loss reserves required by tax regulations or pay the losses as they occur. This is one of the reasons that it is necessary to keep track of the accounting method used by a company. The actual loan loss for the year should be collected in IS1640 Actual Loan Loss.

IS1024 Commissions and Fees Paid. As previously explained, IS1024 Commissions and Fees Paid by banks for services received and IS1015 Commissions and Fees Earned should be recorded separately unless the fees paid are directly related to the fees earned. In most instances, services related to commissions and fees earned and those related to commissions and fees paid have nothing in common.

IS1039 Direct Expenses for Other Operating Activities. Account IS1039 includes all direct expenses related to IS1019 Other Operating Revenue.

IS1050 General and Administrative Expenses

Account IS1050 includes all operating expenses, such as depreciation expenses for building and equipment, personnel expenses, supplies, and any other general indirect operating expenses, except those specially itemized in IS1022 Interest Expenses, IS1023 Provision for Loan Losses, IS1024 Commissions and Fees Paid, and IS1039 Direct Expenses for Other Operating Activities.

IS1099 Operating Income

The sum of IS1040 Total Direct Expenses and IS1050 General and Administrative Expenses is subtracted from IS1020 Total Revenue. The result, which is assigned to account IS1099, is comparable to the operating income (loss) of any other business.

4.2.2 Nonoperating Section

Most items in the Nonoperating Section are defined in the Banking Format as in the Industrial Format. Nonoperating activities are those unconnected to a bank's main activities.

IS1130 Loss (Gain) from Associated Companies

IS1140 Other Nonoperating Loss (Gain)

Refer to the explanations in the Industrial Format. Note that in the banking business, however, certain income, such as investment or interest income, should be treated as operating income and should not be entered in account IS1040.

IS1150 Income Tax Expenses (Credits)

IS1160 Reserve Charges (Credits)

Refer to the explanations in the Industrial Format. Note, however, that the banking business is regulated and that reserve charges, although different from those in industrial businesses, still play a significant role in operating results.

IS1199 Income Before Extraordinary Items

4.2.3 Extraordinary Items

Where no comment is provided for a specific account, please refer to the Industrial Format section.

IS1210 Loss (Gain) from Extraordinary Activities Before Tax Effects

For a discussion of account IS1210, refer to the explanations in the Industrial Format. Be cautious about which items constitute extraordinary activities, because many activities relate to a bank's main operating activity.

IS1220 Tax Effects on Extraordinary Items

IS1230 Minority Interests

IS1299 Net Income

4.2.4 Reference Items for EPS

Refer to the Industrial Format for explanations of the following accounts.

IS1310 Cash Dividends to Preferred Stocks

IS1320 Cash Dividends to Common Stocks

IS1323 Appropriation to Capital Reserves

IS1324 Appropriation to Revenue Reserves

IS1325 Distributions to Directors and Officers

IS1330 Dividend per Share (DPS)

IS1340 EPS before Extraordinary Items

IS1350 Primary Earnings per Share

IS1360 Weighted Average Number of Shares for Primary EPS

IS1370 Fully Diluted EPS

IS1380 Number of Shares for Fully Diluted EPS

IS1390 Special EPS

4.2.5 Other Reference Items

Where no comment is provided for a specific account, please refer to the Industrial Format section.

IS1530 Personnel Expenses

IS1620 Revenue from Discontinued Operations

Refer to the explanations in the Industrial Format. Note that the banking business is regulated. The criteria for discontinued operations, such as the closing of a line of business, should be modified to include, for example, closing branch offices in a certain region.

IS1630 Loss (Gain) from Discontinued Operations

Refer to the explanations in the Industrial Format. Consider the comments regarding account IS1620 Revenue from Discontinued Operations for this account in the Banking Format.

IS1640 Actual Loan Loss

As discussed under IS1023 Provision for Loan Losses, provisions made in the normal course of business are affected by local tax regulations and political pressures. However, the actual loan loss, disclosed in account IS1640, is a true number and reflects the actual loan risk. Losses may fluctuate significantly from year to year, depending on changes in the economy.

IS1650 Interest Income from Loans

IS1011 Interest Income includes interest from fixed income bonds as well as loan investments. It would be useful in studying the profitability of loans to separate the interest income from loans and include it in account IS1650.

IS1660 Interest Expenses to Deposits

IS1022 Interest Expenses includes interest paid for long-term borrowing and for deposits from customers. Account IS1660 can isolate the interest paid for deposits only, which is useful in deposit analysis.

IS1670 Unrealized Gain (Loss) on Investments

Unrealized Gain (Loss) on Investments (account IS1670) is a reference item. IS1012 Trading Account Profit (Loss) and Foreign Exchange Revenue includes the realized gain (loss) from the disposition of investments and unrealized gain (loss) from the valuation of the investments. Although it is increasingly common in some accounting circles to regard them similarly, unrealized gains (losses) on investments cannot be compared with realized gain (loss) in terms of the quality of earnings.

IS1700 Number of Days for the Period

4.3 INSURANCE FORMAT

The insurance business charges premiums based on the uncertainties attendant to assets and to human life. The uncertainty regarding assets (property and casualty insurance) and human life (life insurance) is called *risk*. However, the two types of risk are entirely different, and income and expense recognition processes are different as well. Both types of insurance are often provided by the same organization. When the two types of business are intermingled, analysis of financial statements is difficult.

Property and casualty insurance is usually considered short-term, dealing mainly with risks involving property (e.g., automobiles and homes). But it also includes title insurance, liability insurance for professional services, and/or marine and aviation insurance, which are long-term in nature. A more precise term for these various types of insurance is *non-life insurance*.

On the other hand, *life insurance* deals with human life and is usually regulated by separate laws. Such insurance is very long-term in nature and is sometimes known as "long-term insurance." Health insurance is similar to short-term insurance, but in practice is provided by life insurance companies. Any analysis of the life insurance business should therefore include health insurance when a company provides it. Pension fund management is another popular line of life insurance companies, because they have considerable expertise in managing assets of long-term duration. There are a few side businesses in the insurance industry, including the reimbursement of college education expenses, which is similar to pension fund management in that it involves long-term asset management.

In Europe, both life and non-life insurance are often provided by a single organization, as in Universal Banking. However, in the United States, Japan, and Korea, the two types of insurance are clearly separated. Sometimes, in the latter countries, a single organization offers both types of insurance through different subsidiaries, but each business is regulated by different laws and reports on each segment separately.

Many life insurance companies (and some property and casualty insurance companies as well) are operated as mutual cooperative companies in which the interests of policyholders are paramount. They have no shareholders' equity. It would be a great mistake to ignore these mutual life insurance companies in global analysis, because they compete with others that are owned by shareholders. Data compilation should consider such factors when undertaking comparative analysis in this industry.

Recognition of Income and Expenses

Income and expenses in property and casualty insurance are recognized by the passage of time. Prepaid insurance premiums should be recorded as short-term liabilities, and the premature cancellation of such contracts returns the premium to policyholders.

Income from life insurance is recognized when the contract takes effect, rather than by the passage of time, and related expenses are recognized by mathematical actuarial tables. The actuarial tables have no impact on how long the policy will be valid. This means that premiums received for a policy are recognized as revenue when a contract is signed and there is no unearned premium to be accounted for as a liability.

Reinsurance Business

Insurance companies share possible risks to an individual in a pool with other individuals. Moreover, an insurance company may be unable to bear the entire risk involved in any one incident, so risks are distributed among many other insurance companies. This practice, called *reinsurance*, is common in marine, aviation, and other major categories of risk. Reinsurance is more often found in non-life insurance than in life insurance.

Reporting in the reinsurance business varies country by country. Reinsurance premiums received from other companies are treated as normal premium income, and no special accounting procedure is required.

Reinsurance premiums paid to other insurers are treated in one of two ways. If a part of the premium has been paid to other insurers and the designated event occurs, a part of the claim expenses are recovered from the reinsurers. One accounting method reduces the original premium income by the portion reinsured, and claims and loss expenses are likewise reduced by the amount recovered from the reinsurer. The other method is to reduce gross premium income by the net reinsurance results and make no adjustment of claims and loss expenses. Both methods will result in the same amount of operating income, but the implication is different.

The operating margin, based on the first, line-by-line, reduction method, includes the performance of the reinsured premium, which covered the risks not taken by the original insurer. This accounting method is employed by Japanese companies. The second method adjusts the gross premium by the net results of reinsurance activities to derive a net premium income. Conceptually, the analysis of an insurance company's performance should focus on the extent of the risks the company took. On the other hand, ceding reinsurance in fact means transferring risk rather than seeking profit, because reinsurers are also conscious of the risks involved.

The performance of an insurance company should be measured by the extent of risk it takes. Therefore, the first accounting method is adopted by this book.

INCOME STATEMENT IN AN INSURANCE FORMAT

Sections	Data Items			
Operating Section	IS1002	Gross Premium from Life Insurance	IS1005	Gross Premium from Non-Life Insurance
	IS1003	Adjustments for Life Insurance	IS1006	Adjustments for Non-Life Insurance
	IS1004	Net Premium from Life Insurance	IS1007	Net Premium from Non-Life Insurance
	IS1012	Trading Accounts Profit (Loss)		
	IS1013	Income from Real Estate Investments		
	IS1014	Investment Income		
	IS1019	Other Operating Revenue		
	IS1020	**Total Revenue**		
	IS1031	Insurance Claims and Losses for Life Insurance	IS1035	Insurance Claims and Losses for Non-Life Insurance
	IS1032	LT Insurance Charges (Life)		*(continued)*

(continued)	IS1033	Dividends to Policyholders	IS1036 Underwriting and Policy Acquisition Costs for Non-Life Insurance
	IS1034	Underwriting and Policy Acquisition Costs for Life Insurance	

	IS1039	Direct Expenses for Other Operating Activities
	IS1040	**Total Direct Expenses**
	IS1050	General and Administrative Expenses
	IS1099	**Operating Income**

Nonoperating Section	IS1110	Interest Expenses
	IS1130	Loss (Gain) from Associated Companies
	IS1140	Other Nonoperating Loss (Gain)
	IS1150	Income Tax Expenses (Credits)
	IS1160	Reserve Charges (Credits)
	IS1199	**Income Before Extraordinary Items**

Extraordinary Items	IS1210	Loss (Gain) from Extraordinary Activities Before Tax Effects
	IS1220	Tax Effects on Extraordinary Items
	IS1230	Minority Interests
	IS1240	Policyholders' Surplus
	IS1299	**Net Income or Profit (Loss)**

Reference Items for EPS	IS1310	Cash Dividends to Preferred Stocks
	IS1320	Cash Dividends to Common Stocks
	IS1323	Appropriation to Capital Reserves
	IS1324	Appropriation to Revenue Reserves
	IS1325	Distributions to Directors and Officers
	IS1330	Dividend per Share (DPS)
	IS1340	EPS before Extraordinary Items
	IS1350	Primary Earnings per Share
	IS1360	Weighted Average Number of Shares for Primary EPS
	IS1370	Fully Diluted EPS
	IS1380	Number of Shares for Fully Diluted EPS
	IS1390	Special EPS

Other Reference Items	IS1530	Personnel Expenses
	IS1560	Amortization of Deferred Policy Acquisition Costs—Life Insurance
	IS1561	Amortization of Deferred Policy Acquisition Costs—Non-Life Insurance
	IS1620	Revenue from Discontinued Operations
	IS1630	Loss (Gain) from Discontinued Operations
	IS1670	Unrealized Gain (Loss) on Investments
	IS1700	Number of Days for the Period

4.3.1 Operating Section

IS1020 Total Revenue

The revenue-earning process in the insurance business consists of charging premiums based on the levels of risk taken by a company and investing the income in securities. The premium and investment income is used to pay commissions to agents and to settle claims and losses. The premiums alone are not expected to cover the full amount of possible losses, because reasonable returns are anticipated from investments.

As a result, revenue has two major components: premium income from customers and investment income. The premium income from customers is earned as time passes, and the balance of the premium is treated as prepaid income and should be used to adjust the gross premium to obtain a net premium. Some of the premium income is transferred to reinsurers, who share the risks involved, and the premium ceded to reinsurance companies should also be used to adjust gross premiums before establishing the net premium earned.

Even though life insurance and non-life insurance are significantly different, both are often provided by the same company. For purposes of analysis, they must be separated in most major accounts in the operating section. However, premiums from both types of insurance are invested in securities, and here no distinction is made between the two. If a company sells only one form of insurance, obviously the information segment reserved for the other form of insurance will be blank in the database.

Life insurance companies often provide other, similar, services, such as pension fund management, because their time spans are the same and both involve expertise in investing in fixed income securities, a typical requirement for pension fund management. For convenience in analysis, investment income is divided into three sections, IS1012 Trading Account Profit (Loss), IS1013 Income from Real Estate Investments, and IS1014 Investment Income.

IS1002 Gross Premium from Life Insurance. Account IS1002 includes gross premiums for life insurance, which is a long-term insurance, and for health insurance. From an analyst's point of view, these are two very different products. However, both deal with human life and are often provided by a single organization. A further breakdown is analyzed in the product segmentation section in Chapter 7.

IS1003 Adjustments for Life Insurance. Any part of a premium not earned should be classified as IS1003 Adjustments for Life Insurance. Because income and expenses are recognized when a contract takes effect, an adjustment of the premium is not applicable. Reinsurance activities are not common in life insurance, but they are in health insurance.

IS1004 Net Premium from Life Insurance. The net premium from life insurance is included in account IS1004. This account reflects the result of deducting IS1003 Adjustments for Life Insurance from IS1002 Gross Premium from Life Insurance.

IS1005 Gross Premium from Non-Life Insurance. Account IS1005 includes gross premiums from fire, automobile, and other casualty and liability insurance. Marine and aviation insurance, both long-term in nature, are included here as well, because they are related to risks to property. Premiums from title insurance or professional liability insurance are also included.

IS1006 Adjustments for Non-Life Insurance. Adjustments of premiums are the unearned portion of gross premiums, because income is recognized by the passage of time in non-life insurance. Premiums returned or canceled, unearned premiums, and reinsurance ceded are recorded in account IS1006 Adjustments for Non-Life Insurance.

IS1007 Net Premium from Non-Life Insurance. The net premium from non-life insurance is included in account IS1007. This account reflects the result of deducting IS1006 Adjustments for Non-life Insurance from IS1005 Gross Premium from Non-Life Insurance.

IS1012 Trading Accounts Profit (Loss). Refer to the explanations in the Banking Format for account IS1012.

IS1013 Income from Real Estate Investments. Although income from real estate investments is generally included in investment income, it is separated here because it plays a significant part in insurance company investment. Account IS1013 includes rental income as well as gains (losses) from trading in real estate investments. Insurance companies favor real estate investments because they are long-term and match the duration of their liabilities.

IS1014 Investment Income. Dividend income from equity securities and interest income from fixed income securities, mortgage loans, and policy loans are included in IS1014 Investment Income. Each category of investments carries with it different returns and risks which eventually neutralize each other. The level of risk on investment can be measured by the distribution of investment assets on the balance sheet. Unrealized gains (losses) from investment assets, however, should not be assigned to this account but to IS1012 Trading Account Profit (Loss). Refer to IS1012 in the Banking Format for further discussion.

IS1019 Other Operating Revenue. In many countries, other operating activities are limited by regulations. Insurance companies in Europe have more flexibility, however, and the net results from their other operating activities should be included in account IS1019.

IS1040 Total Direct Expenses

Account IS1040 is the sum of all operating expenses from IS1031 through IS1039. Total direct expenses are segregated into two major lines of insurance business, life and non-life. Such segregation is not always clear on the face of consolidated income statements, and analysts should refer to the individual income statement for each line of business. Non-life businesses, especially, are segregated into further details, and aggregation of expenses from each line is required.

IS1031 Insurance Claims and Losses for Life Insurance. IS1031 includes claims and losses paid or due to life insurance policyholders. It also includes claims and loss adjustment costs and expenses related to the claims process. For claims that are not settled, estimated claims should be included here. Expenses in health insurance are dominated by such claims. Unpaid claims and loss expenses will be recorded as unclaimed claims and losses, or as BS2230 Reserve for Outstanding Claims and Losses on the balance sheet.

IS1032 Long-term Insurance Charges (Life). Long-term insurance charges reflect increases or decreases in long-term insurance reserves. As life insurance contracts become effective and the income is recognized, expected claims and losses should be recognized before they actually occur. These expenses are calculated using actuarial tables and are accumulated as BS2235 Reserve for Life Policy Benefits, or as mathematical reserves, on the balance sheet.

IS1033 Dividends to Policyholders. Account IS1033 includes dividends to policyholders, interest to policyholders, and refunds on long-term policies. Although called dividends, interest, or refunds, these are actually expenses in the form of payments to policyholders when certain designated events occur.

IS1034 Underwriting and Policy Acquisition Costs for Life Insurance. The cost of commissions paid to independent agents who sell insurance policies to customers, as well as policy underwriting adjustment costs, are included in account IS1034. The portion of policy acquisition costs paid but not expended are usually significant and are accumulated as prepaid expenses. However, prepaid expenses are directly related to policy acquisition activities and should be accumulated on the balance sheet as BS2030 Net Receivables rather than BS2190 Intangibles and Other Assets. The amortization of deferred policy acquisition costs should be included here and referred to IS1560 Amortization of Deferred Policy Acquisition Costs—Life Insurance.

IS1035 Insurance Claims and Losses for Non-Life Insurance. IS1035 includes claims and loss expenses paid or due to be paid to non-life insurance policyholders. It also includes claims and losses adjustment costs and expenses related to the claims process. When claims are not settled, their estimated expense should be included. The remote possibility that some claims simply are not filed should also be taken into consideration.

Unpaid claims and loss expenses should be recorded either as unclaimed claims and losses, or as BS2230 Reserves for Outstanding Claims and Losses on the balance sheet. Claims and loss expenses recovered from reinsurers should reduce total claims and loss expenses to isolate the expenses to the extent of risk the company takes.

Loss ratio (claims and losses ÷ net premium earned) is an important indicator in non-life insurance analysis. Account IS1035 should be able to produce an appropriate ratio.

IS1036 Underwriting and Policy Acquisition Costs for Non-Life Insurance. Commissions paid to agents who sell policy contracts to customers are included in account IS1036. The portion of policy acquisition costs paid but not expended is usually significant, and these costs are accumulated as a part of BS2030 Net Receivables rather than BS2190 Intangibles and Other Assets on the balance sheet. The amortization of the deferred policy acquisition costs should be included here and referred to IS1561 Amortization of Deferred Policy Acquisition Costs—Non-Life Insurance.

Underwriting expenses should be reduced by the amount recovered from reinsurers. The expense ratio (underwriting and policy acquisition cost ÷ gross premium) should be appropriately computed from this account.

IS1039 Direct Expenses for Other Operating Activities. Account IS1039 includes all direct expenses related to IS1019 Other Operating Revenue.

IS1050 General and Administrative Expenses

IS1050 includes all other operating expenses except itemized major expenses listed in IS1031 through IS1036. These are general personnel expenses, depreciation of fixed assets, and any other operating expenses.

IS1099 Operating Income

Operating Income, account IS1099, consists of IS1020 Total Revenue minus IS1040 Total Direct Expenses minus IS1050 General and Administrative Expenses. The structure of the database design also makes it possible to isolate the profitability of life and non-life insurance. The analysis of each type of business is discussed in Chapter 11, "Research Procedures."

4.3.2 Nonoperating Section

Where no comment is provided for a specific account, please refer to the Industrial Format section. Deciding which activities are operating activities and which are nonoperating activities should be determined by the activity's relationship to the company's core business.

IS1110 Interest Expenses

Refer to the explanations under IS1110 Interest Expenses in the Industrial Format. Note, however, that borrowing from banks is not common in the insurance industry, because insurance companies themselves are major money-lending institutions. Interest expenses should be limited to term loans for general uses. Certain loans specifically related to investment activities should be classified as investment expenses and deducted from the related investment income.

When an insurance company has mortgaged real estate investments, mortgage interest should be entered in account IS1110. The essential point to remember is that insurance companies do not raise capital from customers as do banks or other financial service companies.

IS1130 Loss (Gain) from Associated Companies

IS1140 Other Nonoperating Loss (Gain)

For account IS1140, refer to the explanations in the Industrial Format. However, note that an insurance company's gain or loss from trading investment assets and investment income are treated as operating income and should be excluded here.

IS1150 Income Tax Expenses (Credits)

IS1160 Reserve Charges (Credits)

For an explanation of reserve charges (credits), account IS1160, refer to the Industrial Format. Regulations regarding special reserves for the insurance industry, however, differ from those applied to industrial companies or banks.

IS1199 Income Before Extraordinary Items

Income before extraordinary items is included in IS1199. This account represents IS1099 Operating Income minus IS1110 through IS1160.

4.3.3 Extraordinary Items

Where no comment is provided for a specific account, please refer to the Industrial Format section.

IS1210 Loss (Gain) from Extraordinary Activities Before Tax Effects

Refer to the explanations under IS1210 in the Industrial Format. Be cautious in determining whether items constitute extraordinary activities, which depends on their relationship to the company's main operating activity. Do not include material gains (loss) on policies for customers resulting from natural disasters, which are at the very core of the insurance business.

IS1220 Tax Effects on Extraordinary Items

IS1230 Minority Interests

IS1240 Policyholders' Surplus

Account IS1240, Policyholders' Surplus, is unique to cooperative mutual insurance companies. IS1299 Net Income, defined as the net surplus to shareholders, is not applicable to mutual insurance companies. If a company has policyholders as well as shareholders, the surplus for policyholders should be treated as a minority interest. In computing the net income margin ratio, both surplus to shareholders and surplus for policyholders should be used.

Of what interest are mutual insurance companies that seek no investment? Regulations governing these insurance companies differ significantly from one country to another. Nevertheless, all companies, regardless of their legal form, compete in the market. For example, major life insurance companies have cooperative formats in the U.S. insurance market, but they compete with insurance companies owned by shareholders. (There are countries, the United Kingdom, for example, with separate regulations for life insurance and non-life insurance companies. Transferring earnings from life insurance, which is dominated by policyholders, as in mutual insurance companies, to non-life insurance, which is governed by shareholders, is restricted.) The segregation of earnings for policyholders and shareholders ultimately helps in analyzing earnings available for distribution to shareholders.

Some countries, including Japan, do not allow shareholding companies to enter the life insurance business. In the United States, the cooperative format is allowed in the non-life insurance business.

IS1299 Net Income or Profit (Loss)

For an explanation of account IS1299, refer to the Industrial Format. This account isolates earnings available for distributions to shareholders.

4.3.4 Reference Items for EPS

For a discussion of the following accounts, refer to the corresponding accounts in the Industrial Format.

IS1310 Cash Dividends to Preferred Stocks

IS1320 Cash Dividends to Common Stocks

IS1323 Appropriation to Capital Reserves

IS1324 Appropriation to Revenue Reserves

IS1325 Distribution to Directors and Officers

IS1330 Dividend per Share (DPS)

IS1340 EPS before Extraordinary Items

IS1350 Primary Earnings per Share

IS1360 Weighted Average Number of Shares for Primary EPS

IS1370 Fully Diluted EPS

IS1380 Number of Shares for Fully Diluted EPS

IS1390 Special EPS

4.3.5   Other Reference Items

Most of the accounts classified as Other Reference Items in the Insurance Format are discussed under corresponding account numbers in the Industrial Format. For further explanation, see those sections.

IS1530 Personnel Expenses

IS1560 Amortization of Deferred Policy Acquisition Costs—Life Insurance

Deferred policy acquisition costs are not accounted for separately in most countries. (The United States is an exception.) When this is the case, amortization should be included as a part of underwriting expenses for life insurance and referred to account IS1560.

IS1561 Amortization of Deferred Policy Acquisition Costs—Non-life Insurance

Account IS1561 reflects the amortization of deferred acquisition costs for non-life insurance. The amortization is included as part of underwriting expenses.

IS1620 Revenue from Discontinued Operations

IS1630 Loss (Gain) from Discontinued Operations

IS1670 Unrealized Gain (Loss) on Investments

IS1700 Number of Days for the Period

4.4   OTHER FINANCIAL SERVICES FORMAT

In addition to banking and insurance, there is a wide variety of other financial services. Several are briefly examined in the following paragraphs.

Banking and the insurance industry are major financial services, requiring separate sets of data. All other financial services, none of which is significant enough to be considered an industry segment on its own, should use the format presented in this section. Their diverse sources of revenue and related expenses should be analyzed, with each different line of business taken into consideration. Financial service industries are, by and large, distinguished from industrial companies by the fact that revenue and expenses in all financial services are extremely sensitive to changes in the rate of interest.

Personal/Commercial Lenders: Companies whose business is lending to customers resemble the banking business, but their financing sources are quite different. Banks finance capital for loans from customer deposits, whereas personal/commercial loan companies are financed by such instruments as long-term bonds. All non-depository credit institutions are classified here. These include a few giant diversified financial service companies, such as American Express and other credit card companies.

Leasing and Rental: Companies in this industry also finance their capital through commercial loans or long-term bonds. These companies have a unique characteristic in regard to their assets. Most revenue comes from interest-sensitive real estate leasing or equipment leasing. However, if the titles of objects leased belong to the clients, the business should be classified either as a bank or as a personal/commercial loan company.

It is often difficult to classify this industry as a financial service. If a company develops real estate by constructing shopping malls, for example, and then sells them, the company should be classified as a real estate developer, which is similar to a construction business. If the constructed real estate is leased to users, the leasing income is based on interest and the company is now a provider of financial services. In practice, most companies do both.

Holding Companies: Conglomerates often operate many different businesses through subsidiaries, which are fully consolidated in the financial statements. Holding companies are defined as companies with passive control over subsidiaries. The subsidiaries are not fully consolidated, and the financial statement of the holding company has dividend income from invested subsidiaries in the income statement and investment assets on the balance sheet. South African holding companies often chose this form of reporting. Such information cannot be compared with financial statements of other industrial companies.

Security Brokerage: Theoretically, security brokerages are not much different from other commercial services classified as industrial that provide brokerage services. However, they also provide loans for margin trading and temporary investments in securities in transition. Most of these services are in fact provided by commercial banks, except those in the United States, the United Kingdom, Japan, Korea, and Taiwan. Financial statements of U.S. and U.K. companies resemble the Banking Format, whereas those of businesses in Japan and Korea, which are more similar to other commercial service companies, fit the Industrial Format better.

Other Unique Industries: These include real estate investment trust and public fund management firms, so-called closed-end funds. Their services involve investing money from clients in securities or real estate. A further breakdown of data sets is necessary to reflect the unique characteristics of each industry, but none of them represents a significant industry group. Each of these industries is regulated differently in every country. The data set format is similar to that for banking in the income statement, but investment categories are expanded on the balance sheet. Each company's reports will show only data applicable to its specific industry; all other segments will be blank.

INCOME STATEMENT IN AN OTHER FINANCIAL SERVICES FORMAT		
Sections	**Data Items**	
Operating Section	IS1011	Interest Income
	IS1012	Trading Account Profit (Loss)
	IS1013	Income from Real Estate Investments
	IS1014	Investment Income
	IS1015	Commissions and Fees Earned
	IS1019	Other Operating Revenue
	IS1020	**Total Revenue**
	IS1022	Interest Expenses
	IS1023	Provision for Loan Losses
	IS1024	Commissions and Fees Paid
	IS1039	Direct Expenses for Other Operating Activities
	IS1040	**Total Direct Expenses**
	IS1050	General and Administrative Expenses
	IS1099	**Operating Income**
Nonoperating Section	IS1130	Loss (Gain) from Associated Companies
	IS1140	Other Nonoperating Loss (Gain)
	IS1150	Income Tax Expenses (Credits)
	IS1160	Reserve Charges (Credits)
	IS1199	**Income Before Extraordinary Items**
Extraordinary Items	IS1210	Loss (Gain) from Extraordinary Activities Before Tax Effects
	IS1220	Tax Effects on Extraordinary Items
	IS1230	Minority Interests
	IS1299	**Net Income or Profit (Loss)**
Reference Items for EPS	IS1310	Cash Dividends to Preferred Stocks
	IS1320	Cash Dividends to Common Stocks
	IS1323	Appropriation to Capital Reserves
	IS1324	Appropriation to Revenue Reserves
	IS1325	Distributions to Directors and Officers
	IS1330	Dividend per Share (DPS)
	IS1340	EPS before Extraordinary Items
	IS1350	Primary Earnings per Share

(continued)

(continued)	IS1360	Weighted Average Number of Shares for Primary EPS
	IS1370	Fully Diluted EPS
	IS1380	Number of Shares for Fully Diluted EPS
	IS1390	Special EPS
Other Reference Items	IS1530	Personnel Expenses
	IS1540	Depreciation Expenses
	IS1620	Revenue from Discontinued Operations
	IS1630	Loss (Gain) from Discontinued Operations
	IS1670	Unrealized Gain (Loss) on Investments
	IS1700	Number of Days for the Period

4.4.1 Operating Section

IS1020 Total Revenue

Account IS1020 combines all revenue from operating activities. Operating activities in this format are defined as financial service activities. IS1012 Trading Account Profit (Loss) and IS1014 Investment Income should be net of related losses or expenses. IS1013 Income from Real Estate Investments is isolated to reflect major income in the leasing and rental industries. Revenue from "other financial services" is added to IS1019 Other Operating Revenue, as in the banking industry. This line should also include income from real estate development in the leasing/rental industry, because the income is industrial in nature.

IS1011 Interest Income. For account IS1011, refer to the explanations in the Banking Format. As discussed, loan activities in the personal/commercial loan industry are similar to those in the banking industry, except that capital is financed by issuing bonds rather than by deposits from customers.

If a company is a capital lessor and the titles of the assets are transferred to the lessee, the lease loans should be classified as loans and interest income from the loans should be classified in IS1011 Interest Income. However, if a company is an operating lessor, the rental income should not be included here, but should instead be placed in IS1013 Income from Real Estate Investments. Assets under operating leases should be classified as real estate investments, and depreciation expenses for the assets should be classified as general expense and shown as a reference item in IS1540 Depreciation Expenses.

IS1012 Trading Account Profit (Loss). For a discussion of account IS1012, refer to the explanations in the Banking Format. As in the Banking Format, a new reference account, IS1670 Unrealized Gain (Loss) on Investments, is added to separate unrealized capital gains/losses.

IS1013 Income from Real Estate Investments. For a discussion of account IS1013, refer to the explanations in the Insurance Format.

IS1014 Investment Income. Account IS1014 should include dividend income from long- as well as short-term equity security investments. Unrealized gains (losses) from security investment, however, should be assigned to IS1012 Trading Account Profit (Loss) as in the Banking Format. Dividend income from subsidiaries in holding companies should also be assigned to IS1014.

IS1015 Commissions and Fees Earned. Refer to the explanations in the Banking Format. Commissions and fees earned (account IS1015) will be the major revenue in brokerage activities.

IS1019 Other Operating Revenue. Refer to the explanations in the Banking Format. Income from real estate development in leasing/rental industry should be included in account IS1019.

IS1040 Total Direct Expenses

Refer to the explanations in the Banking Format. Account IS040 also includes IS1039 Direct Expenses for Other Operating Activities.

IS1022 Interest Expenses. Account IS1022 includes interest paid to depositors and lenders. Most financial service companies included in this category have either minimal or no deposits from customers, and interest expenses should be mainly for borrowing.

IS1023 Provision for Loan Losses. Refer to the explanations in the Banking Format. Loan activities for these companies are similar to those in banking, although the types of customers and the securities backing the loans are different from those found in the banking industry.

IS1024 Commissions and Fees Paid. For a discussion of account IS1024, refer to the explanations in the Banking Format.

IS1039 Direct Expenses for Other Operating Activities. The Industrial Format classifies income from financial services as "other operating activities," whereas the Financial Service Format does the opposite. All direct expenses for industrial activities should be included in account IS1039.

IS1050 General and Administrative Expenses

Refer to the explanations in the Banking Format for account IS1050.

IS1099 Operating Income

Refer to the explanations in the Banking Format for account IS1099.

4.4.2 Nonoperating Section

For a discussion of the following accounts, refer to the explanations in the Industrial Format, unless otherwise indicated.

IS1130 Loss (Gain) from Associate Companies

IS1140 Other Nonoperating Loss (Gain)

Refer to the explanations in the Banking Format.

IS1150 Income Tax Expenses (Credits)

IS1160 Reserve Charges (Credits)

Refer to the explanations in the Banking Format.

IS1199 Income Before Extraordinary Items

4.4.3 Extraordinary Items

For a discussion of the following accounts, refer to the explanations in the Industrial Format.

IS1210 Loss (Gain) from Extraordinary Activities Before Tax Effects

IS1220 Tax Effects on Extraordinary Items

IS1230 Minority Interests

IS1299 Net Income or Profit (Loss)

4.4.4 Reference Items for EPS

For a discussion of the following accounts, refer to the explanations in the Industrial Format.

IS1310 Cash Dividends to Preferred Stocks

IS1320 Cash Dividends to Common Stocks

IS1323 Appropriation to Capital Reserves

IS1324 Appropriation to Revenue Reserves

IS1325 Distributions to Directors and Officers

IS1330 Dividend per Share (DPS)

IS1340 EPS before Extraordinary Items

IS1350 Primary Earnings per Share

IS1360 Weighted Average Number of Shares for Primary EPS

IS1370 Fully Diluted EPS

IS1380 Number of Shares for Fully Diluted EPS

IS1390 Special EPS

4.4.5 Other Reference Items

For a discussion of the following accounts, refer to the explanations in the Industrial Format.

IS1530 Personnel Expenses

IS1540 Depreciation Expenses

IS1620 Revenue from Discontinued Operations

IS1630 Loss (Gain) from Discontinued Operations

IS1670 Unrealized Gain (Loss) on Investments

IS1700 Number of Days for the Period

Balance Sheet
5

Whereas a company's income statement discloses its operating performance for a specific reporting period, the balance sheet reports the company's financial position. A more detailed discussion of the balance sheet can be found in Chapter 3. A company launches operations with certain assets and liabilities and adds or uses certain resources. At the end of a reporting period, a new financial position is reached.

In most countries the format of the balance sheet is related to the format of the income statement. The format of the balance sheet is determined by the accounting method used. Although not known by these names in accounting publications, such approaches essentially consist of the Functional Method (current and noncurrent segregation), the Cost Summary Method (segregation by types of assets and liabilities), or the Debit-Credit (Balancing) Format. Reporting formats differ from country to country and by industry within the various countries. For example, financial service companies generally use the Cost Summary Method, and industrial companies apply the Functional Method.

STRUCTURE OF THE BALANCE SHEET	
Assets	**Liabilities and Shareholders' Equity**
Current Assets: Assets likely converted to cash within one operating cycle	Current Liabilities: Obligations to be paid out within one operating cycle
	Noncurrent Liabilities: Obligations to be paid out over multiple operating cycles
Noncurrent Assets: Assets likely converted to cash in multiple operating cycles and assets for nonoperating use	Shareholders' Equity: Capital provided by shareholders and residual values that belong to shareholders

The data set used in this book adopts the Functional Method, consistent with its use in the income statement. Important items under the Cost Summary Method are noted as reference items. Financial services companies generally use the Cost Summary Method, as discussed in Chapter 4, in regard to the income statement, but important aspects of the Functional Format, in regard to financial services, are used in this book to provide some comparability to industrial companies.

The distinction between current and noncurrent is not always clear in the financial services area (banking, insurance, and other financial services), which, as noted, mainly uses the Cost Summary Method.

The arrangement of the balance sheet in order of liquidity (by either increasing or decreasing liquidity) varies by industry and by country. Whichever format is used, the individual data items can be rearranged to suit the priorities of the analyst.

Individual data items reported by a particular company may be very specific, reflecting the unique character of the industry. For example, fuel held in storage by the airline industry, or nuclear materials held by an electric utility, are specifically noted rather than simply labeled as inventory or as depletable fixed assets, respectively. These specifics, however, will appear under the functional headings, ''Inventory'' and ''Fixed Assets.''

Use of the Debit-Credit Format in preparing a balance sheet is limited today. Although the balance sheet will present ''Total Assets'' and ''Total Liabilities,'' the numbers may not actually represent the company's assets and liabilities. For example, accumulated depreciation on the credit side should be moved to the assets side as a negative number to reduce the value of related assets in order to arrive at meaningful total figures. Net assets figures—total assets minus current liabilities—which are emphasized in Commonwealth countries, can be reconstructed for the Functional Format by rearranging individual data items.

In addition to the numbers assigned to each data item it is important to note the valuation methods a company uses in arriving at the numbers it assigns to each asset and liability in order to interpret the balance sheet. For example, inventory can be evaluated by the First-In-First-Out (FIFO) Method, the Last-In-First-Out (LIFO) Method, or the Moving Average Method.

5.1 INDUSTRIAL FORMAT

The Industrial Format embraces all manufacturing and commercial service industries. The data set for the balance sheet is deliberately organized according to the Functional Method, despite the obvious difficulties this creates when converting company balance sheets produced using the Cost Summary Method in the income statement.

Because of the diversity of companies to be converted to the Industrial Format, the account titles actually used by individual companies cannot be carried over to this format. Each of a company's account titles must be analyzed and assigned to one of the accounts in the following table. Some companies use concise aggregated account titles, such as ''Inventory,'' whereas others use detailed accounts such as ''Raw Materials,'' ''Work-in-Process,'' and ''Finished Goods.'' If the accounts on a company's balance sheet are not specific enough for effective analysis, the information must be sought in the related footnotes. Excessively detailed accounts may be combined for the sake of conciseness.

An income statement using the Industrial Format takes into consideration the possibility of financial services subsidiaries and therefore includes "Other Operating Revenue" and "Direct Expenses for Other Operating Activities." Investments in such financial service companies will be difficult to convert if they are fully consolidated. When this is the case, each data item reported by a company should be analyzed in terms of the company's function and the subsidiaries' operating activities.

BALANCE SHEET IN AN INDUSTRIAL FORMAT		
Sections	**Data Items**	
Current Assets	BS2010	Cash and Cash Equivalents
	BS2020	Marketable Securities and Other Short-Term Investments
	BS2030	Accounts and Notes Receivable
	BS2040	Inventory
	BS2090	Other Current Assets
	BS2099	**Total Current Assets**
Noncurrent Assets	BS2110	Gross Tangible Fixed Assets
	BS2120	Accumulated Depreciation
	BS2130	Net Tangible Fixed Assets
	BS2170	Long-Term Investments and Long-Term Receivables
	BS2180	Investments in Associated Companies
	BS2190	Intangibles and Other Assets
	BS2199	**Total Assets**
Current Liabilities	BS2260	Accounts Payable
	BS2270	Short-Term Borrowing
	BS2280	Short-Term Portion of Long-Term Borrowing
	BS2290	Other Current Liabilities
	BS2299	**Total Current Liabilities**
Noncurrent Liabilities	BS2370	Long-Term Borrowing
	BS2390	Other Long-Term Liabilities
	BS2399	**Total Liabilities**

(continued)

(continued) *Shareholders'* Equity	BS2410	Preferred Equity
	BS2420	Minority Interest
	BS2450	Share Capital and Share Premiums
	BS2460	Retained Earnings
	BS2470	(Treasury Stocks)
	BS2499	**Total Shareholders' Equity**
Reference Items	BS2560	Nondepreciable Fixed Assets
	BS2565	Insurance Value of Tangible Fixed Assets
	BS2660	Pension Reserves
	BS2670	Deferred Tax Liabilities
	BS2680	Non-Equity Reserves
	BS2685	Unrealized Gain (Loss) from Investments
	BS2690	Goodwill Written Off
	BS2710	Number of Shares Outstanding
	BS2720	Par Value
	BS2730	Dividend Right Parity
	BS2740	Voting Right Parity
	BS2770	Number of Treasury Stocks
	BS2800	Number of Employees

5.1.1 Current Assets

BS2010 Cash and Cash Equivalents

Account BS2010 includes all cash on hand and short-term deposits immediately convertible to cash. Because it is difficult to distinguish between cash equivalents (including short-term investments of less than three months' duration) and short-term investments, the analyst should rely on the company's classification. Cash restricted to operating uses should be excluded and assigned either to BS2090 Other Current Assets or to BS2190 Intangibles and Other Assets, after comparing the terms with the operating cycle of the company.

BS2020 Marketable Securities and Other Short-Term Investments

When a company temporarily has excess cash, it should be invested without sacrificing liquidity. If the cash is invested in marketable securities, the securities should be entered in account BS2020. The actual duration of an investment in a specific security may be longer than one year, but whether it is classified as a short- or long-term investment depends on the intent of the company. If a company is willing to sell the securities within a reasonable period whenever cash is required or prices are favorable, the securities should be classified as marketable securities.

Often, a company temporarily buys its own stocks to fulfill stock options, rights, or warrants outstanding. These treasury stocks are classified as current assets in some countries, usually as short-term investments. There are strong arguments in favor of this practice in terms of liquidity.

In order to construct a consistent database, however, treasury stocks should not be classified as assets. Further discussion regarding the status of treasury stocks may be found under BS2470 Treasury Stocks.

The valuation method for marketable securities should be noted for further analysis. Marketable securities are usually valued at the lower of cost or market (LCM). The LCM rule is applied to securities on either an individual or an aggregate basis. Marketable securities and short-term investments in financial service industries are valued at Mark-to-Market. A footnote should identify the valuation method.

In a few countries, new regulations allow companies to adopt the market value of their investment securities (SFAS 115, *Accounting for Certain Investments in Debt and Equity Securities,* in the United States, for example). Realized and unrealized gains or losses on marketable securities should be accounted for as investment income in the income statement. Accumulated unrealized gains are treated as a deduction from shareholders' equity in such cases and should be referred to BS2685 Unrealized Gain (Loss) from Investments.

BS2030 Accounts and Notes Receivable

Account BS2030 includes all receivables directly related to the sale of primary products. These are also called "trade receivables." When a company sells its products, sales invoices may be collected in several ways. If invoices are collected in cash, the transaction is complete. Another possibility is to accept promissory notes due on a certain date. These notes can be discounted by a bank in return for cash or kept until due. In the latter case, they are accounted for as "Notes Receivable." A third method allows sales to longstanding trading partners to be settled on a revolving credit basis. Accounts receivable may also be collected by factoring through clearing houses. In a few countries, companies exchange so-called post-dated checks, which are equivalent to a promissory note, in lieu of payment.

The discounted or discountable portion of notes receivable is treated as an interest expense. When notes receivable are collected through factoring, the discounted portion is considered interest expense if the note was transferred "with recourse," and as a sales discount if it was transferred "without recourse." The balance of accounts receivable or notes receivable at the fiscal period end is recorded net of discount and any allowance for doubtful accounts.

Accounts receivable and notes receivable should be recorded as current assets, even though they may remain uncollected for more than a year, because *current* is defined as "one year or an operating cycle, whichever is longer." This standard is unclear in many countries because of confusion about the definition of *short-term* and *current*. Chapter 3 offers a more detailed discussion of this problem.

Receivables not related to trade activities should be divided into short- and long-term. The long-term portion should be classified as BS2170 Long-Term Investments and Long-Term Receivables.

BS2030 Accounts and Notes Receivable may include *trade receivables from related parties*. Receivables from consolidated subsidiaries should be eliminated in the consolidation process, but receivables from unconsolidated subsidiaries or associated companies under the Equity Method should not be eliminated. An investor may have influence on major policy decisions, but he or she most likely does not have the capability to influence day-to-day operations, such as setting the prices of products or changing credit terms. Therefore, trade receivables from associated companies are similar to other trade receivables and should be treated as regular accounts receivable or notes receivable. Of course, nontrade receivables should be included in BS2090 Other Current Assets, if current, and in BS2190 Intangibles and Other Assets, if noncurrent.

BS2040 Inventory

Items included in BS2040 Inventory vary by industry, but inventory generally includes assets held for sale in ordinary trading or production activities. These may be raw materials, work-in-progress, or finished goods. The cost of inventory includes not only the invoice price and production costs, but also any other direct expenses necessary to sell the product, such as freight and hauling charges, storage costs, and any other costs directly related to the individual item. Overhead expenses related to the manufacturing process should be allocated to individual inventory items on a reasonable basis. In many countries long-term inventory interest expenses may be capitalized.

The unit prices and quantities of inventory are recorded by either the Perpetual Inventory System or the Periodic Inventory System. The beginning inventory and inventory purchased during the period, minus the ending inventory, are allocated to the cost of goods sold in the income statement, and the ending inventory is recorded on the balance sheet. The identification of individual items sold may be possible in certain industries.

All inventory items should be recorded as assets when the company has reasonable control over them. Goods in transit and consigned goods should be recorded as assets as long as the company continues to bear the risk for them.

Inventory valuation depends on industry practice, which should reflect the physical movement of inventory in the industry. The most common methods of valuation are the First-In-First-Out (FIFO) and Last-In-First-Out (LIFO) methods, the Moving Average Method, and specific identification. The Retail Method, which values units of inventory based on their retail price rather than purchase or production cost, also may be adopted if an industry deals with a wide range of inventory or high inflation is common. No matter which method is used, the lower of cost or market value (LCM) is always applied to inventory valuation. Obsolescence or shrinkage of inventory items should also be considered. An inventory method is supposed to be consistent industrywide, but that is not the case in practice. The valuation method, which determines each company's cost flow, should be noted each period for further analysis.

If a company has a variety of inventory items, different valuation methods may be employed for different items. The valuation method used for major inventory items should be separately noted for analysis. When consolidated financial statements are prepared, a uniform inventory method is usually used for all companies, including subsidiaries. If not, the valuation method used by the parent company should be separately noted.

In some countries, such as Germany and Austria, *prepayments to suppliers* are treated as inventory. Whether a prepayment should be regarded as inventory or as other current assets is arguable. It depends on industry practice within the particular country. Advance payments for inventory items should not be recorded as inventory until the risks and rewards of inventory ownership are transferred to the company. Only if the payment was made for specific materials, or the purchasing contracts cannot be canceled without severe penalty, should the amount be classified as inventory. All other prepayments for inventory should be classified as BS2090 Other Current Assets.

When *long-term contracts* are involved, the recording of inventory differs slightly by country. Contract sales are recorded either by the Completed Contract Method or by the Percentage of Completion Method, which is gaining increasing acceptance.

In using the Percentage of Completion Method, sales are realized according to the percentage of the contract's completion and expenses are recorded based on actual expense incurred to date. Although the percentage of completion is often tied to expenses incurred, a note should be made indicating the estimated future expenses required to complete the contract. The buyer is billed for the completed portion. In practice, actual completion and the amount billed do not always match. The portion completed but not billed should be recorded at cost in inventory as construction in progress, and the portion not completed but billed is recorded by some companies as negative inventory on the asset side of the balance sheet. Other companies treat the negative inventory as a current liability or as an advance payment for sales. Excess billing is uncommon, and because a negative asset is illogical on the balance sheet, the reduction of other inventory is recommended. An additional point to note in analysis is that excess billing may include a margin added by the company.

BS2090 Other Current Assets

All current assets not itemized in the Current Assets section should be classified as Other Current Assets. These include nontrade receivables, accrued income, prepayments for future expenses, and prepayments to suppliers.

5.1.2 Noncurrent Assets

BS2110 Gross Tangible Fixed Assets

Noncurrent assets include all tangible fixed assets that are employed in more than one operating cycle or are to be employed for operations, such as land, buildings, plant, machinery, equipment, vehicles, and furniture, as well as construction in progress for a company's own uses. Tangible fixed assets that are leased from others should be included here. The depreciation expenses of the leased property should be included in the regular depreciation account. Of course, a leased property represents an asset under operating lease for the lessor. The titles of properties under capital lease contracts should be transferred to the lessee, and the lessor should not record the property but record leasing loan investments. If a company's gross fixed assets do not appear on the balance sheet, a separate fixed asset schedule should be available in a footnote indicating additions and reductions during the period.

Depreciation expenses are usually computed at the highest rates allowed by regulatory bodies rather than by an asset's actual usage. This arbitrary computation must be adjusted using industry statistics to allow comparisons of the competitiveness of companies in different countries. To this end, BS2560 Nondepreciable Fixed Assets must be identified in order to isolate depreciable fixed assets. This determination is extremely important when one considers, for example, that German companies assign a useful life of 5 to 7 years to depreciate a building that may be used for 50 years. Some Swiss companies have been known to set the value of all assets at one franc. The adjustment process, of course, cannot simply rely on publicly available information.

Government subsidies to purchase specific fixed assets can be controversial in analysis. In terms of the Historical Cost Principle, the cost of fixed assets is determined by the amount paid and government subsidies reduce the purchase price. The earning capability of assets, however, is not diminished by government subsidies. In analysis, the subsidies should not diminish the gross fixed assets or depreciation expenses but should be directly added to retained earnings.

If a country's regulations permit *revaluation of fixed assets,* the basis for depreciation—that is, gross fixed assets—will be adjusted and a new basis for depreciation is established. Revaluation in most countries results in adjustments to shareholders' equity. Note that in Europe the term *fixed assets* represents tangible fixed assets, intangible fixed assets, and financial fixed assets.

BS2120 Accumulated Depreciation

Whichever method is used for depreciation, the accumulated depreciation expended from employment of the assets should be included here in account BS2120. Some countries allow companies to claim *excess depreciation*. If excess depreciation expenses are taxed, there is no additional consideration necessary. However, if the excess depreciation is not taxed, a reserve is temporarily established, which should be classified as a non-equity reserve. The reserves are reversed over the years and, as a result, gradually diminish.

BS2130 Net Tangible Fixed Assets

Net tangible fixed assets are recorded in account BS2130. This figure is calculated by subtracting BS2120 Accumulated Depreciation from BS2110 Gross Tangible Fixed Assets.

BS2170 Long-Term Investments and Long-Term Receivables

Account BS2170 includes all long-term investments carried at cost, as well as long-term loan investments and other nontrade receivables. This account assumes that all investments are carried at cost, and that income from the investments is actually distributed by or received from the investees. The income should be classified as IS1140 Other Nonoperating Loss (Gain).

Investments in associated companies are classified under the Equity Method as BS2180 Investments in Associated Companies. However, nontrade receivables from associated companies, with the exception of equity investments and loan investments (assigned to BS2180 Investments in Associated Companies), should be classified here if the nontrade receivables play no controlling role.

Unless their value is determined by the Equity Method, investments are traditionally valued at cost. New accounting methods, however, tend to use their market value. If the market value is used for the valuation of long-term investments, the unrealized gain or loss is assigned to shareholders' equity. The unrealized gain or loss should adjust BS2460 Retained Earnings and BS2685 Unrealized Gain (Loss) from Investments.

BS2180 Investments in Associated Companies

Investments valued by the Equity Method should be classified as BS2180 Investments in Associated Companies. This account also includes long-term loan receivables from these associated companies. It does not include trade receivables, all of which should be assigned to BS2030 Accounts and Notes Receivable. If consolidated financial statements are not prepared for investments representing significant ownership, they should be classified here. Even though a parent company has dominating ownership of another company, the subsidiary may be valued by the Equity Method if it operates a significantly different business or is located in a politically turbulent country where the parent company cannot exercise effective control.

If investments in a joint venture can be fully or proportionally consolidated, they should be disclosed as separate items on the balance sheet. Investments in joint ventures valued by the Equity Method should be included here.

Undistributed earnings from an investment, usually called *equity earnings,* should be classified in the income statement as IS1130 Loss (Gain) from Associated Companies. The performance of investments in associated companies can then be isolated for analysis.

BS2190 Intangibles and Other Assets

All noncurrent assets not classified in the Noncurrent Assets Section should be assigned to account BS2190, including all intangible assets (i.e., patents, copyrights, trademarks, and goodwill). BS2190 Intangibles and Other Assets also includes any assets restricted for operating use or not earning normal returns. Subscription receivables from partially paid stocks or unamortized formation expenses should be classified here as well, because they are to be collected or amortized, respectively, over a longer period.

Goodwill may be claimed for an acquired company (for a definition, see "Goodwill and Intangible Assets" in Chapter 3). The validity of this practice is questioned, however, because of the difficulty in justifying the future contributions of goodwill to operations. Accounting for goodwill varies by country. In Commonwealth countries, businesses write off goodwill against retained earnings when a company is acquired. Other countries allow companies to capitalize and amortize goodwill, but the amortization period varies from 5 to 40 years. The impact of these different accounting treatments on company earnings can be significant in countries where there are frequent mergers and acquisitions. The accounting method used for goodwill should be noted, and the earnings normalization process, which makes earnings more comparable to those of other companies, will neutralize the impact.

BS2190 Intangibles and Other Assets may also include deferred tax assets, which, net of deferred tax liabilities, is a possible tax credit. This practice is uncommon, however, due to the accounting principle of conservatism.

BS2199 Total Assets

BS2199 Total Assets represents the sum of BS2099 Total Current Assets, BS2130 Net Tangible Fixed Assets, BS2170 Long-Term Investments and Long-Term Receivables, BS2180 Investments in Associated Companies, and BS2190 Intangibles and Other Assets. It also represents the balance of liabilities and shareholders' equity for database purposes.

However, total assets are not just a balancing item on the debit or credit side of the balance sheet. This figure represents a company's total resources to provide *future services in money or any service convertible to money*. If any company's reporting structure is incompatible with this database (e.g., one that includes treasury stocks as a part of marketable securities or accumulated depreciation on the credit-side of the balance sheet), BS2199 Total Assets may not agree with the figure reported by the company.

In addition, total assets are often used in ratio computations. For ratio computations, the total asset figure should be adjusted if any contra item is included, as in the case of the banking industry. (See RR4304 and related ratios in Chapter 11.) In Commonwealth countries, net assets (total assets minus current liabilities) are the focus of company balance sheets, but the figures can be easily converted to total assets for global analysis.

5.1.3 Current Liabilities

BS2260 Accounts Payable

Accounts payable include all payables related to trading activities that are usually owed to suppliers of inventory. Since both long- and short-term trade receivables are included in BS2030 Accounts and Notes Receivable, short- and long-term accounts payable should be included in account BS2260. Similarly, trade accounts payable to associated companies should also be included in Accounts Payable.

Notes payable, however, should not be classified as Accounts Payable because a decision was made to postpone payment instead of taking advantage of discounts by paying net. Notes payable should be classified as BS2270 Short-Term Borrowing. When a company elects payment by promissory note, implicit or explicit interest should be taken into account, because the choice of whether to use credit from a bank or from a supplier is a financing, not an operating, decision.

BS2270 Short-Term Borrowing

Short-term borrowing, classified in account BS2270, includes notes payable to suppliers, commercial notes, bank overdrafts, and any other short-term borrowing from banks or other organizations. All borrowing is assumed to bear explicit interest expense. Most companies maintain limited credit lines with partner banks and must pay interest on borrowed funds.

BS2280 Short-Term Portion of Long-Term Borrowing

If a company borrows money long-term from either public or private sources, the obligations eventually come due according to the terms of a contract between the parties. BS2370 Long-Term Borrowing usually includes long-term bank borrowing, privately placed bonds, publicly sold bonds, and other instruments. However, the short-term portion of long-term borrowing is assigned to account BS2280.

The payments due on the short-term portion of long-term borrowing in the following year are different from those required by other short-term borrowing. A company can plan its cash needs for the portion coming due in the following year above and beyond its cash needs for operating activities. This account also includes the portion of capital lease obligations coming due in the following year.

BS2290 Other Current Liabilities

Account BS2290 includes all other payments expected to be made in the following operating cycle, such as income, property and Social Security taxes, interest, refundable deposits and advance payments from customers, and any other accrued liabilities. The amount is usually determinable, and no explicit interest is specified.

The amounts to be paid are easily determined. Estimated deferred tax liabilities expected to be paid in the following year should be included in BS2390 Other Long-Term Liabilities, rather than in BS2290 Other Current Liabilities, until tax authorities confirm the amount. Provisions for pensions and warrants may come due in the following year, but when the amounts are not known the provisions should be included in BS2390 Other Long-Term Liabilities.

Preferred dividends in arrears should not be included in BS2290 Other Current Liabilities until the payment is declared. However, bonus payments to employees, for example, should be accrued as additional wages to be paid and included in account BS2290.

In a few countries, current dividends payable are treated as current liabilities. This is a debatable point, considering the need for consistency in developing a database. Dividends for the current period are declared when the annual report is prepared and submitted to the shareholders' meeting for approval. Only after a proposed dividend is approved will dividends actually be paid to shareholders. Interim dividends already paid out during the year should not be recorded as liabilities. The final dividends payable should be recorded as a liability when the amount is approved.

In practice, there are variations in the treatment of dividends. In the United States, for example, companies do not record dividends to be paid until they are approved at a shareholders' meeting. On the other hand, companies in the United Kingdom record the liability as soon as the dividend is declared. A few European countries prepare their balance sheets both before and after appropriations. To compile information consistently for purposes of comparison, preparation of the balance sheet before appropriations is recommended.

If conversion of "after appropriation" to "before appropriation" figures is necessary, the process is usually not difficult. Dividends payable should be transferred from current liabilities to retained earnings. In addition to the dividends, there may be other appropriations that cannot be reversed, but the database does not differentiate between such reserves and retained earnings.

BS2299 Total Current Liabilities

BS2260 Accounts Payable, BS2270 Short-Term Borrowing, BS2280 Short-Term Portion of Long-term Borrowing, and BS2290 Other Current Liabilities are combined in BS2299 Total Current Liabilities. This account is important in computing working capital.

5.1.4 Noncurrent Liabilities

BS2370 Long-Term Borrowing

BS2370 Long-Term Borrowing includes all interest-bearing financial obligations that are not due in the following year, such as long-term bank loans, debentures, bonds, mortgage debts, and any other long-term obligations that have fixed repayment schedules and explicit interest rates. This account also includes the discounted present value of capital lease obligations, because a competitive interest rate is assumed even though no explicit interest rate is specified. Each of the obligations may be secured by specific assets or sinking fund requirements from future earnings. Some obligations are secured by possible participation in management, with convertible features, if the company is in default. In consolidated financial statements, borrowing by subsidiaries is no different from borrowing by a parent company.

Convertible bonds should be classified as long-term borrowing until they are converted to common stocks. Certain subordinated loan notes are classified as quasi-capital and as a part of shareholders' equity by French companies. They should be classified here as liabilities as long as the substance of the notes requires fixed payment.

As mentioned previously, the short-term portion of long-term obligations should be excluded from account BS2370 and classified as BS2280 Short-Term Portion of Long-Term Borrowing. Any other obligations without explicit interest commitments should be included in BS2390 Other Long-Term Liabilities. Preferred equity, which usually has fixed income features and no fixed repayment schedule, should be excluded here and included in BS2410 Preferred Equity.

BS2390 Other Long-Term Liabilities

Other long-term liabilities are assigned to account BS2390. These include all other long-term obligations that do not require explicit interest payments, such as provisions for warranty, pensions, severance and related payments, and any other future charges estimated. Also included are deferred tax liabilities and any other non-equity reserves.

Pension obligations, the payments retirees will receive, are determined by contractual agreements reached by a company and its employees. Most companies define a systematic plan applicable to all employees, whose pensions are calculated using salary levels, years of service, and other criteria. A previous section on accounting standards discusses how to define the extent of pension obligations. However, pension plans vary tremendously among companies and countries. Indeed, employees working for the same company but in different countries around the world often have pension schemes that vary significantly in value. These differences have a major impact on a company's competitiveness, as later analysis will show.

Regardless of the size of pension obligations, the method of pension funding significantly affects a company's assets and liabilities. The question is whether the pension fund is to be entrusted to an outside organization. When it is, the fund is isolated from the company's future performance and the balance sheet will show no obligations other than those arising from minor timing differences in the contribution process. This situation is typical of pensions in the United States and Switzerland, for example. Some continental European countries, with their extensive social security systems, entrust the pension obligation to government instead of private money managers.

No matter how pensions are funded, whether entrusted to outside organizations or not, in many countries they represent only a fraction of a company's total obligations. Other benefits, such as severance payments, should not be treated differently than pension obligations.

Whichever method is adopted, obligations to employees, whether pensions or severance payments, should be accrued as liabilities if they are not entrusted to outside organizations. These liabilities are long-term and should be included in account BS2390. Specific information on pension obligations should be collected in BS2660 Pension Reserves as a reference item, because the liability does not exist at all in some countries. Note should also be made of the method used to account for funds entrusted to outside organizations.

If pensions are managed through a national social security program, no note regarding the accounting method need be made for a specific company, because all operate in the same way. For example, all companies in Germany must contribute to the national social security system by law. However, these companies may offer an additional package of retirement benefits and severance agreements to its employees. Such additional benefits must be treated as pension obligations, and the method used to account for them should be noted.

Deferred tax liabilities arise from the timing difference between the point at which companies recognize income and expenses for financial reporting purposes and when they recognize these items for tax reporting purposes. As the use of consolidated financial statements has spread, the recognition of deferred tax liabilities has increased. Before consolidated financial statements were adopted, many countries required companies to use the same accounting method in both financial and tax reporting, and there were therefore no deferred tax liabilities. A discussion of deferred tax accounting may be found in Chapter 3. Many countries still require financial and tax reporting to agree.

When the amount of a future tax obligation is established, it should be considered as "taxes payable" and assigned to BS2290 Other Current Liabilities. If the deferred tax liability is disclosed, it should also be noted as a reference item in BS2670 Deferred Tax Liabilities.

Non-equity reserves, discussed in Chapter 3, ("Sonderposten" in Germany) are reported between liabilities and shareholders' equity on the balance sheet. They should be included in account BS2390 along with a reference note in BS2680 Non-Equity Reserves.

Any other reserves or provisions for charges or special reserves required by law should be included here as well. This issue will be addressed later in subsequent, country-specific volumes. The validity of certain liabilities may be questionable. If liabilities are predictable and can be reasonably estimated, they should be recorded in the income statement and on the balance sheet. Less predictable items, such as litigation, guarantees, and repurchase agreements, should be disclosed as off-balance-sheet items.

BS2399 Total Liabilities

Total liabilities are defined in account BS2399. This account represents the sum of BS2299 Total Current Liabilities, BS2370 Long-Term Borrowing, and BS2390 Other Long-Term Liabilities.

5.1.5 Shareholders' Equity

BS2410 Preferred Equity

Preferred equity, defined in account BS2410, includes redeemable and nonredeemable preferred stocks, as well as preferred stocks issued by subsidiaries. Some preferred stocks are hybrids of debt and common equity. Some companies record dividends paid to preferred stocks issued by foreign subsidiaries as expense. The classification of a security as long-term borrowing or as preferred equity should not be judged by its name. The determination depends on whether the dividends are paid from income before or after taxes. Preferred stocks are usually not granted voting rights, except when dividend payments are in arrears or under other special conditions.

Whether additional paid-in capital from preferred stock issues belongs to preferred shareholders or to common shareholders is arguable. If fixed dividends are paid to preferred stockholders who have no other claim on a company's residual value, the premium is the difference between the face rate of the dividend and the expected return. In such a case, the premium is created at a cost to common shareholders and, therefore, belongs to common shareholders.

Preferred stocks that are participating with common stock in dividend distribution should be excluded from account BS2410, because the income is uncertain and depends on the company's performance each year. This judgment can be made based on the established practice in each country. For example, participation certificates issued by Swiss companies participate fully with dividends paid for common stock. However, preferred stocks in Korea and Brazil are preferred stocks that are consistently participating over the years. In such instances the participative stocks should be classified as common stock. "Deferred shares" in U.K. companies can be included in this account if dividend rights are suspended until they are converted to common shares. The deferred shares have some limitation in their privilege as an equity holder until they are converted and should be accounted for as convertible preferred shares without dividend rights. Dividend payments to preferred stocks reported in the income statement should mirror the classification of preferred stocks on the balance sheet.

BS2420 Minority Interest

When subsidiaries are not 100 percent owned by a parent company, their earnings belonging to minority shareholders should be accumulated as minority interest on the balance sheet. There are variations in the treatment of minority interests among countries because of different views of what constitutes capital. For example, German companies report minority interests as an appropriation of earnings in the income statement and as a part of shareholders' equity on the balance sheet. U.S. companies report the share of earnings due to minority interests before net income in the income statement, and outside shareholders' equity on the balance sheet.

BS2450 Share Capital and Share Premiums

Capital provided by common shareholders is included in account BS2450. Before any determination on share capital is made, multiple shares should be appropriately identified. In many countries, preferred stocks and minority interests are often mixed together with paid-in capital for common stocks.
BS2450 Share Capital and Share Premiums should reflect all of a company's undistributable capital.

Capital provided by shareholders has two components. The first consists of the aggregation of the nominal value of the stocks issued. The par value has no meaning for purposes of financial analysis, but there are regulations in some countries regarding the levels of capital a company must maintain.

The second component of capital provided by shareholders includes the share premiums beyond the par value. The second components may be variously named, but analysts should have little difficulty in identifying them. Neither of the two components may be distributed to shareholders before liquidation.

Companies in some countries do not clearly distinguish between preferred and common stocks, but include both as a part of share capital. Some of these stocks are similar to common stock in regard to dividend rights and qualify as a multiple share regardless of their voting rights. Such common share equivalents should be assigned to account BS2450, as mentioned earlier and discussed in Chapter 3 under "Multiple Shares." If they are truly preferred in all respects, they should be isolated and entered in BS2410 Preferred Equity.

Share premiums are also generated by the exchange of stocks in mergers; these are usually known as "redemption reserves." Capital redemption reserves are no different from share premiums and should be included in BS2450 Share Capital and Share Premiums.

BS2460 Retained Earnings

A company's earnings are generally distributed to shareholders, but in many countries there are some restrictions on distributions in order to preserve a company's capital and thereby maintain economic stability.

Such restrictions, reserve requirements before cash distributions, are found in the commercial law of all countries. *Legal and capital reserves* are established to exclude from distribution a certain percentage (5 or 10 percent) of dividends to be distributed up to a set level (e.g., 50 percent) of share capital. Use of these reserves is extremely restricted prior to a company's liquidation. They may be converted to share capital as stock dividends or used to reduce negative retained earnings resulting from accumulated losses. There are some variations in these reserves and each country has its own regulations. They may be referred to as "earnings reserves" or "revenue reserves" and can be maintained for general or specific purposes. The use of revenue reserves is less restricted than use of legal or capital reserves, but they are not available for immediate distribution to shareholders.

The remaining residual value belonging to common shareholders may be kept as unappropriated retained earnings for future appropriations. This account, BS2460 Retained Earnings, should include all reserves generated by a company's earnings.

Thus, retained earnings represent the earnings transferred from the income statement and accumulated from past accounting periods after distribution to shareholders. On the other hand, there are some "earnings" (positive or negative) that do not originate from the income statement but are a direct result of capital transactions. They include, for example, revaluation reserves, goodwill reserves (in Commonwealth countries), consolidation reserves, foreign currency translation differences, and other untaxed reserves.

Such reserves vary according to national regulations, but most of them have common characteristics. All are some form of gain or loss based on historical cost. They are not effected by operating activities, but by changes in business environments or corporate structures. These reserves are a means of filling the gaps between accounting based on the Historical Cost Principle and actual price level changes in the real world.

The distribution of these gains from capital transactions to shareholders could endanger capital preservation. They are usually not treated as gains or losses in the income statement. The following examples will be further explained in later volumes as they apply in specific countries.

Gains from the revaluation of fixed assets are directly added to retained earnings and preserved for later fluctuations in their value. The reserves are reversed when the assets are disposed of or transferred to share capital permanently through the issue of bonus shares. This gain is assumed to be a change in the nominal value of capital provided by shareholders, and regulations heavily restrict distributions. It is difficult to decide whether revaluation reserves should be subject to distribution, because the added value serves not only common shareholders by increasing residual value but also serves debt capital providers by increasing the value of assets used as security. Revaluation information must be compiled consistently and noted in BS2680 Non-Equity Reserves.

Accounting for *unrealized gains or losses from revaluation of investments* is used in a few countries. If the market value is used in the valuation of investment assets (usually long-term investments available for sale), the unrealized gain or loss is directly accounted to shareholders' equity and the amount should be included in retained earnings with a reference note in BS2685 Unrealized Gain (Loss) from Investments.

Gains or losses from foreign currency translation under the Current Rate Method have implications for shareholders similar to those of gains or losses from the revaluation of fixed assets. In the case of currencies, the gain or loss results from changes in exchange rates between the reporting currency and local currency of a subsidiary's financial statements. The gain or loss should be included in Retained Earnings but the amount is usually insignificant and no separate reference item is necessary.

Goodwill reserves and merger reserves are written off to shareholders' equity in Commonwealth countries instead of capitalizing the consolidation differences on the asset-side. It is one of the major differences in reporting practices compared to non-Commonwealth countries. Reserves written off to shareholders' equity must be noted so that the information can be used in the standardization process in analysis.

In a few countries, *consolidation differences* appear in the shareholders' equity section. This is the equivalent of "negative goodwill" in other countries.

When one company purchases another, the payment for assets acquired is not likely to be the sum of the individual assets' value. Excess payment is accounted for as goodwill and is either capitalized as an intangible asset or used to reduce shareholders' equity in the year of purchase. If the payment for the purchase is less than the sum of the individual assets' value, it is called "negative goodwill" or "consolidation differences" and appears as a positive number in the shareholders' equity section. Consolidation reserves or negative goodwill can be set off against negative results from the purchased assets or restructuring expenses. If the negative goodwill is purely the result of a "good deal," it may be distributed to shareholders, but few companies clarify such matters.

In a business combination, under the Pooling of Interest Method, no goodwill arises. Under this method, the combining companies continue as a single corporation, and assets and liabilities are carried forward into the resulting entity at their book value. "Pooling of interest," accepted in only a few countries, including the United States, is heavily restricted, and business combinations must meet rigidly set criteria to qualify.

Untaxed reserves are usually recorded between the shareholders' equity and liability sections but may be included as a part of shareholders' equity if they are regarded as close to capital. Untaxed reserves are restricted by many conditions governing their distribution to shareholders. Possible tax liabilities should also be considered. Eventually, the reserves should be split between liabilities (deferred tax liabilities with the applicable effective tax rate for the specific items) and shareholders' equity (residual value after tax liabilities) in the normalization process for purposes of comparison. All other reserves of a temporary nature should be included in BS2460 Retained Earnings, including reserves for investment subsidies.

A *limited partnership* differs only slightly from stock corporations insofar as the legal responsibility of the limited partners is concerned; there are merely fewer participants involved. Any residual value that belongs to unlimited partners should be included in BS2460 Retained Earnings.

BS2470 (Treasury Stocks) (Always in the negative)

One way corporations raise capital is by issuing stock. Often shares are purchased back by the issuing company. These are known as "treasury stocks" or "own stocks." There are many reasons for such repurchases, including the need to reduce unnecessary capital, to reserve shares to be used for stock options or warrants, and to control stock prices by manipulating supply and demand of a specific stock.

When treasury stocks are purchased for a long-term purpose, usual practice is to reduce outstanding capital by their purchase price. Temporarily owned treasury stocks are disclosed either as current assets or as a negative number in shareholders' equity. Each reporting method has its own rationale.

The reason for disclosing treasury stocks as an asset is to show that they are available to pay debts (*economist's view*). This view assumes that the treasury stocks are insignificant in comparison to the total number of shares outstanding and that they are liquid enough to be converted to cash. The reason for disclosing treasury stocks as a reduction in shareholders' equity is that the company as a legal entity cannot own itself (*lawyer's view*).

Even though full disclosure is an important accounting principle, the simultaneous inflation of both sides of the balance sheet by including receivables and payables to the same party (shareholders) is an exaggeration. The full disclosure principle can be honored by disclosing treasury stocks as a negative number in shareholders' equity. One of these two views must be adopted and used consistently to arrive at total asset figures that are comparable. This book accepts the lawyer's point of view.

If treasury stocks are disclosed as a negative number in shareholders' equity, at what amount must they be recorded? If shareholders' equity is reduced, which part of it? In regard to the first issue, the treasury stock is usually recorded at purchase cost. Taking the economist's point of view to extremes, the purchase of treasury stocks should also account for unrealized gains or losses, but no one argues to this effect.

There is no easy answer to the question of what parts of stockholders' equity should be reduced by treasury stock. For purposes of discussion, consider the intrinsic value of a stock at liquidation. The stockholders will be rewarded after all obligations to third parties are met. Assuming all assets and liabilities are recorded at current market value, the shareholders will have total shareholders' equity available for distribution. Shareholders' equity is, by and large, composed of three components: share capital (nominal value), share premium (extra contributions from shareholders), and retained earnings (undistributed earnings). If a stock is purchased back by the company, the purchase price must comprise these three components. If the repurchased stocks were issued at the time of incorporation, the purchase price can be easily broken down into these components. If there were later issues, segregation by share premium and retained earnings after nominal value is impractical. Therefore, as a practical matter, treasury stocks are best disclosed as a negative number in shareholders' equity in a separate line.

If using BS2470 (Treasury Stocks) seems superfluous because this designation does not appear in financial statements in many countries, an alternative is to reduce retained earnings by the repurchase price of the treasury stocks. If shareholders' equity must be divided between shareholder capital and internally generated equity for purposes of analysis, one of the two must be reduced by the cost of the treasury stocks. In a mature and financially healthy company, retained earnings should represent the bulk of shareholders' equity. Reducing the retained earnings by the entire amount of treasury stocks would not distort the larger picture.

Stocks owned by an Employee Stock Option Plan (ESOP) also should be included in BS2470 (Treasury Stocks). Whether stocks owned by an ESOP should be considered treasury stocks is arguable. The answer lies in the relationship between a company and its pension trust. This book assumes the pension trust is closely related to the company and that its own shares held by its pension trust are treated as treasury stock. The reason for this is that currently dominant consolidation practices include all related parties into one set of financial statements and the pension trust organization is strongly influenced by the funding company.

BS2499 Total Shareholders' Equity

BS2499 Total Shareholders' Equity adds BS2410 Preferred Equity, BS2420 Minority Interest, BS2450 Share Capital and Share Premiums, BS2460 Retained

Earnings, and the negative BS2470 (Treasury Stocks). Total shareholders' equity may be differently defined for purposes of analysis. This is explained in the later section on ratio computation in Chapter 11.

5.1.6 Reference Items

BS2560 Nondepreciable Fixed Assets

In order to standardize depreciation expenses later, it is helpful to isolate nondepreciable fixed assets, including land and construction in progress. Land may include some material improvements and may therefore show some depreciation expense. If the depreciable portion of the land is relatively negligible, the entire amount should be included in BS2560 Nondepreciable Fixed Assets.

BS2565 Insurance Value of Tangible Fixed Assets

In countries that have adopted extremely conservative valuation methods, the depreciation of fixed assets is accelerated. In such countries, tax reporting and financial accounting usually must conform. Tangible fixed assets are then recorded at significantly lower values than actual market values. For example, in Switzerland the entire purchase price of some fixed assets may be depreciated in the year of purchase and a value of Sfr 1 is recorded on the balance sheet. Companies are then required to disclose the value at which these assets are insured, which is a close estimate of their market value and is useful information for further analysis.

BS2660 Pension Reserves

BS2660 Pension Reserves includes all obligations due to retired employees. Such obligations are not limited to unfunded pension provisions and may include provisions for any retirement plan, severance, and other related payments.

BS2670 Deferred Tax Liabilities

Estimated liabilities arising from the timing differences between financial and tax accounting are included in BS2670 Deferred Tax Liabilities. If a company's deferred tax liabilities are greater than its deferred tax assets, the net amount should be included in BS2390 Other Long-Term Liabilities and BS2670 Deferred Tax Liabilities. If deferred tax assets are greater than deferred tax liabilities, the net amount should be included in BS2190 Intangibles and Other Assets, and this amount also should be included in account BS2670 as a negative number. A more detailed discussion can be found in Chapter 3.

BS2680 Non-Equity Reserves

Account BS2680 includes reserves created at the discretion of management rather than for legitimate business reasons. Certain reserves should be referred to BS2390 Other Long-Term Liabilities, or to BS2460 Retained Earnings, with an appropriate note. Typical examples are those reserves resulting from the revaluation of tangible fixed assets of a company in the United Kingdom and the Investment Allowances under Article 10 of the Austrian Income Tax Act. However, unrealized gains or losses from long-term investments should be referred to BS2685 Unrealized Gain (Loss) from Investments. A more detailed discussion of reserves can be found in Chapter 3 and in later, country-specific, volumes.

BS2685 Unrealized Gain (Loss) from Investments

It is not common to use market prices in long-term investment valuation. But if market value is adopted, the accumulated unrealized gain (loss) should be directly added to BS2460 Retained Earnings, and referred to account BS2685. This amount must be differentiated from unrealized gains for tangible fixed assets, which, as revaluation reserves, should be classified as BS2680 Non-Equity Reserves.

BS2690 Goodwill Written Off

Goodwill that is written off in the year another company is purchased and is subtracted from BS2460 Retained Earnings should be included in account BS2690. Negative goodwill or "badwill," which cannot be amortized, should not be included here.

BS2710 Number of Shares Outstanding

The number of shares outstanding at the end of a period should be disclosed in account BS2710. However, treasury shares should reduce the number of shares outstanding. For companies whose current assets include treasury stocks, it may be difficult to establish the exact number of shares outstanding.

If there are changes in capital immediately after the end of a period, the current number of shares outstanding may be emphasized by the company and the number of shares outstanding as of period end, which would be more useful for comparative analysis, may not be made available. When a company has multiple shares, there will be an individual page in the multiple share information set for each type of share, including the number of shares, and BS2710 will show the aggregate number of primary share equivalents.

BS2720 Par Value

The par value of a common share should be included in account BS2720. For multiple shares, the par value of each share should be disclosed on each individual share page, but not on the balance sheet.

Some companies issue shares without a par value. These shares should be assigned some default value, such as − 999.999, with a separate note for database purposes.

BS2730 Dividend Right Parity

The dividend right parity, shown in account BS2730, will always be "one" for a single-share company. For a company with multiple shares, the dividend right parity of a primary share will be one, and the remaining shares will have a value relative to the primary share's parity. However, if the secondary share's dividend is only slightly different, its dividend right parity should be kept as one. Analysis of such shares should consider the variance in dividend payment in order to simplify the computation process. Further discussion can be found in Chapter 3.

In multiple-share companies, the share most active in the market should be treated as the primary share. This is an important consideration in analysis.

BS2740 Voting Right Parity

Voting right parity, assigned to account BS2740, will always be "one" for a single-share company. For companies with multiple shares, voting right parity of a primary share will be one and the rest will have a relative value. Voting rights could be another approach to multiple-share analysis, but it is not addressed in this book. (See Chapter 3 for further discussion.)

BS2770 Number of Treasury Stocks

The number of treasury stocks used to compute the value assigned to BS2470 (Treasury Stocks) should be disclosed here. For multiple shares, the number of each type of share should be included in the multiple-share information set, and this balance sheet account will show the aggregate number of the primary share equivalents.

BS2800 Number of Employees

The full-time equivalent number of employees at the end of a period should be used for account BS2800. Disclosure of the number of employees is irregular, and there is no single definition. For example, the *average number* of employees is often disclosed. Part-time workers may or may not be converted to full-time equivalents. If the number of employees at the end of a period is needed, an approximate average number can be computed by using the numbers reported at the beginning and at the end of the period.

5.2 Banking Format

The importance of the balance sheet remains paramount in the financial services industry. This is also true of banking. As previously noted, industrial companies have shifted their emphasis from the balance sheet to the income statement and the cash flow statement. The segregation of assets and liabilities has evolved from a "types of assets and liabilities" format into a "short-term and long-term" format, which in turn has become "current and noncurrent." However, in the banking industry everywhere, the segregation of assets and liabilities into a short- and long-term format is still common. This book adopts the current/ noncurrent format, to a certain degree, to make the performance of banks comparable to the performance of industrial companies and to simplify the allocation of assets between sectors.

Loans to customers make up 80 percent to 90 percent of a bank's total assets. Although the segregation of loans varies by country, they can be separated in four different ways:

Segregation of loans by type of customer:
   Commercial loans
   Consumer loans
Segregation of loans by maturity:
   Short-term loans (1 year or less)
   Mid-term loans (1 to 5 years)
   Long-term loans (5 years or more)
Segregation of loans by type of security:
   General loans (no specific security)
   Real estate loans (secured by real estate)
   Lease financing loans (secured by property other than real estate)
Segregation of loans by location of lenders:
   Domestic loans
   Foreign loans

In fact, the method of segregating loans in a database is unimportant, because no matter in what order they are listed, they can be interwoven in grids. Bank disclosures vary, with some providing details in the body of the balance sheet and others reporting details in related notes. This book has adopted loan segregation by type of customer. Other details are selectively added as reference items.

Banks frequently borrow or lend money among themselves as a result of temporary cash needs or temporary excesses in cash holdings. Such transactions are respectively known as "Due to Banks" or "Due from Banks" and represent a significant proportion of total assets. Lending or borrowing among banks is essentially wholesale, and profit margins on these activities are nominal. Interbank activities are treated separately from loans to or deposits from customers.

Investments make up the next major category of assets in banking. Because lending is the main operating activity in banking, loan investments are the major investment vehicle. Other capital may be invested temporarily in short-term securities or, in some cases, in long-term securities to maintain a business relationship with a company. Any long-term security investments usually play a minor role, because the source of a bank's capital, customers' deposits, is short-term in nature.

Liabilities in the banking industry are dominated by customer deposits, which are segregated according to their maturity. Customer deposits are made up of demand deposits, savings deposits, and time deposits. Savings deposits do not have a fixed maturity but can be withdrawn upon notice. Time deposits have a fixed maturity; the longer the maturity of a deposit, the higher the interest rate a bank will pay.

Banks do not finance their capital needs with long-term loans from other banks. They issue long-term bonds or subordinated bonds to cover special capital needs, such as mortgage loans.

BALANCE SHEET IN A BANKING FORMAT

Sections	Data	Items
Current Assets	BS2010	Cash and Cash Equivalents
	BS2020	Short-Term Investments
	BS2035	Federal Funds Sold and Securities Purchased Under Resale Agreements
	BS2050	Commercial Loans
	BS2052	Consumer Loans
	BS2054	Other Loans
	BS2055	**Total Loans**
	BS2057	Loan Loss Reserves
	BS2060	**Net Loans**
	BS2065	Due from Banks and Other Interbank Assets
Noncurrent Assets	BS2130	Net Tangible Fixed Assets
	BS2170	Long-Term Investments
	BS2180	Investments in Associated Companies
	BS2190	Intangibles and Other Assets
	BS2195	Customers' Liabilities for Acceptances
	BS2199	**Total Assets**
Current Liabilities	BS2210	Demand Deposits
	BS2212	Savings Deposits
	BS2215	Time Deposits
	BS2219	Other Deposits
	BS2220	**Total Deposits**
	BS2270	Due to Banks and Other Short-Term Borrowing
	BS2275	Federal Funds Purchased and Securities Sold Under Repurchase Agreements
	BS2280	Short-Term Portion of Long-Term Borrowing
	BS2290	Other Short-Term Liabilities
Noncurrent Liabilities	BS2370	Long-Term Borrowing
	BS2390	Other Long-Term Liabilities
	BS2395	Customers' Acceptances
	BS2399	**Total Liabilities**
Shareholders' Equity	BS2410	Preferred Equity
	BS2420	Minority Interest
	BS2450	Share Capital and Share Premiums
	BS2460	Retained Earnings
	BS2470	(Treasury Stocks)
	BS2499	**Total Shareholders' Equity**

(continued)

(continued)		
Reference	BS2510	Short-Term Loans
Items	BS2512	Mid-Term Loans
	BS2515	Long-Term Loans
	BS2520	Real Estate Loans
	BS2522	Lease Financing Loans
	BS2525	Foreign Loans
	BS2529	Nonperforming Assets
	BS2610	Short-Term Deposits
	BS2612	Mid-Term Deposits
	BS2615	Long-Term Deposits
	BS2625	Foreign Deposits
	BS2630	Core Capital (Tier 1)
	BS2632	Risk-Based Capital (Tier 1 + Tier 2)
	BS2635	Leverage Ratio
	BS2660	Pension Reserves
	BS2670	Deferred Tax Liabilities
	BS2680	Nonequity Reserves
	BS2685	Investment Reserves
	BS2690	Goodwill Written-Off
	BS2695	Off-Balance Contingent Liabilities
	BS2710	Number of Shares Outstanding
	BS2720	Par Value
	BS2730	Dividend Right Parity
	BS2740	Voting Right Parity
	BS2770	Number of Treasury Stocks
	BS2800	Number of Employees

5.2.1 Current Assets

Banks do not divide their assets into those that are current and those that are noncurrent. Instead, they list their assets by type. However, a reasonable classification of a bank's assets into current and noncurrent will help in comparing the performance of banks with industrial companies and other businesses.

What banks and industrial companies regard as "current" differs somewhat and is not comparable. Industrial companies define *current* as one year or an operating cycle, whichever is longer. In constructing a database for banking, business loan investments, which are often held longer than a year, should be separately identified as noncurrent assets.

BS2010 Cash and Cash Equivalents

Cash on hand and non-interest-bearing deposits with other banks make up BS2010 Cash and Cash Equivalents. This account also includes deposits with a central bank or with postal banks (which are called giro accounts), as well as cash in transit, such as checks in the clearing process between banks. Significant amounts represented by checks in transit are reported as other assets by companies in many countries and should be reclassified.

BS2020 Short-Term Investments

BS2020 Short-Term Investments includes investments in trading assets, which may be equity securities, fixed-income securities, or government-issued bills. Whether these securities are short-term or not is determined by the company's intended use of them. They must be convertible to cash within a reasonably short time to qualify as short-term investments.

The security investments reported by a company often include the purchase of the company's own shares. These should be excluded to maintain consistency across countries.

BS2035 Federal Funds Sold and Securities Purchased Under Resale Agreements

It is common with "universal banking" in Europe for banks acting as security brokerages to carry a significant amount of federal funds sold and securities purchased under resale agreements. These funds should be included in account BS2035.

BS2055 Total Loans

Assets in banking are mainly composed of loans and other investments, from which revenue is derived. These loans are segregated in many different ways, either on the balance sheet or in related notes. In this database, the balance sheet will segregate the loans by client type and other classifications are attached as reference items. BS2055 Total Loans is the sum of BS2050 Commercial Loans, BS2052 Consumer Loans, and BS2054 Other Loans.

BS2050 Commercial Loans. Account BS2050 includes all loans for commercial and industrial use, including bills of exchange, bills discounted, and overdrafts. Commercial loans are made for reinvestment in further business activities. Clients for commercial loans consist of all types of corporations and may seek all types of loans, including agriculture loans, regardless of their business.

However, short-term loans to other banks should not be included in BS2050 Commercial Loans. These belong in BS2065 Due from Banks and Other Interbank Assets.

BS2052 Consumer Loans. Consumer loans are disclosed in account BS2052. These are loans to consumers for individual use, including credit card loans and installment loans for the purchase of automobiles, equipment, and homes.

BS2054 Other Loans. All loans other than commercial and consumer loans are included in account BS2054.

BS2057 Loan Loss Reserves

Often loans are in default, and the principal or interest cannot be collected. General provisions, as well as provisions for specific loans, are made as a contra account (a deduction from BS2055 Total Loans) based on estimates that rely on past experience in determining how much is actually recoverable. Such provisions are disclosed in BS2057 Loan Loss Reserves.

Although provisions are based on experience, there are no objective criteria available to help establish their appropriate size. The amount is often dictated by local tax authorities or other regulatory bodies.

BS2060 Net Loans

Net loans amounts are calculated by deducting BS2057 Loan Loss Reserves from BS2055 Total Loans. These are shown in account BS2060.

BS2065 Due from Banks and Other Interbank Assets

"Due from banks" are loans to other banks (but not central banks) and are disclosed in account BS2065. They are treated as loan investments but are separated from other loans. Such loans are, in effect, wholesale agreements among banks. Interest margins are minimal on interbank loans. These loans are usually called "due from banks" or, alternatively, "call money" or "receivables from other banks."

5.2.2   Noncurrent Assets

BS2130 Net Tangible Fixed Assets

Net tangible fixed assets are all operating tangible fixed assets after accumulated depreciation and are disclosed in account BS2130. This account also includes property and equipment under lease if the bank is a lessor, because the bank holds the titles to the assets. However, assets under capital leases to customers should not be assigned to this account because they qualify as consumer loans. Leased fixed assets under capital leases, with the bank as a lessee, on the other hand, should be included here.

BS2170 Long-Term Investments

Long-term investments, which are assigned to account BS2170, are made up of all equity and fixed income securities held for investments and carried at cost. It is difficult in practice to say whether long-term security investments are current or noncurrent. Banks need to invest excess cash, and long-term securities may be the best alternative. This account will include any security invested for longer than one year and carried at cost.

BS2180 Investments in Associated Companies

Refer to the explanations under BS2180 in the Industrial Format. BS2180 Investments in Associated Companies includes all investments carried under the Equity Method, including investments in unconsolidated subsidiaries.

BS2190 Intangibles and Other Assets

Account BS2190 consists of all intangible assets, including goodwill, as well as any prepaid expenses or accrued interest income and any other assets that do not earn competitive income. Prepaid expenses and accrued interest expenses may be short-term but are assumed to be minimal. What is important is their nonearning character.

Nonperforming loans and other investments have the characteristics of other assets. They are common in banking. The possible risk attached to these loans and investments is a part of the total risk banks assume and for which they are compensated through interest income and investment income. These assets are usually included with loans and investments on the company balance sheet. Nonperforming assets should be assigned to BS2529 Nonperforming Assets, as well as to BS2190 Intangibles and Other Assets.

BS2195 Customers' Liabilities for Acceptances

Banks are involved in many other services in addition to taking deposits and lending to customers. Most of these involve transferring funds through letters of credit or guarantees on behalf of customers. Such assets, disclosed in BS2195 Customers' Liabilities for Acceptances, are usually linked to contra items in BS2395 Customers' Acceptances. That means banks may be liable to one client at the same time it has claims for the same amount from another client.

Securities in custodial care, trust operations, qualify as assets and are added to this account. In Japanese banks trusted assets are segregated from operating trusted assets, which are treated as general assets.

These customer acceptances and liabilities generate commission income. The amounts of income can be considerable depending on the level of risk. Disclosure of such items varies by country and is inconsistent, ranging from 5 percent to 200 percent of the net assets (total assets minus this contra account BS2195). Even though individual items are listed on or off the balance sheet, they should not be added because each has a different level of risk.

This account includes total contra items disclosed by a bank, and the remaining off-balance sheet items are disclosed in BS2695 Off-Balance Contingent Liabilities. However, the computation of asset profitability should be based on total assets after netting this account.

BS2199 Total Assets

Total assets are the sum of the following items:

> BS2010 Cash and Cash Equivalents
> BS2020 Short-Term Investments
> BS2035 Federal Funds Sold and Securities Purchased Under Resale Agreements
> BS2060 Net Loans
> BS2065 Due from Banks and Other Interbank Assets
> BS2130 Net Tangible Fixed Assets
> BS2170 Long-Term Investments
> BS2180 Investments in Associated Companies
> BS2190 Intangibles and Other Assets
> BS2195 Customers' Liabilities for Acceptances

5.2.3 Current Liabilities

BS2220 Total Deposits

Customer deposits are the chief criterion in defining a commercial bank. Mortgage banks in Germany hold some customer deposits, but most of their capital is financed through bonds backed by public authorities. The capital is used for mortgage loans. These banks, called "Landesbanken," do not qualify as commercial banks.

Account BS2220 adds all customer deposits. Deposits from other banks are separated and disclosed in BS2270 Due to Banks and Other Short-Term Borrowing, for the same reason that BS2065 Due from Banks and Other Interbank Assets is separated from BS2055 Total Loans.

Types of deposits vary by country, depending on the products banks develop. Their classification is based on the substance of each product. Balance sheets usually classify deposits by the restrictions placed on withdrawal. Other classifications are disclosed as reference items. As with loans, current and noncurrent segregation is unclear, and all deposits are included in this account because, in the banking industry, they are assumed to be operating liabilities.

BS2210 Demand Deposits. Customer deposits bearing little or no interest should be included in BS2210 Demand Deposits. Checking account services are widespread in the United States but not elsewhere. Most accounts with minimal interest have no minimum balance requirement and, outside the United States, no restrictions on withdrawal.

Commercial banking functions are separated from central banking functions in most countries. However, these functions are combined at a few banks (e.g., the Hong Kong Shanghai Bank and the Bank of China), generating a unique item, currency notes in circulation. The notes in circulation should be included in this account.

BS2212 Savings Deposits. Savings accounts consist of deposits requiring a specific period of notice prior to withdrawal without significant penalty. They usually have higher interest rates than demand deposits. The rates normally vary according to the extent of restrictions placed on withdrawal. Often, checks may be written against saving accounts. Banks and customers use this kind of account to "park" money to be used in security trading.

BS2215 Time Deposits. Time deposits disclosed in account BS2215, have a fixed maturity, and early withdrawals result in a significant penalty payment. On the other hand, they offer the highest interest rates as compared with demand or savings deposits. They include certificates of deposit and savings certificates and are used as a short-term investment tool by depositors.

BS2219 Other Deposits. Account BS2219 includes any other type of customer deposit, such as escrow deposits for insurance and taxes.

BS2270 Due to Banks and Other Short-Term Borrowing

Account BS2270 includes any amounts owed to other financial institutions and any other short-term interest borrowing. It also includes call money and bills discounted.

BS2275 Federal Funds Purchased and Securities Sold Under Repurchase Agreements

Account BS2275 is established for banks with brokerage activities.

BS2280 Short-Term Portion of Long-Term Borrowing

Banks rarely borrow from other banks for long-term uses but often issue bonds to the public. The portion to be reimbursed in the following year should be included in account BS2280.

BS2290 Other Short-Term Liabilities

Any other short-term liabilities with no explicitly required interest payment should be included in account BS2290. Detailed examples may be found under account BS2290 in the Industrial Format.

5.2.4   Noncurrent Liabilities

BS2370 Long-Term Borrowing

Long-term borrowing amounts are disclosed in account BS2370. Except for special cases, long-term obligations are uncommon in banking. Exceptions may include banks specializing in bonds for mortgage loans. Other examples are intermediary equity capitalization using subordinated loans or convertible bonds. The discounted value of capital lease obligations should also be assigned to this account.

BS2390 Other Long-Term Liabilities

BS2390 Other Long-Term Liabilities includes any other long-term obligations that are not explicitly interest bearing. Details can be found in the explanations in the Industrial Format. This account also includes net obligations in the form of funds held in trust that must be reported in some countries.

BS2395 Customers' Acceptances

BS2395 Customers' Acceptances is the contra item to BS2195 Customers' Liabilities for Acceptances. As discussed under BS2195, items included vary, and adding them is not meaningful. In most cases, BS2195 Customers' Liabilities for Acceptances and BS2395 Customers' Acceptances will nearly match.

BS2399 Total Liabilities

Total liabilities, disclosed in account BS2399, are the sum of the following:

> BS2220 Total Deposits
> BS2270 Due to Banks and Other Short-Term Borrowing
> BS2275 Federal Funds Purchased and Securities Sold Under Repurchase
>   Agreements

BS2280 Short-Term Portion of Long-Term Borrowing
BS2290 Other Short-Term Liabilities
BS2370 Long-Term Borrowing
BS2390 Other Long-Term Liabilities
BS2395 Customers' Acceptances

5.2.5 Shareholders' Equity

Refer to the explanations in the Industrial Format for the following data items.

BS2410 Preferred Equity

BS2420 Minority Interest

BS2450 Share Capital and Share Premiums

BS2460 Retained Earnings

BS2470 (Treasury Stocks)

5.2.6 Reference Items

Loan Classification by Maturity

In this book, assets and liabilities have been organized by customer type, but they may also be classified by their remaining maturity, for example, or in other ways. Classification by maturity is widely used in German banks.

Sometimes, banks disclose a loan's original maturity instead of its remaining maturity. In such cases, reclassification is difficult and may require additional reference items. Loans classified by maturity are defined as follows:

BS2510 Short-Term Loans: Maturity of one year or less.

BS2512 Mid-Term Loans: Maturity of more than one year but not more than five years.

BS2515 Long-Term Loans: Maturity of more than five years.

Loan Classification by Type of Security

Consumer loans are usually secured by specific property but commercial loans are not. The following items should be isolated for future analysis:

BS2520 Real Estate Loans: Loans secured by real estate.

BS2522 Lease Financing Loans: Loans provided to finance leased assets. A bank is usually the lessor, and the lease is capitalized by the lessee.

BS2525 Foreign Loans

Foreign loans, loans provided to foreign customers, should be isolated in account BS2525 for analysis. A significant portion will be reported in foreign currencies. The fiscal year-end rate of exchange is the best rate to use for translation.

BS2529 Nonperforming Assets

BS2529 Nonperforming Assets includes all assets that do not earn competitive profits. Most should be loans in default on interest or principle payments, but investment assets may be included too.

Deposit Classification by Maturity

BS2610 Short-Term Deposits: Deposits with maturity of one year or less

BS2612 Mid-Term Deposits. Deposits with maturity of more than one year but no more than five years

BS2615 Long-Term Deposits: Deposits with maturity of more than five years

BS2625 Foreign Deposits

BS2625 Foreign Deposits includes deposits by foreign customers of which a significant portion will be reported in foreign currency. As in the case of foreign loans, the best exchange rate for translation is the fiscal year-end rate.

Minimum Capital Requirements by Cooke Committee

Because of the public nature of banking and the growing international competition among banks, in 1990 the Cooke Committee issued general guidelines regarding capital requirements.* The guidelines were adopted by banking regulators and have been implemented as of the 1992 fiscal year. Capital strength is measured by comparing assets weighted by risk factors. The assets include off-balance-sheet items and on-balance-sheet items.

The basis of capital limits the risks that banks can take in their asset portfolios. Major banks in many countries disclose such information.

BS2630 Core Capital (Tier 1)

BS2630 Core Capital, also known as Tier 1, includes common shareholders' equity, qualifying perpetual preferred stock, and minority interest in consolidated subsidiaries, less goodwill and any other disallowed intangibles for commercial banks. The sum of capital is compared with adjusted total assets. The internationally agreed-upon rate is 4 percent of adjusted total assets.

---

* These guidelines are also known as the Basle Capital Agreement. Volatility in the international banking system following the severe fluctuations in oil prices in the 1970s led to the creation of a new standing committee to study the stability of international banking. The Committee on Banking Regulations and Supervisory Practices was composed of senior banking regulators from G-10 countries. Its recommendations have been adopted, with local variations, by banking regulators around world. Capital adequacy ratios can be found in the annual reports of major international banks.

The definition of *core capital* for savings institutions is somewhat different. It includes common shareholders' equity, noncumulative perpetual preferred equity and surplus, and minority interest in consolidated subsidiaries less intangible assets other than purchased mortgage servicing rights. The minimum required rates of capital to adjusted total assets is 3 percent.

For savings institutions, tangible capital is separately defined as the core capital less any intangible assets. Its minimum requirement is 1.5 percent of adjusted total assets.

BS2632 Risk-Based Capital (Tier 1 + Tier 2)

Risk-based capital is disclosed in account BS2632. The risk-based capital ratio is the sum of the core capital (Tier 1) and supplementary capital (Tier 2) to adjusted total assets. Supplementary capital (Tier 2) includes perpetual preferred capital stocks ineligible for Tier 1, perpetual debt and mandatory convertible securities, qualifying senior and subordinated debt, redeemable preferred stocks, and loan loss reserves.

The minimum requirement set by U.S. regulators for the risk-based capital ratio was 8 percent in 1992. It is also the rate agreed upon internationally.

BS2635 Leverage Ratio

The leverage ratio, disclosed in account BS2635, is the percentage of Tier 1 capital of adjusted total assets for savings and loans institutions, which are unique to the United States. The minimum ratio was 3 percent in 1992.

Other Reference Items Regarding Long-Term Liabilities

The following are items, regarding BS2390 Other Long-Term Liabilities, designated as reference items because not all are applicable in every country. For example, pension reserves (account BS2660) are either not applicable or minimal in U.S. and U.K. companies, because all pension obligations are funded to outside trustees. However, companies in Japan have significant pension provisions for retirement and severance payments on their balance sheets. Refer to the explanations in the Industrial Format for details on the following accounts.

BS2660 Pension Reserves

BS2670 Deferred Tax Liabilities

BS2680 Non-Equity Reserves

BS2685 Investment Reserves

Long-term investment assets are usually valued at the lower of cost or market. However, in recent years the use of market value has become more prevalent. The market value approach was first adopted by financial service companies, and industrial companies used this system for all investments held for sale in 1994 in the United States. The unrealized gains or losses in investment assets are assigned to BS2460 Retained Earnings, as a part of shareholders' equity. The amount should be referred to BS2685 Investment Reserves.

BS2690 Goodwill Written Off

Refer to the explanations in the Industrial Format.

BS2695 Off-Balance Contingent Liabilities

Items in BS2195 Customers' Liabilities for Acceptances are not consistently defined. In some countries they are included as a part of total assets, and in others they are not. Even though a company may list several items, they may not be added because of the different risk levels involved. Those items not included as a part of total assets should be assigned to BS2695 Off-Balance Contingent Liabilities.

Stock-Related Reference Items

For a discussion of the following accounts, refer to the explanations in the Industrial Format.

BS2710 Number of Shares Outstanding

BS2720 Par Value

BS2730 Dividend Right Parity

BS2740 Voting Right Parity

BS2770 Number of Treasury Stocks

BS2800 Number of Employees

5.3 INSURANCE FORMAT

The major sources of revenue for insurance companies are premium income and investment income, as discussed in Chapter 4 in regard to the income statement. As a result, an insurance company's balance sheet has two distinctive groups of accounts. One is related to investing activities, and the other is made up of liabilities related to insurance operations.

Life insurance and non-life insurance are usually regulated by separate laws. When both types of insurance are offered by a single company, the financial statements for each type are completely distinct. Often, each line of business—for example, life, health, automobile, fire, and professional liabilities—is separated. Researching companies with multiple lines of businesses is not simple. It is not a matter of merely adding similar items to arrive at a total for the company. Moreover, individual earnings must be reconciled and transferred to the main financial statements.

Assets of insurance companies are mainly composed of investments, itemized in detail, which may include, for example, short-term investments, fixed income security investments, equity security investments, and loan investments. When multiple lines of business are operated by one organization, individual income statements are published in the annual reports. However, the balance sheets are often combined, because all the lines of business make similar investments.

Liabilities in insurance companies are essentially provisions for policyholders. They are distinctly separated between liabilities reasonably confirmed and those purely estimated. Liabilities in life insurance depend on actuarial tables involving complicated mathematical computations based on life expectancy.

Shareholders' equity in insurance companies is similar to that in other industries. However, mutual cooperative insurance companies cannot have any shareholders' equity. Their net assets (total assets less total liabilities) should be classified as policyholders' equity instead of shareholders' equity. In fact, most life insurance policies are sold by mutual cooperative companies, and, although they have no shareholders, they should not be excluded from analysis, because they represent a significant proportion of the industry.

BALANCE SHEET IN AN INSURANCE FORMAT

Sections	Data	Items
Current Assets	BS2010	Cash and Cash Equivalents
	BS2030	Net Receivables
	BS2020	Short-Term Investments
	BS2060	Loans and Mortgages
	BS2070	Fixed Income Securities
	BS2080	Equity Securities
	BS2090	Real Estate Investments
	BS2095	Other Investments
	BS2170	**Total Investments**
Noncurrent Assets	BS2130	Net Tangible Fixed Assets
	BS2180	Investments in Associated Companies
	BS2190	Intangibles and Other Assets
	BS2195	Segregated Accounts
	BS2199	**Total Assets**
Current Liabilities	BS2230	Reserve for Outstanding Claims and Losses
	BS2232	Premium Reserve
	BS2235	Reserve for Life Policy Benefits
	BS2237	Other Insurance Reserves
	BS2240	**Total Insurance Reserves**
	BS2270	Short-Term Borrowing
	BS2280	Short-Term Portion of Long-Term Borrowing
	BS2290	Other Short-Term Liabilities

(continued)

(continued) Noncurrent Liabilities	BS2370	Long-Term Borrowing
	BS2390	Other Long-Term Liabilities
	BS2395	Segregated Accounts
	BS2399	**Total Liabilities**
Shareholders' Equity	BS2410	Preferred Equity
	BS2420	Minority Interest
	BS2430	Policyholders' Equity
	BS2450	Share Capital and Share Premiums
	BS2460	Retained Earnings
	BS2470	(Treasury Stocks)
	BS2499	**Total Shareholders' Equity**
Reference Items	BS2540	Deferred Policy Acquisition Costs
	BS2640	Claims and Loss Reserve for Life
	BS2642	Claims and Loss Reserve for Non-Life
	BS2645	Premium Reserve for Life
	BS2647	Premium Reserve for Non-Life
	BS2650	Life Policy in Force
	BS2660	Pension Reserves
	BS2670	Deferred Tax Liabilities
	BS2680	Non-Equity Reserves
	BS2685	Investment Reserves
	BS2690	Goodwill Written Off
	BS2710	Number of Shares Outstanding
	BS2720	Par Value
	BS2730	Dividend Right Parity
	BS2740	Voting Right Parity
	BS2770	Number of Treasury Stocks
	BS2800	Number of Employees

5.3.1 Current Assets

The insurance industry, like other financial service industries, does not distinguish between current and non-current assets. However, assets that are convertible to cash in a reasonably short period are classified as current assets to make possible a comparison between financial services and industrial companies (i.e., an appropriate asset allocation among different sectors).

BS2010 Cash and Cash Equivalents

Refer to the explanations in the Industrial Format for details on account BS2010. The availability of cash is not a major concern to financial service companies, because most of their assets are readily convertible to cash within a reasonably short time.

BS2030 Net Receivables

In general, BS2030 Net Receivables includes all receivables directly related to a company's operating activities. The partners in the operating activities are policyholders, reinsurers, coinsurers, and underwriting agents.

Prepaid commissions to underwriting agents, however, are significant and are additionally disclosed as a separate item. These prepaid expenses should be included in BS2030 Net Receivables, rather than in BS2190 Intangibles and Other Assets, because they are directly related to the insurance business. In addition, the amount should be referred to BS2540 Deferred Policy Acquisition Costs. BS2030 Net Receivables also includes investment income receivables, because investment is an insurance company's operating activity.

BS2170 Total Investments

Total investments, assigned to account BS2170, are the sum of accounts BS2020 Short-Term Investments through BS2095 Other Investments. Investments are the largest component of an insurance company's assets. National regulations may vary but generally require conservative investments such as fixed income securities. The composition of these investment assets is important in measuring the stability of investment income in insurance companies.

In fact, a significant portion of the investments may be long-term even though they are readily marketable. All, however, are classified as current assets because they are an integral part of the insurance business.

Investment assets held by insurance companies that are available for sale are valued at market value in most countries. The unrealized gains or losses on marketable securities are included in IS1012 Trading Account Profit (Loss) in the income statement. Unrealized gains or losses from investments other than marketable securities are treated as shareholders' equity and should be referred to BS2685 Investment Reserves.

BS2020 Short-Term Investments. BS2020 Short-Term Investments includes all short-term investments in marketable equity securities, as well as debt securities that are to be turned over within a year. Marketable securities are valued at market value, and unrealized gains or losses are included in the trading account profit (loss) in the income statement.

BS2060 Loans and Mortgages. Loans and mortgages, disclosed in account BS2060, include loans to policyholders and other customers and are net of provisions for loan losses. Loans to policyholders are usually secured by policies, and mortgage loans may be secured by real estate.

BS2070 Fixed Income Securities. Investments in fixed income securities are most significant in the insurance business. These include publicly traded bonds, privately placed bonds, debentures, and long-term government securities, as well as investments in redeemable and nonredeemable preferred stocks, unless the preferred stocks participate with common stocks in dividend distribution. The classifications used by a specific company are usually not detailed.

BS2070 Fixed Income Securities also includes investments in loans, which are not itemized unless the amount of a particular loan is of major significance. In that case, the loan should be segregated and assigned to BS2060 Loans and Mortgages.

BS2080 Equity Securities. BS2080 Equity Securities includes all investments in equity securities, whether they are traded publicly or not. However, investments in associated companies representing a significant influence should be separated and disclosed in BS2180 Investments in Associated Companies. Investments in unconsolidated subsidiaries should also be classified as BS2180.

BS2090 Real Estate Investments. Insurance companies usually hold significant investments in real estate which, along with investments in fixed income securities, is a conservative option. BS2090 Real Estate Investments should include only income-producing real estate, although it is not always possible to distinguish between real estate held for investment purposes and real estate used for operations. When identifiable, real estate used as an operating fixed asset should be isolated and classified as BS2130 Net Tangible Fixed Assets. Real estate used for operating leases should also be isolated and included in account BS2130. Rental income from leased assets should be assigned in the income statement to IS1019 Other Operating Revenue, and depreciation expenses for those assets should be classified as IS1050 General and Administrative Expenses. The titles of assets under capital leases are, in effect, transferred to the lessees, and the leases should be classified as BS2060 Loans and Mortgages.

BS2095 Other Investments. Account BS2095 includes all other investment assets.

5.3.2 Noncurrent Assets

Further explanation of the following accounts may be found in the Industrial Format.

BS2130 Net Tangible Fixed Assets

BS2130 Net Tangible Fixed Assets includes all tangible fixed assets net of accumulated depreciation. This account also includes construction in progress, even though such assets ultimately will be transferred to BS2090 Real Estate Investments when completed.

BS2180 Investments in Associated Companies

Equity securities held for other than purely investment purposes should be included in BS2180 Investments in Associated Companies. These are usually valued under the Equity Method, and the equity earnings should be classified in the income statement as IS1130 Loss (Gain) from Associated Companies.

BS2190 Intangibles and Other Assets

BS2190 Intangibles and Other Assets includes intangible and all other assets. Deferred tax assets, assuming that the net of deferred tax assets minus deferred tax liabilities is positive, should be included here. However, investment income receivables should be assigned to BS2030 Net Receivables, because investment is the main operating activity of insurance companies.

BS2195 Segregated Accounts

Many insurance companies manage assets for clients. The commissions and fees earned in the process should be classified as IS1019 Other Operating Revenue after netting all related expenses. These assets are assigned to BS2195 Segregated Accounts.

Whether the segregated funds held on behalf of a trust qualify as an insurance company's assets is arguable. The answer depends on the degree of risk the company assumes. If the performance of the investment puts the insurance company at significant risk, the funds qualify as the company's assets. Otherwise, the funds should be assigned to account BS2195. Commissions and fees earned by managing the funds should be assigned to IS1019 Other Operating Revenue after netting all related expenses.

BS2195 should be a contra item with BS2395 Segregated Accounts. The investment assets are kept within the company for the fees earned and should be differentiated from other assets.

BS2199 Total Assets

Total assets, disclosed in account BS2199, are the sum of the following accounts:

BS2010 Cash and Cash Equivalents
BS2030 Net Receivables
BS2170 Total Investments
BS2130 Net Tangible Fixed Assets
BS2180 Investments in Associated Companies
BS2190 Intangibles and Other Assets
BS2195 Segregated Accounts

5.3.3 Current Liabilities

The difficulty in defining current assets is mirrored by the difficulty in defining current liabilities. A life insurance company's operating cycle is a long one. In general, all insurance-related liabilities are classified as operating liabilities, and other liabilities are divided into short- and long-term by the one-year rule.

BS2240 Total Insurance Reserves

All insurance-related liabilities are called *insurance reserves,* which are typically operating reserves. These amounts are disclosed in BS2240 Total Insurance Reserves.

BS2230 Reserve for Outstanding Claims and Losses. BS2230 Reserve for Outstanding Claims and Losses includes all payables related to known claims and losses while they are being estimated or, if an amount has been confirmed, until it is paid. There may also be payables resulting from unreported accidents. These liabilities are equivalent to accounts payable in industrial companies. The amounts for life and non-life businesses should be referred to BS2640 Claims and Loss Reserve for Life and BS2642 Claims and Loss Reserve for Non-Life, respectively.

BS2232 Premium Reserve. Premiums paid by policyholders are earned as time passes. At the end of any given accounting period, a certain proportion of the premiums have yet to be earned. This unearned portion is called a *premium reserve*. It is also known as an unearned premium, incurred premium, or premium carryover and should be included in BS2232 Premium Reserve. The premium reserve is significant in non-life insurance policies, in which revenue is recognized by the passage of time. The amounts for life and non-life businesses should be referred to BS2645 Premium Reserve for Life and BS2647 Premium Reserve for Non-Life, respectively.

BS2235 Reserve for Life Policy Benefits. BS2235 Reserve for Life Policy Benefits represents a major liability in life insurance. The liabilities are computed by actuarial tables, based on the life expectancy of policyholders and the policy amount in force. All expected future payments are discounted to current value and disclosed as a reserve. These reserves are known as a mathematical reserve in Europe, because they are mathematically computed by the actuarial tables. The liabilities are significantly long-term in nature but are classified as current liabilities because an operating cycle in life insurance is so long.

BS2237 Other Insurance Reserves. BS2237 Other Insurance Reserves includes any other liabilities related to operating activities. Liabilities directly related to insurance are itemized in the preceding paragraphs.

BS2270 Short-Term Borrowing

BS2270 Short-Term Borrowing includes short-term borrowing from banks and any other financial institutions, such as bank overdrafts.

BS2280 Short-Term Portion of Long-Term Borrowing

BS2280 Short-Term Portion of Long-Term Borrowing includes the short-term portion of any long-term borrowing and the current portion of capital (finance) lease obligations.

BS2290 Other Short-Term Liabilities

BS2290 Other Short-Term Liabilities includes all other short-term liabilities that do not bear any explicit interest obligations.

5.3.4 Noncurrent Liabilities

BS2370 Long-Term Borrowing

For a discussion of account BS2370, refer to the explanations in the Industrial Format.

BS2390 Other Long-Term Liabilities

Refer to the Industrial Format for a discussion of account BS2390. The detailed information included here should be referred to BS2660 Pension Reserves, BS2670 Deferred Tax Liabilities, or BS2680 Non-Equity Reserves if applicable.

BS2395 Segregated Accounts

There are other liabilities indirectly related to the insurance business. For example, trusted investment activities for annuities and pensions are considered operating activities, and the duration of such investments is similar to that of life policies. If an insurance company takes substantial risks in investments, they should be added to the company's other itemized securities in BS2170 Total Investments. But when few risks are taken and only commissions are earned on the investing activities, the investments should be classified as BS2195 Segregated Accounts and the contra item is established in the liability section, BS2395 Segregated Accounts.

BS2399 Total Liabilities

Total liabilities, assigned to account BS2399, are the sum of the following accounts:

> BS2240 Total Insurance Reserves
> BS2270 Short-Term Borrowing
> BS2280 Short-Term Portion of Long-Term Borrowing
> BS2290 Other Short-Term Liabilities
> BS2370 Long-Term Borrowing
> BS2390 Other Long-Term Liabilities
> BS2395 Segregated Accounts

5.3.5 Shareholders' Equity

Where no comment is provided for a specific account, please refer to the Industrial Format section. Shareholders' equity includes all of a company's residual value. The equity holders are preferred shareholders, minority shareholders in consolidated companies, policyholders, and common shareholders.

BS2410 Preferred Equity

BS2420 Minority Interest

BS2430 Policyholders' Equity

BS2430 Policyholders' Equity is particular to life insurance companies, specifically mutual cooperative insurance companies. In most countries, life insurance companies cannot distribute all residual earnings to shareholders as dividends because of government restrictions. Income in excess of all required expenses is held for future unexpected accidents or is immediately returned to policyholders.

Excess earnings immediately returned to policyholders are known as dividends to policyholders. However, *dividend* is used exclusively to define returns to shareholders in analysis of equity securities. Therefore, in the income statement dividends to policyholders are assigned to IS1033 Dividends to Policyholders as operating expenses. They may be regarded as adjustments to premium, but the company takes all responsibility for managing the premium and excess earnings are generated for the benefit of policyholders.

If excess earnings are accumulated, they should be assigned to BS2430 Policyholders' Equity and should not be classified as a part of common equity. For mutual insurance companies without stocks, all residual value should be classified as BS2430 Policyholders' Equity.

BS2450 Share Capital and Share Premiums

BS2460 Retained Earnings

Refer to the explanations in the Industrial Format. Unrealized gains or losses on investment assets are recognized as income or loss in the insurance industry and are accumulated as a part of shareholders' equity. They should be included in BS2460 Retained Earnings and referred to BS2685 Investment Reserves.

BS2470 (Treasury Stocks)

BS2499 Total Shareholders' Equity

Account BS2499 includes the sum of the residual value of all equity holders, that is, BS2410 Preferred Equity, BS2420 Minority Interest, BS2430 Policyholders' Equity, BS2450 Share Capital and Share Premiums, BS2460 Retained Earnings, and BS2470 (Treasury Stocks).

5.3.6 Reference Items

Insurance Business Related Reference Items

BS2540 Deferred Policy Acquisition Costs

When insurance policies are sold by agents, all commissions are paid to the agents immediately but are expended as the underlying premiums are earned. The prepaid commissions should be assigned to BS2540 Deferred Policy Acquisition Costs, which is included in BS2030 Net Receivables.

BS2640 Claims and Loss Reserve for Life

The reference item BS2640, which is included in BS2230 Reserve for Outstanding Claims and Losses, represents all claims and loss reserves for life insurance.

BS2642 Claims and Loss Reserve for Non-Life

The reference item BS2642, which is included in BS2230 Reserve for Outstanding Claims and Losses, represents all claims and loss reserves for non-life insurance.

BS2645 Premium Reserve for Life

The reference item BS2645, which is included in BS2232 Premium Reserve, represents premium reserves for life insurance.

BS2647 Premium Reserve for Non-Life

The reference item BS2647, which is included in BS2232 Premium Reserve, represents premium reserves for non-life insurance.

BS2650 Life Policy in Force

The reference item BS2650 includes the aggregate of life policies in force, which is the amount to be paid if the conditions designated by contract occur for all policyholders at the same time.

General Reference Items

Refer to the explanations in the Industrial Format for details on the following accounts.

BS2660 Pension Reserves

BS2670 Deferred Tax Liabilities

BS2680 Non-Equity Reserves

BS2685 Investment Reserves

BS2690 Goodwill Written Off

Reference Items for (Multiple) Shares

Refer to the explanations in the Industrial Format for details on the following accounts.

BS2710 Number of Shares Outstanding

BS2720 Par Value

BS2730 Dividend Right Parity

BS2740 Voting Right Parity

BS2770 Number of Treasury Stocks

BS2800 Number of Employees

5.4 OTHER FINANCIAL SERVICES FORMAT

All financial services other than commercial banking and insurance should be compiled in the Other Financial Services Format. These businesses include personal lending, commercial lending, real estate leasing, equipment leasing, financial holding companies, security brokerages, investment management, and any other financial services.

Because many different businesses are included in one format, it is difficult to illustrate all possible data items reflecting the particulars of each. As for the income statement, each data component should be analyzed for the balance sheet in terms of its benefit to analysis.

All businesses that use this format are assumed to be financial services, which means their income and expenses are sensitive to interest rates and force the balance sheet to emphasize investment assets. It is also assumed that these businesses take no deposits or only minimal deposits from customers, which distinguishes them from banks.

BALANCE SHEET IN AN OTHER FINANCIAL SERVICES FORMAT

Sections	Data Items	
Current Assets	BS2010	Cash and Cash Equivalents
	BS2030	Net Receivables
	BS2020	Short-term Investments
	BS2035	Federal Funds Sold and Securities Purchased Under Resale Agreements
	BS2055	**Total Loans**
	BS2057	Loan Loss Reserves
	BS2060	**Net Loans**
	BS2090	Real Estate Investments
	BS2092	Investments in Securities
	BS2095	Other Investments
	BS2170	**Total Investments**
Noncurrent Assets	BS2130	Net Tangible Fixed Assets
	BS2180	Investments in Associated Companies
	BS2190	Intangibles and Other Assets
	BS2195	Custody Securities
	BS2199	**Total Assets**
Current Liabilities	BS2220	Total Deposits
	BS2270	Short-Term Borrowing
	BS2275	Federal Funds Purchased and Securities Sold Under Repurchase Agreements
	BS2280	Short-Term Portion of Long-Term Borrowing
	BS2290	Other Short-Term Liabilities

(continued)

(continued) Noncurrent Equity Liabilities	BS2370 BS2390 BS2395 BS2399	Long-Term Borrowing Other Long-Term Liabilities Customers' Liabilities **Total Liabilities**
Shareholders'	BS2410 BS2420 BS2450 BS2460 BS2470 BS2499	Preferred Equity Minority Interest Share Capital and Share Premiums Retained Earnings (Treasury Stocks) **Total Shareholders' Equity**
Reference Items	BS2660 BS2670 BS2680 BS2690 BS2695 BS2710 BS2720 BS2730 BS2740 BS2770 BS2800	Pension Reserves Deferred Tax Liabilities Non-Equity Reserves Goodwill Written Off Off-Balance Contingent Liabilities Number of Shares Outstanding Par Value Dividend Right Parity Voting Right Parity Number of Treasury Stocks Number of Employees

5.4.1 Current Assets

BS2010 Cash and Cash Equivalents

BS2010 Cash and Cash Equivalents includes cash on hand and investments to be converted to cash within approximately three months. Refer to explanations in the Industrial Format.

BS2030 Net Receivables

Account BS2030 includes all receivables from customers related to operating activities net of any provision for doubtful accounts. Operating activities should be defined by the nature of the particular industry.

BS2170 Total Investments

Account BS2170 is the sum of BS2020 Short-Term Investments, BS2035 Federal Funds Sold and Securities Purchased Under Resale Agreements, BS2060 Net Loans, BS2090 Real Estate Investments, BS2092 Investments in Securities, and BS2095 Other Investments. As discussed earlier, investments in insurance companies are consistently segregated and their distribution is similar because the level of risk taken by insurance companies is similar. However, investment assets in financial services are as diverse as the many businesses included in this category and are distributed according to the particular businesses.

BS2020 Short-Term Investments. For a discussion of account BS2020, refer to the explanations in the Banking Format.

BS2035 Federal Funds Sold and Securities Purchased Under Resale Agreements. Security brokerage activities require a company to hold a significant number of securities for customers, and they should be included in account BS2035. These assets should also be differentiated from BS2195 Custody Securities, for which the company takes no risk.

BS2055 Total Loans. Loans are classified as one line item (account BS2055) in this format, because most financial services companies lending money to customers are restricted to their specific type of lending.

BS2057 Loan Loss Reserves. For a discussion of account BS2057, refer to the explanations in the Banking Format.

BS2060 Net Loans. Net loans, assigned to account BS2060, are calculated by subtracting BS2057 Loan Loss Reserves from BS2055 Total Loans.

BS2090 Real Estate Investments. BS2090 Real Estate Investments includes investments in real estate and land purchased for other than a company's own uses. The real estate may be purchased for rental purposes or for future profit from its sale. Income from real estate investments should be classified in the income statement as IS1013 Income from Real Estate Investments. Leasing and rental companies typically realize their major income from this source.

BS2092 Investments in Securities. BS2092 Investments in Securities includes all investments in equity securities and fixed income securities other than short-term investments. Income from such investments should be classified in the income statement as IS1014 Investment Income after directly related investment expenses are deducted.

BS2095 Other Investments. Account BS2095 includes all other investments.

5.4.2 Noncurrent Assets

Where no comment is provided for a specific account, refer to the Industrial Format section.

BS2130 Net Tangible Fixed Assets

BS2180 Investments in Associated Companies

For a discussion of account BS2180, refer to the explanations in the Industrial Format. Any company may invest significantly in other companies. Undistributed earnings from subsidiaries under the Equity Method should be included here.

For financial holding companies, actually distributed dividend income should be included in the income statement in IS1014 Investment Income, and the undistributed earnings are accumulated in this account according to the percentage of ownership.

BS2190 Intangibles and Other Assets

BS2195 Custody Securities

Account BS2195 Custody Securities is unique to security brokerage firms that trade securities for customers. This is a contra item to BS2395 Customers' Liabilities.

BS2199 Total Assets

Total assets, disclosed in account BS2199, are the sum of the following:

BS2010 Cash and Cash Equivalents
BS2030 Net Receivables
BS2170 Total Investments
BS2130 Net Tangible Fixed Assets
BS2180 Investments in Associated Companies
BS2190 Intangibles and Other Assets
BS2195 Custody Securities

5.4.3 Current Liabilities

Where no comment is provided for a specific account, refer to the Industrial Format section.

BS2220 Total Deposits

For a discussion of account BS2220, refer to the explanations in the Banking Format. As noted in the Banking Format, deposits from customers are the major criterion for the classification of commercial banking. However, if the deposits are only a minor financing source, the company should be classified as a financial service other than banking, and the minor deposits should be assigned here.

BS2270 Short-Term Borrowing

BS2275 Federal Funds Purchased and Securities Sold Under Repurchase Agreements

Account BS2275 applies to companies with security brokerage activities and is a contra item to BS2035 Federal Funds Sold and Securities Purchased Under Resale Agreements. However, these liabilities should also be differentiated from customers' liabilities, account BS2395, on which the company takes no risk.

BS2280 Short-Term Portion of Long-Term Borrowing

BS2290 Other Short-Term Liabilities

5.4.4 Noncurrent Liabilities

Where no comment is provided for a specific account, refer to the Industrial Format section.

BS2370 Long-Term Borrowing

In other financial service businesses the nature of loans may not differ from those in other industries, but the purpose of financing is quite different for this industry group which relies on long-term borrowing as its financing source. In fact, the definition of financial services is that their assets and major income sources are sensitive to interest rates.

BS2390 Other Long-Term Liabilities

BS2395 Customers' Liabilities

Account BS2395 is a contra item to BS2195 Custody Securities. Custody securities are unique to the security brokerage industry. However, customers' liabilities exclude contingent liabilities not shown on the face of the balance sheet. They are assigned to BS2695 Off-Balance Contingent Liabilities. Reporting practices regarding which items are included in the body of the balance sheet differ by country and should be considered in analysis.

BS2399 Total Liabilities

BS2399 Total Liabilities is the sum of the following:

BS2220 Total Deposits
BS2270 Short-Term Borrowing
BS2275 Federal Funds Sold and Securities Purchased Under Resale Agreements
BS2280 Short-Term Portion of Long-Term Borrowing
BS2290 Other Short-Term Liabilities
BS2370 Long-Term Borrowing
BS2390 Other Long-Term Liabilities
BS2395 Customers' Liabilities

5.4.5 Shareholders' Equity

Refer to the explanations in the Industrial Format for details on the following items.

BS2410 Preferred Equity

BS2420 Minority Interest

BS2450 Share Capital and Share Premiums

BS2460 Retained Earnings

BS2470 (Treasury Stocks)

BS2499 Total Shareholders' Equity

5.4.6 Reference Items

Refer to the explanations in the Industrial Format for details on the following items.

BS2660 Pension Reserves

BS2670 Deferred Tax Liabilities

BS2680 Non-Equity Reserves

BS2690 Goodwill Written Off

BS2695 Off-Balance Contingent Liabilities

For a discussion of account BS2695, refer to the explanations in the Banking Format.

Reference Items for (Multiple) Shares

Refer to the explanations in industrial section for details on the following accounts.

BS2710 Number of Shares Outstanding

BS2720 Par Value

BS2730 Dividend Right Parity

BS2740 Voting Right Parity

BS2770 Number of Treasury Stocks

BS2800 Number of Employees

Cash Flow Statement 6

As discussed in Chapter 3, corporate use of the cash flow statement has a short history as compared with the income statement and the balance sheet. This statement has been known by different names as it gradually developed in response to market needs. The purpose of tracking the flow of cash has also changed over time. Thus, because its importance is still not universally recognized, use of the cash flow statement varies.

There is nevertheless, a growing consensus on both the use of the cash flow statement as a measure of a company's cash position and the format in which it should be presented. The cash flow statement consists of two sections, Cash from Operating Activities and Cash from Nonoperating Activities, each of which has two separate reporting formats, as shown in the following table.

STRUCTURE OF THE CASH FLOW STATEMENT		
Sections	**Reporting Formats**	
Operating Activities	**Indirect Approach** Cash from operations starting from net income	**Direct Approach** Cash from operations starting from cash receipts from operations
Nonoperating Activities	**Investing/Financing** Impacts on cash from nonoperating activities by separation between the changes in assets and the changes in liabilities	**Sources/Uses** Impacts on cash from nonoperating activities by separation between increase in cash and decrease in cash.
Focus of the Statement	• Cash and Cash Equivalents or • Working Capital (Current Assets − Current Liabilities) or • Net Liquid Assets or Net Borrowing	

The Operating Activities section reports the cash generated and cash spent by a company's operations, using either the Direct Approach or the Indirect Approach. The latter method is used in most countries.

The Nonoperating Activities section divides the flow of cash into two subcategories, which vary. The subcategories used in most countries are cash flows from Investing Activities and cash flows from Financing Activities. In Europe, the subcategories more often used are Total Sources of Cash and Total Uses of Cash. Any combination of choices, one from the Operating Activities section and another from the Nonoperating Activities section, is possible.

The cash flow statement may focus on cash and its equivalents, on working capital, or on net liquid assets/net borrowing. The focus on cash and its equivalents dominates in countries where merger and acquisition activities are common, but many companies still concentrate on working capital. U.K. companies generally used net liquid assets or net borrowing (cash + short-term investments − short-term borrowing) but have switched in recent years to an emphasis on investing/financing, as in the United States and Canada.

Reporting requirements for the cash flow statement around the world are inconsistent. The United States and the United Kingdom require such a statement as part of a company's financial statements. Many companies wishing to appear attractive to capital markets provide a cash flow statement even when they are not required to do so.

For banks and other financial service companies, a cash flow statement is unimportant. Most of their assets consist of cash or cash equivalents, and their cash positions and need for cash to pay interest or to purchase capital is irrelevant in evaluating their performances.

6.1 INDUSTRIAL FORMAT

The development of the cash flow statement has been spurred by the accounting standards established in the United States and the United Kingdom to meet the needs of a capital market faced with frequent mergers and acquisitions. In both countries, companies on the market with excess cash or substantial cash-generating capacity are often viewed as desirable investments.

Capital markets with sufficient resources, such as the United States, concentrate on a company's marketing aspects rather than its production capabilities because the ability to generate cash from operating activities is crucial to survival. If a company generates enough cash for reinvestment in production facilities, in addition to cash needs for interest and dividend payments, it is regarded as successful. Until the 1960s, the focus was on working capital, but determining the liquidity of the working capital was a matter of trial and error. Working capital does not provide a company sufficient flexibility when cash is needed.

Because of the two different computing methods, formats for both have been designed for data compilation, and the one provided by the specific company under analysis should be used. The net result can be aggregated in CF3099 Cash from Operations. In practice, if a company uses the Direct Approach, the Indirect Approach also is reported. Both sets of information may then be collected.

Many companies do not start the cash flow statement with net income. Commonwealth countries, for example, often start with trading profits. In such cases, use account CF3010 for trading profits, and assign any nonoperating cash

CASH FROM OPERATING ACTIVITIES IN AN INDUSTRIAL FORMAT		
Approach	**Data Items**	
Indirect Approach	CF3010	Net Income
	CF3020	Depreciation and Amortization
	CF3030	Other Non-Cash Adjustments
	CF3040	Changes in Non-Cash Working Capital
	CF3099	**Cash from Operations**
Direct Approach	CF3050	Cash Receipts from Sales
	CF3060	Cash Disbursement for Purchases
	CF3070	Income Tax Paid
	CF3080	Other Cash Receipts and Disbursements
	CF3099	**Cash from Operations**

activities that appear below the trading profits, as well as non-cash operating activities, to account CF3030. In general, CF3099 Cash from Operations is important, but how it was derived is unimportant for analysis.

In fact, the cash from operations is slightly misleading in the format used in the United States. The cash flow statement starts with Net Income, and adjustments are made for non-cash activities, as well as for Changes in Non-Cash Working Capital. This means that Cash from Operations includes cash activities from nonoperating activities such as interest received, interest payment, or cash from extraordinary activities.

Such concerns are reflected in the format established by Financial Reporting Standard (FRS) 1 in the United Kingdom. Based on FRS 1, Cash Flow from Operating Activities starts with Operating Profit and is adjusted by non-cash movements for the operating profit such as depreciation, exchange adjustments, provisions, and charges in working capital. Cash Inflow from Operating Activities is further adjusted, by Income/Expenses from Financing Activities, such as interest received/paid, dividends received/paid, and another category disclosing payment of domestic and foreign taxes, before considering the cash from investing and financing activities.

These approaches show that there is no absolutely right or wrong, better or worse method. At first glance, the U.K. version of "Cash from Operations" seems more refined than its U.S. counterpart. But dividends paid to shareholders also are reflected in the U.K.'s Cash from Operations whereas in most other countries this is regarded as a financing activity. For analysis, the most important rule is to decide on a format and maintain it consistently.

CF3099 Cash from Operations differs somewhat, depending on the format used in the nonoperating section. In the Sources/Uses Approach, CF3099 Cash from Operations includes changes in short-term investment and short-time borrowing. In this approach, both are classified as components of working capital, and this classification suggests that the Sources/Uses Approach was originally designed to reveal changes in working capital. In contrast, as an examination of the following table reveals, changes in short-term investment and short-term borrowing are classified as nonoperating capital sources in the Investing/

Financing Approach. Otherwise, the difference between the two formats lies only in the one's segregation of functions and the other's segregation of cash inflows and outflows.

CASH FROM NONOPERATING ACTIVITIES IN AN INDUSTRIAL FORMAT

Approaches	Data Items	
Investing/ Financing Approach	**Investing Activities**	
	CF3110	Disposal of Fixed Assets
	CF3120	(Capital Expenditure)
	CF3130	Disposal of Long-Term Investments
	CF3140	(Purchase of Long-Term Investments)
	CF3150	Decrease (Increase) in Short-Term Investments
	CF3180	Other Investing Activities
	CF3189	**Cash from Investing Activities**
	Financing Activities	
	CF3210	(Dividends Paid)
	CF3220	Increase (Decrease) in Short-Term Borrowing
	CF3230	Increase in Long-Term Borrowing
	CF3240	(Decrease in Long-Term Borrowing)
	CF3250	Increase in Capital Stocks
	CF3260	(Decrease in Capital Stocks)
	CF3280	Other Financing Activities
	CF3289	**Cash from Financing Activities**
	CF3490	**Net Changes in Cash**
Sources/ Uses Approach	**Sources**	
	CF3310	Disposal of Fixed Assets
	CF3320	Disposal of Long-Term Investments
	CF3330	Increase in Long-Term Borrowing
	CF3340	Increase in Capital Stocks
	CF3380	Other Sources
	CF3389	**Total Sources**
	Uses or Applications	
	CF3410	Dividends Paid
	CF3420	Capital Expenditures
	CF3430	Purchase of Long-Term Investments
	CF3440	Decrease in Long-Term Borrowing
	CF3450	Decrease in Capital Stocks
	CF3480	Other Uses
	CF3489	**Total Uses**
	CF3490	**Increase (Decrease) in Funds**
Reference Items	CF3495	Definition of Funds
	CF3500	Cash Payments for Interest Expenses

6.1.1 Operating Activities

Indirect Approach

CF3010 Net Income. In using the Indirect Approach with cash from operations, the statement begins with the net income in the income statement, and adds back all non-cash activities to derive cash from operations. Depreciation and amortization are isolated in account CF3020, and the remaining non-cash activities are combined in CF3030 Other Non-Cash Adjustments.

However, the starting line is not necessarily the net income, but can also be any other line item between operating income and net income. In that case, CF3010 requires an appropriate adjustment in its title. CF3030 will be the sum of non-cash activities above the line item chosen, and cash activities below the line chosen, except for CF3020 Depreciation and Amortization. Of course, there is a possibility that the researcher's classification of operating and nonoperating activities may be inconsistent with the numbers reported by the company in the income statement.

CF3020 Depreciation and Amortization. Depreciation of fixed assets and amortization of intangible assets are the major non-cash expenses in the computation of net income. Investments in a given year are depreciated or amortized over the useful life of the assets. Depreciation expenses for tangible fixed assets are collected in IS1540 Depreciation Expenses. Both items are used for various ratio computations for analysis in Chapter 11 "Research Procedures." Depreciation expenses also include depletion of consumable tangible fixed assets such as minerals in mining or nuclear bars at electric utilities.

CF3030 Other Non-Cash Adjustments. Account CF3030 includes all other non-cash adjustments for the computation of net income. There are two main categories. One, non-cash expenses and income, includes the following:

Pension provision charges
Charges to provision for doubtful accounts
Deferred tax expenses
Equity earnings from investments in associate companies
Reversal of write-down of investments
Non-cash extraordinary items
Minority interests

The other category of adjustments, to avoid double accounting, includes the gain or loss from the disposal of fixed assets. For data compilation purposes, any positive or negative impacts on cash should be clearly noted.

An Example of Double Accounting

When a company sells equipment with a gross value of 10,000, and an accumulated depreciation of 8,000, for 3,000, the following entries should be made.

(continued)

(continued)

Cash	3,000	
(Debit) Accumulated Depreciation	8,000	
(Credit) Equipment		10,000
Gain from sale of equipment		1,000

Net income for the company already includes the gain of 1,000. When a cash flow statement is prepared, an additional 3,000 in cash receipts is included as a sale of fixed assets in Investing Activities or Sources. Thus, a total of 4,000 in cash is added by the transaction. Because, in fact, only 3,000 in cash was received, the 1,000 must be deducted from net income to arrive at cash from operations. The opposite procedure is used when a loss occurs.

CF3040 Changes in Non-Cash Working Capital. Account CF3040 applies only when the defined funds in CF3490, the last line of the cash flow statement, are less encompassing than working capital. For example, if CF3490 is defined as "change in cash," changes in working capital (other than cash) affect cash. When accounts receivable increase, cash decreases, and when accounts payable increase, cash increases.

Items that increase cash, based on the balance sheet designed for this book, include the following:

Decrease in accounts receivable
Decrease in inventory
Decrease in other current assets
Increase in accounts payable
Increase in other current liabilities

Items that decrease cash include the following:

Increase in accounts receivable
Increase in inventory
Increase in other current assets
Decrease in accounts payable
Decrease in other current liabilities

For a discussion of changes in short-term investments and short-term borrowing, see CF3099 Cash from Operations.

When the statement focuses on working capital, many companies additionally provide a reconciliation of the working capital. In this case, the working capital basis can be converted to a cash basis by isolating the changes in non-cash working capital and assigning them to CF3040 Changes in Non-Cash Working Capital.

Companies in countries where a cash flow statement is not required voluntarily disclose an equivalent statement, but their reporting formats vary. Often, sources and uses from operating activities and from nonoperating activities are mixed and both sides are balanced. It is necessary to reconfigure irregular formats into a standard format to make them useful for purposes of comparison. First, the focus of the cash flow statement must be determined, and then the statement can be reorganized into operating and nonoperating activities. When possible, it is best to focus on cash for worldwide comparison.

Direct Approach

CF3050 Cash Receipts from Sales. In using the Direct Approach to arrive at CF3099 Cash from Operations, the gross cash receipts from sales are assigned to this account. The procedure that follows should be used:

	Beginning balance of accounts receivable
+	Sales for the period
−	Ending balance of accounts receivable
−	Accounts receivable written off

CF3060 Cash Disbursement for Purchases. Used only in the Direct Approach is CF3060 Cash Disbursement for Purchases. The total cash payments for purchase of manufacturing resources should be assigned to this account. The following procedure should be used:

	Ending balance of inventory
+	Beginning balance of accounts payable
+	Cost of goods sold
−	Depreciation and amortization
−	Beginning balance of inventory
−	Ending balance of accounts payable

CF3070 Income Tax Paid. Despite differences of opinion as to whether income tax expenses are operating activities, income taxes paid for the period should be assigned to account CF3070.

CF3080 Other Cash Receipts and Disbursements. This line, account CF3080, includes all other operating cash disbursements. The procedures that follow should be used:

	Beginning accrued expenses
+	Operating expenses
−	Beginning prepaid expenses
−	Ending accrued expenses payable
+	Interest and dividend received
−	Interest paid

CF3099 Cash from Operations. Cash from Operations is the sum of either CF3010 Net Income, CF3020 Depreciation and Amortization, CF3030 Other Non-Cash Adjustments, and CF3040 Changes in Non-Cash Working Capital, or the sum of CF3050 Cash Receipts from Sales, CF3060 Cash Disbursement for Purchases, CF3070 Income Tax Paid, and CF3080 Other Cash Receipts and Disbursements, depending on the approach used by the company. As mentioned earlier, when the Direct Approach is used, information for the Indirect Approach is also disclosed. Then both sets of information may be collected and verified.

The segregation of operating and nonoperating activities should be approached carefully. A number of confusing items include the following:

- An increase in minority interests can result from two factors. One is an increase in the minority shareholders' portion of a subsidiary's earnings for the year. This increase in minority interests is a non-cash adjustment and should be added to CF3030 Other Non-Cash Adjustments. The other factor is an increase in capital provided by minority shareholders, which means that the parent company sold some of its shares in the subsidiary to minority shareholders. In this case, the increase in minority interests should be classified as CF3280 Other Financing Activities or as CF3380 Other Sources.

- Net cash results from discontinued operations are essentially nonoperating activities that are classified as extraordinary items in the income statement. In the income statement, the net results often are disclosed between the operating and nonoperating section. Depending on the approach, they should be included either in CF3030 Other Non-cash Adjustments or in CF3080 Other Cash Receipts and Disbursements.

- Taxation is often classified as a financing activity in Commonwealth countries, because taxes are treated as a distribution similar to dividends paid to shareholders. This reflects the view of government as a profit-sharing partner because it provides infrastructure. For comparative analysis, researchers must make a decision on whether to treat taxes as operating or nonoperating and to follow this determination consistently.

6.1.2 Nonoperating Activities in the Investing/Financing Approach

Investing Activities

Nonoperating investing activities are the changes in noncurrent assets as described in the following paragraphs.

CF3110 Disposal of Fixed Assets. Gross cash receipts from the disposal of fixed assets, including assets in discontinued operations and leased assets, should be included in account CF3110. This is always a positive number, and cash will increase by this amount.

CF3120 Capital Expenditure. Capital expenditure includes cash payments for the purchase of tangible fixed assets. This account, CF3120, will be useful in measuring the excess cash available to a company for expansion. This is always a negative number. Cash will decrease by this amount.

CF3130 Disposal of Long-Term Investments. Account CF3130 reflects the proceeds from the sale of long-term investment assets, including the sale of investments in associated companies. However, decreases in investment in associated companies (by equity earnings = excess dividend payment or loss in specific year) are non-cash adjustments assigned to CF3030 Other Non-Cash Adjustments. The classification should be consistent with the classification on the balance sheet. If subsidiaries are consolidated by a parent company, changes on the balance sheet should be reflected by changes in the individual assets and liabilities. However, U.K. companies disclose the sale and acquisition of subsidiaries as separate lines. This causes confusion in the cash flow statement. The best way to incorporate the disposal of subsidiaries is to include them in CF3130 Disposal of Long-term Investments. This is always a positive number. Cash will increase by this amount.

CF3140 Purchase of Long-Term Investments. Account CF3140 includes cash payments for the purchase of long-term investments, including investments in subsidiaries. However, an increase in investments in associated companies (resulting from equity earnings of undistributed earnings in associated companies) should be treated as a non-cash adjustment (CF3030). This is a negative number. Cash will decrease by this amount.

CF3150 Decrease (Increase) in Short-Term Investments. All changes in short-term investments except cash equivalents should be included in account CF3150. Cash equivalents are defined as highly liquid assets with a maturity of less than three months.

CF3180 Other Investing Activities. Net changes in noncurrent assets other than tangible fixed assets and long-term investments should be included in account CF3180.

CF3189 Cash from Investing Activities. Cash from Investing Activities, disclosed in account CF3189, is the sum of CF3110 Disposal of Fixed Assets, CF3120 Capital Expenditure, CF3130 Disposal of Long-Term Investments, CF3140 Purchase of Long-Term Investments, CF3150 Decrease (Increase) in Short-Term Investments, and CF3180 Other Investing Activities.

Financing Activities

Nonoperating financing activities are basically the changes in noncurrent liabilities and shareholders' equity.

CF3210 Dividends Paid. Dividends Paid (account CF3210) includes total cash dividend payments for preferred as well as common stocks paid in the previous period. In contrast, Dividends Declared are assigned to IS1310 Cash Dividends to Preferred Stocks, and IS1320 Cash Dividends to Common Stocks. The difference arises because dividends are paid only after their approval at a shareholders' meeting, which may be held six to eight months after the fiscal year end. This is always a negative number. Cash will decrease by this amount.

Dividends paid by subsidiaries to minority shareholders are not treated as dividends in this book. The dividends paid to minority shareholders should be classified as CF3280 Other Financing Activities.

CF3220 Increase (Decrease) in Short-Term Borrowing. Account CF3180 includes all changes in short-term borrowing. (For U.K. companies, cash is defined as cash minus short-term borrowing. The short-term portion of long-term borrowing is reflected in CF3240 Decrease in Long-Term Borrowing or in CF3230 Increase in Long-Term borrowing. Therefore, this account is not applicable in the United Kingdom.)

CF3230 Increase in Long-Term Borrowing. Account CF3230 includes cash receipts from issuing long-term debts, including capital lease obligations, which are assigned to BS2370 Long-Term Borrowing. This is always a positive number. Cash will increase by this amount.

CF3240 Decrease in Long-Term Borrowing. Cash payments for reimbursing long-term debts, including capital lease obligations, are assigned to account CF3240. This is always a negative number. Cash will decrease by this amount.

CF3250 Increase in Capital Stocks. Account CF3250 includes cash receipts from the issue of preferred stocks and common stocks. It is always a positive number. Cash will increase by this amount.

CF3260 Decrease in Capital Stocks. Cash payments to retire preferred stocks or repurchase common stocks are disclosed in account CF3260. This is always a negative number. Cash will decrease by this amount.

CF3280 Other Financing Activities. Account CF3280 comprises all other financing activities. It includes effects on cash from foreign currency translations, which are usually reported separately, and changes in minority interest resulting from increased or reduced ownership in subsidiaries.

CF3289 Cash from Financing Activities. Account CF3289, Cash from Financing Activities, is the sum of CF3210 Dividends Paid, CF3220 Increase (Decrease) in Short-Term Borrowing, CF3230 Increase in Long-Term Borrowing, CF3240 Decrease in Long-Term Borrowing, CF3250 Increase in Capital Stocks, CF3260 Decrease in Capital Stocks, and CF3280 Other Financing Activities.

CF3490 Net Changes in Cash. This account, CF3490 Net Changes in Cash, is the sum of CF3099 Cash from Operations, CF3189 Cash from Investing Activities, and CF3289 Cash from Financing Activities. The net changes are usually reconciled with the opening and closing cash balances.

6.1.3 Nonoperating Activities in the Sources/Uses Approach

Sources

In the following accounts all numbers are positive, and cash will increase accordingly.

CF3310 Disposal of Fixed Assets. All cash receipts from the disposal of tangible fixed assets, including discontinued operations and leased assets, make up account CF3310.

CF3320 Disposal of Long-Term Investments. Account CF3320 captures cash proceeds from the sale of long-term investment assets. It also includes any reported disposal of subsidiaries. However, such an account should not appear in a consolidated cash flow statement.

CF3330 Increase in Long-Term Borrowing. Cash proceeds from borrowed funds, including an increase in finance lease obligations, are disclosed in account CF3330.

CF3340 Increase in Capital Stocks. Account CF3340 includes cash receipts from the issue of preferred and common stocks. It also includes increases of common stocks arising from the conversion of bonds.

CF3380 Other Sources. This line (account CF3380) reports any other increase in cash from nonoperating activities.

CF3389 Total Sources. Total Sources, CF3389, is the sum of CF3310 Disposal of Fixed Assets, CF3320 Disposal of Long-Term Investments, CF3330 Increase in Long-Term Borrowing, CF3340 Increase in Capital Stocks, and CF3380 Other Sources, as well as CF3099 Cash from Operations.

Uses or Applications

All numbers in the following accounts are negative, and cash will decrease accordingly.

CF3410 Dividends Paid. All actual cash payments for preferred and common stocks in a given year are assigned to CF3410 Dividends Paid.

CF3420 Capital Expenditures. Capital Expenditures, account CF3420, includes all cash payments made in acquiring tangible fixed assets.

CF3430 Purchase of Long-Term Investments. All cash payments for the purchase of long-term investments are assigned to account CF3430. It also includes the purchase of subsidiaries if this is separately disclosed by a company.

CF3440 Decrease in Long-Term Borrowing. Account CF3440 includes cash payments for the reimbursement of long-term borrowing. It also includes any decreases in convertible bonds resulting from their conversion to common stocks.

CF3450 Decrease in Capital Stocks. Decrease in Capital Stocks, account CF3450, includes cash payments for the repurchase of capital stocks (preferred as well as common stocks).

CF3480 Other Uses. Other Uses, disclosed in account CF3480, covers any other cash disbursement for nonoperating activities.

CF3489 Total Uses. Account CF3489, Total Uses, is the sum of CF3410 Dividends Paid, CF3420 Capital Expenditures, CF3430 Purchase of Long-Term Investments, CF3440 Decrease in Long-Term Borrowing, CF3450 Decrease in Capital Stocks, and CF3480 Other Uses.

CF3490 Increase (Decrease) in Funds. Account CF3490 reflects the result of deducting CF3489 Total Uses from CF3389 Total Sources. The net result of the cash flow statement will always appear in this account no matter which approach is used. Account CF3490, which is both Net Changes in Cash in the Investing/Financing Approach and Increase (Decrease) in Funds in the Sources/ Uses Approach, conveys a similar message to analysts. The amount will be exactly the same when both approaches focus on cash.

Reference Items

CF3495 Definition of Funds. Historically, the definition of "Funds" in the cash flow statement has evolved from Working Capital to Cash reflecting the needs of the capital market. Account CF3495 defines the last line of the cash flow statement as being, for example, either cash and cash equivalents, working capital, net liquid assets, or some other designation. Each of these examples can be explained as follows:

Cash and Cash Equivalents:	Cash on hand plus short-term investments with maturity of less than three months
Working Capital:	Current assets minus current liabilities
Net Liquid Assets:	Cash and cash equivalents minus short-term borrowing (known as Net Borrowing) if the short-term borrowing is greater than cash and cash equivalents

There may be many variations of the definitions listed. Data compilation should follow the basis used by each company. If needed, the data can be reorganized to conform to the basis most useful in analysis, except when the basis radically departs from the norm. Formats used by companies in the same country are likely to be similar, which is useful in making comparisons between companies in that country.

CF3500 Cash Payments for Interest Expenses. Account CF3500 includes actual cash payments for interest expenses during the year.

6.2 BANKING FORMAT

The cash flow statement is not widely used in banking. The obvious reason is that most of a bank's assets are easily convertible to cash. In contrast to industrial companies, banks do not require cash for capital expenditures but rather to pay interest on deposits. A bank's cash position may be worth analysis in examining its interest payments for borrowed funds, although they are generally insignificant. Banks do not finance their capital from borrowing unless they are engaged in specific businesses involving long-term lending, such as mortgage loans.

Because disclosure requirements from country to country are not uniform, cash flow formats also vary. Except for those in the United States, banks do not provide a real cash flow statement. Most banks in other countries reveal their sources and uses of funds in a balanced format, but changes in cash or increases (decreases) in funds are not isolated. For purposes of international comparison, the information provided can be reorganized to construct a cash flow.

When a cash flow statement is prepared, its format should be similar to the industrial format, therefore making comparisons possible. However, the individual data item must reflect the different aspects of a bank's business, and the distribution of such amounts will be significantly different from those in industrial formats.

CASH FROM OPERATIONS IN A BANKING FORMAT

Approach	Data Items	
Indirect Approach	CF3010	Net Income
	CF3020	Provision for Loan Losses and Depreciation
	CF3030	Other Non-Cash Adjustments
	CF3040	Changes in Non-Cash Working Capital
	CF3099	**Cash from Operations**
Direct Approach	CF3050	Cash Receipts from Revenue
	CF3060	Cash Disbursement for Interest Payments
	CF3070	Income Tax Paid
	CF3080	Other Cash Receipts and Disbursements
	CF3099	**Cash from Operations**

The definition of *operating activities* in banking is significantly different from that applied in industrial companies. And, just as there is difficulty in current and noncurrent segregation on the balance sheet, the segregation of operating and nonoperating activities is not clear either.

A bank's major operating assets consist of loans and investment assets, and deposits represent the major operating liabilities. A greater portion of the loans and deposits have a life of more than one year. In practice, changes in loans and deposits are classified as nonoperating activities, which contradicts the classification on the balance sheet, (i.e., operating assets and liabilities are, in general, treated as current assets and liabilities, respectively).

CASH FROM NONOPERATING ACTIVITIES IN A BANKING FORMAT

Approaches	Data Items	
Investing/ Financing Approach	**Investing Activities**	
	CF3110	Disposal of Fixed Assets
	CF3120	(Capital Expenditure)
	CF3130	Disposal of Long-Term Investments
	CF3140	(Purchase of Long-Term Investments)
		(continued)

(continued)	CF3150	Decrease (Increase) in Short-Term Investments
	CF3160	Decrease (Increase) in Loans
	CF3180	Other Investing Activities
	CF3189	**Cash from Investing Activities**
	Financing Activities	
	CF3210	(Dividends Paid)
	CF3220	Increase (Decrease) in Short-Term Borrowing
	CF3230	Increase in Long-Term Borrowing
	CF3240	(Decrease in Long-Term Borrowing)
	CF3250	Increase in Capital Stocks
	CF3260	(Decrease in Capital Stocks)
	CF3270	Increase (Decrease) in Deposits
	CF3280	Other Financing Activities
	CF3289	**Cash from Financing Activities**
	CF3490	**Net Changes in Cash**
Sources/Uses Approach	**Sources**	
	CF3310	Disposal of Fixed Assets
	CF3320	Disposal of Long-Term Investments
	CF3330	Increase in Long-Term Borrowing
	CF3340	Increase in Capital Stocks
	CF3350	Decrease in Loans
	CF3360	Increase in Deposits
	CF3380	Other Sources
	CF3389	**Total Sources**
	Uses or Applications	
	CF3410	Dividends Paid
	CF3420	Capital Expenditures
	CF3430	Purchase of Long-Term Investments
	CF3440	Decrease in Long-Term Borrowing
	CF3450	Decrease in Capital Stocks
	CF3460	Increase in Loans
	CF3470	Decrease in Deposits
	CF3480	Other Uses
	CF3489	**Total Uses**
	CF3490	**Increase (Decrease) in Funds**
Reference Item	CF3495	Definition of Funds

6.2.1 Operating Activities

For an explanation of the following accounts, refer to the corresponding accounts in the Industrial Format, except when there is a special comment. However, each item should be viewed within a banking context.

Indirect Approach

CF3010 Net Income

CF3020 Provision for Loan Losses and Depreciation. Depreciation and amortization expenses are the major non-cash expenses in industrial companies, and they are assigned to account CF3020. In banking, however, provisions for loan losses or their reversals are the major non-cash adjustments in addition to depreciation and amortization.

CF3030 Other Non-Cash Adjustments. In addition to the items listed for industrial companies, unrealized gains or losses on investments should be included in account CF3030.

CF3040 Changes in Non-Cash Working Capital. Account CF3040 may be ignored in banking, because major assets are composed of loans and changes in the loans are classified as a nonoperating activity.

CF3099 Cash from Operations. Cash from Operations, account CF3099, is the sum of CF3010 Net Income, CF3020 Provision for Loan Losses and Depreciation, CF3030 Other Non-Cash Adjustments, and CF3040 Changes in Non-Cash Working Capital. This is perhaps the most significant figure in a bank's cash flow statement. When cash from operations is adjusted by changes in loans and investments, and changes in deposits and cash dividends to shareholders, the amount becomes a useful tool in analysis.

Direct Approach

The Direct Approach is all but nonexistent in the banking industry but, if found, the following items apply.

CF3050 Cash Receipts from Revenue. Account CF3050 includes cash receipts from interest income, investment income, commissions and fees earned.

CF3060 Cash Disbursement for Interest Payments. This line (account CF3060) includes cash payments for interest for deposits and long-term borrowing and commissions paid.

CF3070 Income Tax Paid

CF3080 Other Cash Receipts and Disbursements. Any other cash receipts or disbursement from operating activities, except those included in the accounts itemized previously, are included in account CF3080.

CF3099 Cash from Operations. Account CF3099 is the sum of CF3050 Cash Receipts from Revenue, CF3060 Cash Disbursement for Interest Payments, CF3070 Income Tax Paid, and CF3080 Other Cash Receipts and Disbursements.

6.2.2 Nonoperating Activities in the Investing/Financing Approach

For an explanation of the following accounts, refer to the corresponding account in the Industrial Format, except when there are special comments. However, each item should be viewed within a banking context.

Investing Activities

CF3110 Disposal of Fixed Assets. The amounts assigned to account CF3110 are negligible in banking, because the weight of fixed assets as compared with loans or investment assets is minimal and the disposal of such assets is insignificant.

CF3120 Capital Expenditure. Capital expenditure (account CF3120) by banks is also minimal. Exceptions may include a major expansion in the number of branch offices or the purchase of equipment.

CF3130 Disposal of Long-Term Investments

CF3140 Purchase of Long-Term Investments

CF3150 Decrease (Increase) in Short-Term Investments. This line, account CF3150, includes changes in BS2020 Short-Term Investments and BS2035 Federal Funds Sold and Securities Purchased under Resale Agreements.

CF3160 Decrease (Increase) in Loans. Loans constitute the banking business's major operating assets, but increases and decreases in loans are classified as nonoperating activities because a good number of them have a life of more than one year. This account should include changes in BS2065 Due from Banks and Other Interbank Assets, as well as changes in BS2055 Total Loans. Even though loans to other banks are classified separately, they make up a part of total loan investments.

CF3180 Other Investing Activities

CF3189 Cash from Investing Activities. Cash from Investing Activities (account CF3189) is the sum of CF3110 Disposal of Fixed Assets, CF3120 Capital Expenditure, CF3130 Disposal of Long-Term Investments, CF3140 Purchase of Long-Term Investments, CF3150 Decrease (Increase) in Short-Term Investments, CF3160 Decrease (Increase) in Loans, and CF3180 Other Investing Activities.

Financing Activities

CF3210 Dividends Paid

CF3220 Increase (Decrease) in Short-Term Borrowing. This line, account CF3220, includes changes in short-term borrowing, a major portion of which is due to other banks.

CF3230 Increase in Long-Term Borrowing

CF3240 Decrease in Long-Term Borrowing

CF3250 Increase in Capital Stocks

CF3260 Decrease in Capital Stocks

CF3270 Increase (Decrease) in Deposits. Although they represent the banking business's main operating liability, increases or decreases in deposits are classified as nonoperating activities (account CF3270) because many deposits have a life of more than one year.

CF3280 Other Financing Activities

CF3289 Cash from Financing Activities. Cash from Financing Activities, account CF3289, is the sum of CF3210 Dividends Paid, CF3220 Increase (Decrease) in Short-Term Borrowing, CF3230 Increase in Long-Term Borrowing, CF3240 Decrease in Long-Term Borrowing, CF3250 Increase in Capital Stocks, CF3260 Decrease in Capital Stocks, CF3270 Increase (Decrease) in Deposits, and CF3280 Other Investing Activities.

CF3490 Net Changes in Cash. Net Changes in Cash, account CF3490, is the sum of CF3099 Cash from Operations, CF3189 Cash from Investing Activities, and CF3289 Cash from Financing Activities.

6.2.3 Nonoperating Activities in the Sources/Uses Approach

For an explanation of the following accounts, refer to the Industrial Format, except when special comments are provided. However, each item should be viewed within a banking context. Refer also to the previous section on the Investing/Financing Approach for definitions of unique items in banking.

Sources

CF3310 Disposal of Fixed Assets

CF3320 Disposal of Long-Term Investments

CF3330 Increase in Long-Term Borrowing

CF3340 Increase in Capital Stocks

CF3350 Decrease in Loans. Refer to CF3160 Decrease (Increase) in Loans under "Investing Activities" in the Investing/Financing Approach

CF3360 Increase in Deposits. Refer to CF3270 Increase (Decrease) in Deposits under "Financing Activities" in the Investing/Financing Approach.

CF3380 Other Sources

CF3389 Total Sources. Total Sources (account CF3389) is the sum of accounts CF3310, CF3320, CF3330, CF3340, CF3350, CF3360, CF3380, and CF3099.

Uses or Applications

CF3410 Dividends Paid

CF3420 Capital Expenditures

CF3430 Purchase of Long-Term Investments

CF3440 Decrease in Long-Term Borrowing

CF3450 Decrease in Capital Stocks

CF3460 Increase in Loans. Refer to CF3160 Decrease (Increase) in Loans under "Investing Activities" in the Investing/Financing Approach.

CF3470 Decrease in Deposits. Refer to CF3270 Increase (Decrease) in Deposits under "Financing Activities" in the Investing/Financing Approach.

CF3480 Other Uses

CF3489 Total Uses. Total Uses, account CF3489, is the sum of accounts CF3410, CF3420, CF3430, CF3440, CF3450, CF3460, CF3470, and CF3480.

CF3490 Increase (Decrease) in Funds. Increase (Decrease) in Funds, account CF3490, is calculated by deducting CF3489 Total Uses from CF3389 Total Sources.

Reference Item

CF3495 Definition of Funds

6.3 INSURANCE FORMAT

As in banking, the significance of the cash flow statement in the insurance business is modest. Most assets are made up of investments. Liabilities consist of insurance reserves. The assets and liabilities are relatively long-term, and their segregation into current and noncurrent is difficult.

The important cash issue in the insurance industry is to match the duration of investments and insurance reserves. When a gap develops between the two, investments of relatively long-term duration must be sold, sacrificing an expected income stream to meet immediate cash needs.

CASH FROM OPERATIONS IN AN INSURANCE FORMAT

Approach	Data Items	
Indirect Approach	CF3010	Net Income
	CF3020	Changes in Insurance Reserves and Depreciation
	CF3030	Other Non-Cash Adjustments
	CF3040	Changes in Non-Cash Working Capital
	CF3099	**Cash from Operations**
Direct Approach	CF3050	Cash Receipts from Revenue
	CF3060	Cash Disbursement for Claims and Underwriting Expenses
	CF3070	Income Tax Paid
	CF3080	Other Cash Receipts and Disbursements
	CF3099	**Cash from Operations**

CASH FROM NONOPERATING ACTIVITIES IN AN INSURANCE FORMAT

Approaches	Data Items	
Investing/ Financing Approach	**Investing Activities**	
	CF3110	Disposal of Fixed Assets
	CF3120	(Capital Expenditure)
	CF3130	Disposal of Long-Term Investments
	CF3140	(Purchase of Long-Term Investments)
	CF3150	Decrease (Increase) in Short-Term Investments
	CF3180	Other Investing Activities
	CF3189	**Cash from Investing Activities**
	Financing Activities	
	CF3210	(Dividends Paid)
	CF3220	Increase (Decrease) in Short-Term Borrowing
	CF3230	Increase in Long-Term Borrowing
	CF3240	(Decrease in Long-Term Borrowing)

(continued)

(continued)	CF3250	Increase in Capital Stocks
	CF3260	(Decrease in Capital Stocks)
	CF3280	Other Financing Activities
	CF3289	**Cash from Financing Activities**
	CF3490	**Net Changes in Cash**
Sources/Uses Approach	**Sources**	
	CF3310	Disposal of Fixed Assets
	CF3320	Disposal of Long-Term Investments
	CF3330	Increase in Long-Term Borrowing
	CF3340	Increase in Capital Stocks
	CF3380	Other Sources
	CF3389	**Total Sources**
	Uses or Applications	
	CF3410	Dividends Paid
	CF3420	Capital Expenditures
	CF3430	Purchase of Long-Term Investments
	CF3440	Decrease in Long-Term Borrowing
	CF3450	Decrease in Capital Stocks
	CF3480	Other Uses
	CF3489	**Total Uses**
	CF3490	**Increase (Decrease) in Funds**
Reference Item	CF3495	Definition of Funds

6.3.1 Operating Activities

For an explanation of the following accounts, refer to the corresponding accounts in the Industrial Format, except when special comments are made. Cash generation and cash requirements in the insurance industry are quite different from those in industrial companies. Most cash is generated from premium and investment income, the industry's central operating activity, and most cash is needed to pay claims and underwrite expenses.

Indirect Approach

CF3010 Net Income

CF3020 Changes in Insurance Reserves and Depreciation. In the insurance industry, changes in insurance reserves are the major non-cash adjustments, in addition to depreciation and amortization. These items are disclosed in account CF3020.

CF3030 Other Non-Cash Adjustments. In addition to the items listed for industrial companies, unrealized gains or losses on investments in the insurance industry should be included in account CF3030.

CF3040 Changes in Non-Cash Working Capital. Changes in non-cash working capital can be significant in the insurance industry because of the significant receivables from underwriting agents, clients, and reinsurers. These should be included in account CF3040.

CF3099 Cash from Operations. Cash from Operations, account CF3099, is the sum of CF3010 Net Income, CF3020 Changes in Insurance Reserves and Depreciation, CF3030 Other Non-Cash Adjustments, and CF3040 Changes in Non-Cash Working Capital. This account may indicate a company's ability to generate cash. If cash from operations is adjusted by changes in investments and cash dividends to shareholders, it becomes a useful tool in analyzing a company's cash position.

Direct Approach

The cash flow statement using the Direct Approach may not be common in the insurance industry, but the following accounts can be used to review cash from operations.

CF3050 Cash Receipts from Revenue. Cash Receipts from Revenue, account CF3050, includes cash receipts from premiums, investment income, and any other operating activities.

CF3060 Cash Disbursement for Claims and Underwriting Expenses. All cash disbursement for claims and underwriting commissions should be included in account CF3060.

CF3070 Income Tax Paid

CF3080 Other Cash Receipts and Disbursements

CF3099 Cash from Operations. Cash from Operations, account CF3099, is the sum of CF3050 Cash Receipts from Revenue, CF3060 Cash Disbursement for Claims and Underwriting Expenses, CF3070 Income Tax Paid, and CF3080 Other Cash Receipts and Disbursements.

6.3.2 Nonoperating Activities in the Investing/Financing Approach

For an explanation of the following accounts, refer to the corresponding accounts in the Industrial Format, except when a special comment is provided. Major changes in insurance nonoperating activities result from purchases of investment assets and the sale or maturity of investments.

Investing Activities

CF3110 Disposal of Fixed Assets. Amounts assigned to account CF3110 are negligible in the insurance industry, because the weight of fixed assets as compared with investments is minimal and the disposal of such assets is insignificant.

CF3120 Capital Expenditure. Capital Expenditure (account CF3120) by insurance companies is minimal, except for a possible expansion in the number of branch offices or the purchase of equipment.

CF3130 Disposal of Long-Term Investments. Investment assets owned by insurance companies are not segregated into short- and long-term categories. All investments except those specifically designated as short-term investments are treated as long-term investments. Cash generated from the disposal of long-term investments or the maturity of such investments can be significant and is disclosed in account CF3130. Loans to policyholders or third parties are treated as (loan) investments.

CF3140 Purchase of Long-Term Investments. Control of the turnover of investments is one of the major functions of an insurance company, and cash needed for the purchase of long-term investments can be significant. Such amounts are included in account CF3140.

CF3150 Decrease (Increase) in Short-Term Investments. This line (account CF3150) should include the changes in BS2020 Short-Term Investments. Maintaining a certain level of short-term investments is very important, and changes in short-term investments can be significant.

CF3180 Other Investing Activities

CF3189 Cash from Investing Activities. Cash from Investing Activities, account CF3189, is the sum of CF3110 Disposal of Fixed Assets, CF3120 Capital Expenditure, CF3130 Disposal of Long-Term Investments, CF3140 Purchase of Long-Term Investments, CF3150 Decrease (Increase) in Short-Term Investments, and CF3180 Other Investing Activities.

Financing Activities

CF3210 Dividends Paid

CF3220 Increase (Decrease) in Short-Term Borrowing. This line, account CF3220, includes changes in BS2270 Short-Term Borrowing, as well as in BS2280 Short-Term Portion of Long-Term Borrowing.

CF3230 Increase in Long-Term Borrowing

CF3240 Decrease in Long-Term Borrowing

CF3250 Increase in Capital Stocks

CF3260 Decrease in Capital Stocks

CF3280 Other Financing Activities

CF3289 Cash from Financing Activities. Cash from Financing Activities, account CF3289, is the sum of accounts CF3210, CF3220, CF3230, CF3240, CF3250, CF3260, and CF3280.

CF3490 Net Changes in Cash. Net Changes in Cash, account CF3490, is the sum of CF3099 Cash from Operations, CF3189 Cash from Investing Activities, and CF3289 Cash from Financing Activities.

6.3.3 Nonoperating Activities in the Sources/Uses Approach

For an explanation of the following accounts, refer to the corresponding accounts in the Industrial Format, except when special comments are provided.

Sources

CF3310 Disposal of Fixed Assets. Amounts assigned to account CF3310 are negligible in the insurance industry, because the weight of fixed assets as compared with investments is minimal, and the disposal of such assets is insignificant.

CF3320 Disposal of Long-Term Investments. As discussed earlier, investment assets owned by insurance companies are not segregated into short- and long-term categories. All investments except those specifically designated as short-term investments are treated as long-term investments. Cash generated from the disposal of long-term investments or the maturity of such investments (disclosed in account CF3320) can be significant. Loans to policyholders or third parties are treated as (loan) investments.

CF3330 Increase in Long-Term Borrowing

CF3340 Increase in Capital Stocks

CF3380 Other Sources

CF3389 Total Sources. Total Sources, account CF3389, is the sum of accounts CF3310, CF3320, CF3330, CF3340, CF3380, and CF3099.

Uses or Applications

CF3410 Dividends Paid

CF3420 Capital Expenditures. Capital expenditures, disclosed in account CF3420, are minimal except when an insurance company, for example, expands the number of its branch offices or purchases equipment.

CF3430 Purchase of Long-Term Investments. Control of the turnover of investments is one of the main functions of an insurance company, and the amount of cash needed for purchase of long-term investments, disclosed in account CF3430, can be significant.

CF3440 Decrease in Long-Term Borrowing

CF3450 Decrease in Capital Stocks

CF3480 Other Uses

CF3489 Total Uses. Total Uses, account CF3489, is the sum of accounts CF3410, CF3420, CF3330, CF3440, CF3450, and CF3480.

CF3490 Increase (Decrease) in Funds. Increase (Decrease) in Funds, account CF3490, is calculated by deducting account CF3489 from account CF3389.

Reference Item

CF3495 Definition of Funds

6.4 OTHER FINANCIAL SERVICES FORMAT

Other financial services include all financial service companies except banking and insurance companies. However, most companies in this category depend on interest and investment income for revenue, and their capital is heavily dependent on short- and long-term borrowing. The cash flow statement for such companies is similar to the format used in banking, because it is not practical to include all the unique data items needed to reflect the variety of financial service companies.

CASH FROM OPERATIONS IN AN INSURANCE FORMAT		
Approach	**Data Items**	
Indirect Approach	CF3010	Net Income
	CF3020	Provision for Loan Losses and Depreciation
	CF3030	Other Non-Cash Adjustments
	CF3040	Changes in Non-Cash Working Capital
	CF3099	**Cash from Operations**
Direct Approach	CF3050	Cash Receipts from Revenue
	CF3060	Cash Disbursement for Operating Expenses
	CF3070	Income Tax Paid
	CF3080	Other Cash Receipts and Disbursements
	CF3099	**Cash from Operations**

The definition of "operating activities" in other financial services varies, depending on the major activities of each business. Just as it is difficult to define current and noncurrent segregation on the balance sheet for banking and insurance companies, the segregation of operating and nonoperating activities is likewise unclear for other financial services.

The major assets related to operating activities are loans and investment assets, and short-term and long-term borrowing are the major operating liabilities. Deposits are not major capital sources for other financial services, but personal loan businesses, commercial loan companies, and brokerage firms may have some deposits from customers. Changes in loans and investments are classified as nonoperating activities.

6.4.1 Operating Activities

For an explanation of the following accounts, refer to the corresponding accounts in the Industrial Format, except when special comments are provided.

CASH FROM NONOPERATING ACTIVITIES IN AN OTHER FINANCIAL SERVICES FORMAT

Approaches	Data Items	
Investing/ Financing Approach	**Investing Activities**	
	CF3110	Disposal of Fixed Assets
	CF3120	(Capital Expenditure)
	CF3130	Disposal of Long-Term Investments
	CF3140	(Purchase of Long-Term Investments)
	CF3150	Decrease (Increase) in Short-Term Investments
	CF3160	Decrease (Increase) in Loans
	CF3180	Other Investing Activities
	CF3189	**Cash from Investing Activities**
	Financing Activities	
	CF3210	(Dividends Paid)
	CF3220	Increase (Decrease) in Short-Term Borrowing
	CF3230	Increase in Long-Term Borrowing
	CF3240	(Decrease in Long-Term Borrowing)
	CF3250	Increase in Capital Stocks
	CF3260	(Decrease in Capital Stocks)
	CF3270	Increase (Decrease) in Deposits
	CF3280	Other Financing Activities
	CF3289	**Cash from Financing Activities**
	CF3490	**Net Changes in Cash**

(continued)

(continued) Sources/Uses Approach	**Sources**	
	CF3310	Disposal of Fixed Assets
	CF3320	Disposal of Long-Term Investments
	CF3330	Increase in Long-Term Borrowing
	CF3340	Increase in Capital Stocks
	CF3350	Decrease in Loans
	CF3360	Increase in Deposits
	CF3380	Other Sources
	CF3389	**Total Sources**
	Uses or Applications	
	CF3410	Dividends Paid
	CF3420	Capital Expenditures
	CF3430	Purchase of Long-Term Investments
	CF3440	Decrease in Long-Term Borrowing
	CF3450	Decrease in Captial Stocks
	CF3460	Increase in Loans
	CF3470	Decrease in Deposits
	CF3480	Other Uses
	CF3489	**Total Uses**
	CF3490	**Increase (Decrease) in Funds**
Reference Item	CF3495	Definition of Funds

However, especially in other financial services, each item must be carefully examined and viewed in the context of the specific business.

Indirect Approach

CF3010 Net Income

CF3020 Provision for Loan Losses and Depreciation. Depreciation and amortization are the major non-cash expenses in industrial companies, and they are assigned to account CF3020. However, provisions for loan losses or their reversal are the major non-cash adjustments, exceeding depreciation and amortization, in other financial service companies, because loans to customers are one of their major assets.

CF3030 Other Non-Cash Adjustments. In addition to the items listed for industrial companies, unrealized gains or losses on investments should be included in account CF3030 for other financial services.

CF3040 Changes in Non-Cash Working Capital. The amounts assigned to account CF3040 are negligible in other financial services, because their major assets are composed of loans and changes in the loans are classified as nonoperating activities. However, receivables in the security brokerage business can be significant and should be considered here.

CF3099 Cash from Operations. Cash from Operations, account CF3099, is the sum of CF3010 Net Income, CF3020 Provision for Loan Losses and Depreciation, CF3030 Other Non-Cash Adjustments, and CF3040 Changes in Non-Cash Working Capital. This is perhaps the most important figure in the cash flow statement of other financial service companies. Cash from operations can be adjusted by changes in loans and investments and by cash dividends to shareholders to provide a useful tool for analysis.

Direct Approach

Although a few other financial service companies may produce a significant cash flow statement, use of the Direct Approach is rare.

CF3050 Cash Receipts from Revenue. Account CF3050 includes cash receipts from interest income, investment income, commissions and fees earned, and any other operating activities.

CF3060 Cash Disbursement for Operating Expenses. This line, account CF3060, includes cash payments for interest payments on deposits and for long-term borrowing.

CF3070 Income Tax Paid

CF3080 Other Cash Receipts and Disbursements

CF3099 Cash from Operations. Cash from Operations, account CF3099, is the sum of CF3050 Cash Receipts from Revenue, CF3060 Cash Disbursement for Operating Expenses, CF3070 Income Tax Paid, and CF3080 Other Cash Receipts and Disbursements.

6.4.2 Nonoperating Activities in the Investing/Financing Approach

For an explanation of the following accounts, refer to the corresponding accounts in the Industrial Format, except when special comments are provided. However, each item should be viewed within the context of the various financial service businesses.

Investing Activities

CF3110 Disposal of Fixed Assets. Amounts assigned to account CF3110 are negligible in other financial services, with the exception of equipment leasing companies, because the weight of fixed assets as compared with loans or investment assets is minimal and the disposal of such assets is insignificant.

CF3120 Capital Expenditure. Capital Expenditure, account CF3120, is minimal, unless a financial institution significantly expands the number of its branch offices or purchases equipment.

CF3130 Disposal of Long-Term Investments. Account CF3130 includes changes in BS2090 Real Estate Investments, BS2092 Investments in Securities, and BS2095 Other Investments.

CF3140 Purchase of Long-Term Investments

CF3150 Decrease (Increase) in Short-Term Investments. Account CF3150 includes the changes in BS2020 Short-Term Investments and BS2035 Federal Funds Sold and Securities Purchased Under Resale Agreements.

CF3160 Decrease (Increase) in Loans. In the personal and commercial lending business, loans are a company's major operating assets, but changes in those assets, BS2055 Total Loans, are classified as nonoperating activities because a good proportion of them have a life of more than one year.

CF3180 Other Investing Activities

CF3189 Cash from Investing Activities. Cash from Investing Activities, account CF3189, is the sum of accounts CF3110, CF3120, CF3130, CF3140, CF3150, CF3160, and CF3180.

Financing Activities

CF3210 Dividends Paid

CF3220 Increase (Decrease) in Short-Term Borrowing. This line, account CF3220, includes changes in BS2270 Short-Term Borrowing, BS2275 Federal Funds Purchased and Securities Sold Under Repurchase Agreements, and BS2280 Short-Term Portion of Long-Term Borrowing.

CF3230 Increase in Long-Term Borrowing. The increase in long-term borrowing can be a significant figure to most companies that provide other financial services because they are heavily dependent on long-term borrowing for capital. Account CF3230 should include the changes in BS2370 Long-Term Borrowing.

CF3240 Decrease in Long-Term Borrowing. If long-term borrowing is a company's major source of capital, any change in such borrowing is significant. Any decrease in long-term borrowing is included in account CF3240.

CF3250 Increase in Capital Stocks

CF3260 Decrease in Capital Stocks

CF3270 Increase (Decrease) in Deposits. Deposits are usually insignificant for other financial services companies, and changes in the level of such deposits therefore will be minimal. Any such changes are disclosed in account CF3270.

CF3280 Other Financing Activities

CF3289 Cash from Financing Activities. Cash from Financing Activities, account CF3289, is the sum of accounts CF3210, CF3220, CF3230, CF3240, CF3250, CF3260, CF3270, and CF3280.

CF3490 Net Changes in Cash. Net Changes in Cash, account CF3490, is the sum of CF3099 Cash from Operations, CF3189 Cash from Investing Activities, and CF3289 Cash from Financing Activities.

6.4.3 Nonoperating Activities in the Sources/Uses Approach

For an explanation of the following accounts, refer to the corresponding accounts in the Industrial Format, except when special comments are provided. However, each item should be viewed within the context of the various other financial services. Refer to the preceding section on Investing/Financing for definitions of unique items.

Sources

CF3310 Disposal of Fixed Assets

CF3320 Disposal of Long-Term Investments

CF3330 Increase in Long-Term Borrowing

CF3340 Increase in Capital Stocks

CF3350 Decrease in Loans

CF3360 Increase in Deposits

CF3380 Other Sources

CF3389 Total Sources. Total Sources, account CF3389, is the sum of accounts CF3310, CF3320, CF3330, CF3340, CF3350, CF3360, CF3380, and CF3099.

Uses or Applications

CF3410 Dividends Paid

CF3420 Capital Expenditures

CF3430 Purchase of Long-Term Investments

CF3440 Decrease in Long-Term Borrowing

CF3450 Decrease in Capital Stocks

CF3460 Increase in Loans

CF3470 Decrease in Deposits

CF3480 Other Uses

CF3489 Total Uses. Total Uses, account CF3489, is the sum of accounts CF3410, CF3420, CF3430, CF3440, CF3450, CF3460, CF3470, and CF3480.

CF3490 Increase (Decrease) in Funds. Increase (Decrease) in Funds, account CF3490, is calculated by deducting CF3489 Total Uses from CF3389 Total Sources.

Reference Item

CF3495 Definition of Funds

Diversification of Operating Activities

7

This chapter describes the diversification of revenue, by product and geographic area, and the distribution of a company's subsidiaries. Industrial companies segregate total revenue into IS1001 Net Sales and IS1019 Other Operating Revenue in the income statement. Net Sales is the revenue generated by a company's main operating activity, or, in other words, the revenue from the sale of its chief products or commercial services. Sometimes conglomerates with diverse operating activities additionally provide financial services through subsidiaries. However, the mere segregation of industrial operating activities and financial service activities in the income statement often provides inadequate detail of a company's many activities. A further segregation of operating activities is almost always useful in an analysis of diversification. In addition to diversifying their products, companies can also diversify geographically, maintaining operations in many countries or regions.

7.1 PRODUCT SEGMENTATION

Products may be segregated in many ways. To be effective, the segregation should reduce a company's exposure to economic fluctuations. There are, however, no two companies that provide precisely the same products and, therefore, classifying or grouping such products to study the impact of their diversification is not a simple matter. Yet it would be useful if a sound industry classification system could be established to serve the various needs of analysis.

7.1.2 Classification of Products

One existing and comprehensive approach to classifying products and operating activities is the Standard Industrial Classification (SIC) coding system. It is published by the U.S. Office of Management and Budget, which states, "The

SIC is the statistical standard classification underlying all establishment-based Federal economic statistics classified by industry.''

Such a standardized classification system is necessary because a breakdown of activities is not standardized among companies. However, even when a standardized classification is used, it may be difficult to find information on the exact products in question. This makes comparisons of companies difficult.

For example, product segments in large corporations embrace many broad categories, such as chemicals or electronic products. The most detailed information available should be collected, and its use should take into account any limitations of the data.

On the other hand, product segments in small companies can be too detailed and, although useful in analyzing a single company, cannot be used to make comparisons with others. In fact, the more detailed the data, the greater the flexibility in analysis, because the detailed segments can be recombined in any manner analysts want. However, all classification necessitates a consideration of what level of detail is optimal. A convenient rule is that product segments should not be more detailed than the SIC codes available. For example, a food processing company may list each container size it produces or each brand name it markets. With few exceptions, these can be combined if they belong to the same SIC code category.

Certain categories, such as SIC code 6331, Fire, Marine, and Casualty Insurance, should be further segregated in analysis, because companies offering all three forms of insurance carefully segregate each category themselves.

There are some weaknesses in the SIC table. The codes are grouped by broadly defined divisions that are further subdivided into groups, which, when applied to a company, reflect its horizontal diversification of products. The codes, however, do not reveal any vertical relationships between the products, which is very common in conglomerates. An example is agriculture products, which might include livestock, animal food production, food processing machinery, and wholesale and retail foods. All these individual products appear separately in the SIC table, but they are vertically related to one another. The diversification effect for the group is therefore likely to be relatively low.

The following table lists divisions and groups of SIC codes. More detailed codes can be found in the Standard Industrial Classification. The horizontal relationships between categories may be assigned for analytical purposes.

Basic Structure of SIC Table

Division	Groups	Group Titles
A	**Agriculture, Forest, and Fishing**	
	0100	Agricultural production—crops
	0200	Agriculture production—livestock and animal specialties
	0700	Agricultural services
	0800	Forestry
	0900	Fishing, hunting, and trapping
B	**Mining**	
	1000	Metal mining
	1200	Coal mining
	1300	Oil and gas extraction
	1400	Mining and quarrying of nonmetallic minerals, except fuels

Division	Groups	Group Titles
C	**Construction**	
	1500	Building construction—general contractors and operative builders
	1600	Heavy construction other than building construction contractors
	1700	Construction—special trade contractors
D	**Manufacturing**	
	2000	Food and kindred products
	2100	Tobacco products
	2200	Textile mill products
	2300	Apparel and other finished products made from fabrics and similar materials
	2400	Lumber and wood products, except furniture
	2500	Furniture and fixtures
	2600	Paper and allied products
	2700	Printing, publishing, and allied industries
	2800	Chemicals and allied products
	2900	Petroleum refining and related industries
	3000	Rubber and miscellaneous plastics products
	3100	Leather and leather products
	3200	Stone, clay, glass, and concrete products
	3300	Primary metal industries
	3400	Fabricated metal products, except machinery and transportation equipment
	3500	Industrial and commercial machinery and computer equipment
	3600	Electronic and other electrical equipment and components, except computer equipment
	3700	Transportation equipment
	3800	Measuring, analyzing, and controlling instruments; photographic, medical, and optical goods; watches and clocks
	3900	Miscellaneous manufacturing industries
E	**Transportation, Communications, Electric, Gas, and Sanitary Services**	
	4000	Railroad transportation
	4100	Local and suburban transit and interurban highway passenger transportation
	4200	Motor freight transportation and warehousing
	4300	Postal services
	4400	Water transportation
	4500	Transportation by air
	4600	Pipelines, except natural gas
	4700	Transportation services
	4800	Communications
	4900	Electric, gas, and sanitary services
F	**Wholesale Trade**	
	5000	Wholesale trade—durable goods
	5100	Wholesale trade—nondurable goods

Division	Groups	Group Titles
G		**Retail Trade**
	5200	Building materials, hardware, garden supply, and mobile home dealers
	5300	General merchandise stores
	5400	Food stores
	5500	Automotive dealers and gasoline service stations
	5600	Apparel and accessory stores
	5700	Home furniture, furnishings, and equipment stores
	5800	Eating and drinking places
	5900	Miscellaneous retail
H		**Finance, Insurance, and Real Estate**
	6000	Depository institutions
	6100	Nondepository credit institutions
	6200	Security and commodity brokers, dealers, exchanges and services
	6300	Insurance carriers
	6400	Insurance agents, brokers, and service
	6500	Real estate
	6600	Holding and other investment offices
I		**Services**
	7000	Hotels, rooming houses, camps, and other lodging places
	7200	Personal services
	7300	Business services
	7500	Automotive repair, services, and parking
	7600	Miscellaneous repair services
	7800	Motion pictures
	7900	Amusement and recreation services
	8000	Health services
	8100	Legal services
	8200	Educational services
	8300	Social services
	8400	Museums, art galleries, and botanical and zoological gardens
	8600	Membership organizations
	8700	Engineering, accounting, research, management, and related services
	8800	Private households
	8900	Miscellaneous services
J		**Public Administration**
	9100	Executive, legislative, and general government, except finance
	9200	Justice, public order, and safety
	9300	Public finance, taxation, and monetary policy
	9400	Administration of human resource programs
	9500	Administration of environmental quality and housing programs
	9600	Administration of economic programs
	9700	National security and international affairs
K		**Nonclassifiable Establishments**
	9900	Nonclassifiable establishments

A variety of industry classifications are used by major media companies. A few examples are provided in the following tables.

Industry Classification of *The Financial Times*

Banks	Health Care	Printing, Paper and Packaging
Breweries	Household Goods	Property
Building and Construction	Insurance	Retailers, Food
Building Materials and Merchants	Investment Trusts	Retailers, General
Chemicals	Other Investment Trusts	Spirits, Wines, and Ciders
Distributors	Investment Companies	Support Services
Diversified Industrial	Leisure and Hotels	Telecommunications
Electricity	Life Insurance	Textiles and Apparel
Electronic and Electrical Equipment	Media	Tobacco
Engineering	Merchant Banks	Transport
Engineering, Vehicles	Oil Exploration and Production	Water
Extractive Industries	Oil, Integrated	
Food Manufacturers	Other Financial	
Gas Distribution	Other Services and Businesses	
	Pharmaceutical	

The industries are presented in the sequence in which they appear in the stock lists of *The Financial Times*.

Industry Classification of the Ministry of Finance of Japan

Fishery, Agriculture, and Forestry	Steel Products	Warehousing and Harbor Transport
Mining	Nonferrous Metals	Communication
Construction	Metal Products	Wholesale
Foods	Machinery	Retail
Textiles and Apparel	Electrical Machinery	Banks
Pulp and Paper	Transport Equipment	Securities
Chemicals	Precision Instruments	Insurance
Pharmaceutical	Other Products	Miscellaneous Finance
Oil and Coal Products	Electric Power and Gas	Real Estate
Rubber Products	Land Transport	Services
Glass and Ceramics	Marine Transport	
	Air Transport	

The industries are presented in the sequence in which they appear in the *Japan Company Handbook of Toyo Keizai*.

Industry Classification of Dow Jones

Basic Materials
Aluminum
Other Nonferrous
Chemicals
Chemicals—
    Commodity
Chemicals—Specialty
Forest Products
Mining, Diversified
Paper Products
Precious Metals
Steel

Conglomerate

Consumer, Cyclical
Advertising
Airlines
Apparel
Clothing/Fabrics
Footwear
Automobile
    Manufacturing
Automobile Parts and
    Equipment
Casinos
Home Construction
Home Furnishings
Lodging
Media
Broadcasting
Publishing
Recreation Products
Entertainment
Other Recreational
    Products
Toys
Restaurants
Retailers—Apparel
Retailers—Broadline
Retailers—Drug-based
Retailers—Specialty

Consumer, Noncyclical
Beverages
Consumer Services
Cosmetics/Personal
    Care
Food
Food Retailers
Health Care Providers
Household Products
House—Durable
House—Non-durable
Medical Supplies
Pharmaceutical
Tobacco

Energy
Coal
Oil, Drilling
Oil, Integrated
Oilfield Equipment and
    Services
Pipelines

Financial
Banks, Money Center
Financial Services,
    Diversified
Insurance, Composite
Insurance, Full Line
Insurance, Life
Insurance, Property and
    Casualty
Real Estate Investment
Savings and Loans
Securities Brokers

Industrial
Air Freight/Couriers
Building Materials
Containers and
    Packaging

Electrical Components
    and Equipment
Factory Equipment
Heavy Construction
Heavy Machinery
Industrial and
    Commercial Services
Industrial, Diversified
Marine Transportation
Pollution Control/Waste
    Management
Railroads
Transportation
    Equipment
Trucking

Technology
Aerospace and Defense
Communications
Computers
Diversified Technology
Industrial Technology
Medical and
    Biotechnology
Advanced Medical
    Devices
Biotechnology
Office Equipment
Semiconductor and
    Related
Software and
    Processing

Utility
Telephone Systems
Electric
Gas
Water

The industries are presented in the sequence in which they appear in *Barron's* index on industry performance.

The following table is the industry classification used by The Bloomberg, the terminal used to provide financial data to customers of Bloomberg LP. The groups and industry formats have been adopted by the author for use in later volumes. The groups are used to segregate and select companies as samples in a survey of research procedures.

Industry Classification of Bloomberg Financial Markets

Industries	Form	Industries	Form	Industries	Form
Consumer—Services		Furniture/Home	IN	Mining	IN
Advertising	IN	Appliances		Iron/Steel	IN
Broadcast, Radio and	IN	Homebuilders	IN		
TV		Real Estate	IN	**Utility**	
Entertainment	IN	Development		Utilities—Electric	IN
Leisure Time	IN	Tire and Rubber	IN	Utilities—Gas	IN
Lodging	IN			Utilities—	IN
Publishing/Printing	IN	**Consumer—Noncyclical**		Telecommunication	
Publishing—Newspaper	IN	Beverages	IN	Utilities—Water	IN
Restaurants/Food	IN	Brewery	IN		
Service		Cosmetics/Personal	IN	**Technology**	
		Care		Aerospace/Defense	IN
Consumer—Manufacturing		Pharmaceutical	IN	Biopharmaceutical	IN
Household Products/	IN	Food-Processing	IN	Electronics—	IN
Wares		Commercial Services	IN	Semiconductor	
Jewelry/Watch/	IN	Medical Supplies	IN	Emerging Technology	IN
Gemstones		Medical—Hospital	IN	Computers	IN
Shoes/Leather	IN	Management		Computer Software/	IN
Textiles	IN	Miscellaneous—	IN	Services	
Toys	IN	Manufacturing		Medical—Biotechnology	IN
Bicycles	IN	Sugar Refineries	IN	Office/Business	IN
		Tobacco	IN	Equipment	
Retail/Wholesale		Wine and Spirits	IN	Telecommunications	IN
Food—Wholesale	IN			Telecom Equipment	IN
Miscellaneous—Wholesale	IN	**Industrial**			
Retail—Department	IN	Building Materials	IN	**Financial Services**	
Stores		Electrical Equipment	IN	Financial—Banks,	BK
Retail—Drug Stores	IN	Electronics	IN	Money Center	
Retail—General	IN	Engineering and	IN	Financial—Banks,	BK
Merchandise		Construction		Commercial	
Retail—Grocery	IN	Hand/Machine—Tools	IN	Financial—Savings and	BK
Retail—Special Line	IN	Machine—Construction	IN	Loans/Thrift	
Retail—Apparel	IN	and Mining		Insurance—Life	NS
Retail—Automobiles	IN	Machine—Diversified	IN	Insurance—Multiline	NS
Wholesale—Special	IN	Manufactured Housing	IN	Insurance—Property	NS
Line		Metal Fabrication/	IN	and Casualty	
		Hardware			
Transportation and		Environmental Control	IN	**Miscellaneous Financial Services**	
Related		Industrial	IN	Holding Companies—	FN
Packaging and	IN	Materials—Specialty		Diversified	
Container				Personal/Commercial	FN
Transportation—Rail	IN	**Energy**		Loans	
Transportation—Air	IN	Oil/Gas—Equipment	IN	Financial—Securities	FN
Transportation—	IN	and Services		Brokers	
Miscellaneous		Oil/Gas—Exploration	IN	Financial—Commodities	FN
Trucking and Leasing	IN	Oil/Gas—International	IN	Trading	
Transportation—Marine	IN	Oil/Gas—Domestic	IN	Lease Financing	FN
Storage/Warehousing	IN			Foreign—ADR	FN
		Basic Materials		Closed-End Funds	FN
Consumer—Capital		Agriculture	IN	Real Estate Investment	FN
Goods		Chemicals	IN	Trusts	
Auto Parts—Original	IN	Forest Products and	IN	Country Funds—	FN
Equipment		Paper		Closed End	
Auto	IN	Fisheries	IN	Investment Companies	FN
Parts—Replacement		Metals—Diversified	IN		
Autos and Trucks	IN				

Industries are grouped by the author. (IN: Industrial, BK: Banks, NS: Insurance, FN: Financial Services)

7.1.3 Data Items to Be Collected

Within each product group, both financial and nonfinancial data may be included. Each of the data items should serve in analyzing the unique character of each grouping. The items collected may not be the same in each industry.

However, a few common data items should be useful in comparative analysis across industries.

For *financial data,* a few countries require product segment information to be disclosed in notes in a company's financial statements. For example, regulations in the United States and Canada require that sales, operating income, and identifiable assets be disclosed. U.K. companies must provide turnover (sales), trading profits, and net assets (total assets minus current liabilities), identified for each specific segment. These financial data items are standardized and are comparable among companies within each country. Many countries do not require any segment information or may require only the disclosure of sales or turnover. Regardless of reporting requirements, many companies disclose such information. Often, the disclosure of financial information is extended to include research and development and/or capital expenditures.

Non-financial data may be disclosed in a great variety of combinations of different items in different industries. Usually, conglomerates cannot disclose the quantity of merchandise or services provided because of the sheer complexity of the group's multiple products. However, individual segments with unique characteristics can be measured. Disclosure of non-financial data is unique in specialized industries, such as electric and gas utilities. For data compilation, industry-specific tables should be developed that reflect the special characteristics of each industry. It should be noted, however, that the data tables may not be compatible across countries within an industry.

Suggested common data items for all industries are IS1020 Total Revenue, IS1099 Operating Income, and BS2199 Total Assets, or such variations as Identifiable Assets or Net Assets (total assets minus current liabilities in Commonwealth countries). They should be in the following format:

Year	Date of information
SIC	Standard Industry Classification
Description	Product Description
Sales	Sales or Revenue
Income	Operating Income
Assets	Total Assets (Identifiable Assets)

The definition of each data item to be collected should be matched with accounts in the income statement or balance sheet for further analysis.

Industry-specific financial data items may be consistent within an industry in a single country, but there is no guarantee that consistency will be maintained by the same industry in other countries.

For illustration purposes, the following list illustrates data items of importance to specific industries:

High technology companies	R & D expenditure, capital expenditure
Utilities	Capital expenditure, government subsidies
Insurance companies	Net premium, investment income, claims and losses, underwriting expenses, reserve charges
Wholesale	Exports

Industry-specific, non-financial data items can be very difficult to work with in a database because of the diverse units of measure. However, operating performance can be easily evaluated by the number of units sold or consumed in a year. The following list gives examples of units of measure used in a number of industries:

Electric utilities	Oil consumption for electricity generation, kilowatts sold, Wholesale/retail margin allowed by local authorities
Retail	Number of stores added and closed, floor space
Pharmaceutical	Number of new patents
Air transportation	Number of aircraft in place, number of routes, gas (petroleum) consumption
Forest products	Square miles of wood by its age

Intercompany sales should be eliminated in consolidation. If the figures are not made available, the total sales figure can still be useful for analysis.

7.2 GEOGRAPHIC SEGMENTATION

Although such segmentation can reduce some operating risks and possibly increase others, geographic and product diversification is a fact of life in the global economy. The diversification of sales and/or production facilities in different countries does help some companies overcome regional or national economic fluctuations.

Geographic diversification is classified by *two different criteria,* the destination of sales and the origin of production. A simple example of classification by destination is a company's disclosure of exports by country, assuming all products are produced in the home country. If a company has production facilities in many different countries, more complicated tables are required to compile the data. The two classifications reveal different aspects of diversification, and both sets of information are useful in analysis. However, disclosure of geographic segments is less standardized internationally in comparison with product segments. Companies in some countries classify geographic segments only by origin, and others only by destination.

Diversification by destination is related to the distribution of consumers' disposable income and demographic differences in spending behavior. *Diversification by origin* is related to the availability of raw materials and labor. There is also a relationship between diversification by origin and the use of the Cost Summary Method in preparing the income statement, and between diversification by destination and the use of the Functional Method. Formats for the income statement and the balance sheet are not incidental but consistent with management attitudes, which tend to be consistent with the organizational structure of a company.

Classification of geographic diversification is unlike product segmentation. There are no standard geographic segment codes. However, the world's more than 200 countries are natural entities for classification. At a higher level, classification might be by economic continent, that is, North America, Europe, Asia, Australia/New Zealand, Africa, Latin America, and Emerging Europe and Russia. However, the continents should be segregated into economic, rather than geographic, blocs. For example, the economy of South Africa is more closely related to Europe or Australia than to the rest of Africa, and Mexico's economy is more akin to the nations of Latin America than to North America. (This situation may change following the North American Free Trade Agreement (NAFTA).) The important point is how closely the economies are linked in economic cycles.

The following list gives suggested segmentation codes. The digits in the first column are the code for each continent, and the letters in the second column represent countries or groups of countries within a Continent. These arbitrary codes are assigned for illustration purposes. Analysts may have a preferred coding system of their own. Refer to the complete set of codes in Appendix A.

10	North America	US	United States of America
		CN	Canada
20	Latin America	BS	Brazil
		CS	Chile
30	Asia	JP	Japan
		HK	Hong Kong
40	Oceana	AU	Australia
		NZ	New Zealand
50	Middle East Asia		
60	Africa		
70	Europe	UK	United Kingdom
		GR	Germany
80	Emerging Europe	RU	Russia

Each company, of course, has its own perspective regarding classification, and standardization is difficult. If, for example, a company's main operations are located in Germany and other European countries and it maintains other minor subsidiaries scattered among the other continents, its geographical classification might be Germany, Europe, and the rest of the world. Obviously no meaningful diversification index can be computed using such a broad category as "the rest of world."

As with product diversification, data items for each segment can consist of both financial and non-financial data. Suggested common financial data items include sales, operating income, and identifiable assets or net assets. Sales figures for each segment are often disclosed, but the remaining information is rarely provided. Research and development activities are usually not segregated and are of little use when they are isolated. This is because research and development activities are generally concentrated in one or two locations, no matter in how many locations the company operates. Inter-segment transactions are common and should be eliminated for appropriate segment computation.

7.3 SUBSIDIARIES WITH LIMITED INFORMATION

There are other aspects to risk diversification involving subsidiaries that cannot be quantified but require careful attention nevertheless.

The financial activities of fully consolidated subsidiaries are usually combined with those of the parent company into a single set of financial statements. Most corporations comprise many different organizations, including branch offices, wholly owned subsidiaries, majority owned subsidiaries, and significantly owned associates. There are links between legally separated entities based on ownership, or on their vertical or horizontal relationship.

The geographic distribution of these various related companies represents another aspect of risk diversification. First, each corporation bears only limited legal liability toward its capital providers, even though borrowing by one subsidiary may be guaranteed by another. Second, various local tax and labor regulations apply to each subsidiary. Third, the management of each subsidiary may enjoy some degree of independence in decision making. Each may also have a different strategy arising from the type of products or services it provides. Management policies may also vary because of differing demographic or other factors, even though they cannot be quantified.

In addition, although profitability is the most important aspect in analysis, intercompany transactions often make it difficult to determine the true performance of a subsidiary. Nevertheless, an attempt should be made to gather as much as possible of the following data for each subsidiary.

DATA ITEMS FOR SUBSIDIARIES WITH LIMITED INFORMATION

Year
Name
Location (country)
Industry (SIC)
Percentage of equity ownership (relationship to a parent company)
Sales
Operating Income
Total Assets
Share Capital

The percentage of ownership among companies, in conjunction with the shareholding information discussed in Chapter 9, "Shareholders Information," is very important in macroeconomic analysis when subsidiaries are not wholly owned. The Europe, Asia, and Far-East (EAFE) Index, which is produced by Morgan Stanley and weighs market capitalization, is criticized because it gives excessive weight to the Japanese market. This is unavoidable unless the intercompany ownership among members of each *keiretsu* (group of companies) is eliminated. Such intercompany ownership is not limited to Japanese companies, however. French and Swedish companies, among others, also maintain strong interrelationships. By carefully documenting interownership in a database using this subsidiary data set and the shareholders information given in Chapter 9, overlapping capital between companies can be eliminated for an effective analysis of the capital market.

7.4 SUBSIDIARIES WITH FULL INFORMATION

Whenever possible, a complete set of financial statements—income statement, balance sheet, and cash flow statement—should be compiled for each subsidiary. When a subsidiary's business is consistent with that of its parent company, consolidation of financial statements makes sense. However, conglomerates often expand into many different types of business. Manufacturers, for example, may own financial services subsidiaries, such as General Electric's GE Capital or General Motors's GM Finance.

Financial service companies in the United States are regulated and may not own industrial subsidiaries, yet insurance companies in Europe may own banks and industrial companies. However, financial service subsidiaries in the United States are fully consolidated with industrial companies, whereas other countries are consolidated using the Equity Method.

In dealing with a subsidiary whose activities vary significantly from its parent company, consolidated financial statements are of little use in financial analysis. Interest income in banking and premium income in the insurance business, for example, cannot be added to sales from manufacturing to determine the volume of business. Net earnings or cash flow figures from such consolidated financial statements may be usable, but the operating performance of the subsidiary and its parent should be analyzed separately.

In order to analyze performance, all or nearly all data on each subsidiary should be compiled as if it were a separate company. A good database should be able to accommodate full multiple sets of information on each subsidiary under one company.

Diversification of   8
Capital

The capital structure of corporations has changed over the decades, as have capital markets, yet it remains unclear which is the cause of the change and which is the effect. Debt capital was dominant in the early years of the twentieth century, but equity capital gradually became more important. The degree of change varies by country just as capital structures vary by company.

Current capital markets serve as trading tools for investors in both corporate bonds and equities. However, returns from the two distinctive securities are affected by significantly different factors. Prices of the two securities often move in opposite directions. Whereas the price of equity is directly related to the profitability of a company, the price of bonds is affected by general levels of interest, adjusted for the risk of insolvency for a specific company. Estimates of profitability and liquidity are also related to capital structures. It is essential to understand the capital structures of companies to be able to analyze the relationship between the two securities. This helps in estimating the cost of capital to a company.

This chapter establishes data sets for the effective analysis of long-term capital structures. The major capital resources can be segregated into common equity, preferred equity, and bonds.

8.1 COMMON EQUITY

Common stocks are usually defined as securities with a claim to a company's residual value after fixed obligations are deducted. Common shareholders also participate in management's decision-making process. Most companies have one type of common stock, and the common stock equity is divided into shares. Investors may buy and sell the company's outstanding shares, and shareholders receive a portion of the company's earnings based on the percentage of ownership. Shares are transferred at a price determined by their current residual value and/or by the company's discounted future earnings.

Many companies have more than one type of common stock. These multiple shares have a proportional claim on a company's residual value, as discussed in detail in Chapters 3 and 5. Usually, the multiple shares have a different dividend right parity and/or voting right parity. If a company has multiple common shares, a division of the residual values among its holders may be difficult, adding further complexity to the already difficult computation of the company's total residual value.

Each of the multiple shares may be separately traded in the market, and most investors watch the price movement of each security. Analysis, however, cannot be undertaken separately for each security, because all take part in the earnings of the same company, just as corporate bond analysis cannot be separated completely from common shares. Most data items related to common stocks can be found in Chapter 4, "Income Statement" and Chapter 5, "Balance Sheet."

For single-share companies, data items in the income statement and on the balance sheet should suffice. For multiple-share companies, the following data items from the income statement and balance sheet should be collected for each type of share.

DATA ITEMS TO BE COLLECTED FOR MULTIPLE SHARES

STOCKID	Identification of Security
IS1330	Cash Dividends to Common Stock
IS1340	Dividend per Share
IS1350	EPS Before Extraordinary Items
IS1360	Primary EPS
IS1370	Weighted Average Number of Shares for the Primary EPS
BS2710	Number of Shares Outstanding
BS2720	Par Value
BS2730	Dividend Right Parity
BS2740	Voting Right Parity
BS2790	Number of Treasury Stocks

In addition to the fundamental data collected (as shown in the preceding list), the following information should be obtained from stock exchanges for each security, as illustrated in Chapter 4, "Income Statement."

DAILY STOCK PRICE INFORMATION SET

STOCKID	Identification of security
DATE	Date of transaction
OPENING	Opening price
HIGH	High of the day
LOW	Low of the day

(continued)

> *(continued)*
> CLOSING   Closing price
> VOLUME   Volume traded
> EXCHANGE   Exchange where stock or security is traded
> CURRENCY   Currency of the transaction
> RATIO   Stock dividend or stock split ratio
> TYPE   Type of dilutive activities

A few government-owned French companies and some Austrian companies do not trade their basic common stock but offer secondary shares to the market. (Refer to the discussions in Chapter 3 regarding the complexity of multiple shares and examples of EPS computations.)

8.2 PREFERRED EQUITY

As capital markets develop, instruments in the markets become more diverse and distinctions become blurred. Preferred stocks provide an example. They are usually defined as a security without maturity and voting rights, paying a fixed percentage of dividend income out of after-tax income. When a company performs poorly in a year and skips the dividends, voting rights are usually reinstated, and dividends in arrears are paid when earnings recover.

However, the terms vary and may be defined by mutual agreement between the company and its shareholders. Stocks for which dividends owed from prior years must be paid up are called *cumulative preferred stocks.* Another type of preferred stock, known as *participating preferred stock,* participates in residual earnings if dividends to common stocks exceed a designated amount. Yet another form of stock without voting right—also called preferred, such as participation certificates in Switzerland and preferred stock in Greece—should be classified as a *multiple common share* when its holders fully participate in any dividend paid to other classes of common stock. Some of them are convertible to common stock, and their price is determined by the price of the common stock.

Preferred dividends, granted special tax status to benefit shareholders in some countries, have become a major instrument in intercompany investment by institutional investors. Preferred stocks are rare in Germany and Switzerland. Preferred dividends are usually distributed from after-tax earnings, but preferred dividends from foreign subsidiaries are sometimes treated as expenses in computing taxable income, such as, for example, in the case of a preferred stock issued by the U.S. subsidiary of a French company.

Preferred stocks in some companies are privately issued and owned by a few related persons. These owners have special privileges with regard to earnings and voting rights, such as, for example, priority shares in Dutch companies.

An analysis of preferred stocks can be very important in some industries, such as utilities, where they are a major source of capital, and computations of the cost of capital should include preferred stocks. Data items for preferred stocks should focus on contracted provisions relating to income, voting power, and participation in earnings, if any.

8.3 BONDS/DEBENTURES

Other major sources of capital for corporations are loans from banks or bonds issued to the public. Debt capital provides special benefits to corporations, because interest expenses for loans are tax deductible. Although such debt may have various formal names, it differs in substance from preferred or common stock in the following ways:

- Some bonds are issued to the public and traded on stock exchanges, others are financed through private placement, which may be a single bank or a handful of lenders. If a loan is publicly traded, the terms and conditions are more standardized and the information about the loan is regularly made available to the public.
- Bonds have fixed terms of income. Interest expenses are fixed at a percentage of the face value. If a bond's face interest rate differs from market interest rates when issued, it is offered at a premium or a discount, accordingly, and the premiums or discounts are amortized over the life of the loans. Issuers account for the amortization as a reduction or increase in interest expense.
- Loans and bonds have maximum terms for reimbursement, which is distinctively different from the requirements for preferred stocks. However, the actual period of reimbursement may be reduced by "calling" terms. A company can also refinance unfavorable loans if market conditions change.
- Most bonds or debentures are secured by the assets of the issuers. Bonds that are not secured by specific assets may be considered as being secured by expected future cash inflows from operations.

From the viewpoint of fundamental analysis, loans are a major flexible capital resource that provides funds without the associated interference in a company's decision-making process. However, requirements governing the payment of interest and principle are strict, and any default will put the company in jeopardy.

In return for the strict requirements governing loans, bondholders do not participate in a company's decision-making process. Some hybrids, such as convertible bonds, offer the holder participation through conversion to common stocks. On the other hand, if interest or principal payments are in default, bondholders are forced to participate in and often take over a company.

For fundamental analysis, each loan should be identified and the terms and conditions governing each should be recorded. The terms and maturity dates will provide information on future cash needs in a company. The short-term portion of long-term loans especially should be considered in the evaluation of future liquidity.

Availability of information varies by country and by industry. Companies in some major markets disclose information openly in their financial statements, but there are also differences in the form of disclosure. U.S. companies itemize each of their loans and their remaining maturities, but German companies do not. The utility and transportation industries depend heavily on loan capital and provide extensive lists of debt schedules; other industries do not.

Shareholders Information

9

In addition to information on subsidiaries, as discussed in Chapter 7, details on key players in a company's decision-making process are needed for analysis. The identification of major shareholders is important. If a few shareholders own majority voting rights in a company, the direction of its operating activities will be decided by its relationship to these shareholders.

Not all shareholders, not even a group of minority shareholders, have the same interests in a company. A major shareholder who serves on a company's board of directors does not necessarily share the priorities, for example, of an institutional investor. Neither do the two have the same interests in the corporate decision-making process.

Shareholder information should be compiled in three categories: major shareholders, types of shareholders (i.e., institutions/individuals), and a breakdown of all shareholders by size of ownership.

9.1 MAJOR SHAREHOLDERS

Major shareholders should be identified by type of organization, the number of shares owned, and the percentage of voting rights held. A rule of thumb is that any shareholder with more than a 2 percent share ownership should be identified. In the case of multiple shares, the voting rights of each category should be noted. Any shareholder who is a member of the board of directors or a key officer should be identified, even if he or she owns less than 2 percent.

The following are codes to be used in identifying major shareholders and to allow further analysis:

Codes	Descriptions
SH10	Government or government-related organization
SH20	Institutional investors
SH21	Banks
SH22	Insurance companies
SH23	Brokerage firms
SH24	Managed funds

SH29	Other institutional investors
SH30	Other organizations with operating interest in the company
SH40	Directors/officers
SH50	Employees
SH60	Individual shareholders
SH90	Foreign shareholders (an additional reference item)

Data Structure for Major Shareholders

Stock ID	Identification of a security
Year	Date of information
Codes	Codes for the types of shareholders
Shareholder	Name of the shareholder
Percentage	Percentage of ownership
Shares	Number of shares owned

If a company has multiple common shares, each class of shareholder should be distinguished. Information on major shareholders is disclosed in all countries when any dominant shareholder exists. In a few countries, such as Sweden, Japan, and Korea, the information is provided in structured format. If each shareholder is identified, overlapping assets can be eliminated for macroeconomic research.

In most countries, this information is made available annually. A few organizations continuously track such information, in addition to company reports filed with stock exchanges, in active capital markets such as the United States.

This information set, in conjunction with the information on subsidiaries discussed in Chapter 7, can be used to identify chain relationships between companies, revealing "Who Owns Whom."

9.2 SHAREHOLDERS BY TYPE OF ORGANIZATION

In addition to identifying major shareholders, companies in some countries provide additional details, such as a classification of all shareholders by type of organization. The types of organizations are usually categorized as listed below. This statistical information reveals concentrations of shareholders by types of organizations.

Codes	Descriptions
SG10	Government or government-related organization
SG20	Institutional investors
SG21	Banks
SG22	Insurance companies
SG23	Brokerage firms
SG24	Managed funds
SG29	Other institutional investors
SG30	Other organizations with operating interest in the company
SG40	Directors/officers
SG50	Employees
SG60	Individual shareholders
SG90	Foreign shareholders (an additional reference item)

The structure of the data on shareholders by type of organization is similar to that for major shareholders.

Data Structure for Shareholders by Type of Organizations

Stock ID	Identification of a security
Year	Date of Information
Codes	Codes for the group types of shareholders
Shareholders	Number of shareholders
Percentage	Percentage of ownership
Shares	Number of shares owned

Information by type of organization should identify all shareholders. Information should be separately collected for each type of share in cases of multiple-share companies.

9.3 SHAREHOLDERS BY SIZE OF OWNERSHIP

The third set of information classifies shareholders by the size of individual ownership. Even though size classification is inconsistent from country to country, an approximation will indicate whether there are many small shareholders or a few large shareholders. Typical size categories are as follows:

Codes	Descriptions
SS10	1–1,000
SS20	1,001–5,000
SS30	5,001–10,000
SS40	10,001–50,000
SS50	50,001–100,000
SS60	100,001–500,000
SS70	500,001–1,000,000
SS80	1,000,000 or greater

Data Structure for Shareholders by Size of Ownership

Stock ID	Identification of a security
Year	Date of information
Codes	Codes for the size categories of shareholders
Shareholders	Number of shareholders
Percentage	Percentage of ownership
Shares	Number of shares owned

Management Information

10

Stockholders are a central factor in corporate decision making through their power to elect company officers and their right to vote on company matters at annual shareholder meetings. The other key element in corporate policy decisions is a company's management, the people who direct daily operations, including members of the board of directors.

Academic research on corporate decision making points out fundamental differences in hiring corporate managers in the United States, Europe, and Japan.

These differences are an important aspect of corporate management and worth study in fundamental analysis, because they play a role in the stability of management polices. Managers of Japanese companies, for example, are hired out of college and are then promoted slowly over the course of their professional life. Managers in U.S. companies are often hired from outside organizations with ready-to-use expertise. European companies take a middle course between these two approaches.

Another crucial aspect of management is the role of outside influences. In many countries, members of a company's board of directors may include representatives of major interested parties as disparate as minority shareholders, employees, unions, major trading banks, and the government. The degree of influence such representatives wield varies by law and custom. Different laws and customs also affect management style.

Codes designating relationships to other organizations for data compilation are given in the following list:

Codes	Descriptions
MG10	Government Related
MG20	Independent Major Shareholder
MG30	Major Shareholding Company
MG40	Independent Major Loan Provider
MG50	Major Loan-Providing Company
MG60	Union Representative
MG70	Independent Individual

Data Structure for Management Information

Year	Date of information
Codes	Codes for relationship with outside organizations
Name	Name of management
Title	Title within the company
Title Codes	Codified title

Title codes can be constructed to track a manager's advancement in a company. The code should identify the manager's operational function within the company and his or her relationship to any specific subsidiary.

Research Procedures 11

The goal of financial statement analysis is to forecast each company's future earnings. No matter how much historical information is gathered, estimating future earnings is a difficult task. Indeed, some analysts claim that historical information is useless because security prices are based on future earnings.

Historical information can, however, serve as a basis for an estimation of future earnings. Once historical information on all companies has been gathered, it should then be compared statistically by sector and by country to establish each company's relative strength. When relative strength is determined, the timing of a decision to buy or sell shares should be based on return and risks.

The following seven research procedures should be followed in security analysis:

1. Primary Data Collection
2. Ratio Computation on Each Company
3. Time Series Ratio Analysis
4. Ratio Analysis by Sector
5. Company Analysis by Sector and by Country
6. Earnings Forecast
7. Timing of Final Actions

The next section in this chapter explores issues encountered at each step and how they should be treated. No matter how many illustrations are provided, actual data will never be exactly the same. Solutions to unique issues must be adapted as needed.

11.1 PRIMARY DATA COLLECTION

Previous chapters have discussed many of the issues pertaining to primary data collection. Some centered on a particular data item's conceptual background. Others emphasized the practical use of individual data items. Future volumes will explore primary data collection in greater detail, using examples in specific countries. However, it is clear that the primary data collection process itself is fundamental to any comparative study of company performance.

Primary data collection involves general economic data and company-specific information. Although this book concentrates on the fundamental data of individual companies, no business is conducted in a vacuum. Companies operate in a constantly changing environment, which has an impact on all businesses. Some environmental factors can be gleaned from corporate statistics; others are related to a much wider circle of outside parties, ranging from government and competitive nonprofit organizations to consumer groups and others. Information on entities whose activities have an impact on companies being analyzed should be collected separately.

11.1.1 General Economic Data

Country statistics are usually collected by government. Most researchers rely on this information, which reflects various political priorities and political uncertainties, national economic policies (monetary and fiscal), foreign trade results, overall market size, and market sizes by sector. All of these and other factors have varying degrees of significance to a specific company under study.

Sector statistics are generated by two different approaches. The top-down approach begins with gross national product (GNP) and works its way down to specific sector information. The bottom-up approach begins with examples of specific companies and works it way up to aggregate sector information. Top-down information is deduced from country statistics and cannot be generated by an individual researcher. Researchers should obtain such information from well-known professional organizations.

Bottom-up information is produced by observing individual companies and, if the sample is big enough, drawing a reasonable conclusion. For example, an average price/earnings (P/E) ratio for a specific sector can be calculated with reasonable confidence if most companies in the sector are included in the computation. This type of statistical information can be generated and constantly updated if the researcher has a good sample. The following section focuses on statistics that can be generated by a database.

11.1.2 Company-Specific Information

Gathering company-specific information is a researcher's most labor-intensive job. Previous chapters have discussed various methods in detail. Once collected, the data can be segregated by source and by the date such information becomes available, as described in the following paragraphs.

Earnings estimates for specific companies are made and constantly updated by researchers in brokerage houses or independent research organizations. Such estimates are based on fundamental information and an appraisal of the policies of a company. Other organizations collect these estimates from individual researchers and evaluate them statistically. This research information is useful but expensive because of the costs involved in data collection and distribution. As long as benefits exceed cost, of course, this presents no problem.

The estimates on earnings create expectations among investors, which, in turn, have an impact on stock prices. Stock prices move radically when the actual earnings figures released by a specific company do not meet expectations. Even though historical information does not have an impact on stock prices directly, earnings estimates are hardly a matter of instinct. They are the product of careful analysis of a company's history and its future prospects.

Individual researchers tend to make their own estimates and compare them with the overall market. If a researcher's expectations are higher than the market's, he or she will recommend buying the stock in question. If the researcher's expectations are lower than the market's, a "sell" recommendation will be issued. A researcher's recommendations eventually become a part of the market's expectation, simply adding more complexity to efforts to "beat the market."

In compiling information on companies worldwide, the definitions of all data items should be carefully reviewed. These issues will be discussed country by country in later volumes, but it is important to note here that consistent definitions are required so that items may be added, averaged, or compared. For example, earnings per share (EPS) is used in earnings estimates all over the world, but which earnings are used as the numerator and which number of shares is used as the denominator is not consistent.

Stock exchanges constantly provide trading information on securities, such as stock prices and trading volume, in addition to enforcing regulations to assure fair distribution of information to all parties. Information on dividend announcements, stock splits, and stock dividends is provided by stock exchanges in most countries.

The volume of information depends on the frequency with which the data are collected, which can range from annually to an on-line continuous flow. The frequency of data collection should be determined by research needs.

Stock prices and trading volume statistics are fairly simple and consistent everywhere, but, depending on the country, the dividends per share figure may or may not reflect taxes. Withholding tax rates also vary, as do the ex-dates, effective dates, and payable dates.

Newspapers and news releases also provide pieces of needed information. For example, announcements of earnings or abbreviated financial statements are made available to the public long before actual interim or annual reports are published. The information is usually released a few days before or after the date an audit is formally completed. The time required to complete an audit can range from 40 days to eight months, depending on the country. Familiarity with the frequency and timing of company announcements is essential to the timely compilation of data. Such announcements should be screened for consistency in data definition and must be interpreted appropriately for analysis.

Researchers should accept with caution any unaudited information provided on an interim basis. Quarterly data are widely available in the United States and contain almost all financial information. Elsewhere, however, interim reports are usually produced only semiannually and contain a limited amount of data. No country requires a formal audit of interim reports. The extent to which interim data should be collected and trusted depends on the character of each capital market.

Annual reports offer the most comprehensive information about a company, and in all countries the details provided are verified by public auditors. The approach to analysis in *Fundamental Analysis Worldwide* is based entirely on data disclosed in annual reports. It is assumed that the definition of each item appearing in annual reports is consistently used in any financial information disclosed by the company.

The following paragraphs summarize issues often encountered in acquiring public documents and assembling the information they provide for database entry and further analysis.

Issues Related to Acquiring Public Documents

1. Companies to be researched
2. Matching security information with company information
3. Inconsistent frequency of information
4. Availability of information to public
5. Inconsistent fiscal year ends

Issues Related to Compiling Financial Information

1. Different fiscal year ends
2. Odd periods
3. Audit requirements
4. Restated information
5. Inconsistent interim information
6. Different reporting formats
7. Different accounting standards
8. Inconsistent accounting standards within a country

Issues Related to Acquiring Public Documents

Companies to be Researched

Which Companies Should Be Included in a Research Database? Researchers should start with publicly traded companies, because they are the primary targets of investors buying and selling securities.

Should Companies Owned by Government and Related Agencies in Addition to those Owned Privately, Be Included? Some industries—national airlines are a prime example in many countries—are dominated by government-owned companies. They compete in the market with other publicly traded companies and must be taken into account when analyzing industry behavior. Many of these companies are in the process of being privatized.

In addition, these government-owned companies often issue fixed income securities to the public, and their inclusion in the database becomes even more valuable when researching fixed security investments.

Often, a majority of a company's shares are government owned and the remaining shares are traded on the market. About 10 percent of Nippon Telephone and Telegraph's (NTT) shares in Japan, for example, are traded. The Ministry of Finance owns the rest. In such a case, estimating market capitalization should be approached carefully. The stock price does not fairly represent the company's net value because of the limited supply of publicly available stocks.

What If the Secondary Stock is Traded on the Market but the Primary Shares are Held Privately or by the Government? Many of the giant government-owned companies of France issue "Investment Certificates" to the public even though the common shares are held by the government. The investment certificates behave in the same way as equity securities. It is impossible to evaluate the banking and insurance industries in France without considering the government's role in those businesses.

Should Subsidiaries be Included? Subsidiaries consolidated by a parent company overlap in calculations of industry size if they are treated as independent companies. However, when a company is not 100 percent owned by a parent, the subsidiary's stock is traded on the market. This raises the problem of overlapping capital, as illustrated by the *keiretsu* system in Japan. The issue is less well known but at least as serious in France, where a few giants own more than 90 percent of many publicly traded companies.

Some subsidiaries are majority owned by a parent company but are not consolidated because they operate an entirely different business. Industry research requires that such subsidiaries be treated as separate companies, although studies of market size should exclude them.

Should Companies that Have Merged with Others Some Years Ago Be Included? Research usually focuses on active companies. However, to exclude "merged out" companies in tracking changes in the market over a period of years will bias the study in favor of corporate survivors.

What If a Company and Its Primary Stock Exchange are Located in Different Countries? A few U.S. companies maintain home offices in the Bahamas, and some Hong Kong companies have moved their headquarters out of Hong Kong. To which location should they be assigned in a database? They should be assigned to the country in which their main operations are located. Most of these companies are traded in both the home market and the market abroad.

However, some Israeli companies are listed only on the New York Stock Exchange even though their operations are mainly in Israel. Such companies should be assigned to the United States, because most of the information about them is available there.

Matching Security Information with Company Information

What about Multiple Share Companies? When a company has one type of common share, matching shares with the company is simple. However, many companies have multiple types of shares, each of which has a claim on the company's residual value. In such cases, a company's earnings should be divided by each type of security and evaluated based on its share of earnings. Only one set of fundamental information is needed for the company, but the difficulty arises in linking the earnings to each type of security.

Dividends of some multiple shares are tied to different divisions within a company. These are called *targeted stocks*. For example, earnings for GME and GMH shares are from entirely separate lines of business, Electronic Data Systems and Hughes Electronics, respectively, whereas GM shares are tied to General Motors's automobile manufacturing. The divisions are governed by one legal entity but are operated with significant independence. Such companies usually provide an almost complete set of separate financial statements for each sector. The database must be able to combine or separate such information for different purposes of analysis.

What If a Security is Traded in Many Different Markets? Large multinational companies use many markets to raise their capital. How is such information compiled in a database? Obviously, each stock exchange requires specific information comparable to the data provided by local companies. However, most stock exchanges do not require all the data available in a company's home country.

If the reporting formats of such companies are partially adjusted to a specific market, must multiple sets of data be compiled? In fact, the basic information provided to various exchanges is not much different from the information disclosed in the company's home country. Nevertheless, use of the information disclosed in the home country is recommended unless there are substantial differences because of varying accounting standards.

A few super global companies—Royal Dutch/Shell, Unilever, and Eurotunnel—issue complete sets of securities in several markets. Typically, one set of fundamental information is translated into different languages and different currencies. These securities should be treated as multiple shares, and information must be carefully compiled to assure compatibility with the fundamental data of other companies.

Inconsistent Frequency of Information

Annual company reports are provided everywhere, but the frequency with which interim reports are distributed varies. U.S. companies issue quarterly reports with reasonably complete data. Companies outside the United States usually provide semiannual reports with minimal information. How can such varying information be used in global research? The extent of information offered in semiannual reports cannot be compared with the comprehensive treatment in the more thorough U.S. quarterly reports. Semiannual reports often consist of a "thank-you" letter to investors containing only sales figures. Companies should be encouraged to provide more meaningful information as a matter of course. There are cases in which companies are required to be more forthcoming in foreign markets where they may be expected to report more frequently. This information is also useful to analysts.

Availability of Information to the Public

The delays involved in obtaining information from companies outside the United States can be frustrating. Several factors contribute to this problem. One is that audits may take from 50 days to five months after the fiscal year end, as compared with approximately 40 days in the United States. Another delaying factor is that it often takes one to three months to publish annual reports once an audit is completed. When the audit and publishing delays are combined, it can take six to eights months in many countries to issue an annual report.

The most important problem, however, is the seeming lack of interest of many companies in keeping the public informed. Unlike U.S. companies, which are heavily financed by equity from the public, companies in most European countries are financed by banks or related parties. Consequently, they rarely volunteer information. Some small companies do not respond to requests for information at all.

Sometimes information given to shareholders is significantly lower in quality than that provided to an "inner circle" of related parties. For example, German companies fully disclose data to their bankers while restricting shareholders to the minimum information required by regulations. Companies in Japan and Korea distribute abbreviated leaflets to shareholders but provide full financial statements to their stock exchanges.

Inconsistent Fiscal Year Ends

There is no fixed time for a company to close its books and produce year-end financial statements. Some countries set restrictions on the timing of the end of the fiscal year for tax purposes. Fiscal year-ends are usually determined by the break points in a company's operating activities, which vary by industry. Most companies prefer to synchronize with the calendar year. In Japan, however, 90 percent of all companies close their books at the end of March, which is the government's fiscal year end. The variety of fiscal year ends leads to the complication of comparing financial results in significantly different years.

Issues Related to Compiling Financial Information

The problems related to acquiring public documents may complicate research but can be managed, if not eliminated, with good planning. Nevertheless, if the following issues are handled incorrectly, poor investment decisions may result.

Different Fiscal Year Ends. Differing fiscal year ends create complications. For example, in comparing operating results of two companies in a given year, which close their books in March and December, respectively, the results will be either three or nine months apart. If the fiscal year ends of companies being compared are spread throughout the year, comparisons become difficult no matter which date is used as a cutoff point.

If quarterly information is available for all companies in a sample, we can compute 12 months trailing information (see 11.3.1) and the differences will be one and a half months maximum. Most international companies, however, provide only semiannual reports with limited information.

If an industry under study has no seasonal operating cycle, an artificial fiscal year can be established by reconfiguring year-to-year information. A researcher should be comfortable with such a process before actually proceeding.

Odd Periods. Although corporate restructuring is infrequent, it often produces an odd fiscal year, and information for the odd year cannot be compared with other years. Comparing the numbers as given is one approach, but any ratios will be inaccurate when data from both the income statements and balance sheets are used.

The retail industry, for example, often produces odd periods because it commonly establishes a Sunday as the last day of a fiscal year. This practice can result in either a 52- or 53-week year. The variance may be ignored if business activity at the fiscal year end is average. Otherwise, the year-end results must be annualized.

Odd periods most often arise in quarterly information (i.e., 12 or 13 weeks), and the impact on results is more significant because the one week can represent a 7 or 8 percent discrepancy in gross results. Quarterly information containing an odd period should be annualized for more meaningful comparison.

Odd periods can be adjusted in either of two ways. One way is to annualize given information. Data from the balance sheet do not require annualization, because the information represents the company's status at any given date. Cash flow and income statement information, however, must be projected to 365 days or to 91/92 days' equivalent information.

The other method is to "cut and paste" information across periods to create normal period equivalents. This can require substantial effort and may be inaccurate if the data contain any one-time charges.

Audit Requirements. In all countries, the financial statements of publicly traded companies must be verified by public auditors. Although the Big Six accounting firms dominate auditing worldwide, the degree of verification required in each country varies and the credibility of some information should be considered twice.

Even more caution is needed in dealing with other company information. For example, product segmentation or research and development activities are often disclosed whether required or not. However, such information, without proper review by auditors, can be misleading or imprecise in its use of definitions and may be merely self-serving.

No country requires full auditing of interim company reports. They are, however, reviewed for reasonableness in some countries. If interim reports are not reviewed by auditors at all, their credibility should be questioned.

Restated Information. Most countries require companies to provide the previous year's comparative data in their annual financial statements. When "dramatic" changes have occurred, for example, a change in accounting standards or a change in the scope of a consolidating entity, the current year's data will not be comparable to the previous year's information. It must then be restated. There is no requirement to do this in most countries except the United States. Therefore, any restatements should be treated with caution.

A general comment: When compiling both original and restated data, remember that use of such information should be selectively applied for specific research purposes. Generally, restated information should be used in reviewing operating performance, but original figures should be used in analyzing price performance.

In fact, many countries do not allow any changes in the beginning balances, which means that restatements are not allowed at all. In such cases, if a change in accounting standards takes place, and the cumulative impact on earnings is due to changes recorded as prior period adjustments, the difference should be treated as an extraordinary item. Otherwise the original figures should be used for comparison year to year.

Restatement due to Reorganization. When a company reorganizes, it usually means one or more operations have been discontinued. This may involve the closure of an operating sector, the spin-off of a sector, or perhaps the spin-off of a subsidiary. It does not include closing one of many manufacturing facilities within a sector, which nowadays is common in all businesses (i.e., closing a factory in one area and opening another elsewhere). Discontinued operations reflect serious changes in a company's operating structure.

Results from discontinued operations qualify as an extraordinary gain (loss) in the current year's data, and figures for the previous year may be restated based on the current size of the company. This type of restatement does not add much new information for comparison purposes and should not be regarded as a true restatement. The adjusted information may be collected but should be used for limited purposes only, such as comparisons of current operating sectors, to avoid misleading results.

Consider, for example, a company that decides to discontinue an inefficient and failing sector in a given year. Stock prices in the previous year were based on all significant factors, including the operation closed the following year. When the previous year's earnings are restated to exclude the discontinued operations, the earnings of the surviving operations are isolated. The P/E ratio, using the actual share price and actual earnings of the previous year, as compared with the P/E ratio using the actual share price and the restated earnings, will be much lower. The operating profit margin for the current year should be compared with the operating profit margin of the restated year, so that similarly sized operations are being compared.

Restatement Due to Merger and Acquisition. The main reason for restating a prior year's figures is the acquisition of new businesses or the discontinuation of operations. When a new business is added, or another is closed, all figures in the financial statements should be modified. For analysis purposes, the performance of operating results in the previous year should be compared with current results. However, if the restated information is used, the performance of stock prices, in relation to earnings, and the dividends per share data, will not be comparable because of changes in both the numerator and the denominator in the calculation of earnings per share.

For example, ABC Company acquires DEF Company by issuing one ABC share for one DEF share, as illustrated in the following table.

		Earnings	Number of Shares	EPS
Year XXX0	ABC	15,000,000	3,000,000	5 per share
	DEF	4,000,000	1,000,000	4 per share
Restated XXX0	ABC	19,000,000	3,000,000	6.33 per share
Year XXX1	ABC	20,000,000	4,000,000	5 per share

Even though ABC's actual performance maintained 5 per share in both years, the comparison of restated EPS with current EPS indicates a 21 percent decrease in performance. The 6.33 per share figure has no justification. Similarly illogical figures will be generated in computing dividend per share.

Restatement Due to Changes in Degree of Ownership. When a parent company changes its share of ownership in a subsidiary from between 20 percent and 50 percent to more than 50 percent, the accounting method for the subsidiary, in many countries, will be switched from the Equity Method to the Full Consolidation Method. This will result in changes in sales, cost of goods sold, and total assets. Although the price performance evaluation will be correct despite the use of restated information, the operating performance evaluation may be distorted.

Restatement Due to Changes in Accounting Standards. A change in accounting standards is another reason for restatement. The change may be in the valuation of assets or in the computation of such liabilities as deferred taxes or pension provisions. For example, in changing the valuation method for investment securities from the Lower of Cost or Market to the Mark-to-Market Method, the restated information should reflect the previous year's investment securities by market value so as to provide a comparison with the value of the current year's investment securities.

Such changes are usually recorded as prior period adjustments in the income statement and directly accounted for in the beginning balance of retained earnings. The restated financial statement assumes that the cumulative impacts to the previous year are adjusted to the beginning balance of the current year's retained earnings. The earnings for the last year are restated as if the accounting standard were adopted in the previous year and can then be compared with the current year's earnings.

The restated figures are valid for both price performance and operating performance. In this case, the restated figures should be the only figures employed for analysis.

Inconsistent Interim Information. In addition to their irregular timing, interim reports of financial information pose a problem in that the definitions of data they contain are often inconsistent with those in annual reports. The comprehensive data in U.S. quarterly financial statements are at least compiled or reviewed, if not fully audited, by public auditors and are mostly comparable to the data provided in annual reports.

In many other countries, interim reports differ from annual reports both in definitions of data and in structure. Their use requires extreme caution. Even more annoying for investors relying on consolidated financial statements, Japanese and Korean companies do provide annual consolidated and separate parent company reports, but the interim information is often restricted to the parent company.

Different Reporting Formats. Before a company's income, expenses, assets, and other data can be analyzed, researchers must overcome the hurdles posed by unfamiliar financial reporting formats in different countries. As previously discussed, there are two basic formats used: the Functional Method (sales/cost of goods sold in the income statement and current/noncurrent assets and liabilities on the balance sheet) and the Cost Summary Method (sales/material/personnel expenses in the income statement and no segregation of current/noncurrent assets and liabilities on the balance sheet).

The presentation of order on the balance sheet varies by country and industry. Some present the accounts in descending order of liquidity, and others in ascending order. The use of the Source/Uses Format and the Investing/Financing Format in the cash flow statement also varies. Under U.K. accounting standards, net assets (total assets minus current liabilities), rather than total assets, is the focus of the balance sheet.

Among the format problems encountered by researchers in studying company reports from different countries is the varying placement of key items or the differing combinations of certain accounts in the financial statements. In the United Kingdom, for example, aggregated data items appear in the main body of the financial statements, with details provided in related notes. In Italy, the details are in the main body of the financial statements and no additional notes are provided.

Although these format differences should not change anything of substance, their inconsistency sometimes leads to the omission of important information. To compare companies, therefore, a consistent restructuring process is required. If information is too detailed, it requires considerable effort to combine and restructure it. When information is too concise, either it requires a significant effort to find more detail in related footnotes or relevant information is missing entirely. Detailed examples will be given in the forthcoming country-specific volumes.

Different Accounting Standards. Even though format differences change nothing of substance, they can be a serious complication when combined with accounting standard differences. Accounting standards can be broadly defined to include the reporting format, but this book will use a narrower definition. For example, accounting standards set the guidelines for the valuation of assets and liabilities, segregation of operating versus nonoperating expenses, segregation of current versus noncurrent assets/liabilities, and the treatment of treasury stocks.

A nation's accounting standards evolve to satisfy various needs, including a company's adherence to local tax regulations and the presentation of approximate economic earnings. The latter objective is the more important in stock evaluation. With global investment more active now than at any other time, economic earnings are at the root of the stock price mechanism. However, accounting is based on historical cost, and continuous changes in the purchasing power of a currency and the impracticality of continuous measurement will never let us achieve the goal of measuring true economic earnings.

A more practical reason for the development of accounting standards is the requirement that companies pay taxes. Taxes are based on two basic assumptions. One is the concept of added value, whereby anyone who benefits from value added to a product should pay taxes in some proportion to the benefits. The other is the ability of a company to actually pay the taxes imposed. The first supposes an appropriate measurement of value added, which requires an accounting of both the resources spent on products and the proceeds received from the sale of the products. The process is relatively simple at first glance, but defining the resources spent for the proceeds received is complicated in practice.

The major "schools" of accounting standards consist of the United States and Canada, which emphasize an approximation of economic earnings; the United Kingdom and other Commonwealth countries, which stress net assets; continental European countries, with their accent on tax accounting; East Asian countries, which highlight the parent company; Latin American countries, with inflation accounting; and Eastern European countries, with emerging accounting standards.

Accounting standards are gradually merging to meet the needs of the global investment community. Members of the European Union have harmonized local accounting standards with several Directives since 1990, and some neighboring states are taking Europe's lead. At present, Nordic countries already disclose far more information than other European countries. Commonwealth nations in Asia are still tied to U.K.-style accounting standards of a decade ago, and East Asian countries are gradually switching from tax-based conservative accounting to U.S. accounting standards. The International Accounting Standards Committee, supported by the International Securities Analysts, makes significant efforts to blend accounting standards. The nations in transition from centrally planned economies to market-oriented economies are also adopting Western accounting standards to attract foreign capital. A few dozen global conglomerates provide truly comprehensive data regardless of their home country's accounting standards, which is useful to international investors.

To mitigate the differences in accounting standards, some larger companies reconcile results based on local accounting standards with internationally recognized accounting standards. Companies listed on foreign stock exchanges also reconcile earnings based on local accounting standards with the national accounting standards of the host exchange.

Inconsistent Accounting Standards Within a Country. Variations in accounting standards exist not only across borders but also within a single country, as in Switzerland and the Netherlands. Swiss companies are free to use any of a number of accounting standards for financial reporting purposes, but reporting for tax purposes is, of course, locally regulated. A few Dutch companies are truly global companies and follow international accounting recommendations, but the vast majority of companies in the Netherlands continue to follow local standards. Such flexibility in financial reporting helps investors to compare companies within an industry but does not provide comparability within a country.

11.2 RATIO COMPUTATION FOR EACH COMPANY

This section defines various types of ratios and provides samples using primary data. Flexibility is possible, and the individual components and titles of each ratio can be changed as needed. The application of these ratios to individual industry formats is outlined in the Appendix.

11.2.1 What Are the Ratios?

Once the fundamental information is compiled it can be used for analysis, that is, to judge the relative strength of a company's performance as compared with industry or country averages. The comparison procedures require many different analytical steps and can be quite complicated, depending on the purpose.

To simplify the process, ratios can be computed. Ratios are comparisons of a few related data items expressed as a percentage, multiples, or simply per share information. These help investors to analyze information without having to deal with the complications of differences in absolute amounts or in the currency. Ratios also simplify matters by reducing several factors to a single measuring unit.

This simplification is possible only if the raw data for all countries are consistently defined. As discussed earlier, differences in accounting standards, such as the valuation methods applied to assets and liabilities or the segregation of income and expenses, make comparisons of computed ratios in different countries difficult.

11.2.2 What Are the Issues in Computing Ratios?

Different Definitions of Ratios

Computing ratios is obviously helpful in providing insights to complicated sets of information, but there are no common rules on "how to do it." Considerable literature on the subject is available in textbooks and research papers produced by various institutions. However, there is no consistency among these resources in defining each ratio or in determining what ratios should be used in a particular type of analysis. The issue becomes even more complicated when the focus shifts from a national to an international horizon.

For example, a simple ratio, such as earnings per share, may vary depending on how the raw data items are defined. U.S. companies, for example, clearly define "extraordinary items" by "unusuality, infrequency, and materiality," and EPS is computed using earnings both before and after deducting extraordinary items. However, extraordinary items are not so clearly defined by French or Japanese companies, which instead refer to "exceptional items." Such exceptional items may include some operating expenses, some recurring, non-operating income (expenses), and some items that would also be regarded as "extraordinary items" in the United States. As a result, the EPS computation ignores the important role of extraordinary items. On the other hand, in Germany, companies have been using a definition of extraordinary items similar to that in the United States since the EU Directives were adopted in 1989. The application of the rules in Germany, however, differs sharply from the practice in the United States, where companies report numerous extraordinary items almost every year because of restructuring, reorganization, and changes in accounting standards. German companies virtually ignore such items in their financial statements.

In developing a database for local users, each ratio should be defined in locally familiar terms. But when companies are analyzed for specific purposes, the ratios should be defined to meet the purposes of the analysis regardless of a particular country's conceptual framework. This book assumes the latter, and that the purpose is to compare companies worldwide.

Precomputed Ratios

Approximately 200 raw data items in the income statement, balance sheet, cash flow statement, and other sets of financial information have been defined. When these raw data items are linked, a ratio is created, and with 200 data items a substantial number of useful ratios can be generated, depending on a researcher's specific needs. Certain ratios require extensive computation. Because it is not practical for an analyst to compute such ratios while running complicated applications, it is recommended that such ratio sets be precomputed and stored as a separate set of information.

For efficiency, computed ratios should be clearly documented, especially the units used in each ratio, so that other computations using the same ratios can be made easily. The following units are usually required:

Local currency in millions or billions
Local currency in basic currency unit
U.S. dollar in millions
Basic U.S. dollar currency
Percentage
Multiples
Other neutral index value

For the purposes of quality control, setting a range for each ratio is also useful. For example, the P/E ratio cannot be a negative number, because such numbers are meaningless in analysis even though the mathematical computation can be performed. More meaningful ranges can be established using statistical analysis, although they may differ by country and by industry.

Missing Data or Incompatible Raw Data

For convenience in analysis, all companies should be segregated into four formats: industrial, banks, insurance, and other financial services. Information from each company is then assigned to one or two of the formats. Some companies will fail to provide all needed information and, inevitably, many data fields will be blank.

In programming ratio computation procedures for all companies, missing data items should be anticipated to avoid unreasonable outcomes in the ratio tables. If an appropriate note is made for each type of error, it will help in investigating the problem. The following illustrations of possible error notes may be helpful:

- Not computed if numerator is zero (zero can be valid if actual number is zero).
- Not computed if denominator is zero.
- Not computed if both numerator and denominator are zero.
- Not meaningful if numerator is negative.
- Not meaningful if denominator is negative.
- Not meaningful if both numerator and denominator are negative.

Incomparable ratio outcomes resulting from differences in accounting standards aside, multiples or percentages become unreasonably large when a denominator approaches zero. This results from a weakness in ratios exposed by the mathematical process. Such unreasonable outcomes can be controlled by setting a range for each ratio and either excluding deviant ratios or adjusting them to a reasonable range.

Average Versus Fiscal Year-End Data

The income statement and the cash flow statement represent data accumulated over an entire period, whereas the balance sheet is a snapshot of assets and liabilities at the end of the fiscal period. Ratios computed using data from both the income statement and the balance sheet will therefore be biased by the end-of-period data. To avoid this situation, data from the balance sheet—the beginning balance and the ending balance—should be averaged.

Although averaging does improve the quality of the outcome, the bias is not entirely eliminated. Theoretically, the data should be continuously weighted to obtain more precise results, but this is not practical.

In some countries, a few ratios such as EPS and the P/E ratio are computed and provided by the companies themselves. Researchers should verify each company's computation process and confirm it independently. Recomputing all such ratios independently will obviously result in a more consistent treatment of all companies.

One Common Currency Versus Local Currency

Most ratios are neutral insofar as currencies are concerned, because both the numerator and the denominator are in the same currency. However, price-related ratios and dividend ratios may be computed using the local currency and/or a currency of the researcher's choice.

In the case of investment in a foreign company, the local currency funds transferred by the investor to the company's host country may be significantly affected by fluctuations in exchange rates. For example, dividend yields and returns on investment should be computed in both currencies. This procedure isolates the impact of currency fluctuations.

11.2.3 Raw Data Adjustment Factor

For most companies, the fiscal periods or quarters and year ends fall on specific dates, the quarters on March 31, June 30, and September 30, and the year ends on December 31. The number of days in a period are 91 days for each quarter and 365 days for each year. However, if a company has an irregular period as a result of reorganization or a simple period change, the number of days in the period changes and comparisons between periods then distort ratios.

To overcome irregularities in the lengths of periods, a ''normalization'' of periods is necessary, using the following computations:

RR4001 Number of Days

IS1700   Exact number of days in the period

RR4002 Annualization Factor

1.0	364 to 371 days for annual
RR4001 ÷ 365	Otherwise
1.0	180 to 185 days for semiannual
RR4001 ÷ 183	Otherwise
1.0	91 to 98 days for quarterly
RR4001 ÷ 91	Otherwise
RR4001	Number of days

RR4003 Average Exchange Rate

An average exchange rate from one currency to a user's currency

11.2.4 Preliminary Data for Ratio Computation

The ratio computation process requires compiling sets of variables to create a single ratio, and the same computation should be repeated for similar ratios. The input variables are designed so they need not be repeated, thereby minimizing subtotal items to reduce maintenance. In computing the following additional subtotal items before any further ratio computation, a great deal of computation time can be saved and the intermediate variables themselves can often be useful in analysis. Even raw data that are used often in analysis should be annualized for further computation if an irregular accounting period is involved.

RR4101 Annualized Sales

IS1001 ÷ RR4002

IS1001   Net Sales
RR4002   Annualization Factor

RR4102 Annualized Total Revenue

IS1020 ÷ RR4002

IS1020   Total Revenue
RR4002   Annualization Factor

RR4103 Annualized Operating Income

IS1099 ÷ RR4002

IS1099   Operating Income
RR4002   Annualization Factor

RR4104 Annualized Income Before Extraordinary Items

IS1199 ÷ RR4002

IS1199   Income Before Extraordinary Items
RR4002   Annualization Factor

RR4105 Annualized Net Income

IS1299 ÷ RR4002

IS1299   Net Income
RR4002   Annualization Factor

RR4106 Annualized Total Dividend

Annualization of total dividends is unnecessary unless the dividends are distributed more often than normal. (''Normal'' may be defined by frequency, that is, once for annual, twice for semiannual, and four times for quarterly distribution.)

RR4107 Annualized Income Before Extraordinary Items per Share

IS1340 ÷ RR4002

IS1340   EPS Before Extraordinary Items
RR4002   Annualization Factor

RR4108 Annualized Earnings per Share

IS1350 ÷ RR4002

IS1350   Primary Earnings per Share
RR4002   Annualization Factor

RR4109 Annualized Cash from Operations

CF3099 ÷ RR4002

CF3099   Cash from Operations
RR4002   Annualization Factor

RR4110 Annualized Dividend per Share

IS1330 ÷ RR4002

Only if dividends are distributed more often than normal
RR4002   Annualization Factor

RR4201 Pretax Income

IS1199 + IS1150

IS1199   Income Before Extraordinary Items
IS1150   Income Tax Expenses

RR4202 Annualized Pretax Income

RR4201 ÷ RR4002

RR4201   Pretax Income
RR4002   Annualization Factor

RR4203 Total Interest Expenses

IS1110 + IS1610

IS1110   Interest Expenses
IS1610   Capitalized Interest Expenses

RR4204 EBIT (Earnings Before Interest and Taxes)

IS1199 + IS1110 + IS1610 + IS1150 + IS1160

IS1199   Income Before Extraordinary Items
IS1110   Interest Expenses
IS1610   Capitalized Interest Expenses
IS1150   Income Tax Expenses
IS1160   Reserve Charges

RR4205 Annualized EBIT

RR4203 ÷ RR4002

RR4203   EBIT
RR4002   Annualization Factor

RR4206 EBDIT (Earnings Before Depreciation, Interest and Taxes)

$$IS1199 + IS1110 + IS1610 + IS1150 + IS1160 + CF3020$$

IS1199   Income Before Extraordinary Items
IS1110   Interest Expenses
IS1610   Capitalized Interest Expenses
IS1150   Income Tax Expenses
IS1160   Reserve Charges
CF3020   Depreciation and Amortization

RR4207 Annualized EBDIT

$$RR4206 \div RR4002$$

RR4206   EBDIT
RR4002   Annualization Factor

RR4300 Working Capital

$$BS2099 - BS2299$$

BS2099   Total Current Assets
BS2299   Total Current Liabilities

RR4301 Changes in Working Capital

$$(BS2099 - BS2299) - (BS2099LY - BS2299LY)$$

BS2099   Total Current Assets
BS2299   Total Current Liabilities
LY   Last Year

RR4302 Net Liquid Capital

$$(BS2010 + BS2020 + BS2030) - (BS2299 + BS2370 + BS2410)$$

BS2010   Cash and Cash Equivalents
BS2020   Marketable Securities and Other Short-Term Investments
BS2030   Accounts and Notes Receivable
BS2299   Total Current Liabilities
BS2370   Long-Term Borrowing
BS2410   Preferred Equity

RR4303 Total Investments

$$BS2020 + BS2035 + BS2170$$

BS2020   Marketable Securities
BS2035   Federal Funds Sold and Securities Purchased Under Resale Agreements (applicable to banks and other financial services)
BS2170   Long-Term Investments and Long-Term Receivables

RR4304 Adjusted Total Assets

BS2199 − BS2195 For Banking and Other Financial Services Formats
BS2199   For Industrial and Insurance Formats

RR4305 Total Common Equity

BS2450 + BS2460 + BS2470

BS2450 Share Capital and Share Premiums
BS2460 Retained Earnings
BS2470 Treasury Stocks (always a negative number)

RR4306 Total Capital

BS2270 + BS2275 + BS2280 + BS2370 + BS2499

This ratio represents all sources of capital provided by outsiders.

BS2270 Short-Term Borrowing
BS2275 Federal Funds Purchased and Securities Sold Under Repurchase Agreements (applicable to banks and other financial services)
BS2280 Short-Term Portion of Long-Term Borrowing
BS2370 Long-Term Borrowing
BS2499 Total Shareholders' Equity

RR4307 Total Debts

BS2270 + BS2275 + BS2280 + BS2370

BS2270 Short-Term Borrowing
BS2275 Federal Funds Purchased and Securities Sold Under Repurchase Agreements (applicable to banks and other financial services)
BS2280 Short-Term Portion of Long-Term Borrowing
BS2370 Long-Term Borrowing

RR4400 Free Cash Flow

CF3099 − CF3120 (or CF3420) − CF3210 (or CF3410)

This ratio represents excess cash available for capital investments in addition to routine investment to maintain normal operating levels and dividend payments.

CF3099 Cash from Operations
CF3120 Capital Expenditures in the Investing/Financing Approach
CF3420 Capital Expenditures in the Sources/Uses Approach
CF3210 Dividends Paid in the Investing/Financing Approach
CF3410 Dividends Paid in the Sources/Uses Approach

RR4401 Annualized Free Cash Flow

RR4400 ÷ RR4002

RR4400   Free Cash Flow
RR4002   Annualization Factor

RR4402 Excess Cash Flow

CF3099 − CF3120 (or CF3420)

This ratio represents cash after interest payments and operating needs available for dividend payments and additional capital expenditures.

CF3099   Cash from Operations
CF3120   Capital Expenditures in the Investing/Financing Approach
CF3420   Capital Expenditures in the Sources/Uses Approach

RR4403 Annualized Excess Cash Flow

RR4402 ÷ RR4002

RR4402   Excess Cash Flow
RR4002   Annualization Factor

RR4404 Total Market Capitalization

BS2710 × Price

BS2710   Number of Shares Outstanding
Price   Stock Price at Fiscal Year End

For multiple shares, market capitalization should be the aggregate of market capitalization for all shares. The stock price of a nontraded share among multiple shares may be assumed to be the equivalent of the primary share based on the dividend right parity (BS2730).

RR4500 Sales (Revenue) per Share

RR4102 ÷ IS1360

RR4102   Annualized Sales (Revenue)
IS1360   Weighted Average Number of Shares

RR4501 Operating Income per Share

RR4103 ÷ IS1360

RR4103   Annualized Operating Income
IS1360   Weighted Average Number of Shares

RR4502 EBIT per Share

RR4205 ÷ ISR1360

RR4205   Annualized Earnings Before Interest and Taxes
IS1360   Weighted Average Number of Shares

RR4503 EBDIT per Share

RR4207 ÷ IS1360

RR4207   Annualized Earnings Before Depreciation, Interest, and Taxes
IS1360   Weighted Average Number of Shares

RR4600 Working Capital per Share

RR4300 ÷ BS2710

RR4300   Working Capital
BS2710   Number of Shares Outstanding

RR4601 Net Liquid Capital per Share

RR4302 ÷ BS2710

RR4302   Net Liquid Capital
BS2710   Number of Shares Outstanding

RR4602 Book Value per Share

(BS2450 + BS2460) ÷ BS2710

BS2450   Share Capital and Share Premiums
BS2460   Retained Earnings
BS2710   Number of Shares Outstanding

RR4603 Tangible Fixed Assets per Share

BS2130 ÷ BS2710

BS2130   Net Tangible Fixed Assets
BS2710   Number of Shares Outstanding

RR4700 Cash Flow per Share

RR4109 ÷ IS1360

RR4109   Annualized Cash from Operations
IS1360   Weighted Average Number of Shares

RR4701 Free Cash Flow per Share

$$RR4401 \div IS1360$$

RR4401   Annualized Free Cash Flow
IS1360   Weighted Average Number of Shares

RR4702 Excess Cash Flow per Share

$$RR4403 \div IS1360$$

RR4403   Annualized Excess Cash Flow
IS1360   Weighted Average Number of Shares

11.2.5 Profitability Ratios

RR5000 Effective Tax Rate (%)

$$(IS1150 \div RR4201) \times 100$$

IS1150   Income Tax Expenses
RR4201   Pretax Income

RR5100 Gross Margin (%)

$$(1 - IS1040 \div IS1001) \times 100$$

IS1040   Total Direct Expenses
IS1001   Net Sales

RR5101 Operating Margin (%)

$$(1 - IS1099 \div IS1020) \times 100$$

IS1099   Operating Income
IS1020   Total Revenue

RR5102 Pretax Margin (%)

$$(RR4201 \div IS1020) \times 100$$

RR4201   Pretax Income
IS1020   Total Revenue

RR5103 Net Margin (%)

$$(IS1299 \div IS1020) \times 100$$

IS1299   Net Income
IS1020   Total Revenue

RR5104 Net Margin Before Extraordinary Items (%)

$$(IS1199 \div IS1020) \times 100$$

IS1199   Income Before Extraordinary Items
IS1020   Total Revenue

RR5105 Nonoperating Income Margin (%)

$$((-IS1110 - IS1130 - IS1140 - IS1150 - IS1160) \div IS1020) \times 100$$

IS1110   Interest Expenses (other than Banking and Other Financial Services)
IS1130   Loss (Gain) from Associated Companies
IS1140   Other Nonoperating Loss (Gain)
IS1150   Income Tax Expenses (Credits)
IS1160   Reserve Charges (Credits)
IS1020   Total Revenue

RR5110 Margin on Discontinued Operations

$$(-IS1630 \div IS1620) \times 100$$

IS1630   Loss (Gain) from Discontinued Operations
IS1620   Sales from Discontinued Operations

RR5111 Profitability of Investments in Associated Companies

$$(-IS1130 \div BS2180) \times 100$$

IS1130   Loss (Gain) from Associated Companies
BS2180   Investments in Associated Companies

RR5200 Sales Growth (%)

$$(RR4101CY \div RR4101LY - 1) \times 100$$

RR4101   Annualized Sales
CY   Current Year
LY   Last Year

RR5201 Revenue Growth (%)

$$(RR4102CY \div RR4102LY - 1) \times 100$$

RR4102   Annualized Total Revenue
CY   Current Year
LY   Last Year

RR5202 Operating Income Growth (%)

$$(RR4103CY \div RR4103LY - 1) \times 100$$

RR4103   Annualized Operating Income
CY   Current Year
LY   Last Year

RR5203 Pretax Income Growth (%)

$$(RR4202CY \div RR4202LY) \times 100$$

RR4202   Annualized Pretax Income
CY   Current Year
LY   Last Year

RR5204 Net Income Growth (%)

$$(RR4105CY \div RR4105LY) \times 100$$

RR4105   Annualized Net Income
CY   Current Year
LY   Last Year

RR5300 Return on Assets Before Extraordinary Items

$$(RR4104 \div ((RR4304CY + RR4304LY) \div 2)) \times 100$$

RR4104   Annualized Income Before Extraordinary Items
RR4304   Adjusted Total Assets
CY   Current Year
LY   Last Year

RR5301 Return on Assets (%)

$$(RR4105 \div ((RR4304CY + RR4304LY) \div 2)) \times 100$$

RR4105   Annualized Net Income
RR4304   Adjusted Total Assets
CY   Current Year
LY   Last Year

RR5302 Return on Shareholders' Equity Before Extraordinary Items (%)

$$(RR4104 \div ((BS2499CY + BS2499LY) \div 2)) \times 100$$

RR4104   Annualized Income Before Extraordinary Items
BS2499   Total Shareholders' Equity
CY   Current Year
LY   Last Year

RR5303 Return on Shareholders' Equity (%)

$$(RR4105 \div ((BS2499CY + BS2499LY) \div 2)) \times 100$$

RR4105   Annualized Net Income
BS2499   Total Shareholders' Equity
CY   Current Year
LY   Last Year

RR5304 Return on Common Equity (%)

$$((RR4105 - IS1310) \div ((BS2450CY + BS2460CY$$
$$+ BS2450LY + BS2460LY) \div 2)) \times 100$$

RR4105   Annualized Net Income
IS1310   Cash Dividends to Preferred Stock
BS2450   Share Capital and Share Premiums
BS2460   Retained Earnings
CY   Current Year
LY   Last Year

RR5305 Operating Income to Total Capital (%)

$$(RR4103 \div ((RR4306CY + RR4306LY) \div 2)) \times 100$$

RR4103   Annualized Operating Income
RR4306   Total Capital
CY   Current Year
LY   Last Year

RR5306 Return on Capital (%)

$$((RR4105 + RR4203 \times (1 - RR5000 \div 100)$$
$$+ (IS1230 \div RR4002)) \div ((RR4306CY + RR4306LY) \div 2)) \times 100$$

RR4105   Annualized Net Income
RR4203   Total Interest Expenses
RR5000   Effective Tax Rate
IS1230   Minority Interests
RR4002   Annualization Factor
RR4306   Total Capital
CY   Current Year
LY   Last Year

RR5400 Asset Turnover (X)

$$RR4102 \div ((RR4304CY + RR4304LY) \div 2)$$

RR4102   Annualized Total Revenue
RR4304   Adjusted Total Assets
CY   Current Year
LY   Last Year

RR5401 Tangible Fixed Asset Turnover (X)

$$RR4101 \div ((BS2130CY + BS2130LY) \div 2)$$

RR4101   Annualized Sales
BS2130   Net Tangible Fixed Assets
CY   Current Year
LY   Last Year

RR5402 Asset Growth (%)

$$((RR4304CY \div RR4304LY) - 1) \times 100$$

RR4304   Adjusted Total Assets
CY   Current Year
LY   Last Year

RR5403 Assets per Employee

$$RR4304 \div BS2800$$

RR4304   Adjusted Total Assets
BS2800   Number of Employees

RR5404 Tangible Fixed Assets per Employee

$$BS2130 \div BS2800$$

BS2130   Net Tangible Fixed Assets
BS2800 . Number of Employees

RR5405 Sales per Employee

$$RR4101 \div ((BS2800CY + BS2800LY) \div 2)$$

RR4101   Annualized Sales
BS2800   Number of Employees
CY   Current Year
LY   Last Year

RR5406 Revenue per Employee

$$RR4102 \div ((BS2800CY + BS2800LY) \div 2)$$

RR4102   Annualized Total Revenue
BS2800   Number of Employees
CY   Current Year
LY   Last Year

RR5407 Personnel Expenses per Employee

$$(IS1530 \div RR4002) \div ((BS2800CY + BS2800LY) \div 2)$$

IS1530	Personnel Expenses
RR4002	Annualization Factor
BS2800	Number of Employees
CY	Current Year
LY	Last Year

11.2.6 Financial Stability Ratios

RR6000 Current Ratio (X)

$$BS2099 \div BS2299$$

BS2099	Total Current Assets
BS2299	Total Current Liabilities

RR6001 Quick Ratio (X)

$$(BS2010 + BS2020 + BS2030) \div BS2299$$

BS2010	Cash and Cash Equivalents
BS2020	Marketable Securities and Other Short-Term Investments
BS2030	Accounts and Notes Receivable
BS2299	Total Current Liabilities

RR6002 Accounts Receivable Turnover (X)

$$RR4101 \div ((BS2030CY + BS2030LY) \div 2)$$

RR4101	Annualized Sales
BS2030	Accounts and Notes Receivable
CY	Current Year
LY	Last Year

RR6003 Accounts Receivable Days (Days)

For annual:	$365 \div RR6002$
For semiannual:	$182 \div RR6002$
For quarterly:	$92 \div RR6002$
RR6002	Accounts Receivable Turnover

RR6004 Inventory Turnover (X)

$$IS1520 \div ((BS2040CY + BS2040LY) \div 2)$$

IS1520	Cost of Materials
BS2040	Inventory
CY	Current Year
LY	Last Year

RR6005 Inventory Days (Days)

For annual:	$365 \div$ RR6004
For semiannual:	$182 \div$ RR6004
For quarterly:	$92 \div$ RR6004
RR6004	Inventory Turnover

RR6006 Total Debts to Total Assets (%)

$$(\text{RR4307} \div \text{RR4304}) \times 100$$

RR4307   Total Debts
RR4304   Adjusted Total Assets

RR6007 Common Equity to Total Assets (%)

$$(\text{RR4305} \div \text{RR4304}) \times 100$$

RR4305   Total Common Equity
RR4304   Adjusted Total Assets

RR6008 Total Debts to Shareholders' Equity (%)

$$(\text{RR4307} \div \text{BS2499}) \times 100$$

RR4307   Total Debts
BS2499   Total Shareholders' Equity

RR6009 Long-Term Debts to Shareholders' Equity (%)

$$(\text{BS2370} \div \text{BS2499}) \times 100$$

BS2370   Long-Term Borrowing
BS2499   Total Shareholders' Equity

RR6010 Total Debts to Common Equity (%)

$$(\text{RR4307} \div \text{RR4305}) \times 100$$

RR4307   Total Debts
RR4305   Total Common Equity

RR6011 Long-Term Debts to Common Equity (%)

$$(\text{BS2370} \div \text{RR4305}) \times 100$$

BS2370   Long-Term Borrowing
RR4305   Total Common Equity

RR6012 Shareholders' Equity to Total Assets (%)

$(BS2499 \div RR4304) \times 100$

BS2499   Total Shareholders' Equity
RR4304   Adjusted Total Assets

RR6013 Total Debts to Total Capital (%)

$(RR4307 \div RR4306) \times 100$

RR4307   Total Debts
RR4306   Total Capital

RR6014 Long-Term Debts to Total Capital (%)

$(BS2370 \div RR4306) \times 100$

BS2370   Long-Term Borrowing
RR4306   Total Capital

RR6015 Shareholders' Equity to Total Capital (%)

$(BS2499 \div RR4306) \times 100$

BS2499   Total Shareholders' Equity
RR4306   Total Capital

RR6016 Retained Earnings to Total Assets (%)

$(BS2460 \div RR4304) \times 100$

BS2460   Retained Earnings
RR4304   Adjusted Total Assets

RR6017 Working Capital to Total Assets (%)

$(RR4300 \div RR4304) \times 100$

RR4300   Working Capital
RR4304   Adjusted Total Assets

RR6100 Cash from Operations to Revenue (%)

$(CF3099 \div IS1020) \times 100$

CF3099   Cash from Operations
IS1020   Total Revenue

RR6101 Interest Expense Coverage (X)

RR4206 ÷ RR4203

RR4206   Earnings Before Depreciation, Interest, and Taxes
RR4203   Total Interest Expenses

RR6102 EBIT to Interest Expenses (X)

RR4204 ÷ RR4203

RR4204   Earnings Before Interest and Taxes
RR4203   Total Interest Expenses

RR6103 Times Interest Earned (X)

IS1099 ÷ RR4203

IS1099   Operating Income
RR4203   Total Interest Expenses

RR6104 Cash from Operations to Fixed Charges (X)

CF3099 ÷ (RR4203 × (1 − RR5000 ÷ 100) + IS1310)

CF3099	Cash from Operations
RR4203	Total Interest Expenses
RR5000	Effective Tax Rate
RR4203 × (1 − RR5000 ÷ 100)	Interest Expenses After Taxes
IS1310	Cash Dividends to Preferred Stocks

RR6105 Cash Dividend Coverage (X)

(IS1199 − IS1230 − IS1310) ÷ IS1320

IS1199   Income before Extraordinary Items
IS1230   Minority Interests
IS1310   Cash Dividends to Preferred Stocks
IS1320   Cash Dividends to Common Stocks

RR6106 EBDIT to Total Debts (%)

(RR4206 ÷ RR4307) × 100

RR4206   Earnings Before Depreciation, Interest, and Taxes
RR4307   Total Debts

RR6107 Repayment Ratio (%)

$$(RR4400 \div CF3240 \ (\text{or } CF3440)) \times 100$$

RR4400   Free Cash Flow
CF3240   Decrease in Long-Term Borrowing (Investing/Financing Approach)
CF3440   Decrease in Long-Term Borrowing (Sources/Uses Approach)

RR6108 Dividend Payout Ratio (%)

$$(IS1320 \div (IS1299 - IS1310)) \times 100$$

IS1320   Cash Dividends to Common Stocks
IS1299   Net Income
IS1310   Cash Dividends to Preferred Stocks

RR6109 Retention Ratio (%)

$$100 - RR6108$$

RR6108   Dividend Payout Ratio

RR6110 Net Worth Growth (%)

$$(RR4305CY \div RR4305LY) \times 100$$

RR4305   Total Common Equity
CY   Current Year
LY   Last Year

RR6111 EBIT to Total Assets (%)

$$(RR4205 \div RR4304) \times 100$$

RR4205   Annualized EBIT
RR4304   Adjusted Total Assets

11.2.7. Growth Potential Ratios

RR6500 Earnings per Share Growth (%)

$$((RR4107CY \div RR4107LY) - 1) \times 100$$

RR4107   Annualized Earnings per Share Before Extraordinary Items
CY   Current Year
.LY   Last Year

RR6501 Net Earnings per Share Growth (%)

$$((RR42108CY \div RR4108LY) - 1) \times 100$$

RR4108   Annualized Earnings per Share
CY   Current Year
LY   Last Year

RR6502 Dividend per Share Growth (%)

$$((RR4110CY \div RR4110LY) - 1) \times 100$$

RR4110   Annualized Dividend per Share
CY   Current Year
LY   Last Year

RR6503 Cash Flow per Share Growth (%)

$$((RR4700CY \div RR4700LY) - 1) \times 100$$

RR4700   Cash Flow per Share
CY   Current Year
LY   Last Year

RR6504 Book Value per Share Growth (%)

$$((RR4602CY \div RR4602LY) - 1) \times 100$$

RR4602   Book Value per Share
CY   Current Year
LY   Last Year

RR6505 Growth in Capital (%)

$$((RR4306CY \div RR4306LY) - 1) \times 100$$

RR4306   Total Capital
CY   Current Year
LY   Last Year

RR6506 Reinvestment Rate (%)

$$((IS1299 - IS1310 - IS1320) \div RR4002) \div ((RR4305CY + RR4305LY) \div 2)) \times 100$$

IS1299   Net Income
IS1310   Cash Dividends to Preferred Stocks
IS1320   Cash Dividends to Common Stocks
RR4002   Annualization Factor
RR4305   Total Common Equity
CY   Current Year
LY   Last Year

RR6507 Sustainable Growth Rate (%)

$$RR5200 \times RR5400 \times RR6109 \div RR6007$$

RR5200   Sales Growth
RR5400   Asset Turnover
RR6109   Retention Ratio
RR6007   Common Equity to Total Assets

RR6600 Employee Growth (%)

$$((BS2800CY \div BS2800LY) - 1) \times 100$$

BS2800   Number of Employees
CY   Current Year
LY   Last Year

RR6601 R & D Expenditure to Sales (%)

$$(IS1550 \div IS1001) \times 100$$

IS1550   Research and Development Expenditure
IS1001   Net Sales

RR6602 Accumulated Depreciation to Gross Tangible Fixed Assets (%)

$$(BS2120 \div BS2110) \times 100$$

BS2120   Accumulated Depreciation
BS2110   Gross Tangible Fixed Assets

RR6603 Accumulated Depreciation to Gross Depreciable Fixed Assets (%)

$$(BS2120 \div (BS2110 - BS2560)) \times 100$$

BS2120   Accumulated Depreciation
BS2110   Gross Tangible Fixed Assets
BS2560   Nondepreciable Fixed Assets

RR6604 Depreciation Expenses to Net Tangible Fixed Assets (%)

$$(IS1540 \div ((BS2130CY + BS2130LY) \div 2)) \times 100$$

IS1540   Depreciation Expenses
BS2130   Net Tangible Fixed Assets
CY   Current Year
LY   Last Year

RR6610 Capital Expenditure to Gross Tangible Fixed Assets (%)

$$(((- CF3120 \text{ or } CF3420) \div RR4002) \div BS2110LY) \times 100$$

CF3120   Capital Expenditure (Investing/Financing Approach)
CF3420   Capital Expenditure (Sources/Uses Approach)
RR4002   Annualization Factor
BS2110   Gross Tangible Fixed Assets
LY   Last Year

RR6611 Capital Expenditure to Net Tangible Fixed Assets (%)

$$(((- CF3120 \text{ or } CF3420) \div RR4002) \div BS2130LY) \times 100$$

CF3120   Capital Expenditure (Investing/Financing Approach)
CF3420   Capital Expenditure (Sources/Uses Approach)
RR4002   Annualization Factor
BS2130   Net Tangible Fixed Assets
LY   Last Year

RR6612 Capital Expenditure to Total Assets (%)

$$(((- CF3120 \text{ or } CF3420) \div RR4002) \div RR4304LY) \times 100$$

CF3120   Capital Expenditure (Investing/Financing Approach)
CF3420   Capital Expenditure (Sources/Uses Approach)
RR4002   Annualization Factor
RR4304   Adjusted Total Assets
LY   Last Year

RR6613 Capital Expenditure to Sales (%)

$$((- CF3120 \text{ or } CF3420) \div IS1001) \times 100$$

CF3120   Capital Expenditure (Investing/Financing Approach)
CF3420   Capital Expenditure (Sources/Uses Approach)
IS1001   Net Sales

RR6614 Cash Generations to Cash Requirements (X)

$$CF3099 \div ((- CF3210 \text{ or } CF3410) + (- CF3120 \text{ or } CF3420))$$

CF3099   Cash from Operations
CF3210   Dividends Paid (Investing/Financing Approach)
CF3410   Dividends Paid (Sources/Uses Approach)
CF3120   Capital Expenditure (Investing/Financing Approach)
CF3420   Capital Expenditure (Sources/Uses Approach)

RR6615 Cash Flow to Net Income (X)

CF3099 ÷ IS1299

CF3099   Cash from Operations
IS1299   Net Income

11.2.8 Special Ratios for Banking

RR7000 Net Interest Income Before Provision

IS1011 − IS1022

IS1011   Interest Income
IS1022   Interest Expenses

RR7001 Net Interest Income

IS1011 − IS1022 − IS1023

IS1011   Interest Income
IS1022   Interest Expense
IS1023   Provision for Loan Losses

RR7002 Annualized Net Interest Income

RR7001 ÷ RR4002

RR7001   Net Interest Income
RR4002   Annualization Factor

RR7003 Net Banking Income

IS1011 + IS1012 + IS1014 + IS1015 − IS1022 − IS1023 − IS1024

IS1011   Interest Income
IS1012   Trading Account Profit (Loss) and Foreign Exchange Revenue
IS1014   Investment Income
IS1015   Commissions and Fees Earned
IS1022   Interest Expenses
IS1023   Provision for Loan Losses
IS1024   Commissions and Fees Paid

RR7004 Annualized Net Banking Income

RR7003 ÷ RR4002

RR7003   Net Banking Income
RR4002   Annualization Factor

RR7005 Non-Interest Income

$$IS1020 - IS1011$$

IS1020   Total Revenue
IS1011   Interest Income

RR7006 Total Investments

$$BS2020 + BS2035 + BS2065 + BS2170$$

BS2020   Short-Term Investments
BS2035   Federal Funds Sold and Securities Purchased Under Resale Agreements
BS2065   Due from Banks and Other Interbank Assets
BS2170   Long-Term Investments

RR7007 Earning Assets

$$BS2060 + BS2020 + BS2035 + BS2065 + BS2170$$

BS2060   Net Loans
BS2020   Short-Term Investments
BS2035   Federal Funds Sold and Securities Purchased Under Resale Agreements
BS2065   Due from Banks and Other Interbank Assets
BS2170   Long-Term Investments

RR7010 Net Interest Margin (%)

$$(RR7000 \div IS1011) \times 100$$

RR7000   Net Interest Income Before Provision
IS1011   Interest Income

RR7011 Net Banking Margin (%)

$$(RR7003 \div (IS1011 + IS1012 + IS1014 + IS1015)) \times 100$$

RR7003   Net Banking Income
IS1011   Interest Income
IS1012   Trading Account Profit (Loss) and Foreign Exchange Revenue
IS1014   Investment Income
IS1015   Commissions and Fees Earned

RR7012 Investment Income to Total Revenue (%)

$$((IS1011 + IS1012 + IS1014) \div IS1020) \times 100$$

IS1011   Interest Income
IS1012   Trading Account Profit (Loss) and Foreign Exchange Revenue
IS1014   Investment Income
IS1020   Total Revenue

RR7013 Non-Interest Income to Total Revenue (%)

$$(RR7005 \div IS1020) \times 100$$

RR7005   Non-Interest Income
IS1020   Total Revenue

RR7014 Net Investment Income to Operating Income (%)

$$((IS1011 + IS1012 + IS1014 - IS1022 - IS1023) \div IS1099) \times 100$$

IS1011   Interest Income
IS1012   Trading Account Profit (Loss) and Foreign Exchange Revenue
IS1014   Investment Income
IS1022   Interest Expenses
IS1023   Provision for Loan Losses
IS1099   Operating Income

RR7020 Interest Income to Total Loans (%)

$$((IS1650 \div RR4002) \div ((BS2055CY + BS2055LY) \div 2)) \times 100$$

IS1650   Interest Income from Loans
RR4002   Annualization Factor
BS2055   Total Loans
CY   Current Year
LY   Last Year

RR7021 Provision for Loan Losses to Interest Income (%)

$$(IS1023 \div IS1650) \times 100$$

IS1023   Provision for Loan Losses
IS1650   Interest Income from Loans

RR7022 Provision for Loan Losses to Total Loans (%)

$$(IS1023 \div RR4002) ((BS2055CY + BS2055LY) \div 2)) \times 100$$

IS1023   Provision for Loan Losses
RR4002   Annualization Factor
BS2055   Total Loans
CY   Current Year
LY   Last Year

RR7023 Actual Loan Losses to Provision for Loan Losses (%)

$$(IS1640 \div IS1023) \times 100$$

IS1640   Actual Loan Loss
IS1023   Provision for Loan Losses

RR7024 Loan Loss Coverage (X)

$$(RR4201 + IS1640) \div IS1023$$

RR4201   Pretax Income
IS1640   Actual Loan Loss
IS1023   Provision for Loan Losses

RR7025 Total Interest Income to Loan Equivalents (%)

$$(IS1011 \div RR4002 \times 100) \div (((BS2035 + BS2055 + BS2065)CY$$
$$+ (BS2035 + BS2055 + BS2065)LY \div 2))$$

IS1011   Interest Income
RR4002   Annualization Factor
BS2035   Federal Funds Sold and Securities Purchased Under Resale
           Agreements
BS2055   Total Loans
BS2065   Due from Banks and Other Interbank Assets
CY   Current Year
LY   Last Year

RR7030 Investment Income to Total Investments (%)

$$((IS1012 + IS1014) \div RR4002) \div ((RR7006CY + RR7006LY) \div 2) \times 100$$

IS1012   Trading Account Profit (Loss) and Foreign Exchange Revenue
IS1014   Investment Income
RR4002   Annualization Factor
RR7006   Total Investments
CY   Current Year
LY   Last Year

RR7031 Investment Income to Earning Assets (%)

$$((IS1011 + IS1012 + IS1014) \div RR4002)$$
$$\div ((RR7007CY + RR7007LY) \div 2) \times 100$$

IS1011   Interest Income
IS1012   Trading Account Profit (Loss) and Foreign Exchange Revenue
IS1014   Investment Income
RR4002   Annualization Factor
RR7007   Earning Assets
CY   Current Year
LY   Last Year

RR7032 Efficiency of Earning Assets (%)

$$((((IS1011 + IS1012 + IS1014 - IS1022 - IS1023) \div RR4002)$$
$$\times 100) \div ((RR7007CY + RR7007LY) \div 2)$$

IS1011   Interest Income
IS1012   Trading Account Profit (Loss) and Foreign Exchange Revenue
IS1014   Investment Income
IS1022   Interest Expenses
IS1023   Provision for Loan Losses
RR4002   Annualization Factor
RR7007   Earning Assets
CY   Current Year
LY   Last Year

RR7033 Operating Income to Earning Assets (%)

$$(RR4103 \div ((RR7007CY + RR7007LY) \div 2)) \times 100$$

RR4103   Annualized Operating Income
RR7007   Earning Assets
CY   Current Year
LY   Last Year

RR7034 Net Income to Earning Assets (%)

$$(RR4105 \div ((RR7007CY + RR7007LY) \div 2)) \times 100$$

RR4105   Annualized Net Income
RR7007   Earning Assets
CY   Current Year
LY   Last Year

RR7100 Total Debts

$$BS2270 + BS2275 + BS2280 + BS2370$$

BS2270   Due to Banks and Other Short-Term Borrowing
BS2275   Federal Funds Purchased and Securities Sold Under Repurchase Agreements
BS2280   Short-Term Portion of Long-Term Borrowing
BS2370   Long-Term Borrowing

RR7101 Total Interest-Bearing Liabilities

$$BS2220 + BS2270 + BS2275 + BS2280 + BS2370$$

BS2220   Total Deposits
BS2270   Due to Banks and Other Short-Term Borrowing
BS2275   Federal Funds Purchased and Securities Sold Under Repurchase Agreements
BS2280   Short-Term Portion of Long-Term Borrowing
BS2370   Long-Term Borrowing

RR7110 Interest Expenses to Total Deposits (%)

$$((IS1660 \div RR4002) \div ((BS2220CY + BS2220LY) \div 2)) \times 100$$

IS1660   Interest Expenses to Deposits
RR4002   Annualization Factor
BS2220   Total Deposits
CY   Current Year
LY   Last Year

RR7111 Interest Expenses to Total Debts (%)

$$((((IS1022 - IS1660) \div RR4002) \div ((RR7100LY + RR7100CY) \div 2)) \times 100$$

IS1022   Interest Expenses
IS1660   Interest Expenses to Deposits
RR4002   Annualization Factor
RR7100   Total Debts
CY   Current Year
LY   Last Year

RR7112 Interest Expenses to Interest-Bearing Liabilities (%)

$$((IS1022 \div RR4002) \div ((RR7101CY + RR7101LY) \div 2)) \times 100$$

IS1022   Interest Expenses
RR4002   Annualization Factor
RR7101   Total Interest-Bearing Liabilities
CY   Current Year
LY   Last Year

RR7200 Total Loans to Total Assets (%)

$$(BS2055 \div RR4304) \times 100$$

BS2055   Total Loans
RR4304   Adjusted Total Assets

RR7201 Net Loans to Earning Assets (%)

$$(BS2060 \div RR7007) \times 100$$

BS2060   Net Loans
RR7007   Earning Assets

RR7202 Earning Assets to Total Assets (%)

$$(RR7007 \div RR4304) \times 100$$

RR7007   Earning Assets
RR4304   Adjusted Total Assets

RR7203 Total Loans to Total Capital (%)

$$(BS2055 \div RR4306) \times 100$$

BS2055   Total Loans
RR4306   Total Capital

RR7204 Earning Assets to Total Capital (%)

$$(RR7007 \div RR4306) \times 100$$

RR7007   Earning Assets
RR4306   Total Capital

RR7205 Growth in Total Loans (%)

$$(BS2055CY \div BS2055LY - 1) \times 100$$

BS2055   Total Loans
CY   Current Year
LY   Last Year

RR7210 Nonperforming Assets to Total Loans (%)

$$(BS2529 \div BS2055) \times 100$$

BS2529   Nonperforming Assets
BS2055   Total Loans

RR7211 Nonperforming Assets to Loan Loss Reserves (%)

$$(BS2529 \div BS2057) \times 100$$

BS2529   Nonperforming Assets
BS2057   Loan Loss Reserves

RR7212 Loan Loss Reserves to Total Loans (%)

$$(BS2057 \div BS2055) \times 100$$

BS2057   Loan Loss Reserves
BS2055   Total Loans

RR7213 Foreign Loans to Total Loans (%)

$$(BS2525 \div BS2055) \times 100$$

BS2525   Foreign Loans
BS2055   Total Loans

RR7214 Customers' Liabilities for Acceptances to Total Assets (%)

$$(BS2195 \div RR4304) \times 100$$

BS2195   Customers' Liabilities for Acceptances
RR4304   Adjusted Total Assets

RR7215 Total Customers' Liabilities to Total Assets (%)

$$((BS2195 + BS2695) \div RR4304) \times 100$$

BS2195   Customers' Liabilities for Acceptances
BS2695   Off-Balance Contingent Liabilities
RR4304   Adjusted Total Assets

RR7300 Total Deposits to Total Capital (%)

$$(BS2220 \div RR4306) \times 100$$

BS2220   Total Deposits
RR4306   Total Capital

RR7301 Total Deposits to Shareholders' Equity (%)

$$(BS2220 \div BS2499) \times 100$$

BS2220   Total Deposits
BS2499   Total Shareholders' Equity

RR7302 Growth in Total Deposits (%)

$$(BS2220CY \div BS2220LY - 1) \times 100$$

BS2220   Total Deposits
CY   Current Year
LY   Last Year

RR7303 Foreign Deposits to Total Deposits (%)

$$(BS2625 \div BS2220) \times 100$$

BS2625   Foreign Deposits
BS2220   Total Deposits

RR7304 Total Deposits to Interest-Bearing Liabilities (%)

$$(BS2220 \div RR7101) \times 100$$

BS2220   Total Deposits
RR7101   Total Interest-Bearing Liabilities

RR7310 Total Loans to Total Deposits (%)

$$(BS2055 \div BS2220) \times 100$$

BS2055   Total Loans
BS2220   Total Deposits

RR7311 Total Loans to Total Capital (%)

$$(BS2055 \div RR4306) \times 100$$

BS2055   Total Loans
RR4306   Total Capital

RR7312 Total Loans to Total Available Funds (%)

$$(BS2055 \div (BS2220 + RR4306)) \times 100$$

BS2055   Total Loans
BS2220   Total Deposits
RR4306   Total Capital

RR7313 Total Loans to Interest-Bearing Debts (%)

$$(BS2220 \div RR7101) \times 100$$

BS2220   Total Deposits
RR7101   Interest-Bearing Debts

RR7320 Total Investments to Total Deposits (%)

$$(RR4303 \div BS2220) \times 100$$

RR4303   Total Investments
BS2220   Total Deposits

RR7321 Total Investments to Total Available Funds (%)

$$(RR4303 \div (BS2220 + RR4306)) \times 100$$

RR4303   Total Investments
BS2220   Total Deposits
RR4306   Total Capital

RR7322 Total Investments to Interest-Bearing Debts (%)

$$(RR4303 \div RR7101) \times 100$$

RR4303   Total Investments
RR7101   Interest-Bearing Debts

RR7330 Earning Assets to Total Deposits (%)

$$(RR7007 \div BS2220) \times 100$$

RR7007   Earning Assets
BS2220   Total Deposits

RR7331 Earning Assets to Total Capital (%)

$$(RR7007 \div RR4306) \times 100$$

RR7007   Earning Assets
RR4306   Total Capital

RR7332 Earning Assets to Total Available Funds (%)

$$(RR7007 \div (BS2220 + RR4306)) \times 100$$

RR7007   Earning Assets
BS2220   Total Deposits
RR4306   Total Capital

RR7333 Earning Assets to Interest-Bearing Debts (%)

$$(RR7007 \div RR7101) \times 100$$

RR7007   Earning Assets
RR7101   Interest-Bearing Liabilities

RR7340 Short-Term Loans to Total Loans (%)

$$(BS2510 \div BS2055) \times 100$$

BS2510   Short-Term Loans
BS2055   Total Loans

RR7341 Short-Term Loans to Short-Term Deposits (%)

$$(BS2510 \div BS2610) \times 100$$

BS2510   Short-Term Loans
BS2610   Short-Term Deposits

RR7342 Foreign Loans to Foreign Deposits (%)

$$(BS2525 \div BS2625) \times 100$$

BS2525   Foreign Loans
BS2625   Foreign Deposits

RR7343 Short-Term Earning Assets to Short-Term Funds (%)

$$((BS2020 + BS2035 + BS2510 + BS2065)$$
$$\div (BS2610 + BS2270 + BS2275)) \times 100$$

BS2020   Short-Term Investments
BS2035   Federal Funds Sold and Securities Purchased Under Resale
         Agreements
BS2510   Short-Term Loans
BS2065   Due from Banks and Other Interbank Assets
BS2610   Short-Term Deposits
BS2270   Due to Banks and Other Short-Term Borrowing
BS2275   Federal Funds Purchased and Securities Sold Under Repurchase Agreements

RR7344 Long-Term Earning Assets to Long-Term Funds (%)

$$((BS2055 - BS2510 + BS2170)$$
$$\div (BS2220 - BS2610 + BS2370 + BS2499)) \times 100$$

BS2055   Total Loans
BS2510   Short-Term Loans
BS2170   Long-Term Investments
BS2220   Total Deposits
BS2610   Short-Term Deposits
BS2370   Long-Term Borrowing
BS2499   Total Shareholders' Equity

11.2.9 Special Ratios for Insurance Companies

RR7500 Total Investment Income

$$IS1012 + IS1013 + IS1014$$

IS1012   Trading Account Profit (Loss)
IS1013   Income from Real Estate Investments
IS1014   Investment Income

RR7501 Annualized Total Investment Income

$$RR7500 \div RR4002$$

RR7500   Total Investment Income
RR4002   Annualization Factor

RR7510 Net Premium from Life to Total Net Premium (%)

$$(IS1004 \div (IS1004 + IS1007)) \times 100$$

IS1004   Net Premium from Life
IS1007   Net Premium from Non-Life

RR7511 Net Premium from Non-Life to Total Net Premium (%)

$$(IS1007 \div (IS1004 + IS1007)) \times 100$$

IS1004   Net Premium from Life
IS1007   Net Premium from Non-Life

RR7512 Total Investment Income to Total Revenue (%)

$$(RR7500 \div IS1020) \times 100$$

RR7500   Total Investment Income
IS1020   Total Revenue

RR7513 Operating Income to Total Net Premium (%)

$$(IS1099 \div (IS1004 + IS1007)) \times 100$$

IS1099   Operating Income
IS1004   Net Premium from Life
IS1007   Net Premium from Non-Life

RR7514 Net Insurance Margin (%)

$$((IS1004 + IS1007 - IS1031 - IS1032 - IS1033 - IS1034$$
$$- IS1035 - IS1036) \div (IS1004 + IS1007)) \times 100$$

IS1004   Net Premium from Life
IS1007   Net Premium from Non-Life
IS1031   Insurance Claims and Losses for Life
IS1032   Long-Term Insurance Charges (Life)
IS1033   Dividends to Policyholders
IS1034   Underwriting and Policy Acquisition Costs for Life
IS1035   Insurance Claims and Losses for Non-Life
IS1036   Underwriting and Policy Acquisition Costs for Non-Life

RR7515 Insurance Margin (%)

$$((IS1004 + IS1007 - IS1031 - IS1032 - IS1033 - IS1034$$
$$- IS1035 - IS1036) \div IS1020) \times 100$$

IS1004   Net Premium from Life
IS1007   Net Premium from Non-Life
IS1031   Insurance Claims and Losses for Life
IS1032   Long-Term Insurance Charges (Life)
IS1033   Dividends to Policyholders
IS1034   Underwriting and Policy Acquisition Costs for Life
IS1035   Insurance Claims and Losses for Non-Life
IS1036   Underwriting and Policy Acquisition Costs for Non-Life
IS1020   Total Revenue

RR7516 Non-Insurance Margin (%)

$$((IS1012 + IS1013 + IS1014 + IS1019) \div IS1020) \times 100$$

IS1012   Trading Accounts Profit (Loss)
IS1013   Income from Real Estate Investments
IS1014   Investment Income
IS1019   Other Operating Revenue
IS1020   Total Revenue

RR7520 Loss Ratio for Life (%)

$$(IS1031 \div IS1004) \times 100$$

IS1031   Insurance Claims and Losses for Life
IS1004   Net Premium from Life

RR7521 Expense Ratio for Life (%)

$$((IS1033 + IS1034) \div IS1002) \times 100$$

IS1033   Dividends to Policyholders
IS1034   Underwriting and Policy Acquisition Costs for Life
IS1002   Gross Premium from Life

RR7522 Combined Ratio for Life (%)

$$RR7520 + RR7521$$

RR7520   Loss Ratio for Life
RR7521   Expense Ratio for Life

RR7530 Loss Ratio for Non-Life (%)

$$(IS1035 \div IS1007) \times 100$$

IS1035   Insurance Claims and Losses for Non-Life
IS1007   Net Premium from Non-Life

RR7531 Expense Ratio for Non-Life (%)

$$(IS1036 \div IS1005) \times 100$$

IS1036   Underwriting and Policy Acquisition Costs for Non-Life
IS1005   Gross Premium from Non-Life

RR7532 Combined Ratio (%)

$$RR7530 + RR7531$$

RR7530   Loss Ratio for Non-Life
RR7531   Expense Ratio for Non-Life

RR7600 Profitability of Invested Assets (%)

$$(RR7501 \div ((BS2170CY + BS2170LY) \div 2)) \times 100$$

RR7501   Annualized Total Investment Income
BS2170   Total Investments
CY   Current Year
LY   Last Year

RR7601 Profitability of Real Estate Investments (%)

$$((IS1013 \div RR4002) \div ((BS2090CY + BS2090LY) \div 2)) \times 100$$

IS1013   Income from Real Estate Investments
RR4002   Annualization Factor
BS2090   Real Estate Investments
CY   Current Year
LY   Last Year

RR7602 Claims and Losses Reserves to Claims and Losses Expenses for Life (%)

$$(BS2640 \div IS1031 \div RR4002) \times 100$$

BS2640   Claims and Loss Reserve for Life
IS1031   Claims and Losses for Life
RR4002   Annualization Factor

RR7603 Claims and Losses Reserves to Claims and Losses Expenses for Non-Life (%)

$$(BS2642 \div IS1035 \div RR4002) \times 100$$

BS2642   Claims and Loss Reserve for Non-Life
IS1035   Claims and Losses Expenses for Non-Life
RR4002   Annualization Factor

RR7604 Claims and Losses Reserves to Claims and Losses Expenses (%)

$$(BS2230 \div ((IS1031 + IS1035) \div RR4002)) \times 100$$

BS2230   Claims and Losses Reserves
IS1031   Claims and Losses for Life
IS1035   Claims and Losses for Non-Life
RR4002   Annualization Factor

RR7605 Long-Term Insurance Charges to Life Policy Benefits (%)

$$(IS1032 \div RR4002) \div ((BS2235CY + BS2235LY) \div 2)) \times 100$$

IS1032   Long-Term Insurance Charges (Life)
RR4002   Annualization Factor
BS2235   Reserves for Life Policy Benefits
CY   Current Year
LY   Last Year

RR7700 Fixed Income Investments to Total Investments (%)

$$((BS2060 + BS2070) \div BS2170) \times 100$$

BS2060   Loans and Mortgages
BS2070   Fixed Income Securities
BS2170   Total Investments

RR7701 Equity Investments to Total Investments (%)

$$((BS2080 + BS2090) \div BS2170) \times 100$$

BS2080   Equity Securities
BS2090   Real Estate Investments
BS2170   Total Investments

RR7710 Total Investments to Total Insurance Reserves (%)

$$(BS2170 \div BS2240) \times 100$$

BS2170   Total Investments
BS2240   Total Insurance Reserves

RR7711 Total Investments to Total Assets (%)

$$(BS2170 \div BS2199) \times 100$$

BS2170   Total Investments
BS2199   Total Assets

RR7712 Total Investments to Adjusted Total Assets (%)

$$(BS2170 \div RR4304) \times 100$$

BS2170   Total Investments
RR4304   Adjusted Total Assets

RR7713 Total Investments to Total Capital (%)

$$(BS2170 \div RR4306) \times 100$$

BS2170   Total Investments
RR4306   Total Capital

RR7720 Total Insurance Reserves to Total Assets (%)

$$(BS2240 \div BS2199) \times 100$$

BS2240   Total Insurance Reserves
BS2199   Total Assets

RR7721 Total Insurance Reserves to Adjusted Total Assets (%)

$$(BS2240 \div RR4304) \times 100$$

BS2240   Total Insurance Reserves
RR4304   Adjusted Total Assets

RR7722 Total Insurance Reserves to Total Capital (%)

$$(BS2240 \div RR4306) \times 100$$

BS2240   Total Insurance Reserves
RR4306   Total Capital

RR7723 Life Policy in Force to Life Policy Benefits (X)

$$BS2650 \div BS2235$$

BS2650   Life Policy in Force
BS2235   Reserve for Life Policy Benefits

RR7724 Insurance Reserve Growth (%)

$$(BS2240CY \div BS2240LY - 1) \times 100$$

BS2240   Total Insurance Reserves
CY   Current Year
LY   Last Year

11.2.10 Special Ratios for Other Financial Services

RR7000 Net Interest Income Before Provision

$$IS1011 - IS1022$$

IS1011   Interest Income
IS1022   Interest Expenses

RR7001 Net Interest Income

$$IS1011 - IS1022 - IS1023$$

IS1011   Interest Income
IS1022   Interest Expenses
IS1023   Provision for Loan Losses

RR7002 Annualized Net Interest Income

$$RR7001 \div RR4002$$

RR7001   Net Interest Income
RR4002   Annualization Factor

RR7003 Net Financial Services Income

$$IS1011 + IS1012 + IS1014 + IS1015 - IS1022 - IS1023 - IS1024$$

IS1011 Interest Income
IS1012 Trading Account Profit (Loss)
IS1014 Investment Income
IS1015 Commissions and Fees Earned
IS1022 Interest Expenses
IS1023 Provision for Loan Losses
IS1024 Commissions and Fees Paid

RR7004 Annualized Net Financial Services Income

$$RR7003 \div RR4002$$

RR7003 Net Banking Income
RR4002 Annualization Factor

RR7005 Non-Interest Income

$$IS1020 - IS1011$$

IS1020 Total Revenue
IS1011 Interest Income

RR7008 Total Investment Income

$$IS1011 + IS1012 + IS1013 + IS1014$$

IS1011 Interest Income
IS1012 Trading Account Profit (Loss)
IS1013 Income from Real Estate Investments
IS1014 Investment Income

RR7009 Net Investment Income

$$IS1011 - IS1022 - IS1023 + IS1012 + IS1013 + IS1014$$

IS1011 Interest Income
IS1022 Interest Expenses
IS1023 Provision for Loan Losses
IS1012 Trading Account Profit (Loss)
IS1013 Income from Real Estate Investments
IS1014 Investment Income

RR7010 Net Interest Margin (%)

$$(RR7000 \div IS1011) \times 100$$

RR7000 Net Interest Income Before Provision
IS1011 Interest Income

RR7011 Net Financial Services Margin (%)

$$(RR7003 \div (IS1011 + IS1012 + IS1014 + IS1015)) \times 100$$

RR7003	Net Financial Services Income
IS1011	Interest Income
IS1012	Trading Account Profit (Loss)
IS1014	Investment Income
IS1015	Commissions and Fees Earned

RR7012 Total Investment Income to Total Revenue (%)

$$(RR7008 \div IS1020) \times 100$$

RR7008	Total Investment Income
IS1020	Total Revenue

RR7014 Net Investment Income to Operating Income (%)

$$(RR7009 \div IS1099) \times 100$$

RR7009	Net Investment Income
IS1099	Operating Income

RR7020 Interest Income to Total Loans (%)

$$((IS1011 \div RR4002) \div ((BS2055CY + BS2055LY) \div 2)) \times 100$$

IS1011	Interest Income
RR4002	Annualization Factor
BS2055	Total Loans
CY	Current Year
LY	Last Year

RR7021 Provision for Loan Losses to Interest Income (%)

$$(IS1023 \div IS1011) \times 100$$

IS1023	Provision for Loan Losses
IS1011	Interest Income

RR7022 Provision for Loan Losses to Total Loans (%)

$$(IS1023 \div RR4002) \div ((BS2055CY + BS2055LY) \div 2)) \times 100$$

IS1023	Provision for Loan Losses
RR4002	Annualization Factor
BS2055	Total Loans
CY	Current Year
LY	Last Year

RR7030 Investment Income to Investments Other Than Loans (%)

$$(((\text{IS}1012 + \text{IS}1013 + \text{IS}1014) \div \text{RR}4002) \times 100)$$

$$\div (((\text{BS}2170 - \text{BS}2060)\text{CY} + (\text{BS}2170 - \text{BS}2060)\text{LY}) \div 2)$$

IS1012	Trading Account Profit (Loss)
IS1013	Income from Real Estate Investments
IS1014	Investment Income
BS2170	Total Investments
BS2060	Net Loans
CY	Current Year
LY	Last Year

RR7032 Efficiency of Total Investments (%)

$$((\text{RR}7009 \div \text{RR}4002) \div ((\text{BS}2170\text{CY} + \text{BS}2170\text{LY}) \div 2)) \times 100$$

RR7007	Net Investment Income
RR4002	Annualization Factor
BS2170	Total Investments
CY	Current Year
LY	Last Year

RR7033 Operating Income to Total Investments (%)

$$(\text{RR}4103 \div ((\text{BS}2170\text{CY} + \text{BS}2170\text{LY}) \div 2)) \times 100$$

RR4103	Annualized Operating Income
BS2170	Total Investments
CY	Current Year
LY	Last Year

RR7034 Net Income to Total Investments (%)

$$(\text{RR}4105 \div ((\text{BS}2170\text{CY} + \text{BS}2170\text{LY}) \div 2)) \times 100$$

RR4105	Annualized Net Income
BS2170	Total Investments
CY	Current Year
LY	Last Year

RR7100 Total Debts

$$\text{BS}2270 + \text{BS}2275 + \text{BS}2280 + \text{BS}2370$$

BS2270	Short-Term Borrowing
BS2275	Federal Funds Purchased and Securities Sold Under Repurchase Agreements
BS2280	Short-Term Portion of Long-Term Borrowing
BS2370	Long-Term Borrowing

RR7101 Total Interest Bearing Liabilities

$$BS2220 + BS2270 + BS2275 + BS2280 + BS2370$$

BS2220   Total Deposits
BS2270   Short-Term Borrowing
BS2275   Federal Funds Purchased and Securities Sold Under Repurchase Agreements
BS2280   Short-Term Portion of Long-Term Borrowing
BS2370   Long-Term Borrowing

RR7110 Interest Expenses to Total Deposits (%)

$$((IS1022 \div RR4002) \div ((BS2220CY + BS2220LY) \div 2)) \times 100$$

IS1022   Interest Expenses
RR4002   Annualization Factor
BS2220   Total Deposits
CY   Current Year
LY   Last Year

RR7111 Interest Expenses to Total Debts (%)

$$((IS1022 \div RR4002) \div ((RR7100LY + RR7100CY) \div 2)) \times 100$$

IS1022   Interest Expenses
RR4002   Annualization Factor
RR7100   Total Debts
CY   Current Year
LY   Last Year

RR7112 Interest Expenses to Interest-Bearing Liabilities (%)

$$((IS1022 \div RR4002) \div ((RR7101CY + RR7101LY) \div 2)) \times 100$$

IS1022   Interest Expenses
RR4002   Annualization Factor
RR7101   Total Interest-Bearing Liabilities
CY   Current Year
LY   Last Year

RR7200 Total Loans to Total Assets (%)

$$(BS2050 \div RR4304) \times 100$$

BS2050   Total Loans
RR4304   Adjusted Total Assets

RR7201 Net Loans to Total Investments (%)

$$(BS2060 \div BS2170) \times 100$$

BS2060   Net Loans
BS2170   Total Investments

RR7202 Total Investments to Total Assets (%)

$$(BS2170 \div RR4304) \times 100$$

BS2170   Total Investments
RR4304   Adjusted Total Assets

RR7203 Total Loans to Total Capital (%)

$$(BS2055 \div RR4306) \times 100$$

BS2055   Total Loans
RR4306   Total Capital

RR7204 Total Investments to Total Capital (%)

$$(BS2170 \div RR4306) \times 100$$

BS2170   Total Investments
RR4306   Total Capital

RR7205 Growth in Total Loans (%)

$$(BS2055CY \div BS2055LY - 1) \times 100$$

BS2055   Total Loans
CY   Current Year
LY   Last Year

RR7210 Nonperforming Assets to Total Loans (%)

$$(BS2529 \div BS2055) \times 100$$

BS2529   Nonperforming Assets
BS2055   Total Loans

RR7211 Nonperforming Assets to Loan Loss Reserves (%)

$$(BS2529 \div BS2057) \times 100$$

BS2529   Nonperforming Assets
BS2057   Loan Loss Reserves

RR7212 Loan Loss Reserves to Total Loans (%)

$$(BS2057 \div BS2055) \times 100$$

BS2057   Loan Loss Reserves
BS2055   Total Loans

RR7214 Custody Securities to Total Assets (%)

$$(BS2195 \div RR4304) \times 100$$

BS2195   Custody Securities
RR4304   Adjusted Total Assets

RR7215 Total Customers' Liabilities to Total Assets (%)

$$((BS2195 + BS2695) \div RR4304) \times 100$$

BS2195   Custody Securities
BS2695   Off-Balance Contingent Liabilities
RR4304   Adjusted Total Assets

RR7300 Total Deposits to Total Capital (%)

$$(BS2220 \div RR4306) \times 100$$

BS2220   Total Deposits
RR4306   Total Capital

RR7301 Total Deposits to Shareholders' Equity (%)

$$(BS2220 \div BS2499) \times 100$$

BS2220   Total Deposits
BS2499   Total Shareholders' Equity

RR7302 Growth in Total Deposits (%)

$$(BS2220CY \div BS2220LY - 1) \times 100$$

BS2220   Total Deposits
CY   Current Year
LY   Last Year

RR7304 Total Deposits to Interest-Bearing Liabilities (%)

$$(BS2220 \div RR7101) \times 100$$

BS2220   Total Deposits
RR7101   Total Interest-Bearing Liabilities

RR7310 Total Loans to Total Deposits (%)

$$(BS2055 \div BS2220) \times 100$$

BS2055   Total Loans
BS2220   Total Deposits

RR7311 Total Loans to Total Capital (%)

$$(BS2055 \div RR4306) \times 100$$

BS2055   Total Loans
RR4306   Total Capital

RR7312 Total Loans to Total Available Funds (%)

$$(BS2055 \div (BS2220 + RR4306)) \times 100$$

BS2055   Total Loans
BS2220   Total Deposits
RR4306   Total Capital

RR7313 Total Loans to Interest-Bearing Liabilities (%)

$$(BS2220 \div RR7101) \times 100$$

BS2220   Total Deposits
RR7101   Total Interest-Bearing Liabilities

RR7330 Earning Assets to Total Deposits (%)

$$(RR7007 \div BS2220) \times 100$$

RR7007   Earning Assets
BS2220   Total Deposits

RR7331 Total Investments to Total Capital (%)

$$(BS2170 \div RR4306) \times 100$$

BS2170   Total Investments
RR4306   Total Capital

RR7332 Total Investments to Total Available Funds (%)

$$(BS2170 \div (BS2220 + RR4306)) \times 100$$

BS2170   Total Investments
BS2220   Total Deposits
RR4306   Total Capital

RR7333 Total Investments to Interest-Bearing Liabilities (%)

$$(BS2170 \div RR7101) \times 100$$

BS2170   Total Investments
RR7101   Total Interest-Bearing Liabilities

11.2.11 Price Relevance Ratios

Although definitions of EPS are gradually converging, the EPS ratios in the following paragraphs that conform to the generally accepted EPS(s) in the local market of the company concerned should be used. An example, using RR4107 Annualized Earnings Before Extraordinary Items per Share, has been chosen for illustration purposes.

RR7800 Price Earnings Ratio (X)

Price ÷ RR4107

Price   Stock Price at fiscal year end for a specific share
RR4107   Annualized Earnings Before Extraordinary Items per Share

RR7801 Earnings Yield Ratio (%)

$(RR4107 \div Price(t - 1)) \times 100$

RR4107   Annualized Earnings Before Extraordinary Items per Share
Price(t − 1)   Stock Price at the beginning of a fiscal year for a specific share

RR7802 Dividend Yields (%)

$(RR4110 \div Price(t - 1)) \times 100$

RR4110   Annualized Dividend per Share
Price(t − 1)   Stock Price at the beginning of a fiscal year for a specific share

RR7803 Price to Book Value Ratio (X)

Price ÷ RR4602

Price   Stock Price at the end of a fiscal year for a specific share
RR4602   Book Value per Share

RR7804 Price to Cash (X)

Price ÷ RR4700

Price   Stock Price at the end of a fiscal year for a specific share
RR4700   Cash Flow per Share

RR7805 Price to Sales (X)

Price ÷ RR4500

Price   Stock Price at the end of a fiscal year for a specific share
RR4500   Sales (Revenue) per Share (annualized)

RR7806 Price to EBIT (X)

Price ÷ RR4502

Price   Stock Price at the end of a fiscal year for a specific share
RR4502   EBIT per Share (annualized)
EBIT   Earnings Before Interest Expenses and Taxes

RR7807 Market Capitalization to Total Assets (X)

RR4404 ÷ RR4304

RR4404   Total Market Capitalization
RR4304   Adjusted Total Assets

RR7808 Market Capitalization to Total Liabilities (X)

RR4404 ÷ BS2399

RR4404   Total Market Capitalization
BS2399   Total Liabilities

11.2.12   Ratios with Non-Financial Information

Horizontal Product Diversification Using Standard Industry Classification (SIC) Codes

Refer to the SIC codes in Chapter 7 for the related diversification indices' computation.

RR7850 Unrelated Horizontal Product Diversification (index)

$$I = \sum_{(j=1 \text{ to } m)} \text{of } P_j \times \text{Ln}(1/P_j)$$

Where P_j = size of jth sector/sum of all sectors
     m = total number of sectors

The j should be the number of different sectors (sectors are defined by the first two digits of the SIC codes).

RR7851 Related Horizontal Product Diversification (index)

$$I = \sum_{(j=1 \text{ to } m)} \text{of } P_j \times \left(\sum_{(j=1 \text{ to } n)} \text{of } P_{ij} \times \text{Ln}(1/P_{ij}) \right)$$

Where P_j = size of jth sector/sum of all sectors
     P_{ij} = size of ith segment/sum of all segments within jth sector
     m = total number of sectors
     n = total number of segments in each sector

The j should be the number of different sectors (sectors are defined by the first two digits of the SIC codes).

The i should be the number of differing last two digits of the SIC codes within a j category.

RR7852 Total Horizontal Product Diversification (index)

$$I = RR7600 + RR7601$$

RR7600 Unrelated Horizontal Product Diversification
RR7601 Related Horizontal Product Diversification

Vertical Product Diversification Using Group Industry Codes

Refer to Chapter 7 for the possible regrouping of industries.

RR7860 Unrelated Vertical Product Diversification (index)

$$I = \sum_{(j=1 \text{ to } m)} \text{ of } P_j \times \text{Ln}(1/P_j)$$

Where P_j = size of jth sector/sum of all sectors
   m = total number of sectors

The j should be the number of groups.

RR7861 Related Vertical Product Diversification (index)

$$I = \sum_{(j=1 \text{ to } m)} \text{ of } P_j \times \left(\sum_{(i=1 \text{ to } n)} \text{ of } P_{ij} \times \text{Ln}(1/P_{ij}) \right)$$

Where P_j = size of jth sector/sum of all sectors
   P_{ij} = size of ith segment/sum of all segments within jth sector
   m = total number of sectors
   n = total number of segments in each sector

The j should be the number of groups.
The i should be the number of the different industry codes within a j group.

RR7862 Total Vertical Product Diversification (index)

$$I = RR7610 + RR7611$$

RR7610 Unrelated Horizontal Product Diversification
RR7611 Related Vertical Product Diversification

*Geographic Diversification Using the Geographic Codes
for International Sales*

Refer to Chapter 7 for the classification of geographic codes.

RR7870 Unrelated Geographic Diversification by International Sales (index)

$$I = \sum_{(j=1 \text{ to } m)} \text{of } P_j \times \text{Ln}(1/P_j)$$

Where P_j = size of jth sector/sum of all sectors
m = total number of sectors

The j should be the number of different sectors (sectors are defined by
the first digit of the Geographic Codes).

RR7871 Related Geographic Diversification by International Sales (index)

$$I = \sum_{(j=1 \text{ to } m)} \text{of } P_j \times \left(\sum_{(i=1 \text{ to } n)} \text{of } P_{ij} \times \text{Ln}(1/P_{ij}) \right)$$

Where P_j = size of jth sector/sum of all sectors
P_{ij} = size of ith segment/sum of all segments within jth sector
m = total number of sectors
n = total number of segments in each sector

The j should be the number of different sectors (sectors are defined by
the first digit of the Geographic Codes).
The i should be the number of differing last digits of geographic codes
within a j category.

RR7872 Total Geographic Diversification by International Sales (index)

$$I = \text{RR7700} + \text{RR7701}$$

RR7700   Unrelated Geographic Diversification by International Sales
RR7701   Related Geographic Diversification by International Sales

Geographic Diversification Using Subsidiary Information

RR7880 Unrelated Geographic Diversification by Subsidiary (index)

$$I = \sum_{(j=1 \text{ to } m)} \text{of } P_j \times \text{Ln}(1/P_j)$$

Where P_j = size of jth sector/sum of all sectors
m = total number of sectors

The j should be the number of subsidiaries weighted by the size of each
subsidiary in different continents.
The size of each subsidiary is measured by the sales for industrial sectors
and adjusted total assets for financial services.

RR7881 Related Geographic Diversification by Subsidiary (index)

$$I = \sum_{(j=1 \text{ to } m)} \text{of } P_j \times \left(\sum_{(i=1 \text{ to } n)} \text{of } P_{ij} \times \text{Ln}(1/P_{ij}) \right)$$

Where P_j = size of jth sector/sum of all sectors
P_{ij} = size of ith segment/sum of all segments within jth sector
m = total number of sectors
n = total number of segments in each sector

The j should be the number of subsidiaries weighted by the size of each subsidiary in different continents.
The i should be the number of subsidiaries weighted by the size of each subsidiary within each continent.
The size of each subsidiary is measured by the sales for industrial sectors and adjusted total assets for financial services.

RR7882 Total Geographic Diversification by Subsidiary (index)

$$I = RR7710 + RR7711$$

RR7710   Unrelated Geographic Diversification by Subsidiary
RR7711   Related Geographic Diversification by Subsidiary

Shareholders' Distribution

Refer to Chapter 10 for the shareholders' classification codes.

RR7890 Major Stable Shareholding (%)

The aggregation of the percentage ownership by major shareholders (SH categories)
     An arbitrary percentage (i.e., more than 1%) can be set for each specific market based on each market's definition of significant influence on management decision making.

RR7891 Major Institutional Shareholding (%)

The aggregation of the percentage ownership by major institutional shareholders (SH20 or SH21 through SH29)
     An institutional shareholder is defined as the shareholder without significant intent to manage the decision-making process. Typically, these include banks, insurance companies, security brokerages, and money managers.

RR7892 Concentration Index by Major Shareholders (index)

A statistical variance of the percentage of ownership by major shareholders (SH categories)

RR7893 Insider Ownership by Major Shareholders (%)

The aggregation of the percentage of ownership by major shareholders in the following categories:

SH30	Other Organizations with Operating Interest
SH40	Directors/Officers
SH50	Employees

RR7894 Institutional Ownership by Type of Organization (%)

The aggregation of the percentage of ownership by institutional investors by "type of organization"

SG20	Institutional Investors

or

SG21	Banks
SG22	Insurance Companies
SG23	Brokerage Firms
SG24	Managed Funds
SG29	Other Institutional Investors

RR7895 Insider Ownership by Type of Organization (%)

The aggregation of the percentage of ownership by the following types of organizations:

SG30	Other Organizations with Operating Interest
SG40	Directors/Officers
SG50	Employees

RR7900 Management Stability Index

Various ratios can be designed by using Management Codes for the relationships with outside organizations and Title Codes (ranks within a company). Refer to Chapter 10 for the possible data codes.

11.3 TIME SERIES RATIO ANALYSIS

An analysis of a company's competitiveness should take the following sequential steps:

1. Gather fundamental data.
2. Compute ratios for each year and each company to see the relationships between the individual data items.
3. Analyze each company's raw data and ratios over several years.
4. Compare the raw data and ratios with benchmarks by industry and by country.

Having established a bare database structure and computed valuable ratios, a researcher may now begin to look at changes experienced by companies over several years before comparing their performances with a particular benchmark.

A statistical tool called *Time Series Analysis* is a form of regression analysis with time as an independent variable. The dependent variable is measured sequentially in time, and its trend is analyzed after a consideration of seasonal fluctuations. Such models are widely used in business and economic analysis.

There are two related terms that will be useful in further analysis: "autocorrelation" and "positively correlated." *Autocorrelation* means that the correlation of residuals in a regression model is related to a time factor. If the residuals at consecutive times tend to have the same sign, they are *positively correlated*.

Regression models are widely used in trying to determine a trend in observed events. If similar observations occur at different times, they may be correlated to some other factor occurring at different times. The correlation can be positive or negative to changes that have occurred previously. This method, Time Series Analysis, is used extensively in forecasting.

Before using statistical tools, it is imperative to ascertain that all assumptions are meaningful. To be statistically meaningful, a sufficient number of observations, assumed to be normally distributed, must be gathered for most outcomes, such as mean or deviation. Considering the difficulties with ratios based on accounting observations, the following limitations should be kept in mind:

1. Usually, time intervals are measured in years. Semiannual or quarterly information is available for a limited number of data items.
2. Many businesses fluctuate seasonally. Such fluctuations can be eliminated by statistical analysis.
3. The number of observations of events that have been measured on the same basis is actually too limited to be statistically meaningful. One need only consider the changing accounting regulations or reporting practices around the world.

One method of increasing the number of observations and eliminating imbedded seasonal fluctuations is to create 12 months trailing ratios. This may generate enough observations of events measured in the same way to be statistically useful. If so, standard time series models can be constructed to reveal any trends. Alternatively, a solution might be found using the average of ratios over a reasonable period of three to five years.

11.3.1 Twelve Months Trailing Ratios

If annual accounting information is provided, it is impossible to increase the number of observations for meaningful statistical analysis. However, when quarterly or semiannual information is available, it increases the number of observations and makes possible more serious statistical analysis.

The use of quarterly information can increase from one to four the number of observations per year, through adding the last four quarterly sets of information. This is called *12 months trailing*. The use of semiannual information will obviously double the number of observations per year.

What if a U.S. company provides quarterly information and companies in Japan or the United Kingdom provide semiannual data? One approach to this problem is to adjust the quarterly observations provided by the U.S. company to semiannual observations, thus establishing the same intervals for all companies. Another approach is to convert the semiannual information to quarterly data through interpolation. Theoretically, interpolation is a reasonable approach because sales and production processes are usually continuous activities and seasonal fluctuations are consistent over the years. However, interpolation of balance sheet information is not a sound practice, because the purchase or disposal of noncurrent assets is a discretionary activity. Interpolation is applicable for companies with few fixed assets, including the fast-moving toy manufacturing industry and food processing companies.

Interpolation can also be useful in dealing with annual information. Consider, for example, a company that changes its accounting period. As a result, one or more accounting periods will be something other than 12 months. This book applies interpolation, using an annualization factor, to data for the income statement and the cash flow statement throughout the ratio computation process.

11.3.2 Average Growth Ratios

When there are a limited number of observations for statistical analysis, the average of certain ratios over the time in question can be very useful. The number of years used is a matter of choice as long as all data are measured on the same basis; however, a five-year period will be used in the following explanations. Such ratio averages can be computed in different ways, two examples of which are given here:

Alternative 1: Simple (Arithmetic) Average Growth Rate for Five Years

To simplify the illustration, the percentage is not used.

Sales growth in year 1 = sales in year 1 ÷ sales in year 0 − 1

Sales growth in year 2 = sales in year 2 ÷ sales in year 1 − 1

Sales growth in year 3 = sales in year 3 ÷ sales in year 2 − 1

Sales growth in year 4 = sales in year 4 ÷ sales in year 3 − 1

Sales growth in year 5 = sales in year 5 ÷ sales in year 4 − 1

Simple (arithmetic) average growth rate for 5 years = Σ(sales growth from years 1 to 5) ÷ 5

Alternative 2: Compound (Geometric) Average Growth Rate for Five Years

Compound (geometric) average growth ratio for 5 years = (sales in year 5 ÷ sales in year 0)$^{1/5}$ − 1

In practice, results in using the two alternatives differ slightly because the denominator in Alternative 1 changes over the years, whereas the denominator in Alternative 2 is fixed at year 0. Alternative 1 calculates the annual average growth rate, and Alternative 2 calculates the annual rate of growth for the period.

The approximate compounded average growth ratio can be computed using the precomputed annual sales growth ratio (RR5200). This is true for all ratios with percentage (%) or multiples (X) in the ratio table.

If one of the six years shows a negative number, such as a net loss, Alternative 1 will generate an error unless the year in question is eliminated in the computation process. If the year with a negative number is eliminated, a different result will be generated, but it will be wrong.

Alternative 2, however, will produce a meaningful result except when year 0 or year 6 is a negative number. The possible conflicting results are illustrated in the following table:

NEGATIVE NUMBERS IN RATIO COMPUTATION

The use of negative numbers in the numerator and/or denominator render many ratio computations invalid. Such cases should be identified. The reason is that mathematically computed ratios with negative raw data are not comparable to ratios without negative data items. For example:

1.	From	10,000 to	30,000	Will be	200%
2.	From	30,000 to	10,000	Will be	-66.7%
3.	From	$-10,000$ to	10,000	Will be	-200%
4.	From	10,000 to	$-10,000$	Will be	-200%
5.	From	$-10,000$ to	$-30,000$	Will be	200%
6.	From	$-30,000$ to	$-10,000$	Will be	-66.7%

Cases 1 and 2 are obvious. No one will argue about the increase and decrease, although the ratios are off because of the differences in the denominators.

In case 3 the number has obviously increased, but the computation generates the opposite result. Case 4 appears to make sense, but not exactly.

In cases 5 and 6 the computation generates the opposite result.

The numbers in cases 3 to 6 are neither comparable to cases 1 and 2 nor comparable to each other.

Transformation of Data

There are methods to circumvent such problems. Statistically, the actual distribution of the data's characteristics does not change in transformation processes such as linear transformation and power transformation. Each observation may be included in analysis by transformation, which means adding an absolute value, say, 40,000, to all numbers. Caution should be exercised in interpreting the results, however, because of the changes in the denominator, which is the basis of comparison.

The transformation process allows researchers to work with more data in analysis, but interpretations of such transformed data require care. For example, when an absolute number is added in a linear transformation, the magnitude of changes will be smaller and the magnitude depends on the number added. If such five-year average growth ratios are convenient for users, it is worth storing them in a separate data set to reduce computing time.

11.4 RATIO ANALYSIS BY SECTOR

Investors seek to maximize return on their investments, which need not be limited to equity securities. However, a company's absolute profitability or percentage of growth is meaningless to investors unless some measuring device is provided. The following section suggests some useful benchmarks.

11.4.1 Defining Sectors

Into what sectors should an investor segregate companies in order to compare their performances? No two companies are in exactly the same business or have the same capital structure, yet many companies share similar business environments and compete with one another. Certain regulations apply to all companies in a country, and others only to companies within a specific industry.

One obvious means of segregation is by country. There are many reasons for defining sectors in this way:

1. The market for most companies is domestic. Companies expand to international markets as they grow.
2. Certain regulations apply to all companies in a country.
3. The same financial reporting practices are applied to all companies within a country.

Country sectors may be expanded to regional sectors when business environments are similar to one another, as in the European Union and in North America. As the internationalization of business expands, the differences in regulations and financial reporting practices tend to diminish.

The more intrinsic differences between companies, however, arise from the nature of their businesses. The expansion of capital markets and corporate operations around the world allows companies to compete with one another anywhere. Thus companies also may be seen to be segregated by sectors of industry.

Still, the question is how to segregate the sectors of industry. In terms of macroeconomic analysis, no two companies are completely independent. How many sectors are appropriate? The segregation explained in the product diversification index computation process may serve as an example. One method is to define industrial sectors by SIC codes, which are based on input materials. When segregating, the broadest possible category is totally unrelated segments, when the first two digits of an SIC code are different. Further segregation is possible by considering the remaining two SIC code digits.

Another approach is segregation by vertical business relationship such as textile manufacturing and textile retail. This book also provides industry tables in Chapter 7, showing how each industry is linked in a vertical relationship to industry groups.

Segregation by vertical relationship may seem convenient and relatively simple until one examines any reasonably sized company and asks: Can this company clearly be described as belonging to just one industry or be identified by a single SIC code? If a company has multiple business sectors, the analyst must either choose one of them or include the company in many different sectors (unless a company's operations are clearly segregated by sector). No company, of course, segregates its operating results in detail by sector unless the sectors are significantly different from one another, such as the insurance and industrial sectors of ITT in the United States.

In sector segregation analysis there is no specific dependent variable to be used for segregation. Multiple factors are presumably interrelated, and their similarity and covariances can be identified by factor analysis. Although detailed statistical computations may be delegated to a professional statistician, the following steps will illustrate the process:

1. Identify a few major data items (ratios) by factor analysis, which is based on the covariance between data items. The variables should include raw data, ratios, and macroeconomic variables.
2. Identify companies that behave similarly, using clustering techniques. The purpose of the analysis is to determine the appropriate number of sectors. However, use common sense in making judgments, because any statistical tool has inherent flaws even if it is used correctly.
3. Assign companies to the chosen sectors, using a classification method or discriminant analysis. The groups, once identified, should be maintained for long-term comparison unless, of course, a company in the group is restructured. If a company is reclassified, all related historical analysis should be recomputed to maintain comparability for the period being researched.

Factor Analysis

Factor Analysis is a statistical tool used to identify a relatively small number of factors that represent interrelationships between many variables. It is an extension of Principal Component Analysis. Earlier, in this book, many different ratios were computed to help identify relatively strong performance companies. Many of them are related and measure the same characteristics of a company. This relationship between ratios is sometimes obvious, but ratios are most often related in complex ways, not easily understood or observed. Moreover, the large number of ratios often leads to confusion and contradictory conclusions. Factor Analysis helps to group similar ratios, that is, ratios that are related to one another and measure the same characteristics. Factor Analysis can identify a much smaller number of factors, and each factor usually can be measured by using a linear function of the ratios constituting that factor. Each of the factors is supposed to represent underlying variables. This is achieved through use of Principal Component Analysis or the Maximum Likelihood Method. A good deal of subjectivity is involved in determining an optimal solution, and it requires broad knowledge and experience in the field.

Principal Component Analysis

Principal Component Analysis is a statistical tool to reduce the number of redundant variables by testing each variable against all others. A Sample Principal Component is the variable with the largest covariance with the remaining variables. The process will identify the most contributory variable among many variables, something not possible through ordinary methods of analysis.

Clustering

Although Factor Analysis is an attempt to group ratios, the clustering technique is a statistical tool that may identify groups of companies that behave similarly. Cluster Analysis may be used to define groups of companies as including companies belonging to the same industry that have some common characteristics. The degree of relationship between companies may be drawn as a hierarchical table according to the distances between observations, and we can identify groups that behave similarly. Again, subjective judgment plays a very important role in such analysis.

Classification or Discreminant Analysis

When we have identified a certain number of groups, such as industry sectors, Discriminant Analysis or classification can allocate a company to a specific group (industry). If a new company has many different, interrelated products, Discriminant Analysis helps in assigning it to one of the predefined industry sectors.

No matter which method of segregation is applied, there is no one perfect solution, and there is always a possibility of error. Multiple sets of sectors should be prepared so that a different set is available for each type of analysis.

11.4.2 Normalization of Information

It is common to use industry/country average values of a ratio as a yardstick to measure the representative performance of a company over a number of years or of companies within a sector. It seems a simple task to calculate the mean (average) value of a ratio. Theoretically, an average is calculated by adding the ratio values of all companies within a sector and dividing by the number of companies. Any off-the-shelf statistical software can generate a massive number of results with little effort. However, the distribution of values in each ratio cannot be ignored. There will be some companies with no data, other companies with invalid data. A simple example is the mathematical computation of the P/E ratio with negative earnings, which will generate a negative ratio. But what does it mean? There is no interpretation for a negative P/E ratio. In considering the validity of individual data items included in computing an average, the following issues should be addressed:

1. *Missing Value/Not Available.* A company may not disclose certain data items because they are not required by regulation. Any ratio based on missing data items should be labeled "Not Available" and should be treated as a missing value in any statistical analysis. Missing values may introduce bias in estimates.

2. *Missing Value/Not Meaningful.* Certain ratios, although mathematically computable, may be meaningless in analysis. This is illustrated by a negative P/E ratio or a growth ratio computed from negative numbers. Such ratios should be labeled "Not Meaningful" and should be treated as missing values in any statistical analysis.

3. *Outliers.* Sometimes a ratio value may be meaningful and reasonable when considered individually, but it may be very different from ratio values of other companies in the group under consideration. Ratios using percentage (%) or multiples (X) imply the comparison of a numerator to a denominator, and their outcomes will be incomprehensible if the denominator approaches zero. These ratios are valid only if the basis of comparison, the denominator, is within a reasonable range. A ''reasonable range'' may vary, depending on the nature of the data item, but if any denominator approaches zero it should be labeled ''Out of Reasonable Range'' or ''Outlier.'' For example, if an earnings per share temporarily is close to zero, the P/E will be extremely large and will distort the average significantly.

Some statistical techniques are available to identify outliers. Care must be taken in deciding whether to include outliers in analysis or to reject them as ''not meaningful.'' When data are skewed, a median or mode value may be used to find a representative number.

For example, a debt to equity ratio (RR6008) may range between 50 percent and 500 percent for most companies in a sector, but cannot be 5,000 percent. However, the ratio, mathematically, can be 5,000 percent if net losses for a company are accumulated for several years and total shareholders' equity evaporates as a result of the negative retained earnings. What does this mean for analysis? If a company is established or kept alive for reasons of national prestige or for other political reasons, but is not a serious business enterprise, should it be included in an industry analysis? Possible approaches to outliers include the following:

- Outliers may be eliminated completely from an average computation.
- An outlier may be restated to a maximum allowable limit. For example, if a specific outlier is located far lower than a mean value, the outlier may be restated as three standard deviations from a mean value. This will keep the observation in the computation but reduce its weight.

4. *Sampling Problems.* One of the biggest problems in calculating averages is a lack of data or too much data for some industries. The simple answer to this problem is to take a random sample of companies and use the sample mean to represent the actual mean of all companies. Again, the problem is how to get a true random sample.

To obtain a random sample, a frame, a list of target companies, is needed. This may be difficult in itself. Then, after drawing a random sample from the frame, it may not be possible to collect data for all the companies included in the sample. Small companies and companies with poor performances within a sector will often be left out and, consequently, the sample values will be biased toward large or well-performing companies.

Another problem to be faced after calculating the averages is the interpretation of the outcomes. If the sample is random and large enough, it may be assumed to be normally distributed and may be taken as a good estimate of the real/true mean. The size of a ''large'' sample depends on the variability of the data under consideration. The greater the variability, the larger the sample should be. Well-established statistical techniques are available to determine the necessary size of a sample. If the universe of the data values is not normally distributed and the sample is not large enough, the sample mean may not be a good estimate of true value. In such cases, robust estimates should be used.

It is unfortunate that in a random sample taken without knowledge of the distribution of the data, a mean value of the collected values (whatever is available) is often used as an estimate of the true mean.

As for remedies to this problem, the practicalities of time and cost require use of the best, rather than an ideal, solution. Nevertheless, it is very important to know what assumptions are being violated so that proper caution may be taken in interpreting and drawing conclusions from the results.

Normality

In using statistical results such as averages and standard deviations, the assumption of a sample's normality, the basis of such statistical results, should not be forgotten.

1. The number of observations in the sample must be large enough (approximately 30 or more observations).
2. The observations must be mutually independent.
3. The observations must be homogenous.

Normality can be tested by a Q-Q plot. If a certain set of samples does not indicate a straight line in the Q-Q plot, linear transformation or power transformation may be applied.

Robustification of Data

Robustification is a method of constructing a normal sample set for further meaningful computation by statistically eliminating outliers. It is true that raw data may be manipulated to fit any result wanted, but although false outcomes may be generated mathematically, they make no sense and do not represent any characteristics of the sample.

11.4.3 Computation of Industry Averages

Simple Versus Weighted Averages

A *simple average* is the sum of observations divided by the number of observations. It may provide a true picture in cases in which a sample has a perfectly normal distribution in terms of company size. However, if the sample includes a few large companies and many small companies in a sector, such as the U.S. software industry, the average will represent the many smaller companies although, in reality, the market is dominated by the few larger firms.

To eliminate skewed results, a weight may be assigned to each observation, producing what is known as a *weighted average*. The question is how to assign weights. One possibility is to use sales figures for industrial companies and adjusted total assets for financial service companies. If an average is sought for both industrial and financial service companies, companies in the two sectors may possibly not be assigned the same weights. In such cases, market capitalization, which is neutral, may be considered as a weighing factor. If unlisted companies, for example, mutual insurance companies in the insurance industry, are included in the computation, then market capitalization will not work.

Once a sample data set is prepared, computing averages with the use of statistical software is a simple process. It is important, however, to consider computing time. With a sample of 20,000 to 30,000 companies used to establish worldwide averages, and the need to weigh 100 to 200 ratios by sales or assets, a significant period of computing time, at least a few days with a standard computer, is required.

An average is a synthesized approximation of many observations. Such averages cannot be appropriately interpreted without related standard deviations and the number of observations included in the computation. If raw data or ratios are not convenient and generate substantial standard deviations, the Z Score can be used instead to neutralize significant variations between sectors or countries.

Z SCORE

The Z Score is a statistical measurement that converts the distance of raw data from a mean value to standard units. It simplifies the magnitude of standard deviations as compared with mean values.

$$\text{Z Score} = (x - X) \div \sigma$$

x Observations
X Mean
σ Standard deviation

Averages by Sector

Weighting	Sectors by Products	Sectors by Region
Simple	Industry	Country
Weighted	Industry Group	Region
	Portfolio	Worldwide

Combinations of single items from each of the three columns in the preceding table can generate most required data.

What if a sector includes only a few companies? In constructing huge tables to compute averages, there is a tendency to overlook such issues as the normality of the sample, as discussed earlier. Consider, for example, an industry average in a single country in which the industry consists of five companies or fewer. Computer processing will generate an average in all cases, but how should the average be interpreted? Averages are computed to produce a synthesized abstract out of many underlying observations. Is an average involving five or fewer companies needed at all to understand the data set?

How often should averages be computed? Because of the time it takes to compute averages, the frequency of such computations should be considered. If all companies end their fiscal years at the same time and all information is available four or five months later, a single computation when all data are in hand will suffice. In reality, however, company fiscal year ends vary widely, as does the timing in making data publicly available.

Annual reports for U.S. companies are made available approximately 80 days after the fiscal year end. In continental Europe, it takes 180 days to produce the annual reports. Anyone attempting to compute averages in May or June for companies with calendar years ending on December 31 will have the necessary data for most U.S. companies and a significant amount of data for U.K. companies, but barely any data for continental European companies. Of course, although outdated, data for all Japanese companies with fiscal year ends in March and Australian companies with fiscal year ends in June will also be available.

The following table provides a guide as to the frequency with which averages should be computed.

Frequency of Computation	Averages
On Demand	Simple Industry Within Country Simple Industry Related Within Country Simple Country Simple Industry Within Region Simple Industry Related Within Region Weighted Industry Within Country Weighted Industry Related Within Country Simple Portfolio Weighted Portfolio
Monthly	Simple Industry Worldwide Simple Industry Related Worldwide Simple Worldwide Weighted Country Weighted Industry Within Region Weighted Industry Related Within Region Weighted Region
Quarterly	Weighted Industry Worldwide Weighted Industry Related Worldwide Weighted Worldwide

11.5 COMPANY ANALYSIS BY SECTOR AND BY COUNTRY

So far, preparing for analysis has involved collecting specific raw data from corporate financial statements and computing ratios to establish the relative relationships between data items. Then each company's compounded average (growth) ratio over a number of years was computed. Finally, average values for the raw data, ratios, and their Z Scores were computed, along with a standard deviation. The number of companies included in computing the averages was noted.

It is now possible to take a company's raw data and ratios, make judgments about the company's strength and past performance, and extrapolate future performance, which is the basis of a company's future intrinsic value. Comparing each value with mental benchmarks is one approach, but comparing such ratios with sector averages is more scientific and efficient.

The ultimate goal of the entire process is to establish a company's relative strength in the sector in which that company mainly competes. The following sections outline approaches to making such comparisons through a discussion of ranking, composite ratios, and beta computations and are followed by a few examples of valuation models.

11.5.1 Ranking

If a single ratio can be identified as a prominent indicator for a specific analysis, ranking is a convenient tool. It simply sorts ratios in ascending or descending order and shows the relative position of a company within a sector. For example:

Size of companies:	Sales, Total Assets, Shareholders' Equity, Market Capitalization, etc.
Absolute performance value:	Net Income, Cash from Operations, Free Cash Flow, etc.
Performance ratio:	Operating Income Margin, P/E Ratio, Debt to Equity Ratio, etc.

Advantages

- Ranking can be applied to all raw data and to any ratio.
- The value of variables can be either continuous or discrete as long as the value has an order.
- The value can be positive, negative, or zero.
- The impact of outliers can be neutralized, because the weight of a rank is the same regardless of its distance between two observations.

Disadvantages

- Ranking is applicable only to a single value. If a sector is well defined and the importance of each ranking is similar to the others, a composite ranking can be established for purposes of comparison. However, caution should be exercised in interpreting composite ranking.
- A clearly homogeneous sector must be defined before ranking.
- Distances between ranks are not comparable within a ranking or between rankings. A possible solution is the use of a relative distance, such as

the Z Score. The Z Score is a linear transformation, and the ranks will not change.

11.5.2 Composite Ratios

The most problematic aspect of ranking is that it is applicable only to one ratio at a time even though the performance of a corporation is far more complex. A composite ranking may be useful when a research design is perfect, because the result is not biased in favor of any one ratio. An alternative is composite ratios.

The ratios illustrated use composite raw data and are, therefore, composite ratios. However, a ratio can be broken down into many components, and comparisons of these multiple ratios may reveal relative strengths and weaknesses in a company.

The Du Pont Model is an example.

$$RR5303 = (RR5400 \times RR5103 \div RR6012) \times 100$$

Return on Equity = Asset Turnover

$\times$ Net Income Margin $\div$ Asset to Shareholders' Equity

In this example, each of the ratio's components represents different aspects of corporate performance. The Asset Turnover ratio indicates asset utilization and capital intensity, the Net Income Margin ratio indicates the profitability of operating activities, and the Asset to Shareholders' Equity ratio reveals capital structures in a company. A comparison of each ratio with the industry average or country average will provide a comparison of the composite ratio with the industry or country average.

The following are a few more ratios used in different industries.

For Banks

Return on Assets = $(RR5101 + RR5105) \times RR5400$

RR5101 Operating Margin
RR5105 Nonoperating Margin
RR5400 Asset Turnover

For Insurance Companies

Return on Assets = $(RR7515 + RR7516 + RR5105) \times RR5400$

RR7515 Insurance Margin
RR7516 Non-Insurance Margin
RR5105 Nonoperating Margin

In certain cases, the result of adding or multiplying many ratios may introduce a bias in favor of those with large or small numbers. In such cases, Z Scores, which are standardized to reflect the standard deviation in a industry, may be used. If each component ratio is standardized, additions, multiplications, and average of a company's Z Scores will be more comparable.

11.5.3 Beta Computations

A company's performance can be judged by comparing it with sector averages (industry or country). Almost all of a company's ratios may be compared with the average ratios of target sector(s). If comparison is complicated by different units of measure, standardized Z Scores may be computed.

A company's performance as compared with sector averages is stationary. With an additional step, the volatility of a company ratio may be compared with the volatility of a sector ratio. This measurement is called a *beta* computation. The beta concept is widely applied to stock prices (*price beta*). Stock prices, which reflect all factors, are very homogenous and applicable in any sector. The homogenous character of stock prices is what makes the beta computation popular.

Beta Computation

$$\beta_i = (\sigma_i \div \sigma_M) \times r_{iM}$$

β_i Beta of i

σ_i Standard deviation of i

σ_M Standard deviation of M(market)

r_{iM} Covariance of i to M(market)

It implies the volatility of i as compared with the market volatility.

If we define an appropriate market applicable to a company, the beta computation process can be applied to earnings-related items as well, which is called *accounting beta*. For example, the sales growth ratio fluctuates with economic cycles, and one company's fluctuation may not be exactly the same as that of others. This means that the sales growth volatility of a company may be compared with the sales growth volatility of a related sector. In practice, it is difficult to collect enough observations on the same basis to make such computations, because accounting results are available, at the most, four times a year and accounting standards are often changed over the years.

11.5.4 Application Models

Composite ratios combine a few ratios related to a specific aspect of performance. When composite ratios are integrated for ultimate corporate valuation, they are called *application models*. The differences between composite ratios and application models should be very minor. A few widely used examples are illustrated in the following paragraphs.

Z Value

One of the composite indices or application models is the Z Value by Altman (1983), an early assessment of financial stability.*

$$Z = 1.2X_1 + 1.4X_2 + 3.3X_3 + 0.6X_4 + 1.0X_5$$

X_1	RR6107 ÷ 100	Working Capital to Total Assets
X_2	RR6106 ÷ 100	Retained Earnings to Total Assets
X_3	RR6111 ÷ 100	EBIT to Total Assets
X_4	RR7508	Market Capitalization to Total Liability
X_5	RR5400	Asset Turnover

This model, which provides an early indication of a liquidity problem, has been tested by Altman. The constant values provided are based on his empirical data. The ratios are common financial stability related ratios, and ratios based on annual or quarterly results may be used. If the liquidity problem in a company is stagnant and long-term, five-year averages instead of annual or quarterly ratios may be utilized.

Constants in the computation of Z Value or the cutoff of the discriminant value Z for insolvency may differ from Altman's depending on the samples in different countries. New ratios may be added and others withheld to suit the need. However, the selection of any ratio should be scientific, based on factor analysis, to avoid bias.

Dividend Discount Model

The ultimate goal of all analysis is to establish the intrinsic value of a stock as compared with its current market price and to determine whether it is undervalued or overvalued. One approach, the discounted present value of all benefits from a stock (i.e., dividend), is the Constant Growth Dividend Discount Model by Gordon-Shapiro.

$$PV_0 = D_1 ÷ (k - g)$$

PV_0	Discounted present value of a stock
D_1	Dividend in period 1
k	Discount rate
g	Dividend growth rate

This basic model was chosen to help demonstrate the concept. In practice, many variations should be considered.

The cash dividend for period 1 (D_1) can be easily estimated unless significant changes in a company's dividend policies are expected. It also may be expressed as $D_0(1 + g)$.

The discount rate (k), or required rate of return, is a company's implicit

---

* See E. I. Altman, *Corporate Financial Distress and Bankruptcy*, John Wiley and Sons, 1983, pp. 179–206.

cost of capital. Although some may disagree with this approach, it can be estimated as follows:

Top-Down Approach for *k*

$$k = r_f + \beta(r_m - r_f)$$

r_f	Risk-free rate = pure risk-free rate + inflation premium
$\beta(r_m - r_f)$	Risk premium
r_m	Market return

A *pure risk-free rate* is a theoretical risk-free rate. Much argument surrounds the choice of a "correct" risk-free rate. In the United States, some use the rate for three-month or one-year Treasury bills. Others may pick the rate for 30-year Treasury bills, depending on their investment horizon. The rate might vary significantly from country to country and cannot be easily separated from the inflation premium rate.

The *inflation premium* is another component that may be included as a part of a risk-free rate. It is embedded in the pricing of all assets.

The *risk premium* is a company-specific risk factor. It is the expected premium for risks taken in investing in a specific company.

Under the capital asset pricing model (CAPM), the risk premium has two components (beta × risk premium rate). The risk premium is the premium rate to be paid for the risks involved in operating uncertainty. It is defined as the differential between market return and the risk-free rate ($r_m - r_f$). Market return is the average return of the industry or market segment to which the company belongs. The risk premium may be computed at the industry level. Beta is the volatility of a specific company as compared with the volatility of the market. An accounting beta using net income may be the better choice because it is more predictive, but, as discussed earlier, the accounting beta is not easily computable. Alternatively, the price beta, which reflects all factors, can be used.

Under the Arbitrage Pricing Theory (APT), the risk premium is assumed to be affected by many factors, and the total risk premium is the aggregation of risk premiums for each factor.

Bottom-Up Approach for *k*. The discount rate (k) can also be estimated from industry practices in general or from a company-specific situation. It is the average cost of capital for a specific company. The capital should include short-term debts, long-term debts, preferred equity, and common equity. The after-tax cost of debt equity should be computed, because dividends are considered after taxes. In practice, the discount rate using the bottom-up approach is more conveniently available to researchers.

Dividend Growth Rate (*g*). The dividend growth rate (g) is the future dividend growth rate for a specific company. Estimating future dividend growth is not simple, because it involves estimating future earnings and cash flows.

Dividend growth rates can be estimated by extrapolating historical dividend growth rates, for example, a five-year compounded average growth rate. This method assumes that the historical performance of a company will continue in the future. That is, of course, not always true. Furthermore, this method cannot be applied to emerging companies. Aggressive emerging companies do not pay any dividends in their early years because all internally generated capital is used for investment opportunities. The extremely conservative dividend policies in countries such as Japan, Germany, and Switzerland should also be considered.

Earnings forecasts are essential to incorporating future changes in business environments into a specific company's valuation. An earnings forecast, illustrated in detail in the following section, requires forecasts for sales, profitability, and cash flow. Incorporating dividend policy with the availability of cash will indicate a future dividend growth rate in this model.

Variations of Constant Growth Dividend Discount Model. The model discussed in the preceding paragraphs is extremely simplified. If an investment horizon for a specific portfolio is limited to a specific time period, for example, five years, the dividend discount model can be modified as follows:

$$PV_0 = D_1 \div (1 + k) + D_2 \div (1 + k)^2 + D_3 \div (1 + k)^3$$
$$+ D_4 \div (1 + k)^4 + D_5 \div (1 + k)^5 + PV_5$$

The variations should be adjusted to the specific situations of the portfolio under consideration.

11.6 EARNINGS FORECAST

Earnings forecasts are hardly new. Many researchers provide advice on whether to buy or sell stock based on their estimates of the future earnings of hot investment target companies. A few organizations combine these recommendations and release a consensus of figures through closed information channels. It is very important to isolate good investment targets, because the value of a stock is not determined by how it has performed in the past but how it will perform in the future. This means that the current value of a stock is the discounted future benefits to be received, and the future benefits are defined as cash dividends to be received in the dividend discount model discussed in the previous section.

What is the source of a dividend? Companies can distribute dividends when earnings are available. For discussion purposes, if cash or liquidity is excluded, future earnings estimates determine the price of stocks.

Company managers and brokerage firm researchers routinely estimate future corporate earnings. They base their estimates on historical financial information and extrapolate from it, taking new and expected information into consideration.

11.6.1 Earnings Estimation

The Du Pont Model and its components, used to analyze return on equity, was discussed earlier. As an extension of the Du Pont Model, earnings per share can be broken down as follows:

$$EPS = RR5400 \times RR5204 \times (100 \div RR6012) \times RR4602$$

RR5400 Asset Turnover
RR5204 Net Income Margin
RR6012 Shareholders' Equity to Total Assets
RR4602 Book Value per Share

Each component in the formula reflects a different aspect of business activity, as follows:

Asset Turnover:	Utilization of assets in conjunction with capital intensity
Net Income Margin:	Efficiency of operating activities or expense control
Equity to Assets:	Capital structure
Book Value per Share:	Accumulated net equity to date

Growth of each individual ratio will lead to the EPS growth ratio. The four ratios shown offer many different aspects of a company's status, but they may not be the only alternatives.

Even though historical data have limitations in predicting future earnings, they provide the best place to start. All fundamental analytical tools are based on historical data.

Sales Forecast

The sales forecast is the first and most difficult step in the entire process of earnings estimation. Normally, analysts look first at the economic cycles and growth of sales in a specific sector, as discussed in Chapter 2. Then the market share of the company in question is analyzed by reviewing its competitive position in the sector. In order to obtain more accurate figures, each product line should be analyzed separately. Marketing strategies and management flexibility should be considered as well.

Sales forecasting requires a substantial understanding of the industry, including such aspects as capital equipment and technology involved in manufacturing processes, market participants, customers and key contracts, and regulatory factors faced by the industry. More important, such information must be compiled on the same basis so that the output ratios are comparable among companies competing within the industry. To facilitate comparability, each data item should be tightly defined regardless of its disclosure format in the company's financial statements. Research and Development (IS1550 or RR6601) activities to improve existing products, or to develop new ones that relate to future markets, should not be ignored.

When a company belongs to an industry with many participants, or to a wide range of industries, building an electronic database is essential to efficient research. When research involves many countries, the difficulties multiply because of differences in disclosure formats and reporting standards.

Asset Utilization

Once the market for a company's product is defined, the ability of the company to support the necessary sales must be considered. Plant asset turnover and accounts receivable turnover are the major components.

Asset Turnover (RR5400) and Tangible Fixed Asset Turnover (RR5401) reflect an operating cycle and the labor intensity of a business. These can also be related to Capital Expenditures (CF3120 or CF3420) to examine the long-term stability of a company's production capability. Accounts Receivable Turnover (RR6002) provides indications of a company's financial flexibility and points to possible changes in sales or production capability.

Net Income Margin

To derive the net income margin from operating activities, many aspects of a company should be considered. These include resource availability related to the commodity markets, efficiency of production in conjunction with relative technology accumulation, and efficiency in marketing and administrative activities. Some nonoperating activities, such as financing expenses and foreign exchange risks, should also be reviewed.

The net income margin is a measure of the efficiency of a company's operations and is mainly controlled by its efficiency of production. Efficiency of the production process is affected by Inventory Turnover (RR6004) and managerial and administrative expertise. Net income is eventually derived after deducting nonoperating and extraordinary activities. Nonoperating activities are ruled by financing decisions. Extraordinary activities may be excluded in an evaluation of long-term operating activities.

Appropriateness of Debt Financing

The asset to shareholders' equity ratio depends on the debt equity ratio. Debt financing is quite different from equity financing in many respects. The cost of debt financing is fixed and considered before taxes, whereas equity financing is flexible and considered after taxes. Debt financing also has an impact on stocks by determining a company's systematic risk of defaulting on debt.

To access sources of capital required to support future production, no company can avoid some degree of debt financing. Debt financing entails financing costs as well as possible liquidity issues. Debt capital providers have a priority claim on corporate earnings over dividends to shareholders, and cash shortages to pay interest expenses or principal can place a company in jeopardy.

Some industries, such as electric utilities and telecommunications, rely on extensive debt financing, and constructing the necessarily detailed debt schedules is not a simple task. Many conglomerates also have access to international capital markets.

Appropriateness of Equity Financing

A company's earnings are often measured by comparing them with equity levels such as Return on Equity (RR5302 and RR5303). Book Value per Share (RR4602) is the level of accumulated retained earnings, and the accumulation is decided by Earnings (IS1350) and Retention Ratio (RR6109), which are directly affected by dividend policies.

If all ratios are combined, net income per share (or EPS) is generated, but each component in the formula reflects different aspects of management and the analysis process can be more constructive with the use of component analysis.

11.6.2 Earnings Consensus

Analysts in brokerage houses and research firms for institutional investors try to make the best estimates using various earnings estimation methods. However, such estimates can be ambiguous and very few analysts are ever consistently close to the actual results. A few organizations gather these estimates and analyze them statistically to find the most agreed-upon forecasts.

As we have seen with differences in accounting standards worldwide, consistency of the earnings estimation by international researchers is another prominent issue to be considered in any statistical analysis. Difficulties in maintaining consistency of accounting standards involved in preparing a concensus on earnings expectation can be seen from a few quality control steps being performed by one of the major organizations, Institutional Brokers Estimate System (I/B/E/S), in the United States.

1. Are the analyst's earnings per share (EPS) forecasts primary or diluted?
2. Are EPS forecasts properly adjusted for corporate actions such as splits, stock dividends, spin-offs, etc.?
3. Does the analyst's EPS forecast include any nonrecurring items?
4. Do the analyst's forecasts accurately reflect the accounting standards of the concensus?
5. Are the estimates 1.5 or more standard deviations from the mean?

As results for a specific period become a reality, these estimates are revised and stock prices are adjusted to reflect the new information. Often, however, actual results differ significantly from the most recent estimates and come as a surprise (a "torpedo effect") to investors.

11.7 TIMING OF FINAL ACTIONS

Technical Analysis and Fundamental Analysis are both used to identify undervalued or overvalued stocks by forecasting stock price movements, but in all other respects the two systems of analysis bear no resemblance. Fundamental Analysis seeks to establish the intrinsic value of stocks by studying a company's historical and projected financial performance, its competitive strategy, and its production and distribution capability. It assumes that stock prices will, sooner or later, reflect the company's fundamental strength. Technical Analysis studies price or market movement, with the use of charts and graphs, to project future movements and trends. The technical analyst assumes that the stock price leads the company's fundamentals. Despite its modern-sounding name, Technical Analysis has been traced to seventeenth-century rice traders, whose tradition is carried on today in the form of candle charting.

In Fundamental Analysis, decisions to buy or sell a stock are guided by a comparison of its intrinsic value with its actual price. Obviously, undervalued stocks should be purchased and overvalued stocks should be sold. Buy and sell decisions, however, should also consider the demand and supply of a stock, a task commonly designated to floor traders. At this point, Technical Analysis becomes helpful in determining the best time to trade.

However, Technical Analysis is hardly limited to short-term timing decisions. Expert technical analysts can identify mispriced stocks long in advance by studying the impact on prices of the highly detailed information flowing through the investment community. With the help of a computer, the average technician can search hundreds of indicators with the flip of a switch. Daily, weekly, monthly, and annual data on stocks, bonds, currencies, commodities, and foreign securities can be scanned in a heartbeat for valuable clues.

A major indicator of future price trends in Technical Analysis is the volume of trading. The volume indicator is generally ignored in modern finance theory, which assumes the efficiency of the market and holds that transactions by individuals have no impact on market prices. Technical Analysis concentrates on the three major areas of study: Sentiment, Flow-of-Funds (momentum), and Market Structure.

Sentiment indicators monitor the trading activities of market participants such as stock exchange floor specialists, short sellers, and mutual fund managers. Put/call ratios and advisory services are a few of the tools used. The changes in sentiment indicators are essential to predicting the future movements of prices.

Flow-of-Funds analysis shows the financial positions of major market participants such as insurance companies, trust accounts, and pension funds. Their cash positions lead to potential selling and buying of securities. This type of analysis also considers the control of money by the banking system.

Market Structure analysis examines the volatility of a given market. For example, the number of ''up'' stocks versus ''down'' stocks and the ''up'' volume versus the ''down'' volume are tracked over a given period of time.

Technical Analysis may be applied to any investment object, from stocks and bonds to commodities and currencies. Any of these may be studied separately, or they may be linked.

Technical Analysis subscribes to the following major tenets:

1. Market-price action discounts everything that can possibly influence the current price. A market price is the result of the struggle between buyers and sellers, or demand and supply, respectively. If prices are rising, higher earnings and dividends are anticipated. This does not mean that price increases generate higher earnings, but that the information regarding earnings and dividends are reflected in the price before the fundamental information becomes available to the public.
2. Prices move in trends. Charting (trend analysis) of historical prices helps to identify trends in their early stages of development, allowing investors to capitalize on their movements. Before a significant price change can occur, all of the shares available for sale or purchase must be bought or sold. This process is known as accumulation, when demand exceeds supply, and distribution, when supply exceeds demand. The longer the period of accumulation or distribution, the greater the potential move.
3. Price action and price history repeat themselves. Technical analysts spend a good deal of their time identifying market patterns. Once a trend begins, they assume it will persist until another indicator points to its disruption. These cycles exist and repeat themselves over weeks, months, and years.

One of the many contributors to this school of analytical thought in the late nineteenth century was Charles H. Dow. See the discussion in the following box.

DOW THEORY

Charles H. Dow's first market average was published in 1884 with 11 securities, 9 of which were railroads. It was divided into two indices in 1897, a 12-stock industrial index and a railroad or transportation index of 20 stocks. A utility index was not added until 1929. Dow's theories laid the groundwork for today's technical analysts.

He believed that market averages discount all fundamental information, which is the first tenet of modern Technical Analysis. According to his theory, three trends exist in any market: primary, secondary, and minor trends, in either the upward or the downward movement of prices. Primary trends, the most significant, define the direction of the market. A primary trend may last one year or many, according to Dow. Moreover, a primary trend has three distinct phases: accumulation, acceleration, and distribution.

The accumulation phase is characterized by institutional or well-informed purchasing. Big block trading is led by large institutional investors. The longer the accumulation phase, the greater the potential price movement will be.

The acceleration phase attracts the attention of technical analysts, and price movements are further accelerated. Fundamental information begins to reach the public.

The final phase, distribution, reveals increased public trading and participation by nonblock traders as a result of growing public awareness through the media. Institutional investors who noticed the early indications take profits.

Secondary trends are corrections to a primary trend. These bounces may last three or four weeks to three or four months. Intermediate fluctuations have the ability to erase one- to two-thirds of the primary movements.

Minor trends usually last for three weeks or less as fluctuations in secondary trends.

The most important element in successful Technical Analysis is the identification of a primary trend as early as possible. Early indications of stabilization should be confirmed by other indicators. For example, a movement in the industrial average eventually should be confirmed by the transportation and utility averages.

The new trend should also be confirmed by changes in volume, which is emphasized in Technical Analysis. In a bullish market, for example, volume traded expands in an upward primary trend and contracts in a downward trend.

Identification of primary trends, which is difficult because of the fluctuations of secondary and minor trends, is emphasized by the Dow Theory. This ambiguity is overcome by using moving averages and momentum indicators to help clarify the prevailing trend.

Stocks tend to move with the prevailing trend of the overall market, which is the correction process from one saddle point to a new saddle point resulting from new events. The impact of new information on prices takes effect gradually, and the stabilization process creates a trend. Technical analysts try to pinpoint such indicators as early as possible.

Fundamental strengths and weaknesses reflected in historical data and future projections will, sooner or later, have an impact on stock prices. Analysts must learn to recognize to what degree these strengths and weaknesses are reflected in current stock prices. This information will serve as a guide in deciding when and in what amounts shares should be purchased or sold.

Appendix A

Data Structures for Database Development

A.6   Ratios Defined in Chapter 11 352

A.1 INDUSTRIAL FORMAT

<table>
<tr><td colspan="3" align="center">**INDUSTRIES APPLICABLE TO AN INDUSTRIAL FORMAT**</td></tr>
<tr>
<td>

Consumer—
Services
Advertising
Broadcast, Radio,
  and TV
Entertainment
Leisure Time
Lodging
Publishing/Printing
Publishing—
  Newspaper
Restaurants/Food
  Service

Consumer—
Manufacturing
Household
  Products/Wares
Jewelry/Watches/
  Gemstones
Shoes/Leather
Textiles
Toys
Bicycles

Retail/Wholesale
Food—Wholesale
Miscellaneous—
  Wholesale
Retail—Department
  Stores
Retail—Drug
  Stores
Retail—General
  Merchandise
Retail—Grocery
Retail—Special
  Line
Retail—Apparel
Retail—
  Automobiles

</td>
<td>

Wholesale Special
  Lines

Transportation and
Related
Packaging and
  Containers
Transportation—
  Rail
Transportation—
  Air
Transportation—
  Miscellaneous
Trucking and Leasing
Transportation—
  Marine
Storage/Warehousing

Consumer—Capital
Goods
Auto Parts—Original
  Equipment
Auto Parts—
  Replacement
Autos and Trucks
Furniture/Home
  Appliances
Home Builders
Real Estate
  Development
Tires and Rubber

Consumer—
Noncyclical
Beverages
Breweries
Cosmetics/Personal
  Care
Pharmaceuticals
Food Processing
Commercial Services

</td>
<td>

Medical Supplies
Medical—Hospital
  Management
Misc.—Manufacturing
Sugar Refineries
Tobacco
Wine and Spirits

Industrial
Building Materials
Electrical Equipment
Electronics
Engineering and
  Construction
Hand/Machine—Tools
Machines—
  Construction and
  Mining
Machines—
  Diversified
Manufactured
  Housing
Metal Fabrication/
  Hardware
Environmental
  Control
Industrial Materials—
  Specialty

Energy
Oil/Gas—Equipment
  and Services
Oil/Gas—Exploration
Oil/Gas—International
Oil/Gas—Domestic

Basic Materials
Agriculture
Chemicals
Forest Products and
  Paper

(continued)

</td>
</tr>
</table>

(continued)		

Fisheries
Metals—Diversified
Mining
Iron/Steel
 	
Utility
	Utilities—Water
	
	Technology
	Aerospace/Defense
	Biopharmaceutical
	Electronics—
	   Semiconductor
	Emerging
	   Technologies
	Computers
		Computer Software/
		   Services
		Medical—
		   Biotechnology
		Office/Business
		   Equipment
		Telecommunications
		Telecom Equipment

A.1.1   Income Statement in an Industrial Format

Sections	Data Items	
Operating Section	IS1001	Net Sales
	IS1019	Other Operating Revenue
	IS1020	**Total Revenue**
	IS1021	Cost of Goods Sold or Cost of Sales
	IS1039	Direct Expenses for Other Operating Activities
	IS1040	**Total Direct Expenses**
	IS1050	Selling, General, and Administrative Expenses
	IS1099	**Operating Income**
Nonoperating Section	IS1110	Interest Expenses
	IS1120	Foreign Exchange Loss (Gain)
	IS1130	Loss (Gain) from Associated Companies
	IS1140	Other Nonoperating Loss (Gain)
	IS1150	Income Tax Expenses (Credits)
	IS1160	Reserve Charges (Credits)
	IS1199	**Income Before Extraordinary Items**
Extraordinary Items	IS1210	Loss (Gain) from Extraordinary Activities Before Tax Effects
	IS1220	Tax Effects on Extraordinary Items
	IS1230	Minority Interests
	IS1299	**Net Income**
Reference Items for EPS	IS1310	Cash Dividends to Preferred Stocks
	IS1320	Cash Dividends to Common Stocks
	IS1323	Appropriation to Capital Reserves
	IS1324	Appropriation to Revenue Reserves
	IS1325	Distributions to Directors and Officers
	IS1330	Dividend per Share (DPS)
	IS1340	EPS Before Extraordinary Items
	IS1350	Primary Earnings per Share
		(continued)

Sections	Data Items	
(continued)		
	IS1360	Weighted Average Number of Shares for the Primary EPS
	IS1370	Fully Diluted EPS
	IS1380	Number of Shares for Fully Diluted EPS
	IS1390	Special EPS
Other Reference Items	IS1510	Export Sales
	IS1520	Cost of Materials
	IS1530	Personnel Expenses
	IS1540	Depreciation Expenses
	IS1550	Research and Development Expenditure
	IS1610	Capitalized Interest Expenses
	IS1620	Sales from Discontinued Operations
	IS1630	Loss (Gain) from Discontinued Operations
	IS1700	Number of Days for the Period

A.1.2 Balance Sheet in an Industrial Format

Sections	Data Items	
Current Assets	BS2010	Cash and Cash Equivalents
	BS2020	Marketable Securities and Other Short-Term Investments
	BS2030	Accounts and Notes Receivable
	BS2040	Inventory
	BS2090	Other Current Assets
	BS2099	**Total Current Assets**
Noncurrent Assets	BS2110	Gross Tangible Fixed Assets
	BS2120	Accumulated Depreciation
	BS2130	Net Tangible Fixed Assets
	BS2170	Long-Term Investments and Long-Term Receivables
	BS2180	Investments in Associated Companies
	BS2190	Intangibles and Other Assets
	BS2199	**Total Assets**
Current Liabilities	BS2260	Accounts Payable
	BS2270	Short-Term Borrowing
	BS2280	Short-Term Portion of Long-Term Borrowing
	BS2290	Other Current Liabilities
	BS2299	**Total Current Liabilities**

(continued)

(continued)

Sections	Data Items	
Noncurrent Liabilities	BS2370	Long-Term Borrowing
	BS2390	Other Long-Term Liabilities
	BS2399	**Total Liabilities**
Shareholders' Equity	BS2410	Preferred Equity
	BS2420	Minority Interest
	BS2450	Share Capital and Share Premiums
	BS2460	Retained Earnings
	BS2470	(Treasury Stocks)
	BS2499	**Total Shareholders' Equity**
Reference Items	BS2560	Nondepreciable Fixed Assets
	BS2565	Insurance Value of Tangible Fixed Assets
	BS2660	Pension Reserves
	BS2670	Deferred Tax Liabilities
	BS2680	Non-Equity Reserves
	BS2685	Unrealized Gain (Loss) from Investments
	BS2690	Goodwill Written Off
	BS2710	Number of Shares Outstanding
	BS2720	Par Value
	BS2730	Dividend Right Parity
	BS2740	Voting Right Parity
	BS2770	Number of Treasury Stocks
	BS2800	Number of Employees

A.1.3 Cash from Operations in an Industrial Format

Approaches	Data Items	
Indirect Approach	CF3010	Net Income
	CF3020	Depreciation and Amortization
	CF3030	Other Non-Cash Adjustments
	CF3040	Changes in Non-Cash Working Capital
	CF3099	**Cash from Operations**
Direct Approach	CF3050	Cash Receipts from Sales
	CF3060	Cash Disbursement for Purchases
	CF3070	Income Tax Paid
	CF3080	Other Cash Receipts and Disbursements
	CF3099	**Cash from Operations**

A.1.4 Cash from Nonoperating Activities in an Industrial Format

Approaches	Data Items
Investing/ Financing Approach	**Investing Activities** CF3110 Disposal of Fixed Assets CF3120 (Capital Expenditure) CF3130 Disposal of Long-Term Investments CF3140 (Purchase of Long-Term Investments) CF3150 Decrease (Increase) in Short-Term Investments CF3180 Other Investing Activities **CF3189 Cash from Investing Activities** **Financing Activities** CF3210 (Dividends Paid) CF3220 Increase (Decrease) in Short-Term Borrowing CF3230 Increase in Long-Term Borrowing CF3240 (Decrease in Long-Term Borrowing) CF3250 Increase in Capital Stocks CF3260 (Decrease in Capital Stocks) CF3280 Other Financing Activities **CF3289 Cash from Financing Activities** **CF3490 Net Changes in Cash**
Sources/Uses Approach	**Sources** CF3310 Disposal of Fixed Assets CF3320 Disposal of Long-Term Investments CF3330 Increase in Long-Term Borrowing CF3340 Increase in Capital Stocks CF3380 Other Sources **CF3389 Total Sources** **Uses or Applications** CF3410 Dividends Paid CF3420 Capital Expenditures CF3430 Purchase of Long-Term Investments CF3440 Decrease in Long-Term Borrowing CF3450 Decrease in Capital Stocks CF3480 Other Uses **CF3489 Total Uses** **CF3490 Increase (Decrease) in Funds**
Reference Items	CF3495 Definition of Funds CF3500 Cash Payments for Interest Expenses

A.2 BANKING FORMAT

A.2.1 Industries Applicable to a Banking Format

Financial—Banks, Money Centers
Financial—Banks, Commercial
Financial—Savings and Loans/Thrifts

A.2.2 Income Statement in a Banking Format

Sections	Data Items	
Operating Section	IS1011	Interest Income
	IS1012	Trading Account Profit (Loss) and Foreign Exchange Revenue
	IS1014	Investment Income
	IS1015	Commissions and Fees Earned
	IS1019	Other Operating Revenue
	IS1020	**Total Revenue**
	IS1022	Interest Expenses
	IS1023	Provision for Loan Losses
	IS1024	Commissions and Fees Paid
	IS1039	Direct Expenses for Other Operating Activities
	IS1040	**Total Direct Expenses**
	IS1050	General and Administrative Expenses
	IS1099	**Operating Income**
Nonoperating Section	IS1130	Loss (Gain) from Associated Companies
	IS1140	Other Nonoperating Loss (Gain)
	IS1150	Income Tax Expenses (Credits)
	IS1160	Reserve Charges (Credits)
	IS1199	**Income Before Extraordinary Items**
Extraordinary Items	IS1210	Loss (Gain) from Extraordinary Activities Before Tax Effects
	IS1220	Tax Effects on Extraordinary Items
	IS1230	Minority Interests
	IS1299	**Net Income**
Reference Items for EPS	IS1310	Cash Dividends to Preferred Stocks
	IS1320	Cash Dividends to Common Stocks
	IS1323	Appropriation to Capital Reserves
	IS1324	Appropriation to Revenue Reserves
	IS1325	Distributions to Directors and Officers
	IS1330	Dividend per Share (DPS)
	IS1340	EPS Before Extraordinary Items
	IS1350	Primary Earnings per Share
	IS1360	Weighted Average Number of Shares for the Primary EPS

(continued)

Sections	Data Items	
(continued)		
	IS1370	Fully Diluted EPS
	IS1380	Number of Shares for Fully Diluted EPS
	IS1390	Special EPS
Other Reference Items	IS1530	Personnel Expenses
	IS1620	Revenue from Discontinued Operations
	IS1630	Loss (Gain) from Discontinued Operations
	IS1640	Actual Loan Loss
	IS1650	Interest Income from Loans
	IS1660	Interest Expenses to Deposits
	IS1670	Unrealized Gain (Loss) on Investments
	IS1700	Number of Days in the Period

A.2.3 Balance Sheet in a Banking Format

Sections	Data Items	
Current Assets	BS2010	Cash and Cash Equivalents
	BS2020	Short-Term Investments
	BS2035	Federal Funds Sold and Securities Purchased Under Resale Agreements
	BS2050	Commercial Loans
	BS2052	Consumer Loans
	BS2054	Other Loans
	BS2055	Total Loans
	BS2057	Loan Loss Reserves
	BS2060	Net Loans
	BS2065	Due from Banks and Other Interbank Assets
Noncurrent Assets	BS2130	Net Tangible Fixed Assets
	BS2170	Long-Term Investments
	BS2180	Investments in Associated Companies
	BS2190	Intangibles and Other Assets
	BS2195	Customers' Liabilities for Acceptances
	BS2199	**Total Assets**
Current Liabilities	BS2210	Demand Deposits
	BS2212	Savings Deposits
	BS2215	Time Deposits
	BS2219	Other Deposits
	BS2220	Total Deposits
	BS2270	Due to Banks and Other Short-Term Borrowing
		(continued)

(continued)		
	BS2275	Federal Funds Purchased and Securities Sold Under Repurchase Agreements
	BS2280	Short-Term Portion of Long-Term Borrowing
	BS2290	Other Short-Term Liabilities
Noncurrent Liabilities	BS2370	Long-Term Borrowing
	BS2390	Other Long-Term Liabilities
	BS2395	Customers' Acceptances
	BS2399	**Total Liabilities**
Shareholders' Equity	BS2410	Preferred Equity
	BS2420	Minority Interest
	BS2450	Share Capital and Share Premiums
	BS2460	Retained Earnings
	BS2470	(Treasury Stocks)
	BS2499	**Total Shareholders' Equity**
Reference Items	BS2510	Short-Term Loans
	BS2512	Mid-Term Loans
	BS2515	Long-Term Loans
	BS2520	Real Estate Loans
	BS2522	Lease Financing Loans
	BS2525	Foreign Loans
	BS2529	Nonperforming Assets
	BS2610	Short-Term Deposits
	BS2612	Mid-Term Deposits
	BS2615	Long-Term Deposits
	BS2625	Foreign Deposits
	BS2630	Core Capital (Tier 1)
	BS2632	Risk-Based Capital (Tier 1 + Tier 2)
	BS2635	Leverage Ratio
	BS2660	Pension Reserves
	BS2670	Deferred Tax Liabilities
	BS2680	Non-Equity Reserves
	BS2685	Investment Reserves
	BS2690	Goodwill Written Off
	BS2695	Off-Balance Contingent Liabilities
	BS2710	Number of Shares Outstanding
	BS2720	Par Value
	BS2730	Dividend Right Parity
	BS2740	Voting Right Parity
	BS2770	Number of Treasury Stocks
	BS2800	Number of Employees

A.2.4 Cash from Operations in a Banking Format

Approaches	Data Items	
Indirect Approach	CF3010	Net Income
	CF3020	Provision for Loan Losses and Depreciation
	CF3030	Other Non-Cash Adjustments
	CF3040	Changes in Non-Cash Working Capital
	CF3099	**Cash from Operations**
Direct Approach	CF3050	Cash Receipts from Revenue
	CF3060	Cash Disbursement for Interest Payments
	CF3070	Income Tax Paid
	CF3080	Other Cash Receipts and Disbursements
	CF3099	**Cash from Operations**

A.2.5 Cash from Nonoperating Activities in a Banking Format

Approaches	Data Items	
Investing/ Financing Approach	**Investing Activities**	
	CF3110	Disposal of Fixed Assets
	CF3120	(Capital Expenditure)
	CF3130	Disposal of Long-Term Investments
	CF3140	(Purchase of Long-Term Investments)
	CF3150	Decrease (Increase) in Short-Term Investments
	CF3160	Decrease (Increase) in Loans
	CF3180	Other Investing Activities
	CF3189	**Cash from Investing Activities**
	Financing Activities	
	CF3210	(Dividends Paid)
	CF3220	Increase (Decrease) in Short-Term Borrowing
	CF3230	Increase in Long-Term Borrowing
	CF3240	(Decrease in Long-Term Borrowing
	CF3250	Increase in Capital Stocks
	CF3260	(Decrease in Capital Stocks)
	CF3270	Increase (Decrease) in Deposits
	CF3280	Other Financing Activities
	CF3289	**Cash from Financing Activities**
	CF3490	**Net Changes in Cash**
Sources/Uses Approach	**Sources**	
	CF3310	Disposal of Fixed Assets
	CF3320	Disposal of Long-Term Investments

(continued)

Sections	Data Items
(continued)	
	CF3330 Increase in Long-Term Borrowing
	CF3340 Increase in Capital Stocks
	CF3350 Decrease in Loans
	CF3360 Increase in Deposits
	CF3380 Other Sources
	CF3389 Total Sources
	Uses or Applications
	CF3410 Dividends Paid
	CF3420 Capital Expenditures
	CF3430 Purchase of Long-Term Investments
	CF3440 Decrease in Long-Term Borrowing
	CF3450 Decrease in Capital Stocks
	CF3460 Increase in Loans
	CF3470 Decrease in Deposits
	CF3480 Other Uses
	CF3489 Total Uses
	CF3490 Increase (Decrease) in Funds
Reference Item	CF3495 Definition of Funds

A.3 INSURANCE FORMAT

A.3.1 Industries Applicable to an Insurance Format

Insurance—Life
Insurance—Multiline (Life and Property & Casualty)
Insurance—Property & Casualty

A.3.2 Income Statement in an Insurance Format

Sections	Data Items		
Operating Section	IS1002 Gross Premium from Life		IS1005 Gross Premium from Non-Life
	IS1003 Adjustments for Life		IS1006 Adjustments for Non-Life
	IS1004 Net Premium from Life		IS1007 Net Premium from Non-Life
			(continued)

(continued)

Sections	Data Items			
	IS1012 Trading Accounts Profit (Loss) IS1013 Income from Real Estate Investments IS1014 Investment Income IS1019 Other Operating Revenue **IS1020 Total Revenue**			
	IS1031 Insurance Claims and Losses for Life IS1032 LT Insurance Charges (Life) IS1033 Dividends to Policyholders IS1034 Underwriting and Policy Acquisition Costs for Life		IS1035 Insurance Claims and Losses for Non-Life IS1036 Underwriting and Policy Acquisition Costs for Non-Life	
	IS1039 Direct Expenses for Other Operating Activities **IS1040 Total Direct Expenses** IS1050 General and Administrative Expenses **IS1099 Operating Income**			
Nonoperating Section	IS1110 Interest Expenses IS1130 Loss (Gain) from Associated Companies IS1140 Other Nonoperating Loss (Gain) IS1150 Income Tax Expenses (Credits) IS1160 Reserve Charges (Credits) **IS1199 Income Before Extraordinary Items**			
Extraordinary Items	IS1210 Loss (Gain) from Extraordinary Activities Before Tax Effects IS1220 Tax Effects on Extraordinary Items IS1230 Minority Interests IS1240 Policyholders' Surplus **IS1299 Net Income**			
Reference Items for EPS	IS1310 Cash Dividends to Preferred Stocks IS1320 Cash Dividends to Common Stocks IS1323 Appropriation to Capital Reserves IS1324 Appropriation to Revenue Reserves IS1325 Distributions to Directors and Officers IS1330 Dividend per Share (DPS) IS1340 EPS Before Extraordinary Items IS1350 Primary Earnings per Share			

(continued)

Sections	Data Items	
(continued)		
	IS1360	Weighted Average Number of Shares for the Primary EPS
	IS1370	Fully Diluted EPS
	IS1380	Number of Shares for Fully Diluted EPS
	IS1390	Special EPS
Other Reference Items	IS1530	Personnel Expenses
	IS1560	Amortization of Deferred Acquisition Costs—Life
	IS1561	Amortization of Deferred Acquisition Costs—Non-Life
	IS1620	Revenue from Discontinued Operations
	IS1630	Loss (Gain) from Discontinued Operations
	IS1670	Unrealized Gain (Loss) on Investments
	IS1700	Number of Days for the Period

A.3.3   Balance Sheet in an Insurance Format

Sections	Data Items	
Current Assets	BS2010	Cash and Cash Equivalents
	BS2030	Net Receivables
	BS2020	Short-Term Investments
	BS2060	Loans and Mortgages
	BS2070	Fixed Income Securities
	BS2080	Equity Securities
	BS2090	Real Estate Investments
	BS2095	Other Investments
	BS2170	Total Investments
Noncurrent Assets	BS2130	Net Tangible Fixed Assets
	BS2180	Investments in Associated Companies
	BS2190	Intangibles and Other Assets
	BS2195	Segregated Accounts
	BS2199	**Total Assets**
Current Liabilities	BS2230	Reserve for Outstanding Claims and Losses
	BS2232	Premium Reserve
	BS2235	Reserve for Life Policy Benefits
	BS2237	Other Insurance Reserves
	BS2240	Total Insurance Reserves
	BS2270	Short-Term Borrowing
	BS2280	Short-Term Portion of Long-Term Borrowing
	BS2290	Other Short-Term Liabilities
		(continued)

(continued)

Sections	Data Items	
Noncurrent Liabilities	BS2370	Long-Term Borrowing
	BS2390	Other Long-Term Liabilities
	BS2395	Segregated Accounts
	BS2399	**Total Liabilities**
Shareholders' Equity	BS2410	Preferred Equity
	BS2420	Minority Interest
	BS2430	Policyholders' Equity
	BS2450	Share Capital and Share Premiums
	BS2460	Retained Earnings
	BS2470	(Treasury Stocks)
	BS2499	**Total Shareholders' Equity**
Reference Items	BS2540	Deferred Policy Acquisition Costs
	BS2640	Claims and Loss Reserve for Life
	BS2642	Claims and Loss Reserve for Non-Life
	BS2645	Premium Reserve for Life
	BS2647	Premium Reserve for Non-Life
	BS2650	Life Policy in Force
	BS2660	Pension Reserves
	BS2670	Deferred Tax Liabilities
	BS2680	Non-Equity Reserves
	BS2685	Investment Reserves
	BS2690	Goodwill Written Off
	BS2710	Number of Shares Outstanding
	BS2720	Par Value
	BS2730	Dividend Right Parity
	BS2740	Voting Right Parity
	BS2770	Number of Treasury Stocks
	BS2800	Number of Employees

A.3.4 Cash from Operations in an Insurance Format

Approaches	Data Items	
Indirect Approach	CF3010	Net Income
	CF3020	Changes in Insurance Reserves and Depreciation
	CF3030	Other Non-Cash Adjustments
	CF3040	Changes in Non-Cash Working Capital
	CF3099	**Cash from Operations**
Direct Approach	CF3050	Cash Receipts from Revenue
	CF3060	Cash Disbursement for Claims and Underwriting Expenses
	CF3070	Income Tax Paid
	CF3080	Other Cash Receipts and Disbursements
	CF3099	**Cash from Operations**

A.3.5 Cash from Nonoperating Activities in an Insurance Format

Approaches	Data Items
Investing/ Financing Approach	**Investing Activities**
	CF3110 Disposal of Fixed Assets
	CF3120 (Capital Expenditure)
	CF3130 Disposal of Long-Term Investments
	CF3140 (Purchase of Long-Term Investments)
	CF3150 Decrease (Increase) in Short-Term Investments
	CF3180 Other Investing Activities
	CF3189 Cash from Investing Activities
	Financing Activities
	CF3210 (Dividends Paid)
	CF3220 Increase (Decrease) in Short-Term Borrowing
	CF3230 Increase in Long-Term Borrowing
	CF3240 (Decrease in Long-Term Borrowing)
	CF3250 Increase in Capital Stocks
	CF3260 (Decrease in Capital Stocks)
	CF3280 Other Financing Activities
	CF3289 Cash from Financing Activities
	CF3490 Net Changes in Cash
Sources/Uses Approach	**Sources**
	CF3310 Disposal of Fixed Assets
	CF3320 Disposal of Long-Term Investments
	CF3330 Increase in Long-Term Borrowing
	CF3340 Increase in Capital Stocks
	CF3380 Other Sources
	CF3389 Total Sources
	Uses or Applications
	CF3410 Dividends Paid
	CF3420 Capital Expenditures
	CF3430 Purchase of Long-Term Investments
	CF3440 Decrease in Long-Term Borrowing
	CF3450 Decrease in Capital Stocks
	CF3480 Other Uses
	CF3489 Total Uses
	CF3490 Increase (Decrease) in Funds
Reference Item	CF3495 Definition of Funds

A.4 OTHER FINANCIAL SERVICES FORMAT

A.4.1 Industries Applicable to an Other Financial Services Format

Holding Companies—Diversified
Personal/Commercial Loans

Financial—Securities Brokers
Financial—Commodities Trading
Lease Financing
Foreign—ADR
Closed-End Funds
Real Estate Investment Trusts
Country Funds—Closed End
Investment Companies

A.4.2 Income Statement in an Other Financial Services Format

Sections	Data Items	
Operating Section	IS1011	Interest Income
	IS1012	Trading Account Profit (Loss)
	IS1013	Income from Real Estate Investments
	IS1014	Investment Income
	IS1015	Commissions and Fees Earned
	IS1019	Other Operating Revenue
	IS1020	**Total Revenue**
	IS1022	Interest Expenses
	IS1023	Provision for Loan Losses
	IS1024	Commissions and Fees Paid
	IS1039	Direct Expenses for Other Operating Activities
	IS1040	**Total Direct Expenses**
	IS1050	General and Administrative Expenses
	IS1099	**Operating Income**
Nonoperating Section	IS1130	Loss (Gain) from Associated Companies
	IS1140	Other Nonoperating Loss (Gain)
	IS1150	Income Tax Expenses (Credits)
	IS1160	Reserve Charges (Credits)
	IS1199	**Income Before Extraordinary Items**
Extraordinary Items	IS1210	Loss (Gain) from Extraordinary Activities Before Tax Effects
	IS1220	Tax Effects on Extraordinary Items
	IS1230	Minority Interests
	IS1299	**Net Income**
Reference Items for EPS	IS1310	Cash Dividends to Preferred Stocks
	IS1320	Cash Dividends to Common Stocks
	IS1323	Appropriation to Capital Reserves
	IS1324	Appropriation to Revenue Reserves
	IS1325	Distributions to Directors and Officers
	IS1330	Dividend per Share
	IS1340	EPS Before Extraordinary Items
	IS1350	Primary Earnings per Share

(continued)

(continued)	
Sections	**Data Items**
	IS1360 Weighted Average Number of Shares for the Primary EPS
	IS1370 Fully Diluted EPS
	IS1380 Number of Shares for Fully Diluted EPS
	IS1390 Special EPS
Other Reference Items	IS1530 Personnel Expenses
	IS1540 Depreciation Expenses
	IS1620 Revenue from Discontinued Operations
	IS1630 Loss (Gain) from Discontinued Operations
	IS1670 Unrealized Gain (Loss) on Investments
	IS1700 Number of Days for the Period

A.4.3 Balance Sheet in an Other Financial Services Format

Sections	**Data Items**
Current Assets	BS2010 Cash and Cash Equivalents
	BS2030 Net Receivables
	BS2020 Short-Term Investments
	BS2035 Federal Funds Sold and Securities Purchased Under Resale Agreements
	BS2055 Total Loans
	BS2057 Loan Loss Reserves
	BS2060 Net Loans
	BS2090 Real Estate Investments
	BS2092 Investments in Securities
	BS2095 Other Investments
	BS2170 Total Investments
Noncurrent Assets	BS2130 Net Tangible Fixed Assets
	BS2180 Investments in Associated Companies
	BS2190 Intangibles and Other Assets
	BS2195 Custody Accounts
	BS2199 Total Assets
Current Liabilities	BS2220 Total Deposits
	BS2270 Short-Term Borrowing
	BS2275 Federal Funds Purchased and Securities Sold Under Repurchase Agreements
	BS2280 Short-Term Portion of Long-Term Borrowing
	BS2290 Other Short-Term Liabilities
	(continued)

Sections	Data Items	
(continued)		
Noncurrent Liabilities	BS2370	Long-Term Borrowing
	BS2390	Other Long-Term Liabilities
	BS2395	Customers' Liabilities
	BS2399	**Total Liabilities**
Shareholders' Equity	BS2410	Preferred Equity
	BS2420	Minority Interest
	BS2450	Share Capital and Share Premiums
	BS2460	Retained Earnings
	BS2470	(Treasury Stocks)
	BS2499	**Total Shareholders' Equity**
Reference Items	BS2660	Pension Reserves
	BS2670	Deferred Tax Liabilities
	BS2680	Non-Equity Reserves
	BS2690	Goodwill Written Off
	BS2695	Off-Balance Contingent Liabilities
	BS2710	Number of Shares Outstanding
	BS2720	Par Value
	BS2730	Dividend Right Parity
	BS2740	Voting Right Parity
	BS2770	Number of Treasury Stocks
	BS2800	Number of Employees

A.4.4 Cash from Operations in an Other Financial Services Format

Approaches	Data Items	
Indirect Approach	CF3010	Net Income
	CF3020	Provision for Loan Losses and Depreciation
	CF3030	Other Non-Cash Adjustments
	CF3040	Changes in Non-Cash Working Capital
	CF3099	**Cash from Operations**
Direct Approach	CF3050	Cash Receipts from Revenue
	CF3060	Cash Disbursement for Operating Expenses
	CF3070	Income Tax Paid
	CF3080	Other Cash Receipts and Disbursements
	CF3099	**Cash from Operations**

A.4.5 Cash from Nonoperating Activities in an Other Financial Services Format

Approaches	Data Items
Investing/ Financing Approach	**Investing Activities**
	CF3110 Disposal of Fixed Assets
	CF3120 (Capital Expenditure)
	CF3130 Disposal of Long-Term Investments
	CF3140 (Purchase of Long-Term Investments)
	CF3150 Decrease (Increase) in Short-Term Investments
	CF3160 Decrease (Increase) in Loans
	CF3180 Other Investing Activities
	CF3189 Cash from Investing Activities
	Financing Activities
	CF3210 (Dividends Paid)
	CF3220 Increase (Decrease) in Short-Term Borrowing
	CF3230 Increase in Long-Term Borrowing
	CF3240 (Decrease in Long-Term Borrowing)
	CF3250 Increase in Capital Stocks
	CF3260 (Decrease in Capital Stocks)
	CF3270 Increase (Decrease) in Deposits
	CF3280 Other Financing Activities
	CF3289 Cash from Financing Activities
	CF3490 Net Changes in Cash
Sources/Uses Approach	**Sources**
	CF3310 Disposal of Fixed Assets
	CF3320 Disposal of Long-Term Investments
	CF3330 Increase in Long-Term Borrowing
	CF3340 Increase in Capital Stocks
	CF3350 Decrease in Loans
	CF3360 Increase in Deposits
	CF3380 Other Sources
	CF3389 Total Sources
	Uses or Applications
	CF3410 Dividends Paid
	CF3420 Capital Expenditures
	CF3430 Purchase of Long-Term Investments
	CF3440 Decrease in Long-Term Borrowing
	CF3450 Decrease in Capital Stocks
	CF3460 Increase in Loans
	CF3470 Decrease in Deposits
	CF3480 Other Uses
	CF3489 Total Uses
	CF3490 Increase (Decrease) in Funds
Reference Item	CF3495 Definition of Funds

A.5   DATA STRUCTURES COMMON TO ALL FORMATS

A.5.1   Multiple Share Information

STOCKID	Identification of Security
IS1330	Cash Dividends to Common Stock
IS1340	Dividend per Share
IS1350	EPS Before Extraordinary Items
IS1360	Primary EPS
IS1370	Weighted Average Number of Shares
BS2710	Number of Shares Outstanding
BS2720	Par Value
BS2730	Dividend Right Parity
BS2740	Voting Right Parity
BS2790	Number of Treasury Stocks

A.5.2   Daily Stock Price Information Set

STOCKID	Identification of security
DATE	Date of transaction
OPENING	Opening price
HIGH	High of the day
LOW	Low of the day
CLOSING	Closing price
VOLUME	Volume traded
EXCHANGE	Stock exchange on which the security is traded
CURRENCY	Currency of the transaction
RATIO	Stock dividend or stock split ratio
TYPE	Type of the dilution activities

A.5.3   Product Segmentation

Year	Date of Information
SIC	Standard Industry Classification
Description	Product Description
Sales	Sales or Revenue
Income	Operating Income
Assets	Total Assets (Identifiable Assets)

SIC tables appear in the *Standard Industrial Classification Manual,* published by the Office of Management and Budget, U.S. Department of Commerce (JIST Works, Inc., 720 North Park Avenue, Indianapolis, IN 46202-3431, U.S.A.). Phone 1-800-648-JIST or 1-317-264-3720; Fax 1-800-JIST-FAX or 1-317-264-3709.

An abbreviated version of SIC tables is provided in Section A.5.4. Further discussion may be found in Chapter 7 of this book.

A.5.4 Basic Structure of SIC Tables

Division	Group	Group Titles
A		**Agriculture, Forestry, and Fishing**
	0100	Agricultural production—crops
	0200	Agricultural production—livestock and animal specialties
	0700	Agricultural services
	0800	Forestry
	0900	Fishing, hunting, and trapping
B		**Mining**
	1000	Metal mining
	1200	Coal mining
	1300	Oil and gas extraction
	1400	Mining and quarrying of nonmetallic minerals, except fuels
C		**Construction**
	1500	Building construction—general contractors and operative builders
	1600	Heavy construction other than building construction contractors
	1700	Construction—special trade contractors
D		**Manufacturing**
	2000	Food and kindred products
	2100	Tobacco products
	2200	Textile mill products
	2300	Apparel and other finished products made from fabrics and similar materials
	2400	Lumber and wood products, except furniture
	2500	Furniture and fixtures
	2600	Paper and allied products
	2700	Printing, publishing, and allied industries
	2800	Chemicals and allied products
	2900	Petroleum refining and related industries
	3000	Rubber and miscellaneous plastics products
	3100	Leather and leather products
	3200	Stone, clay, glass, and concrete products
	3300	Primary metal industries
	3400	Fabricated metal products, except machinery and transportation equipment
	3500	Industrial and commercial machinery and computer equipment
	3600	Electronic and other electrical equipment and components, except computer equipment
	3700	Transportation equipment
	3800	Measuring, analyzing, and controlling instruments; photographic, medical, and optical goods; watches and clocks
	3900	Miscellaneous manufacturing industries

(continued)

(continued)

Division	Group	Group Titles
E		**Transportation, Communications, Electric, Gas, and Sanitary Services**
	4000	Railroad transport
	4100	Local and suburban transit and interurban highway passenger transportation
	4200	Motor freight transportation and warehousing
	4300	Postal services
	4400	Water transportation
	4500	Transportation by air
	4600	Pipelines, except natural gas
	4700	Transportation services
	4800	Communications
	4900	Electric, gas, and sanitary services
F		**Wholesale Trade**
	5000	Wholesale trade—durable goods
	5100	Wholesale trade—nondurable goods
G		**Retail Trade**
	5200	Building materials, hardware, garden supply, and mobile home dealers
	5300	General merchandise stores
	5400	Food stores
	5500	Automotive dealers and gasoline service stations
	5600	Apparel and accessory stores
	5700	Home furniture, furnishings, and equipment stores
	5800	Eating and drinking places
	5900	Miscellaneous retail
H		**Finance, Insurance, and Real Estate**
	6000	Depository institutions
	6100	Nondepository credit institutions
	6200	Security and commodity brokers, dealers, exchanges, and services
	6300	Insurance carriers
	6400	Insurance agents, brokers, and services
	6500	Real estate
	6600	Holding and other investment offices
I		**Services**
	7000	Hotels, rooming houses, camps, and other lodging places
	7200	Personal services
	7300	Business services
	7500	Automotive repair, services, and parking
	7600	Miscellaneous repair services
	7800	Motion pictures
	7900	Amusement and recreation services
	8000	Health services
	8100	Legal services
	8200	Educational services
	8300	Social services

(continued)

(continued)

Division	Group	Group Titles
	8400	Museums, art galleries, and botanical and zoological gardens
	8600	Membership organizations
	8700	Engineering, accounting, research, management, and related services
	8800	Private households
	8900	Miscellaneous services
J		**Public Administration**
	9100	Executive, legislative, and general government, except finance
	9200	Justice, public order, and safety
	9300	Public finance, taxation, and monetary policy
	9400	Administration of human resource programs
	9500	Administration of environmental quality and housing programs
	9600	Administration of economic programs
	9700	National security and international affairs
K		**Nonclassifiable Establishments**
	9900	Nonclassifiable establishments

A.5.5 Geographic Segmentation

Year	Date of Information
Geo Codes	Geographic Codes
Description	Geographic Description
Sales	Sales or Revenue
Income	Operating Income
Assets	Total Assets (Identifiable Assets)

The following are examples of the first two (numerical) characters for Geo Codes:

10	North America
20	Latin America
30	Asia
40	Oceana
50	Middle East Asia
60	Africa
70	Europe
80	Emerging Europe and Russia
90	The Rest of World

The second two (alphabetic) characters for Geo Codes can be systematically constructed for database purposes.

A.5.6 Subsidiary Information

Year
Name
Location (country)
Industry (Standard Industry Classification codes)

Percentage of equity ownership (relationship to a parent company)
Sales or Revenue
Operating income
Total Assets
Share Capital

A.5.7 Data Structure for Major Shareholders

Stock ID	Identification of a security
Year	Date of information
Codes	Codes for the types of shareholders
Shareholder	Name of a shareholder
Percentage	Percentage of ownership
Shares	Number of shares owned

The following are examples of codes for types of shareholders:

Codes	Description
SH10	Government or government-related organizations
SH20	Institutional investors
SH21	Banks
SH22	Insurance companies
SH23	Brokerage firms
SH24	Managed funds
SH29	Other institutional investors
SH30	Other organizations with operating interest in the company
SH40	Directors/officers
SH50	Employees
SH60	Individual shareholders
SH90	Foreign shareholders (an additional reference item)

A.5.8 Data Structure for Shareholders by Type of Organization

Stock ID	Identification of a security
Year	Date of information
Codes	Codes for the group types of shareholders
Shareholders	Number of shareholders
Percentage	Percentage of ownership
Shares	Number of shares owned

The following are examples of codes for shareholders by type of organization:

Codes	Description
SG10	Government or government-related organizations
SG20	Institutional investors
SG21	Banks
SG22	Insurance companies
SG23	Brokerage firms
SG24	Managed funds

SG29   Other institutional investors
SG30   Other organizations with operating interest in the company
SG40   Directors/officers
SG50   Employees
SG60   Individual shareholders

SG90   Foreign shareholders (an additional reference item)

A.5.9   Data Structure for Shareholders by Size of Ownership

Stock ID   Identification of a security
Year   Date of information
Codes   Codes for the size categories of shareholders
Shareholders   Number of shareholders
Percentage   Percentage of ownership
Shares   Number of shares owned

The following are examples of codes for shareholders by size of share ownership:

Codes	Description
SS10	1–1,000
SS20	1,001–5,000
SS30	5,001–10,000
SS40	10,001–50,000
SS50	50,001–100,000
SS60	100,001–500,000
SS70	500,001–1,000,000
SS80	1,000,000 or greater

A.5.10   Data Structure for Management Information

Year   Date of information
Codes   Codes for relationship to outside organizations
Name   Name of management
Title   Title within the company
Title Codes   Codified title

The following are examples of codes for management relationship with outside organizations:

Codes	Description
MG10	Government related
MG20	Independent major shareholder
MG30	Major shareholding company
MG40	Independent major loan provider
MG50	Major loan-providing company
MG60	Union representative
MG70	Independent individual

A.6 RATIOS DEFINED IN CHAPTER 11

A.6.1 Raw Data Adjustment Factors

Ratios	Ratio Titles	Unit	Ind*	Bank	Ins	Fin
RR4001	Number of Days	Days	√	√	√	√
RR4002	Annualization Factor	Rate	√	√	√	√
RR4003	Average Exchange Rate	Rate	√	√	√	√

* Ind, industrial format; Bank, banking format; Ins, insurance format; Fin, other financial service format.

A.6.2 Preliminary Data for Ratio Computation

Annualization of Data Collected in the Financial Statements

Ratios	Ratio Titles	Unit	Ind	Bank	Ins	Fin
RR4101	Annualized Sales	mil or bil	√			
RR4102	Annualized Total Revenue	mil or bil	√	√	√	√
RR4103	Annualized Operating Income	mil or bil	√	√	√	√
RR4104	Annualized Income Before Extraordinary Items	mil or bil	√	√	√	√
RR4105	Annualized Net Income	mil or bil	√	√	√	√
RR4106	Annualized Total Revenue	mil or bil	√	√	√	√
RR4107	Annualized Income Before Extraordinary Items per Share	currency	√	√	√	√
RR4108	Annualized Earnings per Share	currency	√	√	√	√
RR4109	Annualized Cash from Operations	mil or bil	√	√	√	√
RR4110	Annualized Dividend per Share	currency	√	√	√	√

Additional Subtotal Items and Their Annualization

Ratios	Ratio Titles	Unit	Ind	Bank	Ins	Fin
RR4201	Pretax Income	mil or bil	√	√	√	√
RR4202	Annualized Pretax Income	mil or bil	√	√	√	√
RR4203	Total Interest Expenses	mil or bil	√			
RR4204	EBIT (Earnings Before Interest and Taxes)	mil or bil	√			
RR4205	Annualized EBIT	mil or bil	√			
RR4206	EBDIT (Earnings Before Depreciation, Interest, and Taxes	mil or bil	√			
RR4207	Annualized EBDIT	mil or bil	√			
RR4300	Working Capital	mil or bil	√			
RR4301	Changes in Working Capital	mil or bil	√			
RR4302	Net Liquid Capital	mil or bil	√			
RR4303	Total Investments	mil or bil	√	√	√	√
RR4304	Adjusted Total Assets	mil or bil	√	√	√	√
RR4305	Total Common Equity	mil or bil	√	√	√	√
RR4306	Total Capital	mil or bil	√	√	√	√
RR4307	Total Debts	mil or bil	√	√	√	√
RR4400	Free Cash Flow	mil or bil	√			
RR4401	Annualized Free Cash Flow	mil or bil	√			
RR4402	Excess Cash Flow	mil or bil	√			
RR4403	Annualized Excess Cash Flow	mil or bil	√			
RR4404	Total Market Capitalization	mil or bil	√	√	√	√

A.6.3 Additional per Share Data Computation

Ratios	Ratio Titles	Unit	Ind	Bank	Ins	Fin
RR4500	Sales (Revenue) per Share	currency	√	√	√	√
RR4501	Operating Income per Share	currency	√	√	√	√

(cont'd)

(continued)

Ratios	Ratio Titles	Unit	Ind	Bank	Ins	Fin
RR4502	EBIT per Share	currency	√			
RR4503	EBDIT per Share	currency	√			
RR4600	Working Capital per Share	currency	√			
RR4601	Net Liquid Capital per Share	currency	√			
RR4602	Book Value per Share	currency	√	√	√	√
RR4603	Tangible Fixed Assets per Share	currency	√			
RR4700	Cash Flow per Share	currency	√	√	√	√
RR4701	Free Cash Flow per Share	currency	√			
RR4702	Excess Cash Flow per Share	currency	√			

A.6.4 Profitability Ratios

Operating Margin

Ratios	Ratio Titles	Unit	Ind	Bank	Ins	Fin
RR5000	Effective Tax Rate (%)	percent	√	√	√	√
RR5100	Gross Margin (%)	percent	√			
RR5101	Operating Margin (%)	percent	√	√	√	√
RR5102	Pretax Margin (%)	percent	√	√	√	√
RR5103	Net Margin (%)	percent	√	√	√	√
RR5104	Net Margin Before Extraordinary Items (%)	percent	√	√	√	√
RR5105	Nonoperating Income Margin (%)	percent	√	√	√	√
RR5110	Margin on Discontinued Operations (%)	percent	√	√	√	√
RR5111	Profitability of Investments in Associated Companies (%)	percent	√	√	√	√

Sales Growth

Ratios	Ratio Titles	Unit	Ind	Bank	Ins	Fin
RR5200	Sales Growth (%)	percent	√			
RR5201	Revenue Growth (%)	percent	√	√	√	√
RR5202	Operating Income Growth (%)	percent	√	√	√	√
RR5203	Pretax Income Growth (%)	percent	√	√	√	√
RR5204	Net Income Growth (%)	percent	√	√	√	√

Return on Assets

Ratios	Ratio Titles	Unit	Ind	Bank	Ins	Fin
RR5300	Return on Asset Before Extraordinary Items (%)	percent	√	√	√	√
RR5301	Return on Asset (%)	percent	√	√	√	√
RR5302	Return on Shareholders' Equity Before Extraordinary Items (%)	percent	√	√	√	√
RR5303	Return on Shareholders' Equity (%)	percent	√	√	√	√
RR5304	Return on Common Equity (%)	percent	√	√	√	√
RR5305	Operating Income to Total Capital (%)	percent	√	√	√	√
RR5306	Return on Capital (%)	percent	√	√	√	√

Asset Utilization

Ratios	Ratio Titles	Unit	Ind	Bank	Ins	Fin
RR5400	Asset Turnover (X)	multiple	√	√	√	√
RR5401	Tangible Fixed Asset Turnover (X)	multiple	√			

(cont'd)

(continued)

Ratios	Ratio Titles	Unit	Ind	Bank	Ins	Fin
RR5402	Asset Growth (%)	percent	✓	✓	✓	✓
RR5403	Assets per Employee	mil or bil	✓	✓	✓	✓
RR5404	Tangible Fixed Assets per Employee	mil or bil	✓			
RR5405	Sales per Employee	mil or bil	✓			
RR5406	Revenue per Employee	mil or bil	✓	✓	✓	✓
RR5407	Personnel Expenses per Employee	mil or bil	✓	✓	✓	✓

A.6.5 Financial Stability Ratios

Liquidity of Assets

Ratios	Ratio Titles	Unit	Ind	Bank	Ins	Fin
RR6000	Current Ratio (X)	multiple	✓			
RR6001	Quick Ratio (X)	multiple	✓			
RR6002	Accounts Receivable Turnover (X)	multiple	✓			
RR6003	Accounts Receivable Days	days	✓			
RR6004	Inventory Turnover (X)	multiple	✓			
RR6005	Inventory Days	days	✓			

Leverage Ratios

Ratios	Ratio Titles	Unit	Ind	Bank	Ins	Fin
RR6006	Total Debts to Total Assets (%)	percent	✓	✓	✓	✓
RR6007	Common Equity to Total Assets (%)	percent	✓	✓	✓	✓
RR6008	Total Debts to Shareholders' Equity (%)	percent	✓	✓	✓	✓
RR6009	Long-Term Debts to Shareholders' Equity (%)	percent	✓	✓	✓	✓

(cont'd)

(continued)

Ratios	Ratio Titles	Unit	Ind	Bank	Ins	Fin
RR6010	Total Debts to Common Equity (%)	percent	√	√	√	√
RR6011	Long-Term Debts to Common Equity (%)	percent	√	√	√	√
RR6012	Shareholders' Equity to Total Assets (%)	percent	√	√	√	√
RR6013	Total Debts to Total Capital (%)	percent	√	√	√	√
RR6014	Long-Term Debts to Total Capital (%)	percent	√	√	√	√
RR6015	Shareholders' Equity to Total Capital (%)	percent	√	√	√	√
RR6016	Retained Earnings to Total Assets (%)	percent	√	√	√	√
RR6017	Working Capital to Total Assets (%)	percent	√	√	√	√

Coverage Ratios

Ratios	Ratio Titles	Unit	Ind	Bank	Ins	Fin
RR6100	Cash from Operations to Revenue (%)	percent	√	√	√	√
RR6101	Interest Expense Coverage (X)	multiple	√			
RR6102	EBIT to Interest Expenses (X)	multiple	√			
RR6103	Times Interest Earned (X)	multiple	√			
RR6104	Cash from Operations to Fixed Charges (X)	multiple	√			
RR6105	Cash Dividend Coverage (X)	multiple	√	√	√	√
RR6106	EBDIT to Total Debts (%)	percent	√			
RR6107	Repayment Ratio (%)	percent	√			
RR6108	Dividend Payout Ratio (%)	percent	√	√	√	√
RR6109	Retention Ratio (%)	percent	√	√	√	√
RR6110	Net Worth Growth (%)	percent	√	√	√	√
RR6111	EBIT to Total Assets (%)	percent	√			

A.6.6 Growth Potential Ratios

Per Share Growth

Ratios	Ratio Titles	Unit	Ind	Bank	Ins	Fin
RR6500	Earnings per Share Growth (%)	percent	√	√	√	√
RR6501	Net Earnings per Share Growth (%)	percent	√	√	√	√
RR6502	Dividend per Share Growth (%)	percent	√	√	√	√
RR6503	Cash Flow per Share Growth (%)	percent	√	√	√	√
RR6504	Book Value per Share Growth (%)	percent	√	√	√	√
RR6505	Growth in Capital (%)	percent	√	√	√	√
RR6506	Reinvestment Rate (%)	percent	√	√	√	√
RR6507	Sustainable Growth Rate (%)	percent	√	√	√	√

Capital Accumulation Ratios

Ratios	Ratio Titles	Unit	Ind	Bank	Ins	Fin
RR6600	Employee Growth (%)	percent	√	√	√	√
RR6601	R & D Expenditure to Sales (%)	percent	√			
RR6602	Accumulated Depreciation to Gross Tangible Fixed Assets (%)	percent	√			
RR6603	Accumulated Depreciation to Gross Depreciable Fixed Assets (%)	percent	√			
RR6604	Depreciation Expenses to Net Tangible Fixed Assets (%)	percent	√			
RR6610	Capital Expenditure to Gross Tangible Fixed Assets (%)	percent	√			
RR6611	Capital Expenditure to Net Tangible Fixed Assets (%)	percent	√			
RR6612	Capital Expenditure to Total Assets (%)	percent	√			

(cont'd)

Ratios	Ratio Titles	Unit	Ind	Bank	Ins	Fin
(continued)						
RR6613	Capital Expenditure to Sales (%)	percent	✓			
RR6614	Cash Generations to Cash Requirements (X)	multiple	✓			
RR6615	Cash Flow to Net Income (X)	multiple	✓	✓	✓	✓

A.6.7   Special Ratios for Banking and Other Financial Services

Preliminary Data for Special Ratios

Ratios	Ratio Titles	Unit	Ind	Bank	Ins	Fin
RR7000	Net Interest Income Before Provision	mil or bil		✓		✓
RR7001	Net Interest Income	mil or bil		✓		✓
RR7002	Annualized Net Interest Income	mil or bil		✓		✓
RR7003	Net Banking Income	mil or bil		✓		✓
RR7004	Annualized Net Banking Income	mil or bil		✓		✓
RR7005	Non-Interest Income	mil or bil		✓		✓
RR7006	Total Investments	mil or bil		✓		
RR7007	Earning Assets	mil or bil		✓		
RR7008	Total Investment Income	mil or bil				✓
RR7009	Net Investment Income	mil or bil				✓

Income Distributions in Banking Operations

Ratios	Ratio Titles	Unit	Ind	Bank	Ins	Fin
RR7010	Net Interest Margin (%)	percent		✓		✓
RR7011	Net Banking Margin (%)	percent		✓		✓
RR7012	Investment Income to Total Revenue (%)	percent		✓		✓
						(cont'd)

	Ratios	Ratio Titles	Unit	Ind	Bank	Ins	Fin
(continued)							
	RR7013	Non-Interest Income to Total Revenue (%)	percent		√		
	RR7014	Net Investment Income to Operating Income (%)	percent		√		√

Profitability of Loans

Ratios	Ratio Titles	Unit	Ind	Bank	Ins	Fin
RR7020	Interest Income to Total Loans (%)	percent		√		√
RR7021	Provision for Loan Losses to Interest Income (%)	percent		√		√
RR7022	Provision for Loan Losses to Total Loans (%)	percent		√		√
RR7023	Actual Loan Losses to Provision for Loan Losses (%)	percent		√		
RR7024	Loan Loss Coverage (X)	multiple		√		
RR7025	Total Interest Income to Loan Equivalents (%)	percent		√		

Profitability of Investments

Ratios	Ratio Titles	Unit	Ind	Bank	Ins	Fin
RR7030	Investment Income to Total Investments (%)	percent		√		√
RR7031	Investment Income to Earning Assets (%)	percent		√		
RR7032	Efficiency of Earning Assets (%)	percent		√		√
						(cont'd)

Ratios	Ratio Titles	Unit	Ind	Bank	Ins	Fin
(continued)						
RR7033	Operating Income to Earning Assets (%)	percent		√		√
RR7034	Net Income to Earning Assets (%)	percent		√		√

Cost of Capital

Ratios	Ratio Titles	Unit	Ind	Bank	Ins	Fin
RR7100	Total Debts	mil or bil		√		√
RR7101	Total Interest-Bearing Liabilities	mil or bil		√		√
RR7110	Interest Expenses to Total Deposits (%)	percent		√		√
RR7111	Interest Expenses to Total Debts (%)	percent		√		√
RR7112	Interest Expenses to Interest-Bearing Liabilities (%)	percent		√		√

Investment Assets Allocation

Ratios	Ratio Titles	Unit	Ind	Bank	Ins	Fin
RR7200	Total Loans to Total Assets (%)	percent		√		√
RR7201	Net Loans to Earning Assets (%)	percent		√		√
RR7202	Earning Assets to Total Assets (%)	percent		√		√
RR7203	Total Loans to Total Capital (%)	percent		√		√
RR7204	Earning Assets to Total Capital (%)	percent		√		√
RR7205	Growth in Total Loans (%)	percent		√		√

Loans' Exposure to Risks

Ratios	Ratio Titles	Unit	Ind	Bank	Ins	Fin
RR7210	Nonperforming Assets to Total Loans (%)	percent		√		√
RR7211	Nonperforming Assets to Loan Loss Reserves (%)	percent		√		√
RR7212	Loan Loss Reserves to Total Loans (%)	percent		√		√
RR7213	Foreign Loans to Total Loans (%)	percent		√		
RR7214	Customers' Liabilities for Acceptances to Total Assets (%)	percent		√		√
RR7215	Total Customers' Liabilities to Total Assets (%)	percent		√		√

Deposits to Total Capital

Ratios	Ratio Titles	Unit	Ind	Bank	Ins	Fin
RR7300	Total Deposits to Total Capital (%)	percent		√		√
RR7301	Total Deposits to Shareholders' Equity (%)	percent		√		√
RR7302	Growth in Total Deposits (%)	percent		√		√
RR7303	Foreign Deposits to Total Deposits (%)	percent		√		
RR7304	Total Deposits to Interest-Bearing Liabilities (%)	percent		√		√

Duration of Assets and Liabilities

Ratios	Ratio Titles	Unit	Ind	Bank	Ins	Fin
RR7310	Total Loans to Total Deposits (%)	percent		√		√
RR7311	Total Loans to Total Capital (%)	percent		√		√
RR7312	Total Loans to Total Available Funds (%)	percent		√		√
RR7313	Total Loans to Interest-Bearing Debts (%)	percent		√		√
RR7320	Total Investments to Total Deposits (%)	percent		√		
RR7321	Total Investments to Total Available Funds (%)	percent		√		
RR7322	Total Investments to Interest-Bearing Debts (%)	percent		√		
RR7330	Earning Assets to Total Deposits (%)	percent		√		√
RR7331	Earning Assets to Total Capital (%)	percent		√		√
RR7332	Earning Assets to Total Available Funds (%)	percent		√		√
RR7333	Earning Assets to Interest-Bearing Debts (%)	percent		√		√
RR7340	Short-Term Loans to Total Loans (%)	percent		√		
RR7341	Short-Term Loans to Short-Term Deposits (%)	percent		√		
RR7342	Foreign Loans to Foreign Deposits (%)	percent		√		
RR7343	Short-Term Earning Assets to Short-Term Funds (%)	percent		√		
RR7344	Long-Term Earning Assets to Long-Term Funds (%)	percent		√		

A.6.8 Special Ratios for Insurance Companies

Preliminary Data for Special Ratios

Ratios	Ratio Titles	Unit	Ind	Bank	Ins	Fin
RR7500	Total Investment Income	mil or bil			✓	
RR7501	Annualized Total Investment Income	mil or bil			✓	

Income Distributions in Insurance Operations

Ratios	Ratio Titles	Unit	Ind	Bank	Ins	Fin
RR7510	Net Premium from Life to Total Net Premium (%)	percent			✓	
RR7511	Net Premium from Non-Life to Total Net Premium (%)	percent			✓	
RR7512	Total Investment Income to Total Revenue (%)	percent			✓	
RR7513	Operating Income to Total Net Premium (%)	percent			✓	
RR7514	Net Insurance Margin (%)	percent			✓	
RR7515	Insurance Margin (%)	percent			✓	
RR7516	Non-Insurance Margin (%)	percent			✓	
RR7520	Loss Ratio for Life (%)	percent			✓	
RR7521	Expense Ratio for Life (%)	percent			✓	
RR7522	Combined Ratio for Life (%)	percent			✓	
RR7530	Loss Ratio for Non-Life (%)	percent			✓	
RR7531	Expense Ratio for Non-Life (%)	percent			✓	
RR7532	Combined Ratio (%)	percent			✓	

Profitability Ratios

Ratios	Ratio Titles	Unit	Ind	Bank	Ins	Fin
RR7600	Profitability of Invested Assets (%)	percent			√	
RR7601	Profitability of Real Estate Investments (%)	percent			√	
RR7602	Claims and Losses Reserves to Claims and Losses Expenses for Life (%)	percent			√	
RR7603	Claims and Losses Reserves to Claims and Losses Expenses for Non-Life (%)	percent			√	
RR7604	Claims and Losses Reserves to Claims and Losses Expenses (%)	percent			√	
RR7605	Long-Term Insurance Charges to Life Policy Benefits (%)	percent			√	

Distribution of Investments

Ratios	Ratio Titles	Unit	Ind	Bank	Ins	Fin
RR7700	Fixed Income Investments to Total Investments (%)	percent			√	
RR7701	Equity Investments to Total Investments (%)	percent			√	
RR7710	Total Investments to Total Insurance Reserves (%)	percent			√	
RR7711	Total Investments to Total Assets (%)	percent			√	

(cont'd)

Ratios	Ratio Titles	Unit	Ind	Bank	Ins	Fin
(continued)						
RR7712	Total Investments to Adjusted Total Assets (%)	percent			√	
RR7713	Total Investments to Total Capital (%)	percent			√	

Distribution of Insurance Reserves

Ratios	Ratio Titles	Unit	Ind	Bank	Ins	Fin
RR7720	Total Insurance Reserves to Total Assets (%)	percent			√	
RR7721	Total Insurance Reserves to Adjusted Total Assets (%)	percent			√	
RR7722	Total Insurance Reserves to Total Capital (%)	percent			√	
RR7723	Life Policy in Force to Life Policy Benefits (X)	multiple			√	
RR7724	Insurance Reserve Growth (%)	percent			√	

A.6.9 Price Relevance Ratios

Ratios	Ratio Titles	Unit	Ind	Bank	Ins	Fin
RR7800	Price Earnings Ratio (X)	multiple	√	√	√	√
RR7801	Earnings Yield Ratio (%)	percent	√	√	√	√
RR7802	Dividend Yields (%)	percent	√	√	√	√
RR7803	Price to Book Value Ratio (X)	multiple	√	√	√	√
RR7804	Price to Cash (X)	multiple	√	√	√	√
RR7805	Price to Sales (X)	multiple	√	√	√	√
RR7806	Price to EBIT (X)	multiple	√			
						(cont'd)

(continued)						
Ratios	**Ratio Titles**	**Unit**	**Ind**	**Bank**	**Ins**	**Fin**
RR7807	Market Capitalization to Total Assets (X)	multiple	√	√	√	√
RR7808	Market Capitalization to Total Liabilities (X)	multiple	√	√	√	√

A.6.10   Ratios with Non-Financial Information

Diversification of Operating Activities

Ratios	**Ratio Titles**	**Unit**	**Ind**	**Bank**	**Ins**	**Fin**
RR7850	Unrelated Horizontal Product Diversification with SIC Codes	index	√	√	√	√
RR7851	Related Horizontal Product Diversification with SIC Codes	index	√	√	√	√
RR7852	Total Horizontal Product Diversification with SIC Codes	index	√	√	√	√
RR7860	Unrelated Vertical Product Diversification with Group Industry Codes	index	√	√	√	√
RR7861	Related Vertical Product Diversification with Group Industry Codes	index	√	√	√	√
RR7862	Total Vertical Product Diversification with Group Industry Codes	index	√	√	√	√
RR7870	Unrelated Geographic Diversification by International Sales	index	√	√	√	√
						(cont'd)

(continued)

Ratios	Ratio Titles	Unit	Ind	Bank	Ins	Fin
RR7871	Related Geographic Diversification by International Sales	index	√	√	√	√
RR7872	Total Geographic Diversification by International Sales	index	√	√	√	√
RR7880	Unrelated Geographic Diversification by Subsidiary	index	√	√	√	√
RR7881	Related Geographic Diversification by Subsidiary	index	√	√	√	√
RR7882	Total Geographic Diversification by Subsidiary	index	√	√	√	√

Diversification of Shareholders

Ratios	Ratio Titles	Unit	Ind	Bank	Ins	Fin
RR7890	Major Stable Shareholding (%)	percent	√	√	√	√
RR7891	Major Institutional Shareholding (%)	percent	√	√	√	√
RR7892	Concentration Index by Major Shareholders	index	√	√	√	√
RR7893	Insider Ownership by Major Shareholders (%)	percent	√	√	√	√
RR7894	Institutional Ownership by Type of Organization (%)	percent	√	√	√	√
RR7895	Insider Ownership by Type of Organization (%)	percent	√	√	√	√

Disk Installation Instructions

ABOUT THE SOFTWARE

The software was developed for the readers of *Fundamental Analysis Worldwide*. Volume I, Financial Statement Analysis, of *Fundamental Analysis Worldwide* defines all input data items and sample ratios for general research purposes while maintaining the coherent international comparison purposes. The goal of financial statement analysis is to provide a basis to forecast each company's future earnings. Once historical information on a company has been gathered, it can then be compared statistically by sector and by country to establish each company's relative strength. Preparing analysis involves collecting specific raw data from corporate financial statements and computing ratios to establish the relationships between data. The goal of the software is to establish a company's relative strength globally in the sector in which that company mainly competes.

The accompanying software is an Excel 5.0 macro. Once a company profile is prepared, users can compute ratios developed in Chapter 11 of Volume I and also append it for future updates.

COMPUTER REQUIREMENTS

- IBM, PC/AT 386 or higher computer or compatible computer
- 4 MB of RAM
- 2 MB of hard disk space
- PC DOS or MS DOS Version 3.1 or later
- Microsoft Windows 3.1 or later
- Excel for Windows Version 5.0
- 3.5″ high-density floppy drive

INSTALLATION

To install the files on the enclosed disk, you will need at least 2 Mb of free space on your hard disk.

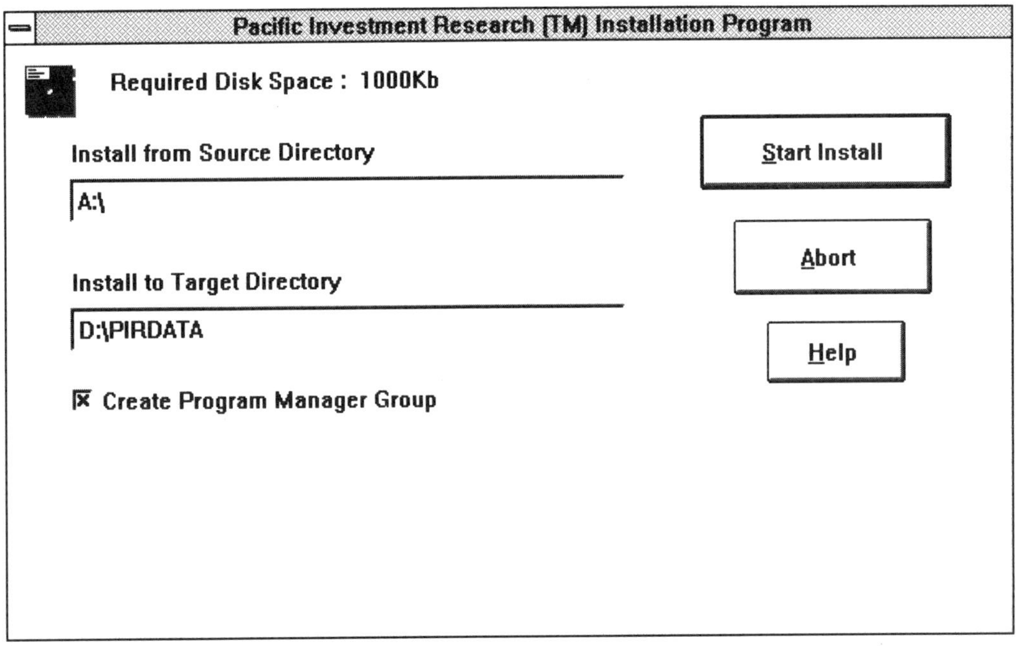
Pacific Investment Research (TM) Installation Program
Required Disk Space : 1000Kb
Install from Source Directory
A:\
Install to Target Directory
D:\PIRDATA
Create Program Manager Group
Start Install
Abort
Help

Figure 1: Install to Target Directory

1. Start your computer and Windows.
2. Insert the *Fundamental Analysis Worldwide* disk into drive A of your computer. (If you are using drive B, make the appropriate substitutions.)
3. From the Program Manager, select File, Run, and type A:\SETUP and click on Enter.
4. The target directory that needs to be created is **C:\PIRDATA** or **D:\PIRDATA** (depending on the hard disk drive installed to). If the user has two hard drives, it is recommended that the software be installed to the hard disk drive that contains data applications. The installation program will then create the PIRDATA directory on the designated hard disk. Under the section titled, *Install to Target Directory,* type in the destination drive. (See Figure 1.)

The installation will create a program group called **FAW** (*Fundamental Analysis Worldwide*). The group will contain one icon, **PIR.** To access the model, double click on the **PIR** icon. This action will open Excel and automatically load the macro to create a new company profile.

GETTING STARTED

Once the application has been loaded, the first page with General Information will be prompted. The following information must be entered before the user is able to proceed.

- Choose one of the following Company Formats: Industrial, Bank, Insurance, and Other Financial Services.
- Choose the Country where the primary stock is traded.
- Enter the Company name in cell C4.
- Enter the Primary Ticker in cell C5.

Once the information is entered, it will be listed on each page of the program until a new company profile has been created. (See Figure 2.)

The country code hidden behind the country combo box and the primary ticker will be used for a file name of the company profile. In addition to the four data items listed above, additional ticker symbols will be required for multiple share companies (see Chapter 3 of Volume I for the definition of multiple shares). If additional ticker symbols are added in cells D5 to G5 (up to four more tickers in addition to the primary ticker), additional pages for information such as stock prices and dividend will be added on each security. **Do not enter** any additional characters or symbols in the ticker number, such as 1. Because the ticker number is used to create the name, an error will be generated by Excel. Otherwise you may copy the page for a primary share to another sheet as needed.

Additional information such as addresses, phone numbers, and any other special notes may also be entered in this page. The information entered in this page will be carried onto the General Information sheet of the company profile.

ADDITIONAL FUNCTIONS IN THE COMPANY PROFILES

Because the macros were written in Excel 5.0, all of the programs functions and commands are applicable. In addition to the standard Excel functions, three

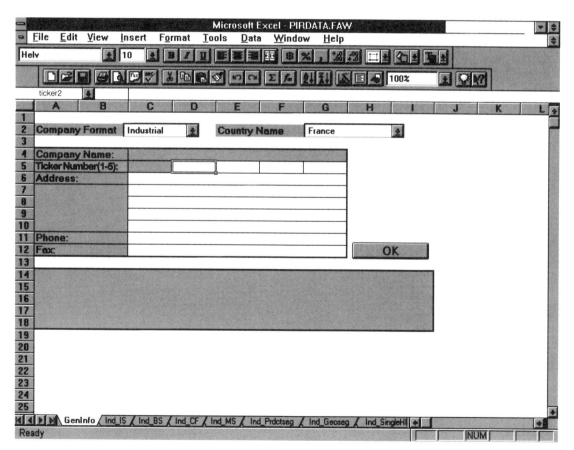

Figure 2: General Information

major functions have been added. They are a printing option, a computation of ratios option, and an addition of a new year option.

Printing and Preview

Due to the multiple pages of layout in a company profile, a **Print** function has been added. The print function allows users to select one or more pages or print the entire company profile to the user's designated printer. Before printing actual pages, the user has the option of previewing the printing ranges.

Computation of Ratios

Once all valid data in the income statement, balance sheet, cash flow statement, and other information has been input, the predefined ratios can be computed for analysis by selecting the **Compute** option from the **PIR** menu. Ratios for all years available in the row for year designation in the income statement will be computed using the information in the financial statements. Refer to Chapter 11 for the predefined ratio samples and also refer to the Appendix for the applicable ratios to a specific data format.

Adding a New Year

By default, each company profile will be prompted with five years from 1990 to 1994. When an additional year is required to update, select **AddYear** from the **PIR** menu. It will add a new column between the column for the account title and the recent year you have with the designation of the following year after the recent year you have in the income statement. Balancing formulas and cell formats will be transferred from the recent year before adding the new year.

TECHNICAL SUPPORT

Technical Support for the Fundamental Analysis Worldwide can be obtained at the following fax number or at the E-Mail address listed below.

1. Fax: 609-799-8464
2. E-Mail: Pacific Investment Research, Inc. using FAWIPIR@AOL.COM

To place additional orders or to request general information about orders or other Wiley products, please call Wiley customer service at (800) 879-4539. Note: Do not call Wiley customer service number for technical support; use the E-Mail address provided above.

Company Index

Subject Index